LEARNING CHINESE

云冈石窟 *Yúngāng Shíkū* 'Yungang Grottoes', 山西 *Shānxī*

汉语基础教材（中级）

Learning Chinese

A FOUNDATION COURSE IN MANDARIN INTERMEDIATE LEVEL

JULIAN K. WHEATLEY 魏久安

Yale UNIVERSITY PRESS NEW HAVEN & LONDON

Yale University Press books may be purchased in quantity for educational, business, or promotional use. For information, please e-mail sales.press@yale.edu (U.S. office) or sales@yaleup.co.uk (U.K. office).

Publisher: Mary Jane Peluso
Editor: Tim Shea
Publishing Assistant: Ashley E. Lago
Manuscript Editor: Jamie Greene
Production Editor: Ann-Marie Imbornoni
Production Controller: Aldo Cupo
Designed by Nancy Ovedovitz
All photographs are by the author.
Set by Toppan Best-set Premedia Limited, Hong Kong.
Printed in the United States of America.

ISBN: 978-0-300-14118-4
Library of Congress Control Number: 2013953756

A catalogue record for this book is available from the British Library.

This paper meets the requirements of ANSI/NISO Z39.48-1992 (Permanence of Paper).

10 9 8 7 6 5 4 3 2 1

谨以此书献给爱妻 Marjorie.

Learning Chinese comes with an extensive set of audio clips that serve as a personal guide to the Chinese language material in the book. These, as well as vocabulary lists (both Chinese-to-English and English-to-Chinese), keys to exercises, and other special features, can be found at the companion Web site **yalebooks.com/wheatley**.

汉语基础教材

CONTENTS

PREFACE

The elementary level of *Learning Chinese* began with two lists: ten basic features of the text and ten general principles for using the text. Except for the third basic feature (which refers to sample schedules provided in Appendix 2 of that volume), both lists also apply to the intermediate level, so they are reproduced here.

A. Ten basic features of *Learning Chinese*

1. Provides instruction in spoken and written Mandarin; no prior background assumed.
2. Serves as a comprehensive resource for the foundation levels of Chinese language study. The elementary level (first year) and intermediate level (second year) cover approximately 200 class hours.
3. Not applicable to the intermediate level.
4. Presents rich content (based on the author's own experience learning Chinese) that is presented incrementally and in detail, is carefully sequenced, and builds toward dialogues or narratives that recapitulate important content.
5. Includes a variety of exercises and audio materials for self-study. The companion Web site, **yalebooks.com/wheatley**, provides a full set of audio clips, as well as comprehensive vocabulary lists, exercise keys, and other features.
6. Contains content that is easily transformed into class activities, and easily supplemented by online or other materials.

7. Includes conversational lessons and character lessons that can be used separately or together.
8. Includes conversational and character lessons that are related but not identical to each other, and which can be interleaved.
9. Teaches reading with both the traditional (Taiwan) and simplified (Mainland) character sets.
10. Teaches characters inductively, by emphasizing reading in context as much as possible.

《汉语基础教材》：十个主要特点

一、供零起点学生口语和书面语学习的汉语入门教材。

二、这是一套综合性的基础教材。共两册，第一册是初级水平，第二册是中级水平，大约需要修读200个课时。

三、 Not applicable to the intermediate level.

四、作者根据自己的汉语学习经历，精心编排话题，并以循序渐进的方式逐步开展，每课最后还编排了一段对话或叙述以重现该课的重要话题。内容充实，层次分明。

五、为自学者提供多样化的书面练习及录音资料。

六、教材内容易转换成课堂活动，也便于通过网络或其他途径进行补充。

七、会话教材与汉字教材可以分开使用，也可以相互配合使用。

八、会话教材与汉字教材内容相关，但不互相依赖，自成体系。

九、汉字教材以繁简汉字编写。

十、识字教学采用归纳法，透过高重现率的篇章，使学习者能够在真实语境中自然学习。

B. Ten general principles for using *Learning Chinese*

1. Prepare before class, perform in class, and consolidate after class.
2. Move from simple to complex, from familiar to novel, and from rote to realistic.
3. Focus on typical interchanges, personalize them when possible, and compound them into longer conversations.
4. Recognize that Mandarin usage varies as much as English. Regard *Learning Chinese* as a guide, but accept additional input from teachers and your own observations.
5. Learn functional phrases rather than individual words; visualize interactions and match appropriate language; and act out scenarios from cues.
6. Distinguish character recognition from reading, and focus reading activities on comprehension.
7. Write characters to improve recognition ability, but utilize word processing programs to compose texts.
8. Consolidate conversational skills while studying the character units; consolidate character skills while studying the conversational units.
9. As much as possible, learn language in context rather than from lists. (But be mindful that lists can help with recall and review.)
10. Know the core, test the core (i.e., that practiced in class). For character material, test comprehension.

使用《汉语基础教材》的十个基本原则

一、强调课前预习，课中练习以及课后复习。

二、从简单到复杂，从陌生到熟悉，从机械操练到自然交际。

三、先熟记典型的会话，再向个性化延伸，最后扩展为完整的会话。

四、汉语表达同英语一样复杂多变，学生可将本教材作为用法指南使用，不仅应该听取老师的建议，自己也应勤于观察。

五、与其只学习个别生词，不如学习如何使用词组；借助提示，摹拟实际交流情境，演练与之相匹配的表达方式。

六、分清识字和阅读的不同；阅读活动最好以理解为主。

七、通过书写汉字来提高辨认字形的能力，同吋借助拼音输入软件来写作。

八、学习汉字时，同时加强会话能力；学习会话时，同时加强汉字能力，互相促进。

九、与其利用生字表、生词表学习，不如利用有上下文的课文学习。(生字表、生词表可用来回忆与复习。)

十、掌握核心教材，测试核心教材；所谓核心教材指的是课堂教学中所使用的教材。至于汉字教材则主要用来测试理解能力。

ACKNOWLEDGMENTS

Special thanks go to Tong Chen (陈彤), my former colleague at the Massachusetts Institute of Technology. In the course of the heavy teaching load to which lecturers in language programs are accustomed, he made a major contribution to this volume by providing the original drafts of many of the longer narratives and more specialized dialogues. Cooking ranks high among his many skills, and he also contributed greatly to the material on Chinese menus and dining contained in Appendix 1.

Though there might be a fair degree of agreement on usage and style for the written language—and perhaps for language spoken on formal occasions—there is far less agreement about usage in ordinary social intercourse or even in informal narratives. After all, the spoken language is fleeting, and participants think about rhetorical issues rather than the medium of language itself when they talk. So, unless you are a playwright or a linguist with a tape recorder, what constitutes spoken usage is extremely subjective. Actual recordings of speech are instructive, but they are less successful as models for learning at the foundation levels. Ultimately, the only way to settle on usage is to respond to the judgments of colleagues and friends who have spoken Chinese from childhood.

People too numerous to list have been involved in this process, but I do want to give special thanks to the following: Tong Chen (陈彤) and Minmin Liang (梁敏敏), both former colleagues at MIT; Xiuqiong Bi (毕秀琼) in Kunming and Yu Zhang (章予), originally from Shandong but now living in Jackson, Tennessee, who are both my e-mail supporters; William Zhou (周雨) at

Yale University; Hsin-hsin Liang (梁新欣) at the University of Virginia; Yinchen Li from New Orleans; and others too numerous to list, from whom I sought occasional help and advice. Special thanks are also due to Professor Goh Yeng Seng (吴英成), head of the Asian Languages and Cultures Academic Group at the National Institute of Education at the National Technological University in Singapore, who took the time to read a draft of this volume.

The final version of *Learning Chinese* has benefited immeasurably from comments and assistance from the people mentioned above. Improprieties, incongruities, or just plain errors that remain are, of course, my own fault (and when discovered, will be duly noted in the addenda and corrigenda file on the *Learning Chinese* Web site).

As with the elementary level, the people at Yale University Press deserve special accolades for outstanding work on the second volume of *Learning Chinese*. They are: Mary Jane Peluso, publisher, who had the courage to support such an unorthodox project in the first place; Tim Shea, editor, whose steady hand ensured completion of the venture even as deadlines came and went; Ashley Lago, publication assistant, who served as coordinator and kept channels open; Ann-Marie Imbornoni, the production editor, who worked behind the scenes to guide the manuscript through to print; and Jamie Greene, manuscript editor, whose magnificent effort brought clarity to a complicated, unruly manuscript—and whose unerring eye caught errors, inconsistencies, and omissions in both the Chinese and the English and saved me from untold embarrassments.

Finally, I would also like to thank Nora Guo for carefully adding the microcalligraphic numbers to the mega-characters in Appendix 4.

INTRODUCTION

"Wǒ pà wǒ bú dà dǒng," Ālìsī shuō. *Hūndìdūndì huídá tā shuō, "Dǐxià jiù róngyi diǎnr le."*
—From *Zǒu Dào Jìngzi Lǐ* (*Through the Looking Glass*), translated by Yuen Ren Chao

The intermediate level of *Learning Chinese* continues along the same lines as the elementary level, with spoken and character units of related—but not identical—content designed to be interleaved or used independently. Chinese material in the spoken units is transcribed in Hanyu pinyin, whereas material in the character units is written primarily in the simplified set of characters (though the traditional set is used occasionally). This division of spoken and written language allows for faster acquisition of vocabulary, and—more generally—it ensures that the development of speaking ability is not adversely affected by factors related to character acquisition, which involves an entirely different set of skills.

Organization

The spoken units in the intermediate level (Units 14–19) are organized like those in the elementary level. Each of the six units introduces a progression of grammatical and notional topics, commentary and exercises, conversations and narratives, and a variety of rote material ranging from epigraphs to rhymes and rhythms. (These spoken units are supported by audio clips provided on the *Learning Chinese* Web site.)

The bilingual format, with Chinese and English in parallel columns (*duìzhào*), provides a convenient comparative perspective and allows learners to practice retelling the material as a step toward internalizing it and, ultimately, making use of it in novel settings both in and out of the classroom. The intermediate level differs from the elementary level in that it makes greater use of narrative material along with dialogues for the oral component. This narrative material includes personal accounts and presentations on subjects of general interest, such as regional languages and geography. The narratives should be regarded as informal oral presentations, transcribed into pinyin for ease of reference and vocabulary retrieval.

The character units introduce characters from both the traditional set (in use in Hong Kong, Taiwan, and many overseas Chinese communities) and the simplified set (now standard on the Mainland and in use in Singapore and some overseas communities). Actual reading is conducted mostly with the simplified set. The traditional set is limited to occasional, clearly demarcated examples and exercises. Character material is presented inductively as much as possible. Individual graphs are introduced in large format, a few dozen at a time, with notes to provide a level of analysis and to assist with recognition. Reading begins with compounds and phrases, proceeds to sentences in context (typically comment and response), and where feasible, culminates in longer selections. The focus is on reading, though writing (by hand or keyboard) is recognized as an important support for character recognition, particularly in the early stages of learning. Writing in the sense of composition is mostly left to later stages of learning, though some guided composition exercises appear in the oral units.

The sequence of units

The intermediate level contains six spoken-language units, two character units, and four appendices. Learners who have used the elementary level of *Learning Chinese*, and whose initial course met three to four hours a week in class, will probably begin this level at the beginning of their third semester of study (second year). Others with more hours per week at the elementary level will begin this level late in their second semester (first year).

Learners who are studying only the spoken language and have completed Unit 7, the last of the spoken units in the previous volume, can continue with Units 14–19. Learners who are interleaving spoken and character units have a choice. Since the last lesson of the previous volume was a spoken unit (Unit 7), strict sequence would be to follow with the next character unit (Unit 20) and then continue with Units 14, 21, 15, and so on. However, it is also possible—and perhaps preferable—to delay Unit 20 for one lesson. That would mean starting with a spoken unit (Unit 14), before picking up the sequence with Unit 20 and continuing with Units 15, 21, 16, and so on. One reason for this is that some learners may prefer to begin a new semester or a new phase with a spoken lesson. Another reason is that Unit 21 anticipates the shift to other published readers or texts by introducing material not covered in previous spoken units—thus violating the general principle that character lessons apply characters to words and grammatical patterns introduced in earlier spoken units. For this reason, delaying Unit 21 has advantages.

The two options are (with character units marked *):

> Strict order: (Unit 7) → 20* → 14 → 21* → 15 → reader of choice → 16 → reader of choice → etc.
> Relaxed order: (Unit 7) → 14 → 20* → 15 → 21* → 16 → reader of choice → 17 → reader of choice → etc.

Appendix 1 contains information about cuisine, dining, and menus, and it has no fixed place in the sequence. The long menu, which includes both pinyin and characters, can be used for recitation practice as well as a prop in dialogues. Select parts can also be used to supplement the sections on food in the regular units. Appendix 2 lists measure words. Appendix 3 lists the characters introduced in *Learning Chinese* for reference. Simplified characters are organized by total number of strokes and are matched to pinyin. Traditional characters (that contrast with their simplified equivalents) are also organized by number of strokes, but they are matched to the corresponding simplified characters. This appendix also includes a section that introduces general principles of simplification. Appendix 4 gives stroke orders for characters introduced in the intermediate level.

The intermediate level has two character units. They are geared to the first two or three spoken units (that is, Units 14, 15, and 16). The eight character units (including the six from the elementary level) constitute a foundation. After completing Unit 21, you will be familiar with roughly 500 commonly used characters; you will have become accustomed to the actual process of reading in Chinese; you will know a great deal about the construction of characters that can be applied to new material; and you will be familiar enough with traditional graphs to make the shift from simplified to traditional when needed. With this foundation in place, further progress with reading is best obtained by turning to good textbooks that already exist—with traditional Chinese stories that are graded for level and edited for learners and with annotations and vocabulary lists (and in many cases, exercises and recordings). A number of these are recommended in the coda to Unit 21.

Sūzhōu

THE CORE UNITS

Pinyin

In many Chinese language textbooks, pinyin appears in small script above or below individual characters, where it functions as a diacritical system to indicate pronunciation. Questions of word division and punctuation do not arise. However, in *Learning Chinese*, pinyin is used to transcribe continuous oral text, so certain writing conventions, designed to make reading easier, are followed. These conventions are enumerated in a document that was first published in 1996, an English translation of which, entitled "Basic Rules for Hanyu Pinyin Orthography," is reprinted as Appendix 1 of John DeFrancis's *ABC Chinese-English Comprehensive Dictionary* (Honolulu: University of Hawai'i Press, 2003).

Word division

According to the basic rules outlined in this article, capitalization and punctuation more or less follow English practice. However, the article leaves some cases of word division unaddressed. Ideally, these issues would be resolved by reference to dictionaries, as they would be in English. In Chinese, however, pinyin conventions are not strongly established, and dictionaries vary in their usage. *Learning Chinese* follows the conventions of the *ABC Chinese-English Comprehensive Dictionary*, which has the virtue of at least focusing on pinyin usage for its organization and retrieval system.

Most pinyin rules for word division are unsurprising and seem to conform to intuitions about what constitutes a word (even if the notion of a 'word' is not so highly profiled in Chinese as it is in English). However, the rules for writing certain kinds of complex verbs in pinyin deserve comment. The Basic Rules state that "when both a verb (or adjective) and its complement are monosyllabic, they are to be written together; otherwise the two are to be separated". Thus: *tīngdǒng* 'understand' ('listen-understand'); *xuéhuì* 'to master' ('study-master'), but *zǒu jìnqu* 'walk in' ('walk enter-go'); *ná qǐlai* 'lift up' ('take rise-come').

Extending the 'monosyllabic' rule to the potential forms gives *tīngdedǒng* 'can understand' and *xuébuhuì* 'cannot master'—written as wholes. Extending the non-monosyllabic rule to the potential forms gives *zǒu bu jìnqu* 'cannot walk in' and *ná de qǐlai* 'can lift up'—written with spaces. The 'monosyllabic rule' is not exemplified for all cases in the Basic Rules; the ABC dictionary consistently follows the rule for the monosyllabic type (writing *tīngdǒng* and *tīngdedǒng*), but it is inconsistent with the non-monosyllabic type (*zǒu jìnqu*). (Careful readers will have noted that in the elementary volume, this distinction was not adhered to. The author now prefers to minimize exceptions to the norm to the few described in the next paragraph.)

In a few cases, the intermediate level of *Learning Chinese*, like the elementary level, will go against pinyin conventions for the sake of pedagogy. These cases are as follows:

1. Changed tones are indicated for the words *bù* 'not' and *yī* 'one; a' (and derivatives). Thus, we see *bú duì* but *bù hǎo*; *yí ge* and *yíkuàir* but *yì běn* and *yìdiǎnr*. Changed tones that result from the regular rule that affects two low-toned words are not specially indicated (hence, *hěn hǎo*).

2. The particle that connects verbs to adjective complement structures is distinguished from *de* with other functions by a plus: *shuō+de hěn hǎo* but *tā shuō de huà*.

Hyphens

Hyphens are employed in ordinal numbers (*dì-yī kè* 'lesson 1'), in coordinate constructions (*sān-sìshí kuài qián* 'thirty or forty dollars'), in certain kinds of abbreviations (*Yīng-Hàn zìdiǎn* 'English-Chinese dictionary'), in reduplicated coordinate constructions (*qīngqing-chǔchǔ*, from *qīngchu* 'clear; distinct'), and in certain types of four-syllable idioms where each disyllable is a segment (*gūlòu-guǎwén* 'ignorant and ill-informed', composed of *gūlòu* 'ignorance' and *guǎwén* 'of limited experience'; but *mòmíngqímiào* 'inexplicable' ['not-understand-its-subtlety']). Where there is uncertainty, particularly regarding four-syllable expressions, *Learning Chinese* strays on the side of more hyphens rather than fewer, so as to improve readability.

Syllables without tone

Syllables without tone are called *qīngshēng* in Chinese, literally 'light-tone' but often translated as 'neutral tone'. Three types of *qīngshēng* can be distinguished: unstressed particles, such as the *de* of *wǒ de* or the *le* of *gòu le*, which never appear with full tone; unstressed syllables in compounds, such as *qīngchu* 'clear', which appear fully toned in other contexts (*qīngqing-chǔchǔ*); and unstressed syllables that result from destressing in casual speech (*zhuōzi shàng > zhuōzi shang*).

Learning Chinese follows the common convention of indicating *qīngshēng* by simply omitting the tone mark. Another method of indicating *qīngshēng* is with a preceding dot (a convention introduced by Yuen Ren Chao, though he originally made use of another Romanization, called Gwoyeu Romatzyh). Thus, *qīngchu = qīng.chǔ*, indicating a neutral tone while still signaling the underlying tone. However, given the amount of pinyin text in *Learning Chinese*, the profusion of dots would damage the readability of the transcription. The only exceptions you will see are in compounds such as *xiǎojiě*, *kěyǐ*, or *nǎlǐ*, in which the third-tone shift interacts with destressing to give *xiáojie*, *kéyi*, and *náli* (a transcription that removes the underlying tone of both syllables). Words such as this are written with the dot convention. Therefore, we write *xiǎo.jiě* (= *xiáojie*), *kě.yǐ* (= *kéyi*), and *nǎ.lǐ* (= *náli*).

Variation in Mandarin

Orthographies provide enough information for readers to recognize words (and phrases) and activate internalized rules of pronunciation. That is why Australians, Scots, and Americans can retain their own pronunciations when reading aloud from a book written in standard English orthography. Under certain conditions, English spelling can be modified to represent accents or local usage, but readers usually read out standard spelling in their own accents.

Pinyin can also operate as a standard orthography, allowing for accents and pronunciations within the range of standard Mandarin. The transient neutral tone would not need to be indicated, nor would the suffixed *r* of northern speech. *Yīdiǎn* would represent *yìdiǎn* (southern) or *yìdiǎnr* (northern); *shì bù shì* would represent *shì bú shì* (careful speech), *shì bu shì* (casual speech), or *shì bu shi* (fast); *mànmàn zǒu* would represent *mànmàn zǒu* (southern speech) or *mànmānr zǒu* (northern); and *bā gè* would represent the occurring alternatives *bā ge* and *bá ge*. Variant Mandarin pronunciations (still within the range of the standard) would be applied according to the speaker's own speech.

However, pinyin is not usually used as an orthography. Rather, it is used as a transcription system (as well as a diacritic system, as noted above). In teaching materials and, to an extent, in dictionaries and other reference works, variant pronunciations are indicated (so long as they fall within the notion of standard Mandarin)—particularly the major geographical variants such as *yìdiǎnr* and *yìdiǎn* or *mànmàn zǒu* and *mànmānr zǒu*.

Under ideal circumstances, the pinyin material in *Learning Chinese* would transcribe actual spoken material and represent the speech of particular individuals at particular times. For various practical reasons, the material for the spoken units of *Learning Chinese* was composed rather than recorded, but it was composed as if spoken by a particular person in a particular place. In many cases, that person is assumed to be an educated northerner who makes moderate use of the *r* suffix but is in other respects not too local in his or her pronunciation. Learners who prefer a non-northern idiom can, at least, omit the *r* from their pronunciation—one of the more salient hallmarks of northern speech. In any case, learners of Chinese should always be ready to observe language as it is actually spoken (or otherwise used) and adjust or annotate their textbooks and dictionaries accordingly.

Chinese-English translation and glosses

Except for the long narratives, most of the spoken Chinese material in *Learning Chinese* is presented alongside an idiomatic English translation. Translation between languages is far less problematical at the level of utterance (speech in context), so, at foundation levels, a parallel translation serves to clarify meaning in context (which reflects the intention of the speakers), while it also provides the learner with cues to practice producing the Chinese.

Ultimately, it is also useful to break down utterances into phrases, words, and smaller meaningful segments. Unlike utterances, individual words do not match up easily across languages. Nevertheless, at beginning levels, a word-for-word gloss is useful. The usual practice is to provide an English approximation for each Chinese word (*yù* 'jade') or a series of English words that gives a rough sense of the range of the Chinese (*shōushi* 'tidy up; put in order; pack'). In some cases, a definition is required (*lóufáng* 'a building of more than one story').

For compounds (which are prevalent), identification of the component parts (morphemes) helps with recall. For most compounds, *Learning Chinese* includes, in parentheses, an analysis of components, for example, *rènao* 'buzzing with excitement' ('hot-noisy') and *gǎoxiào-túpiàn* 'emoticon' ('make-laugh picture'). The glossaries sometimes identify one component with another by phrasing comparable to the English 'the pen of pigpen'. Thus, for *pǔbiàn* 'widespread', the glossary might say *pǔtōng de pǔ* 'the pu of putong'—'common'. Speakers of Chinese often use this phrasing for identifying characters; learners make use of it for identifying morphemes.

For longer narratives, the intermediate level generally provides a list of annotated phrases. Phrases, in fact, tend to be more effective units of study than individual words: *yào zūnshǒu guīdìng* 'one should obey the rules'; *wèile fāzhǎn diànlì* 'in order to develop electrical power'. Ultimately, these phrases can also be broken down into words: *zūnshǒu* 'observe; abide by'; *guīdìng* 'rule; regulation; stipulation'. It is the phrase, however, that forms the ideal unit of study.

As with the elementary level, cumulative vocabulary lists (along with other material) are provided on the Web site rather than in the book. This not only saves space but also discourages list learning (as opposed to learning material in an authentic context, which is far more effective). Within the book, glossaries of words or phrases are listed after the relevant selection in order of their appearance—whether it is a narrative, a dialogue, or a series of example sentences. There is no need for every word in these lists to become part of your active vocabulary. Some words you may only recognize in the narrow context of the unit material. In any case, the lists often contain a level of redundancy, incorporating words encountered earlier, which allows some flexibility to the order in which unit material is used.

Most of the narratives in the intermediate volume have the following format. They are preceded by a short preview that provides context and introduces key words and expressions. They are followed not by the usual list of words (headed 'Vocabulary') but by a list of citations (headed 'Annotations'), which includes problematical segments of the text and provides analysis, translation, and illustrative examples. The annotations are meant to be consulted while reading or listening to the narratives. They can also serve as a reminder of what has been covered, for purposes of review.

Finally, two other changes are introduced in this volume. One is that part-of-speech labels (noun, adverb, pronoun, and so on) are no longer included in the vocabulary lists. The reason for this is that Chinese usage has undergone many changes in recent years, and there are a significant number of cases where part of speech is neither clear nor unanimously understood. The other change introduced in this volume is relatively minor. In English glosses, pronouns and other words with no explicit correspondent in Chinese are no longer placed in brackets. Therefore, *yīnggāi shuō* . . . is simply glossed as 'they should say . . .' rather than '[they] should say . . .' as was done in the elementary level.

All other conventions used in the first volume are retained, as follows:

( )   Parentheses enclose literal meanings: 'buzzing with excitement' ('hot-noisy').

x y   Spaces separate words: *Hěn duō rén xuǎnzé wàichū dǎgōng.*

x-y   Hyphens are used in standard pinyin transcription to link certain constituents: *dì-yī* 'first' or *Ōu-Gòng-Tǐ* 'the EEC'. In the English glosses, hyphens separate disyllabic constituents of four-syllable compounds: *gǎoxiào-túpiàn* 'emoticon' ('make-laugh picture').

[ ]   Brackets enclose notes on style or other relevant information: *jiákè* 'jacket' [from English].

< >   Angle brackets indicate optional material: *zhào <yì> zhāng xiàng.*

/   A solidus distinguishes speech categories in glosses (without actually labeling them): *tànsuǒ* 'to explore; probe / explorations'.

[coll]   This indicates that the previous word or expression is colloquial:
          shá [coll].

~   A tilde is placed between options: *bǐrú shuō ~ pìrú shuō*.

*   An asterisk is placed before unacceptable or ungrammatical material:
          **bù yǒu*.

Dictionaries

The close match between sound and symbol in pinyin makes the *ABC Chinese-English Comprehensive Dictionary* a particularly useful resource for *Learning Chinese*. This dictionary is the only comprehensive dictionary with strict alphabetical ordering of entries by pinyin spelling. In effect, whatever can be written in pinyin (words overheard in conversation or encountered in the spoken language units of *Learning Chinese*, for example) can be looked up without regard to characters—that is, in the same way English words are looked up. (The ABC also allows you to look up the pronunciation of unknown characters using traditional procedures before proceeding to the alphabetic lookup for glosses.)

Xīnjiāpō

Unit 14

Zuò yǒu lǐxiǎng, yǒu dàodé, yǒu wénhuà, yǒu jìlǜ de gōngmín.
'Be good, moral, disciplined citizens.'
('Be have ideals, have morality, have culture, have discipline DE citizens.')
—Public sign at Kunming Teachers College (1999)

Zhìfù guāngróng.
'To get rich is glorious.'
('Get-wealth bright-honor.')
—Attributed to Dèng Xiǎopíng and regarded as a signal of the shift away from ideology in modern China

This unit, like the units that follow, begins with an informal narrative that serves for review, consolidation, and vocabulary development. Several grammatical topics follow, including the use of verb reduplication to express tentativeness, the *bǎ* construction that serves to spotlight items of current interest, and various means for expressing degree and comparison (for example, 'extremely hot' and 'hotter than'). The unit then shifts to the topic of buying and bargaining, and it includes two dialogues that take place at a fruit stand, which are followed by a discussion of flavors. Toward the end of the unit, there is a section that deals with postverbal *le*, culminating in a dialogue about a visit to one of the more spectacular sections of the Great Wall. The unit ends with some pronunciation exercises, a song, a rhyme, and a rondo.

Contents

14.1 A lighthearted narrative on regional languages and urban development

Fāngyán are regional language groups (*dìfang de yǔyán*). Chinese is said to have seven or eight such groups. (*Hànyǔ yígòng yǒu qī-bā ge dà fāngyán.*) They each have different names. (*Bùtóng de fāngyán yǒu bùtóng de míngzi.*) Lin Mei is a Chinese teacher. Her mother is from Shanghai (*Shànghǎi*), so she speaks (*huì shuō* or *huì jiǎng*) Shanghainese, as well as Mandarin. Shanghainese (*Shànghǎihuà*) is completely unlike Mandarin. (*Gēn Pǔtōnghuà wánquán bùtóng.*) Lin Mei can understand Shanghainese (*tīngdedǒng Shànghǎihuà*), but she doesn't understand Cantonese (*tīngbudǒng Guǎngdōnghuà*). Cantonese and Shanghainese are completely different (*wánquán bù yíyàng*). For example (*bǐfang shuō* or *shuō ge lìzi*): 'he' or 'she' (*tā* in Mandarin) is pronounced 'kœy' in Cantonese and 'ɦ̩' in Shanghainese. (Even without indicating tones, and without knowing quite how to read the transcription, it's clear the two are completely different from each other and quite different from Mandarin.) People from Suzhou and Ningbo (*Sūzhōurén, Níngbōrén*)—cities that are not far from Shanghai—speak varieties of language that are quite similar to (*yǒu yìdiǎnr xiàng*) the language spoken by natives of Shanghai. Now here is the rest of the story.

Lín Měi shi Zhōngwén lǎoshī. Lǎo péngyou dōu guǎn tā jiào Xiǎo Lín,
kěshì xuéshēng dāngrán jiào tā Lín lǎoshī. Yóuyú tā shi Zhōngwén lǎoshī,
tā de xuéshēng dōu shi wàiguó lái de: yǒu Rìběn de, Měiguó de, Ōuzhōu de,
yě yǒu Àozhōu de. Lín Měi chūshēng zài Běijīng; tā fùqin yě shi Běijīngrén.
kěshì mǔqin shi Shànghǎi lái de, suǒ.yǐ Lín Měi yě huì shuō diǎnr
Shànghǎihuà. Huì shuō Pǔtōnghuà de rén bù yídìng tīngdedǒng Shànghǎihuà.
Lín Měi de bàba huì shuō Pǔtōnghuà, bú huì shuō Shànghǎihuà, kěshì
māma Pǔtōnghuà Shànghǎihuà dōu huì jiǎng. Suǒ.yǐ Lín Měi hé māma
shuōhuà, bàba yǒu shíhou dǒng, yǒu shíhou bù dǒng. Hěn yǒu yìsi! Wǒ kě.yǐ
shuō ge Shànghǎihuà de lìzi. Pǔtōnghuà shuō: "Wǎnfàn chīguò le ma?"
Shànghǎihuà shuō: "ɦia.vɛ tɕʰɪ.ku.ləʔ va?" Gēn Pǔtōnghuà wánquán bùtóng,
duì ma?

Nà, wǒmen tántan Shànghǎihuà ba. Nǐ kànkan dìtú. Shànghǎi fùjìn yǒu
hěn duō chéngshì: Sūzhōu, Níngbō, Hángzhōu, Wēnzhōu, Shàoxīng děngděng.
Dōu lí Shànghǎi bù yuǎn. Nà, Sūzhōurén shuō shénme huà ne? Sūzhōurén
dāngrán shuō Sūzhōuhuà. Níngbōrén ne? Yíyàng, Níngbōrén shuō Níngbōhuà.
Kěshì Shànghǎihuà, Sūzhōuhuà, Níngbōhuà dōu hěn xiàng; kě.yǐ shuō dōu
shi tóng yì zhǒng fāngyán. Guǎngdōnghuà, Fújiànhuà, Kèjiāhuà děngděng dōu
shǔyú bùtóng de fāngyán. Fāngyán shi shénme ne? Fāngyán shi dìfang de
yǔyán.

Nà bùtóng de fāngyán yǒu bùtóng de míngzi. Bǐfang shuō, Shànghǎi fùjìn
shi Wú fāngyán. Wèishénme jiào Wú ne? Nà shi yīnwèi yǐqián, zài Chūnqiū
Shídài, nèi ge dìfang yǒu ge Wúguó. Hànyǔ yígòng yǒu qī-bā ge dà fāngyán:
Wú (zài Shànghǎi, Zhèjiāng), Yuè (zài Guǎngdōng, Guǎngxī, Xiānggǎng),
Mǐn (zài Fújiàn, Táiwān, Hǎinán), Kèjiā (zài Guǎngdōng, Fújiàn, Jiāngxī),
Xiāng (zài Húnán), Gàn (zài Jiāngxī, Húnán) hé Běifāng fāngyán (zài
běifāng). Běifāng de shi zuì pǔbiàn de. Pǔtōnghuà ne? Pǔtōnghuà bù néng
shuō shi ge dìfang de yǔyán, shì guójiā de yǔyán, kěshì Pǔtōnghuà gen Běifāng
fāngyán zuì jiējìn.

Lín Měi xǐhuan Běijīng, yě xǐhuan Shànghǎi. Kěshì tā shuō zuìjìn biànhuà
tài duō le. Yǐqián Běijīng yǒu hěn duō hútòngr. Hútòngr shi bǐjiào ānjìng de
dìfang, kě.yǐ zǒuyizǒu, hē chá, kàn péngyou; yǒu fángzi, xiǎo shāngdiàn,
cháguǎnr děngděng. Shànghǎi méiyǒu hútòngr; Shànghǎi yǒu nòngtáng—nà

shi Shànghǎihuà de yí ge cí. Nòngtáng yǒu yìdiǎnr xiàng hútòngr, kěshì bù
zěnme ānjìng, bù zěnme hǎokàn!

Běijīng yǐqián hútòngr hěn duō; Shànghǎi yǐqián nòngtáng yě hěn duō.
Kěshì xiànzài, bù yíyàng. Yǐqián de hútòngr shi xiànzài de gòuwù zhōngxīn le;
yǐqián de nòngtáng shi xiànzài de dàlóu le! Yǒude Zhōngguórén hěn xǐhuan
gòuwù zhōngxīn. Wèishénme ne? Yīnwèi hěn fāngbiàn, dōngxi hěn duō, yǒu
chī de, hē de, wánr de. Gòuwù-zhōngxīn hěn gānjìng, méiyǒu hàozi, méiyǒu
zhāngláng, méiyǒu chóngzi, méiyǒu zhīzhū, méiyǒu wénzi. Xiàng ge gōngdiàn
yíyàng, xiàng ge shìwài-táoyuán yíyàng!

Zhōngguórén, yǒude xǐhuan lǎo de dōngxi, xǐhuan chuántǒng de; tāmen hěn
xǐhuan Běijīng de hútòngr. Yǒude xǐhuan xīn de, xiàndài de, hěn xǐhuan dà
chéngshì de gòuwù-zhōngxīn, mótiān-dàlóu. Bù zhīdao nǐmen Měiguórén,
Ōuzhōurén de kànfǎ zěnmeyàng!

VOCABULARY

guǎn tā jiào . . .	literally, 'charge her with the name of . . .', with both person and name having their own verb. This is a more colloquial version of *jiào* followed by person and name: *Lǎo péngyou dōu jiào tā Xiǎo Lín.*
yóuyú	'owing to; as a result of; due to [the fact that]' ('source-in')
gēn . . . bùtóng	'different from . . .' ('with . . . not same')
tán	'talk; discuss': overlaps with *shuō* 'speak; say; talk about'. *Shuōshuo* would also be possible here, but *tántan* suggests the participation of all parties, hence 'discuss'.
shǔyú	'belong to': cf. *Tā shǔ mǎ* 'She's the year of the horse'.
bǐfang shuō	'for example': also *bǐrú shuō ~ pìrú shuō*
Chūnqiū Shídài	'The Spring and Autumn Period' (770–464 BCE), a historical division of the Zhōu Dynasty, named for the Chunqiu annals of that period.

pǔbiàn	'widespread': *pǔtōng de pǔ*
guójiā	'country' ('nation-home'): *guójí* 'nationality' and *guójì* 'international'
jiējìn	'be close to; be near; be intimate with' ('join-close'): *gēn . . . jiējìn*
biànhuà	'changes': the same *huà* of *huàxué* 'chemistry' ('study of transformations')
hútòng<r>	The name given to a particular type of alley that is typically found in Beijing (*Běijīng*). The Mandarin word is supposedly borrowed from Mongolian.
ānjìng	'peaceful' ('peace-quiet')
cháguǎn<r>	'teashop' ('tea-shop'): *fànguǎn<r>*, *túshūguǎn*
cí<r>	'word': *Tā méi cír le.* 'She's run out of things to say.'
nòngtáng	Mandarin pronunciation of a Shanghai word for 'lane' or 'alley'.
bù zěnme . . .	'not so [adjective]': This is the indefinite use of *zěnme*; cf. *bù zěnme gāo*, *bù zěnme lěng*.
gòuwù zhōngxīn	'goods center': a translation of the English 'shopping center'; cf. *shāngchǎng* 'mall' ('business-gathering place')
dàlóu	'big building': 'Skyscraper' has a literal Chinese equivalent—*mótiān-dàlóu* ('scrape-sky big-building').
fāngbiàn	'be convenient': colloquially, 'to go to the restroom'
gānjìng	'be clean'
lǎoshǔ	'mice': *hàozi* 'rats'; *zhānglǎng* 'roaches'; *chóngzi* 'insects'; *zhīzhū* 'spiders'; *wénzi* 'mosquitoes'
gōngdiàn	'palace'
shìwài-táoyuán	('world-outside peach-garden'): alludes to a well-known tale about a man who discovered a distant, secret garden
xīn de	'new things': cf. *chī de, hē de, wánr de*
xiàndài	'modern times' ('new-age')
kànfǎ	'viewpoint; opinion' ('seeing-way')

Hútòngr (*Běijīng*)

NOTE ON 'OLD'   Chinese has two words that overlap with English 'old'. One is *lǎo* (as in *lǎoshī* 'teacher' and *lǎohǔ* 'tiger', where it is better translated as 'venerable' or 'worthy of respect'); the other is *jiù* (as in *Jiùjīnshān* ['old-gold-mountain']—the Chinese name for San Francisco). In general terms, *lǎo* is the opposite of *shào* 'young', whereas *jiù* is the opposite of *xīn* 'new'. *Lǎo* also means 'tough', as of meat, and is the opposite of *nèn* 'tender'. *Lǎo* has basically positive connotations, but *jiù* tends to have negative ones. The following are some typical examples or collocations.

lǎo	'old; experienced; longstanding; of earlier times': positive in tone
Tā lǎo le.	'He's getting old.'
lǎo dìfang	'the usual place'
lǎo péngyou	'a good friend'
lǎoshǒu	'an old hand; expert'
lǎojiā	'hometown'
lǎorén	'old people'
lǎo gōngrén	'experienced worker'
lǎo chuántǒng	'old customs'

jiù	'used; old-fashioned; deteriorated; out-of-date; former': often negative in tone
Jiù le.	'It's worn out.'
Jīqì jiù le.	'This machine's antiquated.'
jiùchē	'used car'
jiùshū	'used book'
jiùyīfu	'worn-out clothes'
jiùshèhuì	'the old society' [pre-1949]
jiùsīxiǎng	'old-fashioned ideas'
jiùhuò	'second-hand goods; junk'

In 1966, at the beginning of the period known as the Cultural Revolution, Mao Zedong called for the destruction of the *Sì Jiù* 'four olds'—*jiùwénhuà* 'old culture', *jiùsīxiǎng* 'old thought', *jiùfēngsú* 'old customs', and *jiùxíguàn* 'old practices'.

Exercise 1

Answer the following questions about the narrative.

1. *Wèishénme yǒu rén shuō Lín Měi shi Shànghǎi lái de?*
2. *Tā de xuéshēng shi shénme dìfang lái de?*
3. *Tā fùqin huì jiǎng shénme huà?*
4. *Mǔqin zhǐ huì jiǎng Shànghǎihuà ba?*
5. *Bàba yǒu shíhou tīngbudǒng Lín Měi shuō de huà, wèishénme?*
6. *Shénme shi fāngyán?*
7. *Wú fāngyán shi shénme? Wèishénme jiào 'Wú'?*
8. *Hútòngr gēn nòngtáng zěnme bù yíyàng?*
9. *Wèishénme xiànzài de Běijīng hútòngr bù duō le?*
10. *Yǒurén bǐjiào xǐhuan hútòngr, wèishénme?*
11. *Gòuwù zhōngxīn shi shénme?*
12. *Mótiān-dàlóu shi shénme?*

13. *Yǒurén yě xǐhuan gòuwù zhōngxīn, wèishénme?*
14. *Shénme shi shìwài-táoyuán?*
15. *Pǔtōnghuà yě kě.yǐ shuō shi fāngyán ma?*
16. *Nǐ de sùshè lǐmian hàozi, chóngzi, zhāngláng duō bu duō? Zěnme bàn?*

14.2 Verb reduplication and tentativeness

In Chinese, as in other languages, it is sometimes useful to give an impression of wariness or nonchalance by suggesting that an action involves a minimum of effort. One way to achieve this effect is to reduplicate the verb (with the repeated syllable normally unstressed).

> *Shànglai kànkan ba.*   'Come on up and take a look.'

There are a number of variations. With single-syllable verbs, such as *kàn* 'look' or *zuò* 'sit', *yī* 'one' can be inserted between the verbs, as if to say 'look a look' or 'sit a sitting'. In this case, both iterations of the verb can be toned (*kànyikàn*), though in fast speech, the second iteration of the verb will be unstressed (*kànyikan*). The postverbal *le* (see §14.8), if present, appears after the first instance of the verb.

Kànyikàn.	'Take a look.'
Ta kànle yí kàn.	'She took a look.'
Zuòyizuò.	'Sit for a bit.'
Tā zuòle yí zuò.	'He sat for a while.'
Zánmen zǒuyizǒu, hǎo bu hǎo?	'Let's take a walk, how about it?'

The same effect can be achieved by adding the phrase *yíxià<r>* 'one time' instead of the second iteration of the verb. Therefore, the options for single-syllable verbs are as follows.

Děngdeng!	'Hang on!'
Děngyiděng!	'Wait a sec!'
Děngyixiàr!	'Hold on!'

Two-syllable verbs, such as *xiūxi*, are more restricted. They too can be reiterated, or followed by *yíxià<r>*, but they do not accept a medial *yī*. For two-syllable verbs, the options are as follows.

Xiūxi xiūxi ba.
Xiūxi yíxià ba. } 'Let's take a break.'

Wǒ gěi nǐ jièshao jièshao.
Wǒ gěi nǐ jièshao yíxiàr. } 'Let me introduce you.'

Other common examples include the following.

Nǐ chángchang ba.
Nǐ chángyicháng ba. } 'Have a taste, why don't you?'
Nǐ chángyixiàr ba.

Shuìshuijiào ba.
Shuìyixià jiào ba. } 'Sleep for a bit.'

Nǐ cāicai ~ cāiyicāi ~ cāiyixiàr.   'Take a guess.'
Nǐ wènwen tā ba.   'Why don't you just ask her?'
Nǐ de zìdiǎn, néng kànkan ma?   'Can I take a look at your dictionary?'
Mōmo ~ mōyimō ~ mōyixiàr!   'Feel this!'

Certain verbs of cognition and consideration seem especially prone to reduplication patterns.

xiǎng	'think'
kǎolǜ	'think over; consider'
shāngliung	'discuss; consult'
tán	'talk; chat; discuss'

Xiān gēn tā tányitán.	'Talk to her first.'
Zánmen shāngliang shāngliang.	'Let's talk about it.'
Ràng wǒ kǎolǜ yíxiàr.	'Let me think it over.'

Kǎolǜ involves a delay or postponement, so it is not surprising that in certain contexts, sentences such as the last example may serve as an indirect way of denying a request—a way of saying 'no'. There are, of course, other expressions that serve the same purpose of delaying a decision. For example: *Yǐhòu zài shuō ba.* 'Why don't we talk about it later?'

14.3 Complex verbs, the *bǎ* construction, and giving instructions

In certain situations—giving instructions, for example—Chinese will highlight the noun (or noun phrases) of interest ('window' and 'door' in the examples that follow) by placing it before the associated verb and marking it with *bǎ*.

Qǐng bǎ chuānghu dǎkāi.	'Open the window, please.'
Qǐng bǎ mén guānshàng.	'Close the door, please.'
Chūqu de shíhou, qǐng bǎ mén suǒshàng.	'Lock the door when you go out, please.'

Historically, *bǎ* derives from a verb meaning 'take', and it is sometimes possible to get a feel for the function of *bǎ* by translating it as 'take'.

Qǐng bǎ shūbāo fàng zai wàitou.	'Please take your bookbags and put them outside' (i.e., 'Put your bookbags outside, please').

NOTE

Fàng zai wàitou. You have encountered other cases in which *zài* (usually unstressed) is placed after the verb: *Wǒ shēng zai Guǎngzhōu, zhǎng zai Xiāng Gǎng, xiànzài jiā zhù zai Luòshānjī.* With the verbs *shēng, zhǎng,* and *zhù,* the *zài* phrase may also be placed before the verb with a nuance of difference: *Wǒ zài Guǎngzhōu shēng de* 'I was born in Guangzhou'. With the verb *fàng,* however, the place where the thing ends up is consistently mentioned after the verb: *fàng zai zhuōzi shàng, fàng zai qiántou, fàng zai tóu shàng.*

Bǎ typically appears before noun phrases that refer to things moved, changed, or otherwise affected by an action verb. The *bǎ* phrase is drawn close to the verb, so adverbs (such as *xiān* in the next example) tend to appear before it rather than after it.

> *Wǒ xiān bǎ chē kāi guòlai, hǎo bu hǎo?*   'I'll drive my car over first, okay?
> *Nǐmen zài zhèr děng wǒ.*   Wait here for me.'

An effective way to get a feel for the function of *bǎ* is to give instructions to your classmates or friends to move things around, and then have them confirm that they've done it.

> *Xiān bǎ shūbāo fàng zai wàitou.*   'Please put your bookbags outside.'
>
> *Hǎo, wǒ bǎ shūbāo fàng zai wàitou le.*   'Okay, I've put the bookbags outside.'
>
> *Xiànzài bǎ yīfu fàng zai chuáng shang.*   'Now put the clothes on the bed.'
>
> *Hǎo, wǒ yǐjīng bǎ yīfu fàng zai chuáng shang le.*   'Okay, I've already put the clothes on the bed.'
>
> *Xiànzài bǎ yǐzi fàng zai qiánbianr.*   'Now put the chairs in front.'
>
> *Bǎ míngzi xiě zai hēibǎnshang.*   'Write your name on the blackboard.'

Bǎ is never associated with a 'naked' verb, but it typically occurs with combinations of verb plus complement (*xiě* + *zai* phrase, in the last examples; *dǎkāi* 'do' + 'open', *guānshàng* 'close' + 'up' in the earlier ones). 'Directional complements' are another common kind of verb combination that often satisfies the conditions for using *bǎ*.

In the elementary level of *Learning Chinese* (§7.1.3), it was shown that motion (directional) verbs (e.g., *shàng*, *chū*, *guò*) combine with an untoned *lái* or *qù* to form combinations such as *xiàlai*, *guòqu*, and *huílai*. Now you will see that these pairs can combine with compatible verbs such as *ná* 'hold; take'; *tái* 'lift; raise [with palms up]'; *kāi* 'drive'; *fàng* 'put'; and *bān* 'move; remove; take away'. The complete paradigm can be illustrated with *ná* 'carry; bring; take'.

ná shànglai	'bring them up here'
ná shàngqu	'take them up there'
ná xiàlai	'bring them down here'
ná xiàqu	'take them down there'
ná jìnlai	'bring them in here'
ná jìnqu	'take them in there'
ná chūlai	'bring them out here'
ná chūqu	'take them out there'
ná huílai	'bring them back here'
ná huíqu	'take them back there'
ná guòlai	'bring them over here'
ná guòqu	'take them over there'

With other verbs, the same construction applies.

bān jìnlai	'move in here'
fàng jìnqu	'put them in there'
tái chūlai	'carry them out here'
tái chūqu	'carry them out there'
kāi huílai	'drive them back here'
bān huíqu	'move back there'
kāi guòlai	'drive it over here'
kāi guòqu	'drive it over there'

An additional directional complement can be added to the set: *qǐlai* 'rise [here]' (for which there is no corresponding **qǐqu*). The *qǐlai* complement has a number of extended meanings (§15.8.3), but with verbs of motion, it often corresponds to the English verbal particle 'up'.

zhàn qǐlai	'stand up'
ná qǐlai	'hold up'
tái qǐlai	'lift up'

USAGE

a. *Nǐ de dōngxi nàme duō ya!*   'You have so many things! I'll help
     Wǒ bāng nǐ ná chūlai,   you bring them out, okay?'
     hǎo bu hǎo?

     Méi guānxi, wǒ zìjǐ ná ba!   'Never mind, I'll get them!'
     Bù, wǒ bāng nǐ ná.   'No, I'll help you with them.'

b. *Nǐ zhù <zai> jǐ lóu?*   'What floor do you live on?'
     Liù lóu.   'The 6th.'
     Hǎo, wǒ bāng nǐ ná shàngqu ba.   'Okay, let me help you take
                                   them up.'

     Nǐ tài kèqi le. Máfan nín le.   'You're too kind. If you
                                   don't mind then.'

c. *Wǒ xiān bǎ chē kāi guòlai,*   'I'll drive my car over first, okay?'
     hǎo bu hǎo?

     Hǎo, nà wǒ zài zhèli děng nǐ.   'Fine, so I'll wait for you here.'
     Wǒ yìhuǐr jiù dào.   'I'll be back shortly.'

Notice that when the thing moved is explicitly mentioned, it is placed before the verb as an object of the preposition (co-verb) *bǎ*. The following exercise provides more examples.

Dā biànchē? 'Hitching a ride?'

Exercise 2

Using directional verb combos such as those illustrated in §14.3, request that your friend help you in the manner indicated. Notice that objects are mentioned—clothes, shoes, suitcases, and so on—but places are not. How to express these places (e.g., drawers, room) will be covered later.

Please help me put the books down there.   *Qǐng bāng wǒ bǎ shū fàng xiàqu.*

Please help me to take the clothes out [of the drawers].   *Qǐng bāng wǒ bǎ yīfu ná chūlai.*

1. Please put the clothes back [in the drawers].
2. Please bring the flowers up [here].
3. Please carry the luggage down [there].
4. Please lift up this suitcase. (*xiāngzi*)
5. Please take these clothes out [of the drawers].
6. Please take the shoes out [of the room].
7. Please lift this computer up [onto the rack].
8. Please bring the keys back [here].
9. Please carry the musical instruments over [there].
10. Please move the things out [there].
11. Please drive the car over [there].
12. Please lift up the fridge. (*bīngxiāng*)
13. Please put the dictionaries back [there].

14.4 Degree and comparison

14.4.1 Degree of intensity

Questions about degrees of intensity can be asked using the question phrase *yǒu duō* (or *yǒu duōma*) 'to what degree'. In certain cases, *yǒu* can be omitted.

Xiàtiān yǒu duō rè?	'How hot are the summers?'
Tā <yǒu> duō gāo?	'How tall is he?'
Dào fēijīchǎng <yǒu> duō yuǎn?	'How far is the airport?'

Responses often include adverbs or constructions that indicate degree. The examples below are organized into types, and they include a number of new constructions.

a. With the modification placed before the stative verb:

Jīntiān hěn rè.	'Today's quite hot.'
Jīntiān tǐng rè <de>!	'It's really hot today!'
Jīntiān fēicháng rè.	'Today's unusually hot.'
Jīntiān bǐjiào rè.	'It's quite (~ rather) hot today.'
Jīntiān xiāngdāng rè.	'It's relatively (~ rather ~ quite) hot today.'
Jīntiān yǒu diǎnr rè.	'Today's sort of (~ quite) hot.'

b. With the modification placed after the stative verb:

| *Jīntiān rè jíle.* | 'It's really hot today.' ('hot to-the-max') |
| *Jīntiān rè sǐle.* | 'It's boiling today.' ('hot to-death') |

c. With the modification mediated by the particle +*de* 'to the extent that':

Jīntiān rè+de hěn.	'It's very hot today.' ('hot+to very')
Jīntiān rè+de bùdéliǎo.	'It's awfully hot today.' ('hot+to amazing')
Jīntiān rè+de yàomìng!	'It's excruciatingly hot today! ('hot+to want-life')
Jīntiān rè+de yàosǐ!	'It's hot as hell today!' ('hot+to want-death')
Jīntiān rè+de shéi dōu bù xiǎng chūqu!	'Today's so hot that no one wants to go out!'

The first example (under c.) contrasts with *Jīntiān hěn rè* 'It's quite hot today', in which *hěn* has hardly any intensifying function. The last example involves a full sentence *shéi dōu bù xiǎng chūqu* 'no one wants to go out', placed as a complement to *rè+de*. A literal translation would be 'hot to the extent that no one wants to go out'.

14.4.2 'Than' comparatives

Comparison is often implicit in the unmodified stative verb, but it is canceled by the presence of preverbal *hěn* (as noted in the previous paragraph).

Therefore, in the right context, *tā gāo* corresponds to English 'she's taller', but *tā hěn gāo* corresponds to 'she's quite tall'.

Shéi gāo? / *Tā gāo.*	'Who's taller?' / 'She's taller.'
Tā gāo yìdiǎnr.	'She's a bit taller.'
Tā shāowēi gāo yìdiǎnr.	'He's a wee bit taller.'
Gāo duōshao?	'How much taller?'
Tā gāo yí cùn.	'He's an inch taller.' ('taller by an inch')
Tā gāo yí bèi.	'She's twice as tall.' ('taller by one multiple')
Tā gāo yì tóu.	'He's a head taller.' ('taller by a head')

NOTES

a. *Shāowēi* (or more formally, *shāo*) is an adverb meaning 'slightly; a bit'. (For *wēi*, cf. *Wēiruǎn* 'Microsoft'.) Like other adverbs, *shāowēi* appears before a verb or stative verb (adjective) but typically also in conjunction with a postverbal *yìdiǎnr*: *shāowēi lǎo yìdiǎnr* 'It's a bit tough [of meat]'.

b. *Yí bèi* 'by one-fold; twice as'

Explicit comparison is signaled by *bǐ* 'compare; than', which (unlike English counterparts) is placed before the associated verb. By contrast, expressions indicating the degree or amount of comparison are placed after the stative verb. The construction, then, is A—*bǐ*—B—SV (degree). For example, *bǐ Tiānjīn dà yìdiǎnr* 'bigger than Tianjin' ('than Tianjin bigger [by] a-bit').

Běijīng bǐ Tiānjīn dà.	'Beijing is bigger than Tianjin.'
Běijīng bǐ Tiānjīn dà yìdiǎnr.	'Beijing is a bit bigger than Tianjin.' ('Beijing than Tianjin is bigger by a bit.')
Běijīng bǐ Tiānjīn shāowēi dà yìdiǎnr.	'Beijing's a little bit bigger than Tianjin. ('Bj than Tj is somewhat bigger by a bit.')
Běijīng bǐ Tiānjīn dà hěn duō.	'Beijing's a lot bigger than Tianjin.' ('Bj than Tj is bigger by quite a lot.')

Běijīng bǐ Tiānjīn dà +de duō.	'Beijing is much bigger than Tianjin.' ('Bj than Tj is bigger to the extent of a lot.')
Běijīng bǐ Tiānjīn dà duōle.	'Beijing is a lot bigger than Tianjin.' ('Bj than Tj is bigger by a whole lot.')
Běijīng bǐ Tiānjīn dà yí bèi.	'Beijing is twice as big as Tianjin.' ('Bj than Tj is bigger by one-fold.')

NOTES

a. In English, we generally mean 'in terms of population' when we say that one city is bigger than another. Likewise, *dà* in the previous set of sentences is more likely to mean population (*rénkǒu*) than area (*miànjī*).

b. Notice that the various ways of expressing degree with noncomparatives do not overlap with those of the comparatives: *+de hěn, +de bùdéliǎo,* and so on are unique to noncomparatives; *+de duō, duōle,* and so on are unique to comparatives.

DIALOGUE

Jiǎ:	*Shànghǎi shi Zhōngguó rénkǒu zuì duō de chéngshì ba?*	'Shanghai is the city with the largest population in China, right?'
Yǐ:	*Shì, bǐ Běijīng duō.*	'Right, it's got more than Beijing.'
Jiǎ:	*Bǐ Běijīng duō duōshao?*	'How much more than Beijing?'
Yǐ:	*Bǐ Běijīng duō jǐbǎiwàn.*	'Several million more than Beijing.'
Jiǎ:	*Nà, Shànghǎi shi shìjiè shàng zuì dà de ba?*	'So Shanghai's the largest city in the world?'
Yǐ:	*Bù, wǒ xiǎng Mòxīgē Shì gèng dà.*	'No, Mexico City's even bigger, I think.'

	NONCOMPARATIVE			COMPARATIVE		
	PRE-	SV	-POST	(X *BǏ* Y) SV	AMOUNT	
'quite tired'	*hěn*	*lèi*		*gāo*		'taller'
'very'	*fēicháng*	*lèi*		*gāo*	*yìdiǎnr*	'a bit taller'
'rather'	*bǐjiào*	*lèi*		*gāo*	+*de duō*	'much taller'
'quite'	*xiāngdāng*	*lèi*		*gāo*	*hěn duō*	'much taller'
'a bit'	*yǒu yìdiǎnr*	*lèi*		*gāo*	*duōle*	'a lot taller'
'extremely'		*lèi*	*jíle*	*gāo*	*yí cùn*	'an inch taller'
'exhausted'		*lèi*	*sǐle*	*gāo*	*yí bèi*	'twice as tall'
'very'		*lèi*	+*de hěn*			
'awfully'		*lèi*	+*de bùdeliǎo*			
'terribly'		*lèi*	+*de yàomìng*			
'dreadfully'		*lèi*	+*de yàosǐ*			
'so tired that'		*lèi*	+*de . . .*			

14.4.3 'As' comparatives

The claim that 'Beijing is bigger than Tianjin' is usually not negated with 'Beijing isn't bigger' but with 'Beijing isn't as big as'. In other words, rather than *bù bǐ Tiānjīn dà* (which is possible in certain contexts), the negative is usually *méi<yǒu> Tiānjīn <nàme> dà*. In actual conversation, the *bǐ* versus *méiyǒu* patterns may serve to shift perspective.

1. *Běijīng méiyǒu Shànghǎi*   'Beijing's not as big as Shanghai.'
    <nàme> dà.

    Duì a, Shànghǎi bǐ Běijīng   'Right, Shanghai's a lot bigger than
    dà duōle.   Beijing.'

2. *Miǎndiàn méiyǒu Tàiguó*   'Burma's not as developed as
   <nàme> fādá.   Thailand.'

   Shì a, Miǎndiàn bǐjiào luòhòu.   'Right, Burma's less developed.'

3. *Kūnmíng de hǎibá méiyǒu*   'Kunming's elevation isn't as high
   Xīníng de <nàme> gāo.   as Xining's.'

   Shì a, Xīníng de hǎibá shi   'That's right; Xining is over 3,000
   sānqiān duō mǐ.   meters high.'

   Kěshì Lāsà de gèng gāo. Zài Lāsà   'But Lhasa is even higher. In Lhasa,
   hūxī hěn kùnnan.   breathing's quite difficult.'

4. *Yúnnán de lǎnhóu hěn kě'ài, dànshi*   'The sloths in Yunnan are quite
   méiyǒu xióngmāo kě'ài.   cute, but they're not as cute as
                                 pandas.'

   Shì a, xióngmāo zuì kě'ài.   'True, pandas are the cutest.'

5. *Yúnnán de Shí Lín hěn*   'The Stone Forest of Yunnan is
   zhuàngguān, kěshì méiyǒu   spectacular, but it's not as
   Guìlín de nàme zhuàngguān.   spectacular as Guilin.'

VOCABULARY

luòhòu	'less developed': Countries are often characterized as *fādá* 'developed' or *luòhòu* 'less developed' ('fall-back').
hǎibá	'elevation; height' ('sea-exceed')
hūxī	'to breathe' ('breathe out-breathe in')
kùnnan	'difficult; laborious' ('hard pressed-difficult')
lǎnhóu	'sloths' ('lazy-monkey')
xióngmāo	'pandas' ('bear-cat')
zhuàngguān	'be spectacular' ('robust-sight')

Even in spoken language, the more formal expression *bùrú* ('not resemble') can substitute for *méiyǒu . . . <nàme>*. When *bùrú* is not followed by a stative verb, it is understood to mean 'as good as'.

> *Hànyǔ ne, Wáng Xiǎobīn bùrú Léi Hànbó. = Hànyǔ ne, Wáng Xiǎobīn*
> *méiyǒu Léi Hànbó <nàme> hǎo.*

Otherwise, a stative verb may be explicitly mentioned.

> *Lǎoshī bùrú xuéshēng*   'The teachers aren't as intelligent as
>   *cōngmíng, kěshì xuéshēng*   the students, but the students aren't
>   *bùrú lǎoshī yǒu jīngyàn.*   as experienced as the teachers.'

About ten years ago, a Nanjing (*Nánjīng*) newspaper, *Yángzǐ Wǎnbào*, had the following headline, directed to the youth of Nanjing.

> *Shàngxiāng bùrú*   'Better to surf the Web than get stoned; better
>   *shàngwǎng, qiúshén*   to seek knowledge than get religion.' ('Go on-
>   *bùrú qiúzhī.*   incense not-like go on-web, seek-divinity not-
>   like seek-knowledge.')

POSITIVE PERSPECTIVE	NEGATIVE PERSPECTIVE
Shànghǎi bǐ Běijīng dà + de duō.	*Běijīng méiyǒu Shànghǎi \<nàme\> dà.* [*Běijīng bùrú Shànghǎi dà.*]
'Shanghai's much bigger than Beijing.'	'Beijing isn't as big as Shanghai.'

Něi zuò zuì gāo? (*Shànghǎi*)

14.4.4 Comparing abilities

Comparing how well people do something ('You speak Chinese better than I do') combines the comparative construction ('better than') with V+*de* ('speak better'). There are a number of options; the comparison can be mentioned first ('you than me speak better'), or V+*de* can be mentioned first ('you speak better than I do').

V+*de* before *bǐ*

Tā <shuō Yīngyǔ> shuō+de bǐ wǒ hǎo.	'He speaks English better than I do.'
Tā <chànggēr> chàng+de bǐ wǒ hǎo.	'She sings better than I do.'

bǐ before V+*de*

Tā <Yīngyǔ> bǐ wǒ shuō+de hǎo.	'He speaks English better than I do.'
Tā <gēr> bǐ wǒ chàng+de hǎo.	'She sings better than I do.'

Since these are comparatives, they are subject to the same modification of degree as simple comparatives.

Tā shuō+de bǐ wǒ hǎo yìdiǎnr.	'She speaks a bit better than I do.'
Tā shuō+de bǐ wǒ hǎo+de duō.	'She speaks much better than I do.'
Tā shuō+de bǐ wǒ hǎo duōle.	'She speaks a lot better than I do.'

As the previous three examples show, an object need not be present. If, for clarity or another reason, an object is stated, then it cannot be placed directly after the verb when the +*de* construction is used. Instead, it has to be mentioned earlier. There are two possibilities. First, the verb and object can be 'exposed' first, and the verb is repeated before +*de*: *Tā chànggēr chàng+de bǐ wǒ hǎo.* This is usual in those cases where the object is closely tied to the verb (*chànggēr, chīfàn, lùyīn*). Second, the object can simply be mentioned before the verb: *Tā Yīngyǔ shuō+de bǐ wǒ hǎo.* Exercise 3 provides practice.

Exercise 3

Get used to the options by trying slight variations on the model sentences cited previously, first without the objects, then with them. Start by writing the answers, and then practice saying them.

> *Tā / wǒ / xiě / hǎo > Tā bǐ wǒ xiě+de hǎo ~ Tā xiě+de bǐ wǒ hǎo.*
> *Tā / wǒ / xiě / zì / hǎo > Tā xiězì bǐ wǒ xiě+de hǎo ~ Tā xiězì xiě+de bǐ wǒ hǎo.*

Now try to form sentences with the following words (two ways for the first, then one way when you add the object).

1. Speaking:
   Nǐ / wǒ / shuō / hǎo →
   Add *Zhōngwén* →
2. Speaking:
   Tā / wǒ / shuō / qīngchu →
   Add *huà* →
3. Driving:
   Tā / wǒ / kāi / kuài →
   Add *chē* →
4. Speaking:
   Tāmen / wǒmen / shuō / biāozhǔn ('proper') →
   Add *sìshēng* ('the four tones') →

Now praise others over yourself; the person in brackets is the other person—the starting point. One answer is fine. There is no need to give variations.

> *dǎ lánqiú* ('play basketball') [*hǎo*] → [*Xiǎo Bì*] . . .
> *Xiǎo Bì <lánqiú> dǎ+de bǐ wǒ hǎo ~ <dǎ lánqiú> dǎ de+bǐ*
> *wǒ hǎo ~ <lánqiú> bǐ wǒ dǎ+de hǎo.*

1. *chànggēr* [*hǎotīng duō le*] → [*nǐ*] . . .
2. *zuòfàn* [*hǎo + de duō*] → [*tā*] . . .
3. *xiězì* [*qīngchu yìdiǎnr*] → [*jiějie*] . . .
4. *yòng kuàizi* [*hǎo*] → [*Xiǎolín Yóuměi*] . . .
5. *bāo jiǎozi* ('wrap dumplings') [*kuài*] → [*Qiánchéng*] . . .
6. *zhǎng* [*gāo*] → [*dìdi*] . . .
7. *pǎo* [*màn*] → [*Lǎnhóu / xióngmāo*] . . .

Write out your answers in preparation for answering aloud in class:

1. Explain that *Yáo Míng* is thirty centimeters taller than Kobe Bryant. (Note: Kobe Bryant is called *Xiǎo Fēi Xiá* 'young flying knight', which is, incidentally, also the Chinese name of Peter Pan. Centimeters are *gōngfēn* or *límǐ*, both of which are M words. Thirty centimeters is roughly one foot.)
2. Explain to your friend that you both like to sing, but she sings much better than you do.
3. Explain that you have an older brother who is five years older than you.
4. Explain that eating your own cooking (*zìjǐ zuò de*) is always much better than eating out.
5. Note that apartments (houses) are twice as expensive in Beijing as they are in Xining (*Xīníng*).
6. Explain that it's frustrating (*tǎoyàn*) your friend doesn't study as hard (*yònggōng*) as you do, but he speaks more fluently.
7. Explain that in the winter in Lhasa, it's so cold that no one (*shéi dōu*) dares (*gǎn*) to go out.
8. Explain that the weather has gotten a bit warmer (*nuǎnhuo*) recently.

14.5 Cities and population

In the course of making comparisons, it is often useful to cite the largest, best, most expensive, or least attractive item in the set—in other words, to form superlatives. In Chinese, these are formed with *zuì*: *zuì hǎo* 'best' and *zuì piányi* 'least expensive' are examples. *Zuì* can also appear before verbs such as *xǐhuan* 'like' and *yuànyi* 'willing'. In addition, *zuì* can be repeated for effect.

Wǒ zuì bù xǐhuan tīngxiě.	'I dislike dictation most of all.'
Wǒ zuì bú yuànyi gēn tāmen yíkuàir qù.	'I'm not at all willing to go with them.'
Wǒ zuì zuì xǐhuan de shi zhè dào cai.	'This is the dish I really, really like best.'
shìjiè shang zuì dà de chéngshì	'the largest city (~ cities) in the world'
shìjiè shang zuì guì de qìchē	'the most expensive car (~ cars) in the world'
shìjiè shang zuì lěng de dìfang	'the coldest place (~ places) in the world'

Chinese uses the expression *zhī yī* 'one of', which contains *zhī*, a relic from classical Chinese that serves—among other things—to mark modification (a little like modern *de*), and *yī* 'one'.

zuì dà de chéngshì zhī yī	'one of the largest cities in the world'
zuì hǎo de Zhōngguó mǐjiǔ zhī yī	'one of the best Chinese rice wines'
Zhōngguó shi wǔ ge Ān-lǐ-huì chéngyuánguó zhī yī.	'China is one of the five permanent member states of the UN Security Council.'

NOTE

The Chinese equivalents to what are called acronyms in alphabetic languages (e.g., NATO or WTO) are shortened or so-called telescoped phrases. They are typically made up of the first syllables added to a generic. Thus, *Àolínpǐkè Yùndònghuì* 'Olympic Games' gets shortened to *Ào-yùn-huì*; *Ānquán Lǐshìhuì* 'Security Council' ('Security Directorship Organization') gets shortened to *Ān-lǐ-huì*; and *Shìjiè Màoyì Zǔzhī* 'World Trade Organization' gets shortened to *Shì-mào Zǔzhī*.

The same pattern with *zhī yī* is also the basis of fractions and percentages. One-third is rendered in Chinese as *sān fēn zhī yī* 'one of three parts', one-fourth is *sì fēn zhī yī* 'one of four parts', and 75 percent is *bǎi fēn zhī qīshíwǔ* 'seventy-five parts of one hundred'.

sān fēn zhī yī	'one-third'
sì fēn zhī yī	'one-fourth'
wǔ fēn zhī èr	'two-fifths'
bǎi fēn zhī wǔ	'5 percent'
bǎi fēn zhī èrshí	'20 percent'
bǎi fēn zhī qīshíwǔ	'75 percent'

14.5.1 Approximate numbers

Large numbers and figures are usually approximations. There are several expressions that may be used to indicate a figure is a rough estimate. *Chàbuduō* and *dàgài* have been used in earlier units, and both are placed before the amount. *Dàyuē* 'about; around; approximately' ('big-about') also appears before the amount. *Zuǒyòu*, on the other hand, combines roots for left and right to mean 'more or less' and is placed after the amount.

Shí Lín zài Kūnmíng de dōngbianr, chàbuduō yǒu yìbǎi sānshí gōnglǐ.	'The Stone Forest is about 130 kilometers east of Kunming.'
Dàlǐ zài Kūnmíng de xībianr, dàgài yǒu sìbǎi gōnglǐ.	'Dali is about 400 kilometers west of Kunming.'
Měi nián, dàyuē yǒu yìbǎiwàn nóngmíngōng jìnchéng.	'About one million rural workers move to the cities every year.'
Xīchāng zài Kūnmíng de běibianr yǒu wǔbǎi gōnglǐ zuǒyòu.	'Xichang is about 500 kilometers north of Kunming.'

14.5.2 Large numbers

In addition to the numerals 0–9, Chinese has simple words for five powers of ten: *shí* 'ten', *bǎi* 'hundred', *qiān* 'thousand', *wàn* 'ten thousand', and *yì* 'hundred million'. (For extremely large numbers, hundred million can also be expressed as *wànwàn* 'ten thousand ten thousands'.) Notably missing   at least from an English perspective—is 'million', which in Chinese is expressed only as a compound: *bǎiwàn* ('hundred-ten thousand'). Nowadays, large numbers are often written out in Arabic numerals (without commas) rather than characters, though they are, of course, read out in Chinese. (Arabic numerals are logograms, like Chinese characters, which represent words but do not indicate pronunciation.)

One important rule to note is that in stating large numbers, the highest possible power of ten is always used. In other words, 1,500 is always expressed in Chinese as *yìqiān wǔbǎi* rather than as **shíwǔbǎi*. The key to forming large numbers, then, is to keep the five basic powers of ten in mind and work down from the largest power to the smallest. Empty tens and hundreds slots (whether one or more than one) that are not final in the figure are signaled by *líng* 'zero'. Therefore, 1,000,300 is *yìbǎiwàn líng sānbǎi*.

yìbǎi líng wǔ	105
jiǔbǎi líng èr	902
jiǔbǎi bāshí'èr	982
yìqiān èrbǎi (~liǎngbǎi) líng yī	1,201
yíwàn yìqiān líng sìshíwǔ	11,045
sìwàn wǔqiān jiǔbǎi líng sì	45,904
shíwàn	100,000
sānshísìwàn wǔqiān jiǔbǎi bāshíwǔ	345,985
yìbǎiwàn líng jiǔ	1,000,009
yìbǎiwàn líng sānbǎi	1,000,300
bābǎiwǔshíwàn líng bābǎi	8,500,800
yìqiān yìbǎi wǔshíwàn	11,500,000
yíyì sìqiānwàn	140,000,000
shísānyì sìqiānwàn	1,340,000,000

Exercise 4

One of the more common occasions to cite very large numbers is when you are talking about population, so here are some rough figures to practice with. (*Zhōngguó rénkǒu shi shísānyì.*) You can cite them as approximations, using *zuǒyòu*.

China	1.3 billion	Canada	35 million
Hong Kong	8 million	India	1.2 billion
Iraq	24 million	Indonesia	238 million
Singapore	4.5 million	Thailand	61.5 million
United Kingdom	59 million	United States	310 million
Beijing	14 million	Shanghai	18 million
New York City	8 million	Chicago	2.8 million

Write Chinese equivalents for the following sentences.

1. The Jin Mao Building (*Jīn Mào Dàshà*) in Shanghai is one of the tallest buildings (*dàlóu*) in the world. The Oriental Pearl Tower (*Dōngfāng Míngzhū Tǎ*) is also one of the tallest; it is 468 meters tall.
2. Walmart (*Wò'ěrmǎ*) is one of the largest companies in the world.
3. Thirty percent of MIT graduate students are from abroad.
4. Although everyone in our Chinese class has been abroad, about 15 percent of us have never studied a foreign language before.
5. Louis Cha (*Jīn Yōng*) is one of the most popular authors in the world; his books have sold more than one hundred million copies.

NOTES

a. *gōngsī* 'company'; *gǔfèn yǒuxiàn gōngsī* 'limited company' ('stocks limited company'); *màoyì gōngsī* 'trading corporation' ('trade company')

b. Louis Cha is the English name of author *Zhā Liángyōng*, whose pen name is *Jīn Yōng* (*Gām Yùhng* in Cantonese). He has resided in Hong Kong for most of his life.

14.5.3 Comparing cities

The following four short interchanges give you a chance to combine comparison with large numbers as you talk about some of the world's largest urban conglomerations.

a. *Shànghǎi shi bu shi Zhongguó zuì*   'Is Shanghai the largest city in
    dà de chéngshì?   China?'
   Nǐ shi shuō rénkǒu ma?   'Are you talking about population?'
   Shì.   'Yes.'

   Nà dàgài Shànghǎi bǐ Běijīng dà   'I guess Shanghai's a bit bigger than
    yìdiǎnr. Tīngshuō xiànzài shi   Beijng. I hear it has eighteen
    yìqiān bābǎiwàn.   million nowadays.'

b. *Měiguó zuì dà de chéngshì shi něi*   'What is the largest city in the United
    ge?   States?'
   Shì Niǔyuē; Luòshānjī dì-èr.   'It's New York; Los Angeles is
                                              second.'

   Zhījiāgē bú shi bǐ Luòshānjī dà   'Isn't Chicago bigger than Los
    ma?   Angeles?'
   Bù, Zhījiāgē shi dì-sān...huòzhě   'No, Chicago is number three . . . or,
    xiànzài Xiūsīdùn [Háosīdùn]   now, perhaps Houston's a little
    kěnéng bǐ Zhījiāgē shāowēi dà   bigger than Chicago.'
    yìdiǎnr.

c. *Zhōngguó ma, Shànghǎi zuì dà,*   'As for China, Shanghai's the largest,
    kěshì dì-èr, dì-sān wǒ bú tài   but I'm not sure about which is
    qīngchu.   second and third.'
   Běijīng shì bu shì dì-èr?   'Is Beijing second?'
   Yǒurén shuō Chóngqìng yěshì   'Some say that Chongqing is also
    Zhōngguó zuì dà de chéngshì zhī   one of the biggest cities in China.'
    yī.
   Kěshì Chóngqìng hǎoxiàng méiyǒu   'But Chongqing doesn't seem to be
    Běijīng nàme dà.   as big as Beijing.'
   Chóngqìng shi ge zhíxiáshì, duì   'Chongqing is a directly administered
    ma?   city, isn't it?'

> *Duì a, Běijīng, Tiānjīn, Shànghǎi, Chóngqìng dōu shi zhíxiáshì.*
>
> 'Right, Beijing, Tianjin, Shanghai, and Chongqing are all directly administered cities.'
>
> *Běijīng de rénkǒu shi duōshao?*
>
> 'What's Beijing's population?'
>
> *Běijīng de wǒ bù zhīdao, Tiānjīn de rénkǒu shi bābǎiwàn ba.*
>
> 'I don't know what Beijing's is, but Tianjin's is eight million, I guess.'

d. *Zhōngguó shi shìjièshang rénkǒu zuì duō de guójiā, yǒu shísānyì. Yìndù shi dì-èr, rénkǒu shi shíyì zuǒyòu.*

'China is the largest country in the world, with 1.3 billion people. India is second, with a population of about one billion.'

Kěshì yǒu rén shuō zài 2050 (èrlíng wǔlíng nián), Yìndù huì yǒu shíliùyì, Zhōngguó shísìyì. Nèi yàng, Yìndù huì shi zuì dà de.

'But people say that by 2050, India will have 1.6 billion, and China will have 1.4 billion. That'll make India the largest country.'

14.6 At the fruit stand: Buying and bargaining

Purchases in China, as in many countries, can be subject to bargaining. This requires a certain amount of time and engagement, but it also offers a chance for language practice. The rules for bargaining are difficult to make explicit. In any case, outsiders (to say nothing of foreigners) cannot really know local prices, so the best hope is to get within a few percentage points of a good price. Chinese friends will generally say you overpaid (*Nǐ gěi tài duō le*), but you can respond that you got a free language lesson in return: *Yǒu jīhuì liànxí Zhōngwén!* ('have opportunity to practice Chinese').

Bargaining for expensive items—such as jewelry or crafts—is a rather different skill from making minor purchases of commodity items. There may be a 'give' of a few percentage points built into the asking price of fruit or vegetables at your local market, which might increase to 10–20 percent in the price of cotton material at your local bazaar. However, the difference between asking price and best price for an expensive item sold in a market or shop may be upwards of 300 percent—particularly at notorious bargain markets frequented by tourists, such as *Yǎxiū Fúzhuāng Shìchǎng* 'Yaxiu Clothing Market' in east Beijing or *Xiāngyáng Shìchǎng* in Shanghai.

Merchants know that if you make an absurdly low counter offer of, say, 30 percent of asking price, then that constitutes a promise, and you are stuck with the goods even if you eventually figure out they are only worth 10 percent of the original asking price. With this in mind, it's always wise to respond to the question 'What are you willing to pay?' with the counter question 'What's your best price?' Many people claim that, for more expensive purchases, it's best to get help from a local friend.

For low-intensity bargaining, the following examples include some useful phrases with which to begin.

Starting out
Wǒ jiùshi kànkan.   'I'm just looking.'
Wǒ kànkan, kěyǐ ma?   'Can I take a look at this [pointing]?'

Resisting
Wǒ zài xiǎngxiang.   'I'm thinking about it.'
Wǒ zài zhuànzhuan.   'I'm just strolling about.'
Wǒ zài guàngguang.   'I'm just looking around.'

Seeking a reduction
Kěyǐ piányi yìdiǎnr ma?
Piányi yìdiǎnr, xíng ma?   } 'Can you make it a bit cheaper?'
Néng bu néng piányi yìdiǎnr?
Tài guì le, piányi diǎnr ba?   'Too expensive; make it a bit cheaper, okay?'

Finding the bottom
Nǐ zuì dī duōshao qián?   'How much is your lowest (best) price?'
Ni gěi wǒ ge zuì dī jià.   'Give me your best (lowest) price.'
Shuō ge zuì dī jià ba.   'Tell me your best price.'

Discounts
Dǎzhé ma?   'Do you give a discount?'
Yǒu zhékòu ma?   'Any discount?'

Xíng, dǎ ge jiǔzhé.	'Okay, I'll give it to you for 90 percent.' (10 percent off)
Chéng, gěi nǐ ge bāwǔzhé.	'Okay, I'll give it to you for 85 percent.' (15 percent off)
Hǎo, dǎ ge qīzhé.	'Okay, I'll give it to you for 70 percent.' (30 percent off)

Seller's strategies

Nǐ yuànyi chū duōshao?	'How much are you willing to pay?'
Huòzhēn-jiàshí, méi piàn nǐ!	'The goods are true, and the price is right—I'm not taking you for a ride!'
Yì fēn jiàqian yì fēn huò.	'You get what you pay for.' ('One cent of price, one cent worth of thing')
Yí kuài sān, wǒ jiù méi dé zhuàn le.	'At ¥1.30, I won't be making anything.'
Jìnkǒu de bǐjiào guì.	'Imported things cost a bit more.'

Agreeing to the sale

Nà hǎo ba, mài gei nǐ ba.	'Okay, that's fine, I'll sell it to you.' [seller]
Dé dé dé, nǐ názǒu ba.	'Okay, okay, okay, you've got it.' [seller]
Xíng, xíng, xíng ~ Hǎo, hǎo, hǎo. Jiù zhèi jià le.	'Fine, at that price then.' [buyer]

VOCABULARY

dī	'low': *zuì dī jià* 'lowest price', with *jià* short for *jiàgé* 'price'
dǎzhé	'to offer a price break, give a discount': cf. *zhékòu* 'discount'
yuànyi	'be willing to'
zhuàn	'profit; to earn'
jìnkǒu	'import' ('enter-port')
dé dé dé	*Dé* as a full verb often means 'get; obtain', as in *dé zhuàn* 'obtain profit'; here, the sense is 'go ahead; all right; fine'.

NOTES

a. *Zhé* has a range of meanings, from 'snap' to 'fold', but in combination with *dǎ*, it means 'break' or 'discount'. Although English typically focuses on the amount of reduction ('10 percent off'), Chinese states the resulting discounted price ('90 percent'). It indicates this with a numerical modifier before *zhé*: *jiǔzhé* '90 percent'; *bāshíwǔzhé*, '85 percent'.

b. *Chéng* is an alternative to *xíng* or *hǎo*. As a full verb, *chéng* means 'become; accomplish; succeed', but as a response, it means 'agreed; fine; okay'.

c. *Chū duōshao*, with *chū* 'go out' in this context means 'cause to go out' or 'give; spend'.

d. *Méi dé zhuàn* 'won't get any profit': *dé* 'get; obtain' is the verb, and *zhuàn* is a noun.

e. With transactional verbs that involve movement away from the possessor, such as *mài* 'sell' or *dì* 'to pass; to forward', the recipient—the person who ends up with the object in question—can be introduced with *gěi* (often untoned), which is placed directly after the verb: *mài gei tā* 'sell to him' or *dì gei tā* 'pass it to her'.

14.6.1 Buying fruit

Here are two plausible conversations between a foreign customer (*gùkè* 'customer') and the proprietor of an open-air fruit stand (*lǎobǎn* 'owner; boss').

Lǎobǎn:	*Kuài lái, kuài lái, hǎochī de Tiānjīn lí.*	'Quick, come and get 'em, tasty Tianjin pears.'
Gùkè:	*Tián bu tián?*	'Are they sweet?'
Lǎobǎn:	*Bǎo tián, yòu dà yòu tián. Lái, shìyixiàr.*	'Guaranteed sweet, big and sweet. Here, have a taste.'
Gùkè:	*Ng, hǎo tián. zěnme mài a?*	'Hm, pretty sweet. How are they sold?'
Lǎobǎn:	*Yí kuài wǔ yì jīn.*	'¥1.50 a catty.'
Gùkè:	*Nà, dàgài yǒu jǐ ge?*	'So, about how many is that?'
Lǎobǎn:	*Sì dào wǔ ge ba.*	'About four or five.'
Gùkè:	*Lǎobǎn, yí kuài sān yì jīn kě.yǐ ma?*	'Laoban, how about ¥1.30 a catty?'
Lǎobǎn:	*Mǎi liǎng jīn suàn nǐ yí kuài sì yì jīn.*	'Buy two catties, and I'll make it ¥1.40 each.'
Gùkè:	*Hǎo, ná liǎng jīn.*	'Good, I'll take two catties.'

VOCABULARY

bǎo	'to be assured, to guarantee'
jīn	'jin, catty': a unit of weight equal to one-half a kilogram (*liǎng* 'ounce' is equivalent to 0.05 kg, so 10 liangs = 1 jin)
yòu . . . yòu . . .	'both . . . and . . .': *yòu dà yòu tián* 'big and sweet'
shì	'to try': *shìshi kàn* 'try it and see'
zěnme mài	'how much' ('how are they sold')
suàn	'calculate, count, make it [an amount]'

NOTE

Shì 'try' adds another member to a large set of homophones that, even ignoring parts of compounds (e.g., *diànshì* 'television'; *kǎoshì* 'test'), includes *shì* 'be', *shì* 'thing' (*shìqing*), *shì* 'room' (*jiàoshì* 'classroom'), and *shì* 'market, municipality'.

Lǎobǎn:	*Guòlai kànkan, yòu xīnxiān yòu piányi de shuǐguǒ.*	'Come and take a look— fresh, inexpensive fruit.'
Gùkè:	*Nǐ hǎo, lǎobǎn, wǒ yào mǎi píngguǒ.*	'Hi, Laoban, I want to buy some apples.'
Lǎobǎn:	*Yō! Wàiguó péngyou a? Lái, nín tiāotiao.*	'Wow! A friend from abroad? Here, choose one.'
Gùkè:	*Nǎ zhǒng tián?*	'Which are the sweetest?'
Lǎobǎn:	*Nín chángchang zhè zhǒng.*	'Taste this one.'
Gùkè:	*Ng, hǎo tián. Hǎo de, wǒ yào zhè zhǒng. Duōshao qián yì jīn?*	'Mm, quite sweet. Okay, I'd like these. How much per catty?'
Lǎobǎn:	*Wǔ kuài qián yì jīn.*	'¥5 a catty.'
Gùkè:	*Tài guì le, piányi diǎnr. Bié gěi wǒ wàiguórén jiàgé.*	'That's too much; reduce it a bit. Don't give me foreigner prices.'
Lǎobǎn:	*Yō! Nín de Zhōngwén zhēn hǎo, hái huì kǎnjià.*	'Hey! Your Chinese is pretty good—you can even bargain.'
Gùkè:	*Nǎ.lǐ, nǎ.lǐ, mǎmahūhū. Sì kuài qián yì jīn, zěnmeyàng?*	'Nah, it's just so-so. How about ¥4 for a catty?'

Lǎobǎn:	*Bù xíng, zuì dī sì kuài wǔ.*	'Can't do; my best is ¥4.50.'
Gùkè:	*Hǎo ba, wǒ yào wǔ ge.*	'Okay, I'll take five.'
Lǎobǎn:	*Yígòng sān jīn, shísān kuài wǔ.*	'That's three catties, ¥13.50.'
Gùkè:	*Gěi nín yìbǎi kuài.*	'Here's ¥100.'
Lǎobǎn:	*Nín yǒu língqián ma?*	'Do you have any change?'
Gùkè:	*Wǒ zhǎozhao. Ng, hǎo, yǒu liǎng zhāng liǎng kuài de hé liǎng zhāng wǔ kuài de. Zhèng hǎo shísì kuài.*	'Let me see. Umm, okay, here are two twos and two fives. Just right, ¥14.
Lǎobǎn:	*Tài hǎo le, zhǎo nín wǔ máo.*	'Great, here's ¥0.50 in change.'
Gùkè:	*Xièxie, zàijiàn.*	'Thanks, goodbye.
Lǎobǎn:	*Màn zǒu, xià cì zài lái.*	'Take it easy—come again.'

VOCABULARY

xīnxiān	'fresh' ('new-fresh')
Yō!	'What have we here?' 'Wow': exclamation of surprise
tiāo	'choose; select'
jiàgé	'price'
kǎnjià	'to beat down the price; bargain' ('chop-price') [coll]; cf. *tǎojià-huánjià* 'to haggle' ('give-price return-price'); *jiǎng jiàqian* 'to bargain' ('talk-price')
língqián	'small change' ('odd bits-money')

NOTES

a. *Zhǎo nín wǔ máo* literally means 'find you ¥0.50', but in English one would say 'Here's ¥0.50 in change.'

b. *Màn zǒu, xià cì zài lái* is a conventional phrase.

14.6.2 The names of fruit

Fruit names can vary from place to place in the Chinese-speaking world. Pine-apple, for example is usually cited as *bōluó* in standard Mandarin dictionaries. In Taiwan, however, it is called *fènglí* ('phoenix-pear'), and in Singapore, it is called *huánglí* ('yellow-pear'). The names cited in this section are those that seem to have the broadest currency.

Mài shuǐ.guǒ de. (*Shànghǎi*)

Many kinds of fruit can be counted with the general measure word *gè*: *liǎng ge píngguǒ* 'two apples', *shí ge shìzi* 'ten persimmons', *liǎng ge xiāngjiāo* 'two bananas'. In shops and at stalls, though, fruit can often be bought in slices (*piàn*) or cubes (*kuài*). Grapes and bananas are generally bought in bunches (*chuàn*). Single grapes are counted with *kē*.

bōluó	'pineapple'
chéngzi	'orange'
gānjú	'mandarin orange'
gānzhé	'sugar cane'
hāmìguā	'muskmelon' ('Hami-melon')
huǒlóngguǒ	'red pitaya; dragon fruit' ('fire-dragon-fruit')
júzi	'tangerine'
lí	'pear'
liúlián	'durian'
lìzhī	'lychee'
lǐzi	'plum'
lóngyǎn	'longan' ('dragon-eye')

mángguǒ	'mango'
míhóutáo	'kiwi' ('macaque-peach')
mùguā	'papaya' ('wood-melon')
níngméng	'lemon'
píngguǒ	'apple'
pútao	'grapes'
shíliu	'pomegranate'
shìzi	'persimmon'
táo<zi>	'peach'
xiāngjiāo	'banana' ('frangant-plantain')
xīguā	'watermelon' ('west-melon')
xìngr	'apricot'
yángtáo	'starfruit' ('sun-peach')
yēzi	'coconut'
yòuzi	'pomelo'

NOTES

a. Hami, a place in Xinjiang Province, gives its name to the *hāmiguā*—the muskmelon. Muskmelons have a raised network over their yellowish outer rinds, giving rise to the alternative English names 'netted melon' and 'nutmeg melon'. Their flesh is yellowish to greenish and tastes like cantaloupe.

b. *Huǒlóngguǒ*, sometimes called *lóngzhūguǒ* ('dragon-pearl-fruit'), is the fruit of a cactus native to Central and South America, but it is now also cultivated in Southeast Asia, southern China, and other places.

c. *Míhóu* 'macaque' is a kind of monkey. The Chinese name for kiwi is *míhóutáo*. The kiwi fruit may seem well named, for it has the color and look of a kiwi bird's body, and most of the kiwi fruit we eat in the United States comes from New Zealand—the home of the kiwi bird. However, the fruit is, in fact, native to central and southern China, where it goes under a variety of names, including *míhóutáo* ('macaque-monkey peach') and *míhóulí* ('macaque-monkey-pear'). Supposedly, the fruit is a favorite of monkeys.

d. The fruit called *lìzhī* in Mandarin is rendered into English spelling as 'litchee', 'lichee', or 'lychee'.

e. The name *liúlián* is borrowed, probably first into Cantonese, from Malay *durian*. Note how the strongly voiced Malay *d* and *r* were not heard as pinyin *d* and *r*, but rather as *l*. The durian is known for it offensive smell (for which it is generally banned from hotel rooms and public transportation) and its thick, creamy fruit. In Chinese, the smell would be described as *hěn chòu* 'foul' but the taste as *hěn xiāng* 'fragrant'.

14.7 Tastes and 'adding more to'

With fruit—and with food in general—it is useful to be able to describe and compare flavors. In English, we talk about the four basic flavors: bitter, salty, sour, and sweet. Some would add a fifth: savory or piquant. There are also words for lack of taste, such as bland. Chinese, with its predilection for sets of five, recognizes *wǔwèi* 'five flavors'. In fact, in Chinese, it is possible to add one or two other flavors to the basic five (*má* and *sè*). Here is a list of words for tastes, along with typical substances associated with those tastes.

TASTES	TYPICAL FOOD
là 'hot'	*làjiāo* 'chilies'
	jiāng 'ginger'
suān 'sour'	*cù* 'vinegar'
tián 'sweet'	*táng* 'sugar'
xián 'salty'	*yán* 'salt'
	jiàngyóu 'soy sauce'
kǔ 'bitter'	*kǔguā* 'bitter melon'
má 'numbing'	*huājiāo* 'Sichuan pepper'
sè 'astringent;	*bù shú de shìzi* 'unripe persimmons'
puckery'	*hǎishuǐ* 'sea water' (which is also considered *kǔ* and *xián*)

NOTES

a. Related words (that are not quite tastes) include *dàn* 'bland', *xiāng* 'fragrant', and *chòu* 'smelly'.

b. Other groups of five include the *wǔsè* 'five colors' (red, yellow, blue, white, and black) and the *wǔxiāng* 'five aromas' (of fennel, brown pepper, aniseed, cinnamon, and cloves). Both sets are associated with cooking and cuisine. There are also the *wǔjīn* 'five metals' (gold, silver, copper, iron, and tin)—as in *wǔjīn shāngdiàn* 'ironmongers, hardware store'—and the *wǔgǔ* 'five cereals' (rice, spiked millet, panicled millet, wheat, and beans). The predilection for sets of five is probably a legacy of concepts such as the *wǔxíng* 'five elements' that are so important to traditional notions of health and medicine in China.

c. As a list, the five flavors (*wǔwèi*) are often ordered as *là, suān, gān, kǔ, xián*, with the bound word *gān* 'sweet' instead of *tián*.

d.   The Chinese word for black pepper is *hújiāo* 'foreign pepper'. *Hújiāo* is not used as much in Chinese cooking as *huājiāo* 'flower pepper'—also called fagara, brown pepper, or Sichuan pepper. Unlike the sharp heat of *làjiāo* 'chilies', which are associated with Hunan cuisine, *huājiāo* has a slightly numbing effect and, mixed with *làjiāo*, is characteristic of Sichuan food. Recall Sichuan dishes that begin with '*málà*', such as *málà ěrduo* ('numbing-spicy pig-ears') and *málà jīsī* ('numbing-spicy shredded-chicken').

e.   *Sè* is also the taste of unripe pears and peaches (*lí, táo*).

We will end this section with a short comment in praise of Chinese cuisine.

> *Zhōngguó rén shuō xīfāng cài kǒuwèir tài dàn, méiyǒu wèidao; tāmen yě shuō nánfāng cài (xiàng Yìndù de, Tàiguó de) kǒuwèir tài zhòng. Xīfāng de tài dàn, nánfāng de tài zhòng, kěshì Zhōngguó de zhèng hǎo!*

'The Chinese say that Western food tastes too bland—it doesn't have any flavor. They say southern food (such as Indian and Thai) tastes too rich. Western food is too bland, southern is too rich, but Chinese is just right!'

14.7.1 Adding or subtracting amounts

If the food is not salty enough, then you can request more salt to be added: *Qǐng duō fàng yìdiǎnr yán.* If you need another drink, then you can ask the server to bring another glass: *Qǐng duō lái yì bēi.* Though this pattern also occurs with *zǎo* 'early' and *wǎn* 'late', it is most common with *duō* and *shǎo*, which are normally stative verbs, but here fill the adverbial position. The pattern is as follows—note the contrast with English.

ADVERB	VERB	AMOUNT
duō / shǎo	*fàng*	amount
	gěi	amount

Here are some relevant verbs, followed by examples.

gěi	'give'
fàng	'put'
ná	'hold; take'
lái	'bring' [cause to come]
niàn	'read'

1. *Duō chī yìdiǎnr cài!*   'Have some more food!'
   Xièxie, chībǎo le, chībǎo le.   'Thank you, I'm fine, I'm full.'

2. *Tài dàn le, gāi duō fàng yìdiǎnr*   'It's too bland; you should add more
      yán / jiàngyóu.   salt / soy sauce.'
   Bù, bù, hái hǎo, zhè yàngr hái   'No, it's fine; it's fine as is.'
      hǎo.

3. *Qǐng duō fàng yí kuài táng.*   'Another cube of sugar please.'
   Yí kuài gòu le ma?   'One more is enough?'
   Gòu le, gòu le.   'Yeah, that's fine.'

4. *Qǐng duō lái sān píng*   'Please bring three more bottles of
      kuàngquánshuǐ.   mineral water.'

5. *Qǐng duō lái liǎng ge bēizi.*   'Please bring two more glasses.'

6. *Qǐng zài tiān shuāng kuàizi.*   'Please bring another pair of
                                             chopsticks.' ('again add pair
                                             chopsticks')

7. *Qǐng duō dú ~ niàn yì háng /*   'Please read one more line /
      yí duàn / yí yè.   paragraph / page.'

8. *Wǒ duō ná liǎng ge, hǎo bu hǎo?*   'I'll take two more, okay?'

9. *Wǒ duō mǎi yí gè.*   'I'll take (buy) another.'

10. *Nà tài zhòng le, shǎo ná yì-liǎng* 'That's too heavy; take one or two
       běn, hǎo bu hǎo?   fewer books, okay?'

When only one item is involved, the effect of the *duō* pattern can be achieved with *zài* 'again; more'.

11. *Zài chī yìdiǎnr ba.*   'Eat some more.'
12. *Qǐng zài lái yì píng kělè.*   'Please bring another bottle of cola.'
13. *Nǐ zài ná yí gè, hǎo bu hǎo?*   'Take another one, okay?'

In fact, *zài* and *duō* can co-occur.

14. *Qǐng zài duō lái yìdiǎnr cài!*   'Please have some more food!'
                                        ('please again additionally eat some
                                        food')

Exercise 5

Provide Chinese equivalents for the following sentences.

1. Sichuan food is hot, but it isn't as hot as Hunan food. Thai food is even hotter, I feel.
2. If you prefer a saltier taste, then put more soy sauce in.
3. I'm not used to hot food, so please put fewer chilies in, so please don't cook it too spicy.
4. Lychees are a bit too sweet for me; I prefer plums or peaches.
5. Durian is cheaper in southern regions than it is in the north. Durian tastes a bit sour.
6. Cantonese food tends to be a little sweet, with not much soy sauce. Sichuan food is hot and numbing.
7. If durian is even a tiny bit overripe [*shú*], then it stinks to high heaven. However, if it's too unripe [*shēng*], then it doesn't taste good. When you buy it, it should be fragrant.

14.8 Verb-*le* and an excursion to the Great Wall

As noted in earlier units, *le* may appear at the foot of a sentence to signal a change in phase (*xiànzài hǎo le*; *yǐjīng chīfàn le*), or it may intervene between a verb and its object to signal priority or completion. (Of course, if no object is present, then *le* can only be distinguished by context or meaning.) The following sections deal with the latter type, which can be designated 'verb-*le*' (V-*le*).

Historically, the two types—or two positions—of *le* are thought to have different sources, a fact which sheds some light on their modern functions.

Postverbal *le* (perfective *le*) is said to derive from destressing the verb *liǎo* 'finish; settle' (which, like *le*, is also written 了). In fact, in recitation styles, *le* is read as *liǎo*. A good example is the following line from the song *Dōngfāng Hóng* 'The East is Red', in which *chūliǎo* is used, rather than the normal colloquial *chūle*.

> *Zhōngguó chūliǎo yí ge Máo Zédōng*   'From within China there
>   appeared a person named
>   Mao Zedong'

Sentence *le*, on the other hand, is thought to derive from destressing the verb *lái* 'come'. Therefore, *lěng le*, in an etymological sense, indicates 'to have come into a state of being cold'. The following sections deal with V-*le*, whose general function is to indicate completion.

14.8.1 Sequence of events

One particularly clear manifestation of V-*le* is found in sequences (cf. §5.12.2), where the second event is conditional on the completion of the first, and the first verb is marked with *le*. Often, the second clause contains the adverb *jiù* 'then' [temporal or logical] (which is often unstressed/untoned).

> *Shénme shíhou mǎi piào?*   'When do we buy our tickets?'
> *Shàngle chē jiù mǎi piào.*   'You buy tickets after you board.'

Where the conditions are more severe, *cái* (cf. §7.7) may substitute for *jiù*.

> *Néng chūqu wánr ma?*   'Can I go out to play?'
> *Nǐ chīle fàn cái néng chūqu wánr.*   'Not until you've eaten can you go
>   out to play.'
> *Wǒ zǎoshang chīle xiànrbǐng cái*   'Mornings—I can't function until
> *yǒu jīngshen.*   I've had a meat-stuffed
>   pancake.'

In such cases, the 'V-*le* O' (V-*le* + object) construction occupies the same position in the sentence as a time word.

> *Wǒ sān diǎn huíjiā.*   'I'm going home at 3:00.'
> *Wǒ chīle fàn jiù huíjiā.*   'I'm going home after I eat.'
> *Wǒ xiàle kè cái huíjiā.*   'I'm not going home until after class.'

Le used after the first verb in these sentences serves much the same purpose as *yǐhòu* 'afterwards'. In fact, when the second event is less likely to follow immediately on the first, *yǐhòu* may be preferred.

Tā bìyè yǐhòu dǎsuàn qù	'He's planning to go abroad to study
Zhōngguó liúxué.	in China after he graduates.'

Even with the presence of the postverbal *le* in the first clause (*chīle fàn; xiàle kè*), you can still find the other *le*—sentence *le*—modifying the whole sentence. Contrast the following sets of questions and answers.

Nǐ jīntiān jǐ diǎn huíjiā?	'When are you going home today?'
Wǒ xiàle kè jiù huíjiā.	'I'm going home right after class.'
Tā jīntiān jǐ diǎn huíjiā le?	'When did she go home today?'
Tā xiàle kè jiù huíjiā le.	'She went home right after class.'
Tāmen hái zài ma?	'Are they still here?'
Bù, tāmen xiàle kè jiù zǒu le.	'No, they left after class.'

14.8.2 Verb *le* in simple sentences

Verb *le* offers the speaker a way to highlight those events in a narrative that are of particular significance because they have been completed before the time of speaking.

Tāmen mǎile hěn duō dōngxi.	'They bought a lot of things.'
Tā zǒule yí ge xiǎoshí.	'She walked for an hour.'

If an object is present (*hěn duō dōngxi*), *le* will generally follow the verb but precede the object or other noun complement (e.g., *mǎile hěn duō dōngxi; zǒule yí ge xiǎoshí*). Note the position of *le* in the following examples.

Wǒmen zài Chángchéng shang pále	'We walked along the Great
liǎng ge zhōngtou.	Wall for a couple of hours.'
Tā shuìle bā ge xiǎoshí<de> jiào.	'She slept eight hours <of
	sleep>.'
Tā dào chéng lǐ qù bànle yìxiē	'He went into town to do some
shìqing.	things.'
Tā bìngle sān tiān.	'She was ill for three days.'

More illustrations:

1. Jiǎ: *Lèi ma?*   'Tired?'
   Yǐ: *Hěn lèi, shuì+de bù hǎo.*   'Sure am; I didn't sleep well.'
   Jiǎ: *Zāogāo!*   'Too bad!'
   Yǐ: *Zhǐ shuìle sān-sì ge zhōngtou!*   'I only slept three or four hours!'
   Jiǎ: *Nà, nǐ yīnggāi xiūxi yíxiàr.*   'You should take a break then.'

2. Jiǎ: *Mǎile yìxiē shénme?*   'What sort of things did you buy
                                                      ~ have you bought?'

   Yǐ: *Mǎile ge táidēng, yí ge*   'I bought a lamp, a radio, a
       shōuyīnjī, yì běn zìdiǎn. . . .   dictionary. . . .'

3. *Shíjiān hěn jǐnzhāng, wǒmen qùle*   'The time was tight! We got to
   Xīníng, kěshì méi dào Lāsà.   Xining, but we didn't make it
                                                      to Lhasa.'

4. *Wǒ xiān dǎle diànhuà, ránhòu*   'I made a phone call first and
   qù chīle fàn.   then went and finished my
                                                      meal.'

5. *Tā chīle mǐfàn, yě chīle miàn.*   'She ate the rice as well as the
                                                      noodles.'

6. *Tā gānggāng chīle fàn.*   'She just now finished her meal.'

14.8.3 *Le* and nonduration

It's appropriate to make one last point while we are dealing with *le*. As you
know, duration is expressed by a phrase placed after the verb (and before associated objects).

Zuótiān wǎnshang wǒ zhǐ shuìle   'I only slept three hours last night;
   sān ge xiǎoshí, jīntiān hěn hútu.   today, I'm quite muddled.'

Duìbuqǐ, nǐ děngle hěn jiǔ le!   'Sorry, you've been waiting a long
                                                      time!'

Bù, gāng dào.   'No, just got here.'

However, not doing something for a period of time is treated differently in
Chinese. The time of deprivation is treated as though it were 'time when' and

placed before the verb. Final *le* (i.e., sentence *le*) underscores the fact that the deprivation continues to the present.

Wǒ sān ge yuè méi jīhuì shuō Hànyǔ le.	'I haven't had a chance to speak Chinese for three months.'
Nǐ zuì hǎo duō fùxí yíxià.	'You'd better review some more then.'
Wǒ sān tiān méi shuìjiào le.	'I haven't slept for three days.'
Nà nǐ yídìng hěn lèi ba.	'You must be tired.'
Wǒ èrshí duō xiǎoshí méi chīfàn le.	'I haven't eaten for over twenty hours.'
Nà nǐ yídìng hěn è ba!	'You must be hungry!'

Therefore, not having done something for a time is not treated the same way as having done something for a time. Sentences such as the following, in which the duration is denied or corrected, are not exceptions to the rule—the duration happened and is questioned.

Wǒ méi shuì jiǔ ge xiǎoshí; wǒ shuō shuìle liù ge xiǎoshí.	'I didn't sleep nine hours; I said I slept six hours.'

Summary of *le* (and related patterns)

S-*le*	*xiànzài hǎo le*	it's okay now	change of state
S-*le*	*bù zǎo le*	it's getting late	change of state
S-*le*	*yǐjīng xiàkè le*	class is over already	new phase
S-*le*	*qù Chángchéng le*	went to the Great Wall	earlier event
Neg	*méi qù Chángchéng*	didn't go to the GW	didn't happen
V-*guo*	*qùguo Chángchéng*	has been to the GW	had the experience

Neg	*méi qùguo Chángchéng*	haven't ever been to GW	hasn't had the experience
V-*le*	*bànle yìxiē shìqing*	took care of some business	(quantified object)
Shi . . . de	<*shi*> *zuótiān qù de*	went yesterday	focus on when
V-*le* O	*xiàle kè*	after class gets out	conditional action
V-*le* O	*dàole Xīníng*	made it to Xining	accomplished

Exercise 6

Explain the following situations in Chinese.

1. You generally sleep eight hours a night.
2. But last night you only slept three hours.
3. You generally get up at 7:30.
4. But this morning you didn't get up until 9:00.
5. After you eat breakfast, you walk (*zǒulù*) for thirty minutes.
6. Every day you do an hour of Chinese homework.
7. You haven't eaten for ages—you're starving.
8. On Mondays, Wednesdays, and Fridays, your first class is at 11:00.
9. You eat lunch after you get out of class.
10. Yesterday you didn't go home until after you'd eaten dinner.
11. You had to study last night, so you only slept four hours.
12. Yesterday afternoon you went to Xidan and bought some souvenirs.
13. You're not buying a standing ticket ever again—you haven't slept for thirty hours.

Sīmǎtái

To Sīmǎtái

Jiǎ:	*Zuótiān gànmá le?*	'What did you do yesterday?'
Yĭ:	*Wǒ qù mǎi xiézi le.*	'I went to buy some shoes.'
Jiǎ:	*Shì ma? Qù nǎr mǎi de?*	'Really? Where'd you go?'
Yĭ:	*<Zài> Xīdān.*	'Xidan.'
Jiǎ:	*Duōshao qián?*	'How much?'
Yĭ:	*85 kuài.*	'¥85.'
Jiǎ:	*Bú guì.*	'Not bad.'
Yĭ:	*Hái mǎile jǐ jiàn chènyī.* *Ránhòu wǒmen chīle lāmiàn.* *Nǐmen ne?*	'I also bought some shirts. Then we had some noodles. How about you?'
Jiǎ:	*Wǒmen qù pá Chángchéng le.*	'We went and climbed the Great Wall.'
Yĭ:	*Zuò huǒchē qù de ma?*	'Did you go by train?'
Jiǎ:	*Bù, huǒchē tài màn le, wǒmen shi zuò gōngjiāo qù de.*	'No, the train's too slow; we went by public bus.'

Yǐ:	*Huǒchē shì tài màn.*	'The train *is* too slow.'
Jiǎ:	*Wǒmen méi qù Bādálǐng, wǒmen qùle Sīmǎtái. Zài Chángchéng shàng zǒule jǐ ge xiǎoshí.*	'And we didn't go to Badaling, we went to Simatai. We walked for a few hours on the Great Wall.'
Yǐ:	*Sīmǎtái, Běijīng de dōngběi biānr—nàme yuǎn!*	'Simatai, northeast of Beijing— so far!'
Jiǎ:	*Bādálǐng rén tài duō le, Sīmǎtái shì yuǎnle yìdiǎnr, kěshì rén méi Bādálǐng nàme duō.*	'There are too many people at Badaling; Simatai is a little farther, but there aren't as many people there.'
Yǐ:	*Ǹg. Nà, jīntiān dǎsuàn gànmá?*	'Hm. And what are you doing today?'
Jiǎ:	*Jīntiān wǒ děi xuéxí.*	'Today I have to study.'
Yǐ:	*Wǒ yě shì. Xià xīngqī yǒu qīmò kǎoshì!*	'Me too; I have finals next week!'

VOCABULARY

gànmá	'What are you doing? What are you up to?' [coll]
Xīdān	a shopping district in western Beijing
chènyī	'shirt' [coll.]: (M is *jiàn*) The more formal word is *chènshān*.
lāmiàn	('pull-noodles') noodles made by pulling strips off a lump of dough
pá	'climb; crawl'
Bādálǐng	Because it is relatively close to Beijing (about 70 km slightly northwest of the city), and is now served by an expressway (as well as a railway), Badaling is still the most popular tourist site on the Great Wall.
Sīmǎtái	The site of a much more impressive portion of the Great Wall, northeast of Beijing, farther away (110 km), and harder to reach—but now also becoming very popular. There are, of course, other Great Wall sites near Beijing, off the beaten path, but still accessible.

dǎsuàn   'plan; intend to' ('hit-calculate')

qīmò   'end of term' ('term-end')

NOTE

Notice the position of *le* in *yuǎnle yìdiǎnr* 'is little father off'. With stative verbs (such as *yuǎn*), *le* appears before the amount and directly after the stative verb For example, *hǎole hěn duō* 'feel much better now' and *zhòngle sān gōngjīn* 'put on three kilos [i.e., I gained weight]', with *zhòng* 'heavy'.

Exercise 7

Rearrange the words and phrases to form sentences.

1. *xiǎng / wǒmen / qù / kàn / jiǔyuèfen / dào / míngnián / Xī'ān / qīnqi*
2. *xiūxi xiūxi / huíjiā / yào / xiànzài / wǒ*
3. *túshūguǎn / xiǎng / bu / jīntiān / wǒ / qù / xiǎng / wǒ / chéng li / mǎi / qù / dōngxi /qù*
4. *jǐnzhāng / dōu / lǎoshī / suǒyǐ / yán / yīnwèi / hěn / xuéshēng / hěn*
5. *fànguǎnr / xīngqīliù /qù / kè / dōu / de / xuéshēng / chīfàn / èrniánjí / qù / méiyǒu / suǒyǐ*
6. *lěng / Běijīng / suǒyǐ / tiānqì / fēng / dà / hěn / bu / wǒmen / shūfu / qiūtiān / yǒu diǎnr / yě / hěn*
7. *fùmǔ / kěshì / Zhōngwén / tā / shuō / bu / huì / huì*
8. *lái de / tā / shì / lǎo Běijīng / Běijīng / suǒyǐ / jiào /péngyou / dōu / tā*

14.9 Pronunciation

Practice reading aloud the following tone sets. Read down, then across.

gòuwù	*fāngyán*	*kǔguā*	*làjiāo*
sùshè	*zhāngláng*	*hǎixiān*	*zhuàngguān*
shìjiè	*fēngsú*	*Yǎxiū*	*jiànkāng*
shǔyú	*zìjǐ*	*xióngmāo*	*mángguǒ*
lǎnhóu	*fùmǔ*	*guójiā*	*mǐjiǔ*
hǎibá	*shàngwǎng*	*huíjiā*	*lǐxiǎng*

Now practice full tone plus *qīngshēng*.

qīngchu	*chóngzi*	*lǐzi*	*lìzi*
gūniang	*wénzi*	*běnzi*	*hàozi*

Practice reading these three-syllable words (including some common nouns and some proper nouns) slowly and carefully.

Wò'ěrmǎ	*Sīmǎtái*	*Bādálíng*	*kuàngquánshuǐ*
hāmìguā	*huǒlóngguǒ*	*zhíxiáshì*	*Wángfǔjǐng*
guójìhuà	*quánqiúhuà*	*lǚxíngshè*	*yǔyánxué*

Finally, practice reading these words with *érhuà*. Definitions are provided out of interest, as well as to give you a sense of the kind of colloquial, familiar, local words that show the *r* suffix.

gùnr	'rod; stick'
miáor	'sprouts'
gǔxuèr	'one's offspring' ('bone-blood')
zhàopiānr	'photograph': also *zhàopiàn* with falling tone on *piàn* 'slice'
xìngrénr	'almond; apricot kernal' ('apricot-kernal')
miànbāozhār	'breadcrumbs' ('bread-scraps')
miànbāopír	'crust' ('bread-skin')
qiányuànr	'front courtyard'
qiǎohuór	'tricky work, requiring some finesse'
tuōr	'something serving as support; a tout' [for a business]
sháor	'spoon; ladle'
shùchàr	'fork in a tree'
chuànménr	'drop in on someone' ('string together-door')
yíngmiànr	'head on; face-to-face; from the opposite direction' ('receive-face')
tóufèngr	'part or parting of combed hair' ('head-seam,fissure')
nǎizuǐr	'pacifier; nipple [on a baby's milk bottle]' ('milk-mouth')
chàngpiānr	'phonograph record; disk' ('song-disk')
gǔnguār	'rotund; something plump' ('roly-gourd')
xiāngchángr	'sausage' ('fragrant-intestine')

zhàlánr	'railings; bars'
shuǐniūr	'snail' ('water-ox'): cf. *shuǐniú* 'water buffalo'
jiǎoyìnr	'footprint; tracks' ('foot-print')
méicír	'be at a loss for words' ('without-words')
méidǐr	'be unsure' ('without-basis')
duìjìnr	'compatible; to one's liking' ('to-strength')
bīngguàr	'icicle' ('ice-hang')
zhēnbír	'eye of a needle' ('needle-nose')

Exercise 8

Place the following words in short phrases that demonstrate your undertanding of the differences among them. Proceed down the columns.

1	2	3	4	5	6
shìjiè	*qīngchu*	*Yīngyǔ*	*niánjí*	*yǒumíng*	*guójí*
shíjiān	*qīngcài*	*yǐjing*	*biāozhǔn*	*yǒu yìsi*	*lǎojiā*
shíhou	*cāntīng*	*yǐqián*	*cháodài*	*yǒu dàoli*	*guójiā*

14.10 Rhymes and rhythms

Singing and dancing, in addition to language, are considered part of one's cultural identity in China. In case you are asked to sing (at a banquet or on a tour bus), here is a song for you to fall back on—just in case you have not prepared anything else.

This is a song that is very popular in China, with a tune you should find easy to remember. Its Chinese title is *Hóng Hé Gǔ* (红河谷), which translates literally as 'Red River Valley'. This is not the Red River that flows through Yunnan and across northern Vietnam, which, incidentally, is called *Hóng Hé* 'red river' or *Yuán Hé* 'primary river' in Chinese and *Sông Hồng* ('river-red') in Vietnamese. No, this Red River Valley is, apparently, in Manitoba, Canada. The song, which seems to have originated in the late 19th century, has passed into the North American folk repertoire.

Tián Hàojiāng, the opera bass at the New York Metropolitan Opera, recorded a fine version of the song on his 2009 CD: Zàijiàn Xiǎolù (再见小路) 'Songs of Our Generation'. Here are the lyrics for the first verse and refrain, along with a literal translation.

Rénmen shuō, nǐ jiù yào líkāi cūnzhuāng,	('people say, you then will leave village')
wǒmen jiāng huáiniàn nǐ de wēixiào,	('we will miss your DE smile')
Nǐ de yǎnjing bǐ tàiyang gèng míngliàng,	('you DE eyes than sun more bright')
Zhàoyào zài wǒmen de xīn shàng.	('shine LOC our heart on')
Zǒu guòlái nǐ zuò zài wǒ de shēn páng,	('come over-here, you sit at my DE body beside')
bú yào líbié+de zhèyàng cōngmáng,	('not want leave+DE so hastily')
yào jìzhù Hóng Hé Cūn, nǐ de gùxiāng,	('must remember RRV, your hometown')
hái yǒu nà rè'ài nǐ de gūniang.	('still have that ardent-love you DE girl')

Wǒmen jiang huáiniàn nǐ de wēixiào.

Now, back to tradition, with a rhyme about the moon.

Yuè guāngguāng, zhào gǔchǎng,	('moon bright, shine+on grain-fields')
gǔchǎng shàng, nóngrén máng.	('grain-fields on, farmers busy')
Jīnnián dàogǔ shōuchéng hǎo,	('this-year rice harvest good')
Jiājiā-hùhù lètáotáo.	('every household full+of+joy')

Finally, a story (with measure words) that has the virtue of being brief but endless, so it can be easily remembered and recited line-by-line around a class.

Cóngqián yǒu yí zuò shān,	('Formerly be a M mountain')
shān lǐ yǒu ge miào,	('mountain on have M temple')
miào lǐ yǒu ge héshang jiǎng gùshi;	('temple in have M priest tell story')
jiǎng de shénme gùshi?	('tell DE what story')
Cóngqián yǒu yí zuò shān . . .	('Formerly be a M mountain . . .')

Summary

Owing to [the fact]	*yóuyú tā shi Zhōngwén lǎoshī*
Different; not the same	*bùtóng de fāngyán / wánquán bù yíyàng*
For example	*shuō ge lìzi / bǐfang shuō*
Old	*lǎo chuántǒng / jiùchē*
Tentative	*Qǐng děngyíxiàr / Zánmen shāngliang shāngliang.*
Directionals	*Wǒ bāng nǐ ná shàngqu, hǎo bu hǎo?*
Bǎ	*Qǐng bǎ mén guānshang.*
	Wǒ yǐjīng bǎ yīfu fàng zai chuáng shang le.
Noncomparative	*Jīntiān xiāngdāng rè / Jīntiān rè+de bùdéliǎo.*

Comparatives	*Běijīng bǐ Tiānjīn dà yìdiǎnr ~ dà duōle.*
	Bǐ Běijīng duō jǐ bǎiwàn.
	Běijīng méiyǒu Shànghǎi <nàme> dà.
	Běijīng bùrú Shànghǎi dà.
	Tā Hànyǔ jiǎng+de bǐ wǒ hǎo (de duō, etc.).
One of . . .	*shìjiè shang zuì dà de chéngshì zhī yī*
Large numbers	*bābǎiwàn*
Approximately	*Yǒu yìbǎi gōnglǐ zuǒyòu.*
Bargaining	*Kěyǐ piányi yìdiǎnr ma? / Shuō ge zuì dī jià ba.*
Discounts	*Yǒu zhékòu ma? / Xíng, dǎ ge jiǔzhé.*
Some more	*Duō chī yìdiǎnr cài! / Xièxie, chībǎo le, chībǎo le.*
	Qǐng zài lái yì píng kělè.
Sequence	*Wǒ xiàle kè jiù huíjiā. / Wǒ xiàle kè jiù huíjiā le.*
	Wǒ xiān dǎle diànhuà, ránhòu qù chīle fàn.
Duration	*Zuótiān shuìle bā ge xiǎoshí <de jiào>.*
Deprivation	*Wǒ sān tiān méi shuìjiào le.*

Unit 15

Jiànshè yǒu Zhōngguó tèsè de shèhuìzhǔyì!
'Establish a socialism with special Chinese characteristics!'
('Establish [possess Chinese special-quality DE] socialism!')
—Slogan on the wall of a factory outside Shanghai, 1998

Unit 15 begins with the usual warm-up narrative and then focuses on patterns that involve the co-verb *duì* 'to; in; on'. A series of short travel accounts follows, designed to draw attention to ways of maintaining temporal and logical cohesion over longer stretches of discourse. Conversational material is provided in a section on the family and professions, and then there is a relatively long introduction to a third common verbal suffix (after *guò* and *le*): *zhe*. *Fāngyán*—regional languages—and the *bǎ* construction are revisited, we dive into a third set of verb combos, and then there are short sections on 'waiting' and 'rushing'. The unit winds down as it begins, with a narrative on the topic of cigarettes and smoking, which should elicit some good discussion. The unit closes with a classical Chinese poem and a traditional rhyme about New Year's activities.

Contents

15.1 The literature teacher

Wáng Xuéyīng was born in Nanjing. *Nanjing* means 'southern capital', a name that reflects the fact that at various times in its history, the city has been China's capital (*shǒudū*)—most recently during the Ming Dynasty. *Xuéyīng*'s parents are from Shaoxing (*Shàoxīng*), so he regards Shaoxing as his ancestral home (*lǎojiā*). Shaoxing's local specialty (*tèchǎn*) is a rice wine called *Shàoxīngjiǔ*. Shaoxing has its own local dialect, which, when you hear it (*tīng qǐlai*), you'll find is quite like the Shanghai dialect. *Wáng Xuéyīng* teaches modern Chinese literature (*Zhōngguó xiàndài wénxué*) and is well-informed about famous Chinese authors (*duì Zhōngguó de xiàndài zuòjiā hěn yǒu yánjiū*), such as *Lǔ Xùn*, *Lǎo Shě*, and *Dīng Líng*. He's also studied abroad (*liúguo xué*).

Wáng Xuéyīng shi Lín Měi de hǎo péngyou. Tā shēng zai Nánjīng, kěshì yīnwèi tā fùmǔ shi Shàoxīngrén, suǒ.yǐ Zhōngguórén yě shuō Shàoxīng shi tā de lǎojiā. Shàoxīng zài nǎr? Shàoxīng zài Zhèjiāng, lí Hángzhōu hěn jìn, lí Shànghǎi yě bù yuǎn. Shàoxīnghuà tīng qǐlai hěn xiàng Shànghǎihuà. Shàoxīng zuì yǒumíng de tèchǎn shi Shàoxīngjiǔ, nà shi yì zhǒng mǐjiǔ. Hēguo de rén dōu shuō Shàoxīngjiǔ hěn tián, hěn chún.

Wáng Xuéyīng yīnwèi shēng zai Nánjīng, suǒ.yǐ yě kě.yǐ shuō shi Nánjīngrén. Nánjīng zài Jiāngsū, zài Cháng Jiāng biān shang. Nánjīng nèi ge chéngshì xiāngdāng dà, rénkǒu dàgài sān-sìbǎiwàn. Dànshi shi bǐjiào ānjìng de chéngshì, méiyǒu Shànghǎi nàme rènao, nàme xuānnào. Nǐ kěnéng xiǎng zhīdao Nánjīng wèishénme jiào 'Nánjīng'? Shi zhèyàngr de: 'Jīng' shi shǒudū de yìsi. Nánjīng shi nánbiānr de shǒudū. Xiànzài de shǒudū shi Běijīng, kěshì yǐqián Nánjīng yě zùoguo shǒudū. Suǒ.yǐ Nánjīng fùjìn de gǔjī hěn duō! Nǐ yīnggāi qù kànkan, hěn yǒu yìsi!

Wáng Xuéyīng, hé Lín Měi yíyàng, yě jiāoshū. Tā jiāo Zhōngguó wénxué, Zhōngguó xiàndài wénxué. Nǐ xiǎng liǎojiě Zhōngguó zuì yǒumíng de xiàndài zuòjiā, nà nǐ kě.yǐ qǐngjiào tā. Tā duì Lǔ Xùn, Lǎo Shě, Dīng Líng, Shěn Cóngwén, Cán Xuě děng.děng nèi xiē yǒumíng de xiàndài zuòjiā dōu hěn yǒu yánjiū!

Wáng Xuéyīng 1986 nián céng zài Yīngguó liúguo xué. Tā Yīngwén jiǎng+de hěn hǎo. Tīng-shuō-dú-xiě dōu xíng. Tā yě zhīdao yìdiǎnr guānyú Měiguó hé Ōuzhōu de shìqing. Tā shuō tā shi Zhōngguórén, dāngrán zuì xǐhuan chī Zhōngguó cài, kěshì tā yě xǐhuan chī wàiguó cài, xiàng Fǎguó de, Yìdàlì de, Měiguó de. Měiguó de kuàicān tā yě xǐhuan, xiàng hànbǎobāo, règǒu, pīsàbǐng! Tā shuō tā zhīdao kuàicān duì shēntǐ bù hǎo, kěshì yīnwèi hěn hǎochī, tā háishi hěn xǐhuan chī. Tā de kànfǎ shi xiǎng chī shénme jiu chī shénme, zhǐ yào nǐ bù chī tài duō. Nǐ juéde tā zhèyàng shuō yǒu dàoli ma?

VOCABULARY

tián	usually 'sweet,' but here, 'smooth'	
chún	'mellow' [of wine]	
Cháng Jiāng	'Yangtze River' ('long river'): cf. *Chángchéng*	
xuānnào	'bustling, noisy' ('hubbub-noise'): characterizes the noise of a city better than *rènao*	
kěnéng	'possibly; probably; maybe': cf. *dàgài*, *yěxǔ*	
shǒudū	'capital city' [of a country]. A provincial capital is *shǒufǔ*.	
zuòguo	'has done': in the sense of 'has played the part of; has been'	
gǔjī	'historical site' ('ancient-remains')	
liǎojiě	'understand; get to know; acquaint oneself with' ('complete-explain')	
zuòjiā	'author' ('do/write-expert')	

qǐngjiào	'please enlighten me' ('request-instruction'): Used deferentially to ask for instructions from a superior. It is a verb + object compound, hence the falling tone on *jiào* 'instruction'; cf. *jiàoshòu*.
céng	'before; in the past; ever': often in conjunction with V-*guo*
guānyú	'about; concerning': here introducing the object *shìqing*
kuàicān	'fast food' (e.g., *hànbǎobāo*, *règǒu*, *pīsàbǐng*)
zhǐ yào	literally, 'only want,' but the corresponding English expression is 'as long as; provided that': *Zhǐ yào duì shēntǐ hǎo, wǒ kěyǐ chī.* 'As long as it's good for me, I can eat it'.
yǒu dàoli	'make sense; be rational, right': The whole phrase acts as a stative verb. For example, *hěn yǒu dàoli*; the negative is *méi<yǒu> dàoli*.

NOTES

a. *Lǎojiā* 'hometown; land of one's ancestors' ('old-home'): In the Chinese view, you are from the place that your ancestors came from; cf. *gùxiāng* 'native place, hometown' ('old-country').

b. *Tīng qǐlai* 'when it comes to listening to it': Note the extended meaning of the suffix *qǐlai* rather than its literal meaning of 'rise up'; cf. *zhàn qǐlai* 'stand up'.

c. *Hěn tián, hěn chún; nàme rènao, nàme xuānnào*: The narrator adopts a very natural strategy of honing in on the right word. For example, *tián* 'sweet' isn't quite the right word; *chún* is more apt. Similarly, *rènao* isn't quite the right word for characterizing the noise of a city; *xuānnào* is better. This synonym strategy works well for learners who can gain time and feedback by trying out words of similar meanings.

d. *Rènao* combines the roots for 'hot' and 'noise'. For Chinese, the word connotes a lively family gathering or the hubbub of a packed restaurant or well-lit street with lots going on—all positive associations. English 'lively' or 'buzzing with excitement' capture something of the same sense: *jiē shang hěn rènao* 'it's buzzing on the street'. In addition to its adjectival (stative verb) sense, *rènao* may also function as a verb meaning 'to party; have a jolly time' (*Dàjiā zài yìqǐ rènao rènao*) and as a noun meaning 'excitement' or 'buzz'; cf. *kàn rènao* 'enjoy the excitement; go where the crowds are'.

e. *Duì . . . yǒu yánjiū* 'to be well informed about . . .' ('to have knowledge of . . .'): See below for other patterns that involve the co-verb *duì*.

f. *Liúxué* 'study abroad' ('remain-study'); cf. *chūguó liúxué* 'go abroad to study' and *liúxuéshēng* 'overseas student'. In dictionaries, *liúxué* is classified as a compound verb. However, the label— even if it is appropriate—does not tell the full story, for certain types of material can intervene between the two parts of the compound. For example, *tā liúguo xué* 'he's studied abroad' and *wo zài Táiwān liúle yì nián xué* 'I studied in Taiwan for a year'. In many respects, *xué* in this compound acts like a generic object (cf. *chīfàn, chànggē*).

Exercise 1

Prepare spoken or written answers to the following questions about the story about *Wáng Xuéyīng*.

1. *Qǐng nǐ tántan lǎojiā shi shénme yìsi.*
2. *Shàoxīngrén shuō shénme huà? Yǒu shénme tèdiǎn?*
3. *Shàoxīng zuì yǒumíng de tèchǎn shi shénme? Wèidao zěnmeyàng?*
4. *Nánjīng rénkǒu dàgài shi duōshao?*
5. *Nánjīng wèishénme jiào Nánjīng?*
6. *Zhōngguó háiyǒu shénme chéngshì yě zuòguo shǒudū?*
7. *Wáng Xuéyīng duì shénme hěn yǒu yánjiū?*
8. *Xiǎng liǎojiě Zhōngguó yǒumíng de zuòjiā kě.yǐ qǐngjiào shéi?*
9. *Wáng Xuéyīng Yīngyǔ jiǎng + de hěn hǎo; wèishénme?*
10. *Guānyú chī kuàicān nǐ yǒu shénme kànfǎ?*

15.2 Patterns with *duì*

You have encountered a number of constructions that make use of the co-verb *duì*. Here, they are reviewed with examples.

Duì . . . hǎo	'good for . . .'
Yǒu rén shuō niúnǎi duì shēntǐ hǎo.	'Some people feel milk is good for you.'
Tīngshuō niúnǎi duì pífū hǎo, xiāngjiāo duì nǎozi hǎo.	'I've heard it said that milk is good for the skin and bananas are good for the brain.'

Duì . . . yǒu ~ gǎn xìngqu	'be interested in' ('toward . . . have ~ feel interest')
Duì xià wéiqí gǎn xìngqu ma?	'Are you interested in playing Go?'
Hěn gǎn xìngqu, dànshi duì xiàngqí gèng yǒu xìngqu.	'I'm very interested, but I'm even more interested in chess.'
Wǒ cóng xiǎo duì huàhuàr yǒu xìngqu.	'I've been interested in drawing since I was small.'
Tīngshuō Qīngcháo de Kāngxī huángdì duì tiānwén fēicháng gǎn xìngqu.	'I heard that Emperor Kangxi of the Qing Dynasty was very interested in astronomy.'
Duì . . . yǒu yánjiū	'be informed about; be well versed in' ('to . . . have research')
Tā duì Zhōngguó de xiàndài lìshǐ hěn yǒu yánjiū.	'She's well versed in modern Chinese history.'
Duì . . . yǒu bāngzhù	'be of help'
ABC zìdiǎn duì Hànyǔ xuéxí dà yǒu bāngzhù.	'The ABC dictionary is a great help in studying Chinese.'

VOCABULARY

xià wéiqí	'play Go' ('put+down encircling-chess')
xiàngqí	'chess' ('elephant/ivory-chess')
huàhuàr	'to paint; draw' ('paint-paintings')
huángdì	'emperor'
tiānwén<xué>	'astronomy' ('heaven-inscriptions')
bāngzhù	'help'

15.3 Temporal and logical sequence

In previous units, you encountered adverbs (*yǐjīng, jiù, cái*) and conjunctions (*yīnwèi, suīrán, yǐhòu*), all of which make explicit certain temporal or logical connections between sentences (or utterances). This section provides additional material incorporated in longer and more complicated chunks. Let's first look at some relevant vocabulary.

VOCABULARY

xiān	'first': *qǐxiān* 'at first; originally' ('raise-first')	
ránhòu	'and then; after that' ('thusly-after') [of past events or future ones]	
hòulái	'later on; afterward' ('after-come') [only when retelling the past]	
zài	'again; go on to' [anticipated repetition; postponement]	
yòu	'once again; go on to' [with an event that has happened or is destined to happen]	
yīncǐ	'because of this; for that reason; so' ('because-this')	
jiéguǒ	'as a result' ('to form-fruit/result')	

Wǒmen xiān qù Běijīng kànwàng wǒ qīzi de qīnqi, ránhòu qù Shànghǎi kāihuì. Yuè dǐ jiu huílai.	'First we're going to Beijing to visit my wife's relatives, and then we're going to Shanghai for a conference. We'll be back at the end of the month.'

VOCABULARY

kànwàng	'visit; call on; see [people]' ('look-view'): *xīwàng de wàng*	
běnyuè	'this month' ('root-month'): *běnyuè dǐ* 'at the end of the month'	

Jīběnshang, wǒmen dǎsuàn dào Xī'nán qù dāi jǐ ge xīngqi cānguān yìxiē Yízú nóngcūn. Ránhòu wǒmen qù Mínzú Xuéyuàn zuò yí ge yuè de yánjiū.	'Basically, we plan to go to the Southwest to spend a few weeks visiting some Yi villages. After that, we're going to do a month's research at the Minority Peoples' Institute.'

VOCABULARY

jīběnshang	'basically' ('base-root-on')
dāi	'stay over' [coll]
cānguān	'visit; tour; see places': cf. *cānjiā* 'participate in'

NOTES

a. The *Yízú* are the Yi people, a non-Han people with extensive presence in southwest China. The Yi call themselves by a variety of names (*zìchēng* 'autonyms'), including those transcribed as Norsu or Nasu.

b. *Mínzú Xuéyuàn* are Minority Institutes. Two of the better known ones are in Chengdu and Beijing.

Wǒmen běnlái dǎsuàn shàngwǔ jiǔ diǎn chūfā, kěshì yīnwèi liǎng ge rén dùzi dōu bù shūfu, wǒmen xiàwǔ sì diǎn cái líkāi Lìjiāng. Jiéguǒ, dào Báishā de shíhou, tiān yǐjīng hēi le. Wǒmen zài xiǎo lǚguǎn shuìle yí yè; dì-èr tiān zǎoshang kāishǐ shàngshān. Lùshang wǒmen pèngdàole yìxiē Nàxīzú de rén; tāmen gěi wǒmen zhǐle lù.	'Originally, we had planned to start at 9:00 in the morning, but because two people got upset stomachs, we didn't leave Lijiang until 4:00. As a result, when we got to Baisha, it was already dark. We spent the night in a small inn; then the morning of the next day, we started up the mountain. On the way, we met some Naxi people; they showed us the route.'

VOCABULARY

chūfā	'start off [on a journey]' ('leave-issue forth')
dùzi bù shūfu	'have upset stomachs'
lǚguǎn	generic term for 'hotel', but in this case, more of a hostel
yí yè	'one night'
pèngdào	'run into; meet up with' ('bump-to')
zhǐ lù	'indicate the route; provide directions' ('indicate road')

NOTES

a. *Báishā* is a village about 15 kilometers north of Lijiang at the base of a chain of peaks that go under the name of *Yùlóng-xuěshān* 'Jade Dragon Snow Mountain'.

b. *Nàxīzú*: the Naxi (~ Nahsi) are a non-Han, minority people with their own language and writing system who live in and around Lijiang in northwest Yunnan.

Wǒmen bā hào fēi dào Xiāng Gǎng, dì-èr tiān, zuò huǒchē dàole Guǎngzhōu. Zài Guǎngzhōu dāile liǎng tiān kànle kàn; ránhòu shíyī hào zuò fēijī dào Chéngdū qù le. Wǒmen zài Chéngdū dāile	'We flew to Hong Kong on the 8th, and the next day took a train to Guangzhou. We stayed in Guangzhou for two days to look around; then, on the 11th, we flew to Chengdu. We stayed

yí ge xīngqi mǎi dōngxi, hòulái zuò huǒchē qùle Xīchāng. Xīchāng zài Dàliáng Shān, zài Chéngdū xīnán biānr wǔ bǎi gōnglǐ de dìfang.

in Chengdu for a week to buy supplies then later on took a train to Xichang. Xichang is about 500 kilometers southwest of Chengdu, in the Great Snowy Mountains.'

NOTE

Xīchāng is a city in the Great Snowy Mountains in the southern part of Sichuan. It is now best known for the satellite launch and tracking facilities that are some 50 kilometers from town. Historically, it is an important center of the Yi people.

Hánjià, wǒ xiān huíjiā kànwàng jiārén. Dāile yí ge xīngqī yǐhòu wǒ jiu qù Táiběi kāihuì. Zài Táiběi zhǐ dāile sān tiān, méiyǒu shíjiān qù kàn hěn duō dìfang. Míngnián hěn xiǎng zài huíqu yí cì duō liǎojiě yíxiàr Táiwān de wénhuà, duō kàn yìdiǎnr Táiwān de fēngjǐng, duō chī yìdiǎnr Táiwān de xiǎochī. Yīncǐ, wǒ xiànzài zhèngzài xiǎng bànfǎ jìnyibù tígāo wǒ de Zhōngwén shuǐpíng. Zhèyàng wǒ kě.yǐ gēn Táiwān rén duō liáotiān, duō gōutōng.

'Over winter break, first I went home to visit my family. After a week there, I went to Taipei for a meeting. I only stayed three days in Taipei, so I didn't have time to see a lot of places. Next year, I want to go back once again to get to know more about Taiwanese culture, see more of Taiwan's scenery, and eat more Taiwanese snacks. That's the reason I'm now thinking about how I can raise my Chinese level. That way, I'll be able to chat with more people from Taiwan and communicate with them more.'

VOCABULARY

hánjià	'winter break' ('cold-holiday')
kāihuì	'attend, hold, open a meeting' ('open-meeting')
fēngjǐng	'scenery' ('wind-view')
zhèngzài	'be in the process of' ('right now-be at')

jìnyíbù	'go a step further; raise a notch' ('go forward-one-step')
tígāo	'raise' ('raise-high')
shuǐpíng	'level' ('water-level')
gōutōng	'communicate' ('channel-through')

NOTE

Duō liǎojiě <yíxiàr> . . . 'get to know more about . . .'; *duō kàn* . . . 'see more of . . .'; *duō chī* . . . 'eat more . . .' In each case, *duō* appears before the verb in the adverbial position—as if it were an adverb of degree, such as 'get to know to a greater degree' (cf. §14.7.1).

Exercise 2

Prepare narratives along the following lines.

1. Itinerary: I arrived in Shanghai at 5:30 and got the #4 bus to the Shanghai train station. I planned to take the subway to the hotel on *Zhàojiābāng* Road, but I was tired with lots of luggage, so I took a cab instead. Later on, I moved once again to a hotel in *Zhá Běi* (district) near the train station. That way, it's easier to get to the airport.

2. Daily schedule: I generally get up at 7:30, shower, and have some rice gruel. I bike to *Běijīng Yǔyán Dàxué* for a 10:00 class. At noon, I eat lunch in the cafeteria with classmates. From 1:00 to 3:00, I have two more classes. After class, I go off to the library to study. I usually eat dinner at a local restaurant. Sometimes, in the evening, I go into town or hang out at bars and coffee shops with my friends. I don't get home until quite late.

3. Over the New Year, I spent a few days with friends in Guilin (*Guìlín*) and then went on to Kunming (*Kūnmíng*) by train. Originally, I planned to visit Dali (*Dàlǐ*) and Lijiang (*Lìjiāng*) in the northwest of Yunnan (*Yúnnán*) as well, but I didn't feel well, so I just stayed in Kunming at the Camellia Hotel (*Cháhuā Bīnguǎn*). I wrote letters and rested. Later on, I went with *Bì Xiùqióng* to visit the Stone Forest (*Shí Lín*) and Zheng He Park (*Zhèng Hé Gōngyuán*) on the southern shore of Lake Dian (*Diān Chí*).

Translate as you fill in the blanks with either *zài*, *yòu*, *jiù*, or *cái*.

1. *Duìbuqǐ, wǒ méi tīng qīngchu, qǐng nǐ _____ shuō yí cì.*
2. *Lù hěn yuǎn, zuò huǒchē qù yěxǔ sān tiān _____ dào.*
3. *Nǐ děi xiān mǎi piào _____ néng shàngche.*
4. *Nǐ xiān shàngchē _____ bǔ piào ('top up ticket'), hǎo bu hǎo?*
5. *E, zhēnshi de! Tā zuótiān méi lái, jīntiān _____ méi lái.*
6. *Xiànzài méiyǒu shíjiān, wǒmen míngtiān _____ shuō, hǎo bu hǎo?*
7. *Zhè bú shì cái ('only') liǎng diǎn ma, nǐ zěnme _____ chīshang le.*
8. *Píngcháng wǒ sì diǎn huíjiā, kěshì jīntiān yīnwèi yǒu kǎoshì wǒ wǔ diǎn _____ huíjiā de.*
9. *Liǎng nián qián wǒ xuéle liù ge yuè de Zhōngwén, yǐhòu méiyǒu _____ xué le.*
10. *Píngcháng tā chī bàn wǎn fàn _____ bǎo le, kěshì jīntiān hěn è, liǎng wǎn _____ bǎo!*
11. *Nǐ bù duō zuò yìhuǐr le ma? _____ hē yì bēi kāfēi!*
12. *Rén bù duō, liù píng _____ gòu le.*
13. *Rén bù shǎo, shí'èr píng _____ gòu!*
14. *Zài Xī'ān dāile yí ge lǐbài, ránhòu _____ huídào Běijīng gōngzuòle liǎng ge yuè.*

Xióngmāo zuì kě'ài!

15.4 Family and professions

Talking about family naturally leads to talking about professions. Now we will take some time to expand vocabulary and usage for both subjects. For family, terms and usage reflect traditional ideas about status. Therefore, males are mentioned before females (*fùmǔ, xiōngdì-jiěmèi*), and terms referring to older people are mentioned before those for younger (*jiěmèi*). This applies not just to words but also to phrases. When reporting on your own family, it would be customary to present them from oldest to youngest and from male to female. Birth sequence is also important, and you will see that the question of where you fall in the birth sequence is easier to ask in Chinese than it is in English. We begin with a short interview designed to elicit basic information about the family. *Jiǎ* is Chinese, and *Yǐ* is a foreigner working in China.

Jiǎ:	*Nǐ jiālǐ yǒu jǐ kǒu rén?*	'How many people are in your family?'
Yǐ:	*Liù kǒu, wǒ àiren hé sì ge háizi.*	'Six, my spouse and four children.'
Jiǎ:	*Sì ge háizi? Jǐnán-jǐnǚ?*	'Four children? How many boys, how many girls?'
Yǐ:	*Dōu shi nǚ'ér.*	'They're all girls.'
Jiǎ:	*Ó, sì ge nǚháizi—sìqiān jīn a! Nǐ yǒu zhàopiānr ma?*	'Oh, four girls—4,000 pieces of gold! Do you have photos?'
Yǐ:	*Yǒu, nǐ kàn . . . wǒ tàitai, lǎodà, lǎo'èr, lǎosān, lǎoxiǎo.*	'I do, take a look . . . my wife, my oldest, my second, third, and youngest.'
Jiǎ:	*Nǐ zhèi sì ge háizi dōu hěn kě'ài.*	'Those four kids of yours are really cute.'
Yǐ:	*Nǎ.lǐ, dōu hěn tiáopí.*	'Nah, they're all quite mischievous.'
Jiǎ:	*Wǒ bú tài xiāngxìn, kàn qǐlai dōu hěn guāi!*	'I don't believe you, they all look very well behaved!'

VOCABULARY

kǒu	M word for people treated as one part of a group, such as a family or village
zhàopiān<r>	'photograph; picture' ('photograph-slice'): sometimes also *xiàngpiān<r>*; in both cases, the presence of an *r* suffix is usually associated with a level tone. Without the *r* suffix, both words are pronounced with a falling tone on *piàn*: *zhàopiàn, xiàngpiàn*.
tiáopí	'naughty; mischievous; unruly' ('stir up-skin') [esp. of children]: The word is slightly derogatory.
xiāngxìn	'believe' ('mutual-believe')
kàn qǐlai	'when it comes to looking at them; to look': cf. §14.1, *tīng qǐlai*
guāi	'well behaved' [esp. of children]

NOTES

a. *Jǐnán-jǐnǔ*: the symmetry of the question allows a reduction of the full pattern (*jǐ ge érzi, jǐ ge nǚ'ér*) to the favored four-syllable format.

b. *Qiān jīn* is literally '1,000 <pieces of> gold', a (now) tongue-in-cheek reference to daughters, so *liǎngqiān jīn* '2,000 <pieces of> gold' refers to 'two daughters'. In some southern regions, daughters are called *jīnhuā* 'golden flowers'. A similar phrase is *sì duǒ jīnhuā* ('four M gold-flowers').

c. *Lǎodà*: Children (sons or daughters) can be referred to as *lǎodà, lǎo'èr, lǎosān*, and so on, according to relative age. The youngest is often referred to as *lǎoxiǎo*.

Now we can proceed to a longer dialogue in a more natural setting. *Zhāng Guóróng*, a local, is taking *Bái Jiéfēi*, a Canadian student studying Chinese medicine, to see his mother's clinic. They have just run into Guorong's sister, *Zhāng Mǐnmǐn*, which leads to a conversation about their families.

Guóróng: *Ēi, dàjiě, lái, nǐmen rènshi yíxiàr: Zhè shi Bái Jiéfēi, Jiānádà de, lái liúxué yì nián le, zhuānyè shi Zhōngyī.*

'Hey, sis, come over and meet someone: this is Bai Jiefei from Canada. He's been here studying for a year; his specialty is Chinese medicine.'

Mǐnmǐn:	*Zhōngyī! Lìhai! Ng, nǐ hǎo, wǒ jiào Zhào Mǐnmǐn. Wǒ hǎoxiàng zài shūdiàn jiànguo nǐ.*	'Chinese medicine! Wow! Hello, I'm Zhao Minmin. I think I've seen you in the bookshop.'
Jiéfēi:	*Shì a, wǒ jìdé, nǐ hǎoxiàng bāng wǒ zhǎo shū láizhe.*	'Yes, I remember; you helped me find some textbooks.'
Mǐnmǐn:	*Jiùshi a. Duìbuqǐ, wǒ xiànzài yǒu shìr. Yǐhòu zài liáo ba.*	That's right. Sorry, I have something to do right now. We'll talk again later, okay?
Guóróng:	*Tā jiù zhèyàngr, lǎoshi fēngfēng-huǒhuǒ de.*	'She's like that—always on the go.'
Jiéfēi:	*Nǐ hái yǒu xiōngdì-jiěmèi ma?*	'Do you have any other brothers and sisters?'
Guóróng:	*Bù, jiù wǒmen liǎ. Jiějie bǐ wǒ dà liǎng suì. Nǐ ne? Jiālǐ yǒu xiē shénme rén?*	'No, it's just the two of us. Sister's a couple years older than me. How about you? Who's in your family?'
Jiéfēi:	*Bàba, māma, hái yǒu sì ge xiōngdì jiěmèi.*	'My mother and father, plus four siblings.'
Guóróng:	*Nǐ lǎo jǐ?*	'Where are you in the sequence?'
Jiéfēi:	*<Nǐ shuō> shénme?*	'Huh?'
Guóróng:	*Wǒ shi shuō nǐ lǎo jǐ? Bǐfāng shuō lǎodà, lǎo'èr.*	'I mean what's your ranking; for example, first-born, second-born.'
Jiéfēi:	*O, míngbai le; wǒ <páiháng> lǎo'èr.*	'Oh, I see; I'm second.'
Guóróng:	*Hǎo le, jiù zhèr. Zhè shi zhěnsuǒ. Wǒ mā yīnggāi zài lǐtou.*	'Okay, here we are. This is the clinic. My mom should be inside.'
Jiéfēi:	*Nǐ bàba yě shi yīshēng ma?*	'Is your dad a doctor too?'

Guóróng:	*Bù, tā shi lǎoshī. Tā zài Dì-wǔ Kējì Gāozhōng jiāoshū, jiāole yǒu sānshí nián le.*	'No, he's a school teacher. He's been teaching in #5 High School of Science and Technology for thirty years.'
Jiéfēi:	*Sān shí nián le. Wa! Tā jiāo shénme?*	'Thirty years. Wow! What does he teach?'
Guóróng:	*Wùlǐ.*	'Physics.'
Jiéfēi:	*Guàibude nǐ duì wùlǐ gǎn xìngqu.*	'No wonder you're interested in physics.'
Guóróng:	*Yěxǔ shì. Nǐ bà-mā zěnmeyàng?*	'I guess so. How are your parents?'
Jiéfēi:	*Wǒ mā hái zài; wǒ yǒu ge jìfù. Tāmen kāile yí ge fàndiàn, tèbié shòu huānyíng; zài Xīn'ào'ěrliáng. Wǒ mā guǎn qián, wǒ bà dāng dàchú. Tāmen měitiān dōu děi yìqǐ mǎi cài.*	'My mother's still alive; I have a stepfather. They opened a restaurant that's very popular; it's in New Orleans. My mom deals with the money, and my dad is the chef. Every day, they buy the food together.'
Guóróng:	*Tāmen hěn máng ba.*	'They must be pretty busy.'
Jiéfēi:	*Kě bú shì! Tāmen zhěngtiān dōu zài máng. Xiǎo de shíhou, wǒmen jiù děi zuò jiāwù, mǎi cài, zuòfàn, dǎsǎo, xǐ yīfu, yě zài fàndiàn bāngmáng.*	'That's for sure! They work all day. When we were small, we'd have to do housework, buy the food, cook, clean the floors, wash the clothes, and help out in the restaurant.'
Guóróng:	*Ai, nǐmen zhēn xíng!*	'Hey, you guys are great!'
Jiéfēi:	*Nǐ yě duì fùmǔ dà yǒu bāngzhù, bú shì ma?*	'You help your parents a lot too, no?'
Guóróng:	*Bù, wǒ jiějie gàn+de bǐ wǒ duō duōle.*	'No, my sister does much more than I do.'

VOCABULARY

jìde	'remember' ('note-obtain')
láizhe	See note *c* below.
liáo	'chat' [coll]: common in phrases such as *yǐhòu zài liáo* 'we'll talk more later'
fēngfēng-huǒhuǒ	'in a great hurry; on the go; full of energy' ('wind-fire'): In this case, the component parts are nouns ('wind' and 'fire') rather than the more usual stative verb base.
liǎ	colloquial for *liǎng ge [rén]*, particularly after plural pronouns—*wǒmen liǎ*
páiháng	'rank; position' [among siblings] ('line up-column')
zhěnsuǒ	'clinic' ('treatment-place')
yīshēng	'doctor': cf. *dàifu*, especially in the expression *kàn dàifu* 'see a doctor'
kējì	'science and technology': *kēxué de kē, jìshù de jì*
guàibude	'<so it's> no wonder that; so that's why' ('be strange-not-get')
jìfù	'stepfather': cf. *jìmǔ*
shòu huānyíng	'be popular' ('receive welcome'): *hěn shòu huānyíng*
guǎn	'manage; deal with'
dāng	'work as; act as; be': *dāng mǔqin* 'be a mother'; *dāng lùshī* 'work as a lawyer'; *dāng gōngrén* 'be a worker'; *shì* is frequently an alternative to *dāng*—*tā shi yīshēng*—cf. *Tā zuò shēngyi* 'She's in business.'
dàchú	'chef' ('big-chef'): probably short for *dàchúshī*; cf. *dàshīfu*, a more formal word for 'chef'
zhěngtiān	'the whole day': cf. *zhěnggè* 'the whole thing; entire' [as opposed to 'in pieces' or 'parts of']. *Zhěng* also appears with time expressions, as in *sān diǎn zhěng* 'exactly three o'clock'.
zuò jiāwù	'do household chores' ('do home-things'): In Taiwan, *zuò jiāshì* ('home-things') is more common.

dǎsǎo	'to sweep; to clean': cf. *sǎodì* 'sweep the floor' ('sweep-ground')

NOTES

a. *Nǐmen rènshi yíxiàr* is a colloquial alternative to *Wǒ gěi nǐmen jièshuo yíxiàr*.

b. *Jiàn* 'see; catch sight of': cf. *kàn* 'see; visit' and *kànjiàn* 'see; look at'

c. *Láizhe* 'just; very recently': derived from the verb *lái* 'come' and the verb particle *zhe*, it is best treated as a unit. Its use is confined to northern Mandarin, where it indicates a situation that was ongoing in the recent past. One common usage is asking for a restatement or reminder when something slips your mind: *Tā xìng shénme láizhe?* 'What did you say her name was?' Otherwise it is used in statements, as in the previous dialogue: *Nǐ hǎoxiàng bāng wǒ zhǎo shū láizhe.* 'I recall you were just recently helping me look for some books.'

d. Following an implied 'if,' *jiù* can often be translated as 'then'. With an amount, it can also be translated as 'only; just': *jiù wǒmen liǎ*.

e. *Jiālǐ yǒu xiē shénme rén?* *Xiē* 'several' and *shénme* 'what' often occur together in questions that ask for a listing.

f. *Xiōngdì-jiěmèi* is a collective noun made up of the compounds *xiōngdì* 'older and younger brothers' and *jiěmèi* 'older and younger sisters'. Just as *xiōngdì* makes use of the more restricted root *xiōng* for elder brother (rather than *gē*), there is another compound for sisters—*zǐmèi*—that makes use of a more restricted term for elder sister (rather than *jiě*). *Zǐmèi* is also used metaphorically, as in *zǐmèi<chéng>shì* 'twin cities' or *zǐmèipiān* 'companion volume'.

g. Recall that children are ordered as *lǎodà*, *lǎo'èr*, *lǎosān*, and so on. The question *Nǐ lǎo jǐ?* seeks to find out birth order. Sometimes, the word *páiháng* appears in the question or response, making the 'rank; position' meaning explicit.

h. If you want to ask someone whether his or her parents are still alive, then the respectful question is *nǐ bà-mā hái jiànzài ma*, using *jiànzài* 'be in good health' ('healthy-exist').

i. *Háizimen* 'children': *-men*, the collective suffix, occurs with personal pronouns and nouns referring to human beings, such as *lǎoshīmen* and *tóngxuémen*.

j. *Bāng* 'help': *bāng nǐ zuò*; *bāng nǐ xiě*; *bāng tā xǐ yīfu*; cf. *bāngmáng* 'give a hand' and *bāngzhù* 'help; assist'. In the case of *bāngmáng*, *máng* acts as an object; cf. *bāng ge máng* 'give a hand' or *bāng tā de máng* 'help her out'. *Bāngzhù*, however, does not permit intervening material: *bāngzhù biérén jiùshi bāngzhù zìjǐ*. It may also act as a noun: *dà yǒu bāngzhù*.

ADDITIONAL VOCABULARY

jìfù	'stepfather'
jìmǔ	'stepmother'
zǔfù	'grandfather' [on the father's side]

zǔmǔ	'grandmother' [on the father's side]: *Wàizǔfù* and *wàizǔmǔ* are the grandparents on the mother's side (the 'outside'). In the south, grandfather and grandmother on the mother's side are addressed as *wàigōng* and *wàipó*, respectively. In the north, *lǎoye* and *lǎolao* are more usual.
shuāngbāotāi	'twins' ('pair-placenta-embryo')
dúshēngzǐ	'only child' [boy]
dúshēngnǚ	'only child' [girl]

EMPLOYMENT AND OTHER PROFESSIONS

To cover the employment situation of family (or friends), you will need to be able to talk about those who are not working as well as those who are.

With a job

Tā dāng yīshēng.	'He works as a doctor.'
Tā shi yīshēng.	'She's a doctor.'
Tā zuò diànyuán.	'He's a shop clerk.'
Tā zài bàozhǐ de biānjíbù gōngzuò.	'She works on the editorial staff of the paper.'
Tā shi jūnrén.	'He's a soldier.' [*jiěfàngjūn* 'PLA']

Without a job

Tā tuìxiū le.	'She's retired.' ('retreat-rest')
Tā xiàgǎng le.	'He's been laid off.' ('depart-post')
Tā shīyè le.	'She's lost her job.' ('lose-employment')
Tā bèi chǎo le.	'He's been fired.' [see note]

NOTE

One of the more colorful ways of saying 'fired' in Chinese is *chǎo yóuyú*, whose literal meaning is 'to fry squid' but which is used colloquially to mean 'to fire [someone]': *Lǎobǎn chǎole tāde yóuyú* 'The boss fired him' ('fried his squid'). Often, it is used passively with *bèi* (which, in such cases, has the effect of English 'get'; see §16.7) and without the object *yóuyú*: *Tā bèi chǎo le*.

For reference, here is a selection of jobs or professions.

Based on *shī*
- *gōngchéngshī* — 'engineer'
- *lǜshī* — 'lawyer'
- *jiànzhùshī* — 'architect'

Based on *yuán*
- *shòuhuòyuán* — 'shop assistant'
- [*zhèngfǔ*] *guānyuán* — '[government] civil servant'
- *zhíyuán* — 'clerk; office worker' [e.g., *yínháng de zhíyuán* 'bank clerk']
- *diànyuán* — 'shop assistant'
- *tuīxiāoyuán* — 'salesperson' ('push-sales-person')
- *jiàshǐyuán* — 'pilot'
- *yǎnyuán* — 'actor'
- *móshù-yǎnyuán* — 'magician'

Based on *gōng*
- *xiūlǐgōng* — 'mechanic' ('repair-laborer')
- *diàngōng* — 'electrician' ('electricity-laborer')
- *kuànggōng* — 'miner' ('mine-laborer')
- *wǎgōng* — 'bricklayer' ('tile-laborer')
- *shígōng* — 'mason' ('stone-laborer')
- *guǎndàogōng* — 'plumber' ('pipe-way-laborer')

Based on *rén*
- *jūnrén* — 'soldier'
- *shǒuyìrén* — 'craftsman' ('hand-art-person')
- *gōngrén* — 'factory worker'

Miscellaneous
- *jìzhě* — 'reporter'
- *dàifu ~ yīshēng* — 'doctor'
- *jīnglǐ* — 'manager'

diànzhǔ	'shopkeeper' ('shop-host')
língshòushāng	'retailer'
nóngmín	'farmer'
jǐngchá	'police officer'
dàshīfu ~ dàchú	'cook; chef'
cáifeng	'tailor'
sījī	'driver'
jūnguān	'army officer'
gōngjiàng	'artisan'
gànbu	'cadre; government official'
yìshùjiā	'artist'
xiǎofànzi	'hawker; peddlar'

Mài shuǐguǒ de fùnǚ 'Women selling fruit' (*Běijīng* 2007)

15.5 Setting the stage: Verb-*zhe*

Of the three common verbal suffixes in Chinese, we learned about *guo* early on and *le* (in its postverbal manifestation) more recently. The third, *zhe*, has been almost completely avoided until now. There is a reason for this. Most of the language presented so far has dealt with actions or inner states. The verb-*zhe* (V-*zhe*) is rare in such language and serves primarily to set the scene (e.g., 'the door's open'; 'there's a vase on the table'; 'the blinds are drawn') and indicate the various configurations of the actors (e.g., 'a man is standing at the door'; 'he's wearing a long robe and holding a pipe in his hands'). Like *guo* and *le*, *zhe* precludes other suffixes (*guo* or *le*) or verbal complements (such as *wán* 'finish' or *guòlai* 'over here').

15.5.1 Verbs involving configuration or bodily attitude

Zhàn, zuò, and the words listed below are examples of verbs that involve attitudes or configurations of the body that are compatible with persistant states. Therefore, they are particularly susceptible to the *zhe* suffix.

zhàn	'stand'
zuò	'sit'
tǎng	'lie'
shuì<jiào>	'sleep'
dūn	'squat; crouch'
děng	'wait'
dīng	'watch intently'
lèng	'stare blankly'

EXAMPLES

Tā zài dìbǎn shang shuìzhe ne.	'He's asleep on the floor.'
Tā zài shāfā shang tǎngzhe ne.	'She was lying on the sofa.'
Tāmen zài ménkǒu děngzhe nǐ ne.	'They're waiting for you at the door.'
Bié lèngzhe, lái bāng wǒ ná!	'Don't just stare; give me a hand!'
Duìbuqǐ, wǒ lèi+de bùdéliǎo.	'Sorry, I'm exhausted.'
Zuòzhe bùrú dūnzhe shūfu.	'Sitting isn't as comfortable as squatting.'
Wǒ tóngyì.	'I agree.'

Verbs of wearing (e.g., *chuān* 'wear [clothes, shoes]', *dài* 'wear [hats, and other accessories]', *jì* 'wear [a tie]') and verbs of holding (*ná* 'carry; hold', *dài* 'lead; bring') also commonly appear with *zhe*.

Tā jīntiān chuānzhe yí jiàn hóng dàyī ne.	'Today she's wearing a red coat.'
Tā tóu shang dàizhe yì dǐng qíguài de màozi.	'She was wearing a curious hat on her head.'
Nǐ shǒu.lǐ názhe de shi shénme?	'What are you holding in your hands?'
Nǐ kàn, tā shǒu.lǐ názhe qiāng.	'Look, he's got a gun.'

15.5.2 Patterns with V-*zhe*

In addition to the configurations of people, the arrangement of furnishings and other objects in a room can also be presented with V-*zhe*.

Nouns

yǐzi	'chair'
zhuōzi	'table'
huà<r>	'picture'
dēng	'light'
huāpíng	'vase'
chuānghu	'window'
qiáng	'wall'

Verbs

guà	'hang'
fàng	'put'
bǎi	'arrange; display'
suǒ	'lock'
guān	'close; shut'
kāi	'open'

a. Item + V-*zhe*

Mén kāizhe <ne>.	'The door's open.'
Mén kāizhe—kě.yǐ.	'It's okay open.'
Dēng kāizhe ne.	'The light's on.'
Qǐng bǎ tā guānshang.	'Please switch it off.'
Chuānghu guānzhe ne.	'The window's closed.'
Méi guānxi, tài lěng le.	'Never mind, it's too cold [to have it open].'
Mén suǒzhe ne. Jìnbuqù.	'The door's locked. We can't get in.'
Wǒ yǒu yàoshi.	'I have a key.'

b. Existence: Location + V-*zhe* + Item

V-*zhe* can also provide a more precise substitute for *yǒu* in the existence pattern.

Location + *yǒu* + Item →	Location + V-*zhe* + Item
Chuānghu pángbiānr yǒu yì zhāng zhuōzi.	*Chuānghu pángbiānr fàngzhe yì zhāng zhuōzi.*
'There's a table next to the window.'	'There's a table standing next to the window.' [i.e., 'placed there and remaining']

English often uses the verbs 'stand' or 'sit' in such contexts, extending terms that are otherwise only applied to humans to physical objects. Chinese does not do this.

Zhuōzi shang fàngzhe yí ge huāpíng.	'There was a vase sitting on the table.'
Zhuōzi shang bǎizhe jǐ zhāng míngpiàn.	'A number of business cards were arranged on the table.'
Qiáng shang guàzhe yì fú huàr.	'Hanging on the wall was a painting.'
Shāfā shang zuòzhe yí wèi jǐngchá.	'A police officer was sitting on the sofa.'

| *Zhuōzi dǐxia shuìzhe yí ge xiǎo wáwa.* | 'A baby was sleeping under the table.' |

c. Location: Person + Location + V-*zhe* <*ne*>

The location pattern with *zài* also has its correlate with V-*zhe*.

Tā zài chuáng shang zuòzhe ne.	'They are/were sitting on the bed.'
Tāmen zài shāfā shang shuìzhe ne.	'They're sleeping on the sofa.'
Kèrén zài ménkǒu děngzhe nǐ ne.	'Your guest is waiting for you at the door.'

d. V-*zhe* + Verb

Zhe frequently accompanies the first of two verbs. In such cases, V-*zhe* provides the setting, or context, for the second verb.

Tā názhe huà huíjiā le.	'She went home holding the painting.'
Bù yīnggāi dīzhe tóu zǒulù.	'You shouldn't walk with your head down.'
Tā xiàozhe shuō: Wǒ méi shíjiān gēn nǐ cāizhe wánr.	'She laughed and said, "I don't have time to play guessing games with you."'

VOCABULARY

dī	'to lower': contrast with *dǐxia* 'under; underneath', which has a low tone
xiào	'laugh; smile': cf. *xiàohua* 'a joke'; *kāi wánxiào* 'be kidding; play a joke'
cāi	'guess': *cāiduì* 'guess right'; *cāicuò* 'guess wrong'; *cāibuchū* 'cannot guess; cannot figure out'

e. V-*zhe* in imperatives

Zhe can also appear in imperatives.

Nǐ liúzhe ba.	'Take it.' ('keep-persist')
Názhe ba.	'Hold it, please.' ('hold persist')
Děngzhe ba.	'Hang on.'
Tīngzhe; bié zài shuō le!	'Listen; don't say anything more!'

f. Negation

There seems to be relatively little need to report the negation of a persistent state. Nevertheless, where it occurs, it is formed with *méi<yǒu>* and (usually) without *zhe*.

Mén shì bu shì kāizhe ne?	'Is the door open?'
Méi kāi, guānzhe de.	'It isn't open, it's closed.'
Qǐngwèn, jǐ diǎn?	'What's the time, please?'
Duìbuqǐ, wǒ jīntiān méi dài biǎo.	'Sorry, I'm not wearing my watch today.'

Exercise 3

Provide English paraphrases for each of the following.

1. *Zhànzhe gànmá? Zuòxia ba. / Zhànzhe bǐ zuòzhe shūfu.*
2. *Nǐ kàn, Wèi lǎoshī shǒu shang dàizhe yí ge dà jīn biǎo, shēn shang chuānzhe yí jiàn pídàyī. / Tā gāng zhòngle yí ge dàjiǎng!*
3. *Xuéxiào de dàménkǒu xiězhe 'Hǎohǎo xuéxí, tiāntiān xiàng shàng.'*
4. *Nǐ kuài chūqu kànkan, mén wàitou zhànzhe yí ge lǎowài, shuō shi yào zhǎo nǐ.*
5. *Wàitou xiàzhe xuě, kěshì yìdiǎnr dōu bù lěng!*

VOCABULARY

biǎo	'a watch'
gāng	'just; a short while ago'
pídàyī	'leather coat' ('leather-big-clothing')
zhòngjiǎng	'win the lottery; hit the jackpot' ('hit-prize')
xuéxiào	'school'
xuě	'snow'

Provide Chinese paraphrases for each of the following.

1. When we got there, there were already people waiting for us in front of the door.
2. "The door's open, you can go on in," I said.
3. "The door's locked, we can't get in," they said.
4. Don't stand; the people sitting in the back can't see. There are still seats up front.
5. There was a table by the door with several bottles of soda arranged on it.
6. On the wall above the table was a sign (*páizi*) with characters written on it.

15.5.3 Ongoing acts versus persistent states

First impressions tend to associate V-*zhe* with English verb + -*ing*: *zhànzhe* 'standing'; *zuòzhe* 'sitting'. However, although it is true that many cases of V-*zhe* do correspond to this English construction, the reverse is not true. English verbs ending in -*ing* often do not correspond to V-*zhe* in Chinese. The reason for this is that English uses V-*ing* for both ongoing actions ('We're recording') and for persistent states ('It's hanging on the door'), whereas Chinese uses V-*zhe* only for persistent states. Contrast the following pair of examples.

Action
Tā zhèngzài zhàn qǐlai ne.   She's standing up at this
                                             very moment.

State
Tā bú dòng, jiu zài nàr zhànzhe ne.   She's not moving; she's
                                             just standing there.

In the first sentence, *zhèngzài* supports the directional complement—*qǐlai*—to underscore the fact that the action is happening before our eyes. In other words, it's ongoing. In the second sentence, however, *zhànzhe* indicates that the standing is persistent. Though both are—in a sense—current (at the time of reference), Chinese distinguishes them both as ongoing acts versus persisting states (the latter with *zhe*).

Recall that ongoing or recent actions are often explicitly marked by *zài* in the adverbial position immediately before the verb.

Tāmen hái zài xǐzǎo ne.	'They're still bathing.'
Nǐ zuìjìn zài zuò shénme?	'What have you been doing lately?'
Tāmen tiāntiān zài xuéxí Zhōngwén.	'They've been studying Chinese daily.'

To emphasize how current the action is, the adverb *zhèng* 'exact' can be placed before *zài*.

Tā zhèngzài chīfàn ne Yìhuǐr gěi nǐ dǎ guòqu, xíng ma?	'She's eating right now. Can she phone you back in a short while?'
Xíng, bù jí, bù jí.	'Sure, no hurry.'
Wǒ zhèngzài xǐzǎo de shíhou, jǐngchá gěi wǒ dǎle ge diànhuà.	'The police phoned me just as I was having a bath.'
Tāmen gēn nǐ shuō shénme?	'What did they want?'
Tā zhèngzài gēn tā shuōhuà ne.	'She's talking to him right now.'
Tāmen zài shuō xiē shénme?	'What are they talking about?'

In fact, for some northern speakers, this pattern can be further reinforced by the addition of V=*zhe* and a final *ne*.

Zhèng <zài> xiàzhe yǔ ne!	'It's raining right now!'
Zāogāo, wǒ de sǎn wàng zai jiālǐ le!	'Drat, I've left my umbrella at home!'

The fact that *zài* may co-occur with *zhe* may seem strange, since we have just been viewing V-*zhe* in contrast to the *zài*-V pattern. Apparently, in some cases, the two notions of ongoing and persistent actions can complement each other. The range of the V-*ing* forms in English (the so-called 'progressive tenses')—which includes both ongoing actions (putting on) and persistent states (wearing)—is, after all, a precedent for associating the two notions.

Notice that some situations can be interpreted as ongoing actions or persistent states.

Tā zhèngzài shuìjiào ne.	'She's just going to sleep.'	[action]
Tā shuìzhe ne.	'She's asleep.'	[state]
Tā zài děng chē.	'He's waiting for a bus.'	[action]
Tā děngzhe ne.	'He's waiting.'	[state]
Tāmen zài chīfàn ne.	'They're eating.'	[action]
Tāmen yíkuàir chīzhe fàn ne.	'They're having a meal.'	[state]
Tāmen dōu zài tiàowǔ.	'They're all dancing.'	[action]
Péngyou chàngzhe, tiàozhe, gāoxìng jíle.	'The friends are so happy, singing and dancing.'	[state]
Tā zhèngzài chuān dàyī ne.	'She's putting on her coat right now.'	[action]
Tā chuānzhe dàyī ne.	'She's wearing a coat.'	[state]
Tā zài ná Jīngūbàng.	'He's picking up his Golden Cudgel.' [The Monkey King]	[action]
Tā shǒu.li názhe yì zhī bàngzi.	'He's holding a club.'	[state]
Tā zài bǎ shū fàng zài hézi lǐ.	'He's putting the books in a box.'	[action]
Hézi lǐ fàngzhe hěn duō shū.	'There are lots of books sitting in the box.'	[state]

Exercise 4

Paraphrase the following actions in Chinese.

1. The soup's hot. / The soup's heating up. / The soup's hot now.
2. She's closing the door. / She closed the door. / The door's closed.
3. He's putting on his shoes. / He was wearing slippers (*tuōxié*). / He put on his shoes.
4. I'm just in the process of finishing up my report (*bàogào*).
5. She's in the bath right now; can you come back in twenty minutes?

15.6 More on Chinese regional languages

The colloquial names for regional languages (*fāngyán*, shortened from *dìfang de yǔyán*) are generally formed from the name of the province or city where the language is most current. For example, *Guǎngdōnghuà* for 'Cantonese' or *Shànghǎihuà* for 'Shanghainese'. However, linguists, in order to suggest more accurately the region where the language is spoken, use more specialized terms that are based on the names of historical kingdoms or regions plus *yǔ* (e.g., *Yuèyǔ* 'Cantonese'). Many of the better known Chinese regional languages subsume regional variants. *Yuèyǔ*, for example, includes not only standard Cantonese, associated with the major urban centers of Guangzhou and Hong Kong, but also local dialects such as *Táishānhuà*. In English, *Táishānhuà* would be called a dialect of Cantonese. In colloquial Chinese, it might be called a *fāngyán* or a *tǔhuà* 'local dialect'. Linguists would probably call it a *cìfāngyán* 'secondary regional language'. Even local dialects of *Yuèyǔ* may not be mutually intelligible.

Guǎngdōnghuà 'Cantonese': The dialect grouping called *Yuè* or *Yuèyǔ*. *Yuè* dialects include *Táishān*, also called Toisan after the Cantonese pronunciation and Hoisan after the pronunciation of Taishan itself. It is spoken in a coastal region of Guangdong Province, southwest of Hong Kong. Speakers of *Yuè* are found in many parts of the world. Not so long ago, most Chinese Americans descended from emigrants from Taishan County and adjoining regions known (in Cantonese pronunciation) as *Sze Yup* 'four counties'. (Recent administrative changes have made the *Sze Yup* area actually *Ng Yup* 'five counties'.) In many parts of the Chinese-speaking world, Cantonese commands almost as much prestige as Mandarin, and it is often learned as a second language.

Fújiànhuà 'Fukienese, Hokkien': *Fújiànhuà* is often called Hokkien in English, after the Fukienese pronunciation of the name of its home province, Fujian (*Fújiàn*). The dialect grouping as a whole is called *Mǐn*, and within *Mǐn*, the southern or western group that includes Taiwanese and the languages of Amoy (*Xiàmén* in Mandarin) and Swatou (*Shàntóu* in Mandarin) are often called *Mǐnnányǔ* 'southern Min'. Min speakers and their descendents are found throughout Southeast Asia (notably in Singapore, where they are a majority) and other parts of the world.

Xiāng Gǎng: shāngyè dàjiē 'A commercial street in Hong Kong'

Shànghǎihuà 'Shanghainese': The dialect grouping that includes *Shànghǎihuà*, *Sūzhōuhuà*, *Níngbōhuà*, and others is called *Wú* or *Wúyǔ*.

Kèjiāhuà 'Hakka': The name Hakka is based on the Cantonese pronunciation of the word *kèjiā* 'guests; strangers' ('guest families'). The Hakka are called guests because they settled in places already occupied by Cantonese. Hakka speakers are found in Guangdong Province, southwest Fujian Province, Hong Kong, Taiwan, and many parts of Southeast Asia.

Keep this discussion of *fāngyán* in mind as you read the following dialogue. Place: Beijing. *Jiǎ*, a foreigner studying in China, has been talking to *Yǐ*, a Chinese student.

Jiǎ:	*Nǐ fùmǔ yě zhù zai Běijīng ma?*	'Your parents live in Beijing too?'
Yǐ:	*Shì, tāmen zài zhèr yǒu ge fángzi.*	'Yes, they have an apartment here.'
Jiǎ:	*O, yǒu zìjǐ de fángzi!*	'Oh, so they have their own apartment!'
Yǐ:	*Bú shì zìjǐ de, shi māma de dānwèi fēn gěi tāmen de.*	'It's not their own; it's provided by my mom's unit.'
Jiǎ:	*O, dānwèi fēn gěi tāmen de.*	'Oh, it's provided by the unit.'
Yǐ:	*Shì, zài yí dòng liù céng gāo de dānyuánlóu, wàitou bù qǐyǎnr dànshi wū li hěn bú cuò.*	'Yes, it's in a six-story residential building that's not much to look at on the outside, but the rooms aren't bad inside.'
Jiǎ:	*Fùmǔ shi zài Běijīng zhǎngdà de ma?*	'Were your parents raised in Beijing?'
Yǐ:	*Bù, wǒ fùqin shi Guǎngzhōurén, mǔqin shi Níngbō lái de.*	'No, my father's from Guangzhou, and my mother's from Ningbo.'
Jiǎ:	*Wǒ zhīdao Guǎngdōngrén shuō Guǎngdōnghuà. Nà, Níngbōrén shuō shénme huà ne?*	'I know people from Guangdong speak Cantonese; so what language do Ningbo people speak?'

Yǐ: *Níngbō lí Shànghǎi bù yuǎn.*   'Ningbo's not far from Shanghai.
     Níngbōhuà yǒu diǎnr xiàng   Ningbo dialect is a bit like
     Shànghǎihuà.   Shanghainese.'

Jiǎ: *O, Níngbōrén shuō*   'Oh, Ningbo people speak
     Shànghǎihuà!   Shanghainese!'

Yǐ: *Bù, Níngbōhuà hěn xiàng*   'No, Ningbo speech is a lot like
     Shànghǎihuà, kěshì bù   Shanghai speech, but it's not
     wánquán yíyàng.   completely identical to it. The
     Shànghǎihuà, Níngbōhuà,   languages of Shanghai,
     Sūzhōuhuà děng.děng dōu   Ningbo, Suzhou, and so on are
     shì Wúfāngyán.   all Wu dialects.'

Jiǎ: *'Fāngyán' shi shénme yìsi?*   'What's a *fāngyán*?'

Yǐ: *Fāngyán ne, fāngyán shi*   'A *fāngyán*, well . . . a *fāngyán* is a
     dìfāng de yǔyán, xiàng   regional language, like
     Guǎngdōnghuà, Fújiànhuà,   Cantonese, Fujianese, and
     zhèyàngr de.   such.'

Jiǎ: *Nǐ huì shuō Shànghǎihuà*   'Do you speak Shanghainese?'
     ma?

Yǐ: *Shànghǎihuà wǒ bú huì,*   'I don't speak Shanghainese, but
     dànshi wǒ huì shuō yìdiǎnr   I do speak some Cantonese.'
     Guǎngdōnghuà.

Jiǎ: *Huì shuō Pǔtōnghuà de rén*   'Do people who speak Mandarin
     tīngdedǒng Guǎngdōnghuà   understand Cantonese and
     Shànghǎihuà ma?   Shanghainese?'

Yǐ: *Tīngbudǒng. Pǔtōnghuà shi*   'No. Mandarin's Mandarin,
     Pǔtōnghuà, Guǎngdōnghuà   Cantonese is Cantonese, and
     shi Guǎngdōnghuà,   Shanghainese is Shanghainese;
     Shànghǎihuà shi   they're all different regional
     Shànghǎihuà, dōu shì bù   languages.'
     tóng de fāngyán.

Jiǎ: *Ài, Hànyǔ zhēn fùzá!*   'Wow, Chinese is so
      complicated!'

VOCABULARY

dòng	M for buildings: *yí dòng [liù céng gāo de] dānyuánlóu*
liù céng	'six stories': *céng* is an M for levels, layers, and stories
dānyuánlóu	*dānyuán* 'a residential unit'; also 'a section of a book': *zhè shi dì-shíwǔ ge dānyuán*
qǐyǎnr	'be attractive; striking' ('raise-eyes') [coll]: often used in the negative
děngděng	'and so on': used to close a list. This is a special function of the verb *děng* 'wait'.
fùzá	'be complicated': cf. *bù jiǎndān* 'not simple'

NOTES

a. *Fángzi* 'house' or 'apartment' [Mainland usage with *gè* as M word]: A freestanding house in an urban setting is a rare thing in China, and it is usually called a *biéshù*, often translated as 'villa'. Less commonly (but more so in Taiwan), apartments are also called *gōngyù*.

b. *Fēn gěi* 'distribute to' ('distribute-give'): *Fēn* is one of a number of transactional verbs that are followed by *gěi* 'give' when a personal object is present. Others include *mài* 'sell' (*mài gěi tā* 'sell to him') and *dì* 'pass' (*dì gěi wǒ* 'pass me something').

c. Older Chinese residential blocks are typically six stories high; above that, they are required to have elevators.

d. Ningbo is a city in Zhejiang Province, near the coast and south across the Bay of Hangzhou from Shanghai. Regional dialects in southern Jiangsu and most of Zhejiang are closely related to Shanghainese, and they are all classified as Wu dialects.

15.7 To *bǎ* or not to *bǎ*?

Recall §14.3: Using the stage metaphor, the co-verb *bǎ* was said to draw nouns into the spotlight to prepare them for a special role. A contrast can be made between sentences with *bǎ* which designate particular nouns, and those without *bǎ*, which do not.

Qǐng dǎkāi chuānghu.	'Open a window please.' [any window]
Yǐjīng dǎkāi le.	'I already have.'

The speaker is not designating a specific window—any window will do. However, if the speaker wants to indicate a specific window (as if pointing), then he is more likely to use *bǎ*.

Qǐng bǎ chuānghu dǎkāi.	'Please open the window.' [a specific window]
Wǒ yǐjīng bǎ tā dǎkāi le.	'I've already opened it.'

Instructions that involve manipulation of particular items almost always elicit the grammatical word *bǎ* (or its more formal counterpart, *jiāng*). The items in question will be moved, taken, broken, prepared, hidden, painted, purged, promoted, or otherwise changed in some way. For that reason, *bǎ* is typically associated with verb combos (action plus result), or, at very least, verb-*le* (action done) or a reduplicated verb (*qiēqie* 'cut up'). For the same reason, *bǎ* is not associated with verbs such as *xǐhuan* or *kàn*, whose objects seem unaffected by the attention.

Wǒ hěn xǐhuan nèi bù diànyǐng.	'I love that movie.'
Wǒ yǐjīng kànwánle nèi běn shū.	'I've finished reading the book.'

Bǎ also does not appear with potential verb combos, for which the effect is not actual, only hypothesized.

Tā nèi ge xiāngzi wǒ ná bu qǐlai.	'I can't lift that suitcase of hers.'

Other examples:

Yǒu diǎnr hēi, qǐng bǎ dēng dǎkāi.	'It's a bit dark; put the light on, please.'
Dēng huài le, kāibuliǎo.	'The light's broken; it won't go on.'
Nà, wǒmen bǎ zhuōzi bāndào chuānghu nàr, hǎo bu hǎo?	'Well then, let's move the table over to the window, okay?'
Tài zhòng le, bānbudòng.	'It's too heavy; it can't be moved.'
Nà, bǎ táidēng ná guòlai ba.	'Okay, then let's bring the desk lamp over.'
Hǎo, zhèyàngr kě.yǐ.	'Okay, that's fine.'
Shéi bǎ wǒ de píjiǔ hēle?	'Who drank my beer?'
Méi rén hē nǐ de píjiǔ!	'No one drank your beer!'
Nǐ xiān bǎ niúròu qiēqie.	'First, slice the beef.'

Zěnme qiē, qiē piànr háishi qiē   'How? Into slices or into chunks?'
   kuàir?

Qǐng bǎ zìxíngchē fàng zài   'Please put your bike in the alley.'
   xiǎoxiàng li.
Fàng zài xiǎoxiàng li gòu   'Will it be safe enough if I put it
   ānquán ma?   there?'
Méi wèntí, wǒ huì bāng nǐ   'No problem, I'll help you keep an
   kānzhe.   eye on it.'

VOCABULARY

bù   M for things viewed not as items but as productions,
               such as films, works of literature, and machines:
               nèi bù diànyǐng
táidēng   'lamp' ('platform-light')
qiē   'cut up'
xiǎoxiàng   'alley' ('small-alley')
kān   'watch over; tend': a level-toned relative of (and written
               with the same character as) *kàn* 'look at'; *kān háizi* 'to
               babysit children'

As several of the previous examples show, *bǎ* can be directly negated or modified by adverbs—a vestige of its verbal origin.

Tā méi bǎ chuānghu dǎkāi.   'She didn't open the windows.'
Tāmen yǐjīng bǎ dōngxi názǒu le.   'They've already taken the
                                          things out.'
Bié bǎ shūbāo fàng zai zhuōzi   'Don't put your bookbags on
   shang.   the table.'

15.8 Verb combos (3)

The use of *bǎ* is, as noted, intimately connected to complex verbs, so this is an appropriate place to continue the complex verb survey. First, let's do a review exercise.

Exercise 5

Complete each sentence with one of the listed verb complements (actual or potential—the latter with inserted *bu* or *de*): *wán* and *hǎo* 'finish', *dào* and *zháo* 'manage to; succeed in', *bǎo* 'filled', or *cuò* 'in error'.

1. *Kèrén yào lái le, nǐ fàn zuò _____ le méiyǒu?*
2. *Nǐ zhǎo něi wèi? / Duìbuqǐ, wǒ yěxǔ dǎ _____ le.*
3. *Tā shuō de huà nǐ tīng _____ ma?*
4. *Téng lǎoshī zài chuānghu wàitou, nǐ méi kàn _____ tā ma?*
5. *Nèi běn shū tài cháng le, wǒ kàn _____.*
6. *Wǒ xiǎngdào kǎoshì de shìqing jiu shuì _____ jiào!*
7. *Tā xiǎng zuò de shìr yǐjīng zuò _____ le.*
8. *Wǒ de zìdiǎn zhǎo _____ le ! Nǐ kàn _____ le ma? Méiyǒu zìdiǎn bù néng zuò jīntiān de gōngkè!*
9. *Bié kèqi, duō chī yìdiǎnr cài! / Ài, wǒ chī _____ le, bù néng zài chī le!*
10. *Jīntiān shi yīntiān, kàn _____ tàiyáng!*

15.8.1 Position of objects

As noted earlier, *bǎ* is associated with manipulation or other kinds of actions that affect the position or integrity of objects.

Tā bǎ bǐ ná qǐlai le.	'She picked up the pen.'
Tā bǎ huà ná xiàlai le.	'He took the painting down.'

However, an indefinite object (one that is new to the discourse, and in English typically preceded by an indefinite article such as 'a~an' or 'some') generally appears after the verb combination, and not before with *bǎ*. *Lái* and *qù*, whose function is to indicate direction toward or away from the speaker, are often—but not always—postponed until after the object.

Tā ná qǐ bǐ lai le.	'She picked up a pen.'
Wǒ xiǎng bu qǐ tā de míngzi lái le.	'I can't remember his name.'

Názhù le ma? (Běijīng)

15.8.2 More verb complements

a. *Zhù*, which as a verb means 'live', combines with verbs such as *jì* 'note', *ná* 'hold', and *tíng* 'stop' to convey fixedness.

Tā de diànhuà hàomǎ wǒ lǎo jìbuzhù!	'I can never remember her phone number!'
Tā hěn cōngming, nǐ wènbuzhù tā!	'He's smart; you won't stump him!'
Názhù le ma?	'Got it?'
Jiēzhù! / Jiēzhù le!	'Catch it! / Got it!'
Zhànzhù, bú yào dòng! Jǔ qǐ shǒu lai!	'Stay still; don't move! Hands up!'

VOCABULARY

wènbuzhù	'stump' ('ask-not-stick'): also *wènbudǎo* ('ask-not-collapse')
jiē	'join': *xièxie nǐmen lái jiē wǒmen*

dòng	'move': *yùndòng de dòng*
jǔ	'raise': cf. *jǔzhòng* 'lift weights' or *jǔxíng* 'take place; *bǎ shǒu jǔ qǐlai* is also possible, but the *bǎ* version puts more focus on the hands—"Put your hands up!"

b. *Kāi* as a verb complement means 'open'.

Kāibukāi ~ dǎbukāi chuānghu.	'I can't open the window.'
Zǒukāi! Zhèr méiyǒu nǐ de shìr.	'Get lost! This doesn't concern you.'
Yú líbukāi shuǐ ya, guā líbukāi yāng; rénmín qúnzhòng líbukāi Gòngchǎndǎng.	'Just as fish can't leave the water and melons can't leave the vine, the people can't be separated from the Communist Party.' [from a popular song]

c. *Shàng* and *xià*, in addition to their literal meanings in the directional complements *xiàlai*, *shànglai*, *xiàqu*, and *shàngqu*, also form single-syllable complements.

Bǎ húlur fàngxià!	'Put the gourd down!'
Zhèi jiān jiàoshì zuòbuxià sānshí ge rén.	'This classroom won't seat thirty.'
Zuòxià ba.	'Why don't you sit down?'
Wǒ wàngle dàishàng biǎo.	'I forgot to put my watch on.'
Tā pà tā kǎobushàng dàxué.	'He's afraid he won't pass the university entrance exam.'
Tā zhēn kě'ài; wǒ yǐjīng àishàng tā le.	'She's so cute; I've already fallen in love with her.'
Xiāngzi tài xiǎo le, fàngbuxià dōngxi.	'This case is too small; I can't get the things in.'

d. *Zǒu* 'leave' appears as a complement meaning 'away'.

Tāmen yǐjīng bānzǒu le.	'They've already moved away from here.'
Shéi bǎ wǒ de yàoshi názǒu le?	'Who's gone off with my keys?'

Dōngtiān lái le, niǎo dōu fēizǒu le.	'Winter's here, and the birds have all flown.
Méi guānxi, niǎo shi sìhài zhī yī, zǒu jiu zǒu ba.	Never mind, birds are one of the four pests; if they've gone, they've gone.'

15.8.3 Specialized forms

a. A number of complements appear only in the potential form. *Qǐ* (*qǐlai de qǐ*) is one. As a complement, it shows a considerable shift in meaning from 'rise' to 'worthy of' or 'afford to'.

Duìbuqǐ.	'Sorry.' ('face-not-worthy')
Āiyā, xiànzài Běijīng de shēnghuó fèiyòng tài gāo le, wǒ kě zhùbuqǐ!	'Gosh, the cost of living in Beijing is too high; I can't afford to live here!'
Yànwō, yúchì zhèi lèi de dōngxi tài guì le; wǒ chībuqǐ.	'Things like bird's nest soup and shark fin are too expensive; I can't afford to eat them.'

b. It is also possible to choose to use the potential framework but not commit to a particular complement. In this case, a default complement, *liǎo* (the fully stressed version of the particle *le*) is available. Unlike most of the other verb complements, *liǎo* combines with almost any action verb but only in the potential (-*deliǎo* or -*buliǎo*). It usually suggests 'more than one can be expected to do'.

Dōngxi tài duō le, wǒ yí ge rén zěnme nádeliǎo ne?	'I have too many things; how can I carry them all by myself?'
Wǒ lái bāng nǐ ná ba.	'Let me help you.'
Chē tài duō le, wǒmen wǔ diǎn dàobuliǎo.	'There are too many cars; we won't be able to make it by 5:00.'
Dǎ ge diànhuà gàosu tāmen, hǎo bu hǎo?	'Phone them and let them know, okay?'
Zhème duō cài, wǒ yí ge rén zěnme chīdeliǎo ne?	'So many dishes; how can I eat them all by myself?'

Chàbuliǎo duōshao.   'There's hardly any difference;
                                                       they're more or less the same.'
                                                       ('lack-not-able much')

c. Verb complements, particularly the directional ones, often have extended
   meanings. For example, *qǐlái*, which as a directional complement means 'up
   here' (e.g., *zhàn qǐlai*), also functions on a much more abstract level—in the
   sense of 'when it comes to doing'.

Zhèi jiàn shì shuō qǐlai róngyì,   'This is easy to talk about but
   zuò qǐlai nán.   tough to do.'
Zhèi tiáo lù, kàn qǐlai hěn jìn,   'This route looks short, but when
   zǒu qǐlai hěn yuǎn.   you walk it, it's quite far.'
Shàoxīnghuà tīng qǐlai hěn   'Shaoxing dialect sounds like
   xiàng Shànghǎihuà.   Shanghainese.'

Exercise 6

Do [or write what you would say for] the following situations in Chinese.
If the comment is not about yourself, then you should address the appropriate person, as indicated.

1. Ask him to come down and take a look.
2. Ask him to bring the books in.
3. Ask them when they are moving in.
4. Ask her to bring the books up here.
5. Ask her to come out and take a look at the view.
6. Ask her to drive the car over and pick up the students.
7. Say that someone seems to have taken your bookbag by mistake.
8. Explain that you can't affort to eat seafood because it's so expensive.
9. Explain that your car won't seat seven; suggest taking two cars.
10. Explain that you're full and can't eat any more.
11. Explain that you can't remember his name.
12. Explain that you can't open the door because it's locked.

15.9 Stand a little closer

Not all verb combinations are of the same type. One fairly productive pattern combines an action verb with a comparative adjective: V (SV + *yìdiǎnr*).

Shuō kuài yìdiǎnr.	'Speak a bit faster.'
Zhàn jìn yìdiǎnr.	'Stand a little closer.'
Xiě dà yìdiǎnr.	'Write it a bit bigger.'
Zǒu màn yìdiǎnr.	'Walk a bit more slowly.'

USAGE

Qǐng bǎ chuānghu dǎkāi.	'Open the window, please.'
Chuānghu kāizhe ne.	'The window's open.'
Nà, bǎ tā kāi dà yìdiǎnr.	'Then open it a bit wider.'

Zǒu kuài yìdiǎnr, hǎo bu hǎo,
    huǒchē wǔ diǎn zhōng kāi.
	'Walk faster, okay, the train
	    leaves at 5:00.'

Fàngxīn ba, láidejí.	'Don't worry; we'll make it.'

Kāi màn yìdiǎnr, hǎo bu hǎo,
    ānquán dì-yī.
	'Drive more slowly, okay,
	    safety first.'

NOTES

a. This pattern also works for *dàshēng* 'in a loud voice': *Shuō dàshēng yìdiǎnr* 'Speak louder'.

b. The construction V (SV + *yìdiǎnr*) should be distinguished from the one presented in §14.7 that involved adding (or subtracting) items (*duō* + V + *yìdiǎnr* + N): *Qǐng duō fàng yìdiǎnr táng.*

   Kuài yìdiǎnr and *màn yìdiǎnr* may also stand alone at the beginning of an utterance, urging speed or advising care.

Kuài yìdiǎnr, xiàyǔ le.	'Hurry, it's raining.'
Màn yìdiǎnr, lù hěn huá.	'Slow down, the road's slippery.'

Exercise 7

Provide Chinese paraphrases for the following sentences.

1. Hurry up; it's almost time for class.
2. Stand a bit closer; otherwise, you won't be able to see.

3. I like it sweet; please add some sugar.

4. Sorry to trouble you, would you mind speaking a bit louder? I can't hear.
   (*máfan nǐ* 'trouble you to')

5. Write it bigger, please, so I can count (*shǔ*) the strokes (*bǐhuà*).

15.10 Waiting and rushing

This is a miscellaneous section that deals with two notions that are quite common in conversation: waiting and rushing. First, waiting, which involves the verb *děng*.

děngdeng ~ děngyiděng ~ děngyixiàr	'wait a sec; just a minute'
shāo<wēi> děngyixiàr	'wait for a bit'
děng yìhuǐr	'wait awhile'

Here are the follow-up responses, indicating the wait won't be long.

Mǎshàng jiu lái.	'I'll be right there.'
Shāo děngyixiàr, mǎshàng jiu huílai.	'Please wait, I'll be right back.'
Wǒ yìhuǐr jiu huílai.	'I'll be back shortly.'
Wǒ hěn kuài jiu huílai!	'I'll be back right away!'
Mǎshàng jiu hǎo.	'I'll be done in a jiffy.'

NOTES

a. *Yìhuǐr* is generally the more colloquial pronunciation. *Yíhuìr*, with rising then falling tones, is also heard. Dictionaries, which often favor more formal speech, tend to give the *yíhuìr* pronunciation.

b. *Shāo<wēi>* 'slightly; for a bit': Hotel telephone operators in China tend to say *qǐng shāo děng* when they transfer your call.

c. *Mǎshàng* 'immediately; at once' ('on a horse'): synonymous with *lìkè*

USAGE

Shāo děngyixiàr, wǒ mǎshàng jiu huílai.	'Hold on, I'll be right back.'

Qǐng děngyixiàr, wǒ qù lóushang wènwen tā. Nǐ zuò yìhuǐr ba.	'Just a minute, I'll go upstairs and ask her. Make yourself comfortable.'
Qǐng děngdeng, wǒ qù bàngōngshì zhǎo tā.	'Just a minute, I'll go see if he's in the office.'
Qǐng děng yìhuǐr, wǒ de yàoshi wàng zai bàngōngshì le.	'Hang on a minute; I left my keys in the office.'
Qǐng děngyixiàr, wǒ qù zhǎo tā. Nǐ xiān hē diǎnr chá ba.	'Hold on a minute; I'll go find him. Have some tea first.'
Qǐng děngdeng, tā zài dǎ diànhuà ne.	'Hold on for a minute please; he's on the phone.'
Qǐng shāo děng, wǒ děi qù mǎi yóupiào, mǎshàng jiu huílai. Nín zuòyixiàr ba.	'Hold on for a bit please; I have to go and buy some stamps. I'll be right back. Make yourself at home.'

NOTE

Nín zuòyixiàr ba is literally 'why don't you sit for a bit', but it is often used when someone has to step out for a bit, hence the freer translation of 'make yourself at home'.

15.11 Smoking

Chōuyān 'smoking' ('pull-smoke'), or more formally as *xīyān* ('suck-smoke'), plays a more important role in social etiquette than it now does in the West. Offering *xiāngyān* 'cigarettes' ('fragrant-smoke'), for example, is a gesture of friendship and bonding among males. *Yāncǎo* 'tobacco' ('smoke-grass') is grown in Yunnan Province, and *guǎnggào* 'advertisements' ('broad-announcements') for Yunnan cigarette companies (*yāncǎo gōngsī*) are common. Cigarettes are commonly bought by the pack (*yì bāo*) or even individually (*yì gēn <yān>*) rather than by the carton (*yì tiáo <xiāngyān>*). It is said that roughly two-thirds of males smoke in China, but far fewer females do. The government (*zhèngfǔ*) is concerned about the health problems associated with smoking (*hěn guānxīn zhèi ge wèntí*), and there are now restrictions on smoking in public places (*gōnggòng chǎngsuǒ*). Still, it's hard to avoid breathing in *èrshǒuyān* 'second-hand smoke' ('second-hand-smoke').

Jiǎ: *Dàduōshù Zhōngguó nánren píngcháng dōu chōuyān. Tāmen zhīdao chōuyān duì shēntǐ bù hǎo, kěshì yīnwèi péngyou dōu chōu, suǒ.yǐ tāmen juéde bù chōu bù xíng; péngyou gěi nǐ yān, nǐ zěnme néng bù chōu? Fǎnzhèng, dàjiā dōu xíguàn chōuyān, suǒ.yǐ hěn shǎo yǒu rén fǎnduì. Yǒu péngyou gàosu wǒ, yǒude nánde yì tiān chōu liǎng bāo, nà jiùshi yí ge xīngqī shísì bāo, yí ge yuè liùshí bāo, yì nián qībǎi duō bāo! Xiànzài yì bāo hǎo yān zuì piányi chàbuduō bā kuài qián (Rénmínbì, nà jiùshi yí kuài duō Měijīn), suǒ.yǐ yì nián làngfèi zhème duō qián, tài kěxī le! Zhōngguó zuì yǒumíng de yāncǎo gōngsī zài Yúnnánshěng, zuì yǒumíng de páizi yěxǔ shi Yúnyān, Hóngtǎshān, hé Āshīmǎ. Jiē shang, qìchē shang, nǐ hái huì kànjiàn xiāngyān de guǎnggào!*

Yǒurén chōu Zhōngguó yān, yě yǒurén chōu wàiguó yān, xiàng Wànbǎolù, Luòtuo. Wàiguóyān dōu bǐjiào guì, yìbān de yì bāo yě děi shíjǐ kuài. Suīrán hěn guì, kěshì chōu wàiguó yān de yě bù shǎo. Tīngshuō shi yīnwèi wàiguó yān jìnr bǐjiào dà. Xiànzài hěn duō Zhōngguórén yě zhīdao chōu tài duō yān bù hǎo, kěshì chōuyān de rén háishi hěn duō. Zuìjìn Zhōngguó zhèngfǔ hěn guānxīn zhèi ge wèntí, fābùle yí ge jìnyānlìng. Jìnyānlìng de yìsi shi jìnzhǐ zài gōnggòng chǎngsuǒ chōuyān. Suǒ.yǐ xiànzài zài huǒchēzhàn, fànguǎnr, kāfēitīng, diànyǐngyuàn zhèi lèi de dìfang, zhǐ néng zài zhìdìng de xīyānqū chōuyān, biéde dìfang bù néng chōu. Zhèyàng, bù chōuyān de bú huì xī nàme duō èrshǒuyān. Nà, nǐ kě bu kě.yǐ jièshao yíxiàr Běiměi, Ōuzhōu de qíngkuàng ne?

Yǐ: *Wǒ xiān shuōyixiàr Měiguó de qíngxing. Yǐqián Měiguórén chōuyān de bìng bù shǎo. Wǔshí niándài, liùshí niándài de diànyǐng yǎnyuán bù lǎoshi chōuyān ma? Kěshì zuìjìn èrshí duō nián lái, chōuyān de rén hǎoxiàng yuè lái yuè shǎo. Àobāmǎ zuìjìn bú shì yě jièyān le ma? Wèishénme ne? Nà shi yīnwèi dàjiā dōu zhīdao chōuyān duì shēntǐ bù hǎo, chōuyān de rén bǐjiào róngyì dé áizhèng. Zài shuō, biérén kàn nǐ chōuyān yě huì mà nǐ, tāmen bèipò xī èrshǒuyān, suǒ.yǐ tāmen hěn bù gāoxìng. Méi fǎzi. Suǒ.yǐ xiànzài Měiguó hěn duō dìfang, xiàng jīchǎng, huǒchēzhàn, fànguǎnr, fàndiàn děng gōnggòng chǎngsuǒ dōu bú ràng nǐ chōuyān, měi ge dìfang dōu tiē gàoshì shuō: "Bù zhǔn xīyān." (Xīyān jiùshi chōuyān de yìsi, xīyān nèi ge cí kěnéng bǐjiào zhèngshi, chōuyān bǐjiào kǒuyǔ.)*

Zài Měiguó chōuyān de bǐjiào shǎo yě shi yīnwèi yān hěn guì! Yì bāo sì-wǔ kuài qián (Měijīn, nà jiùshi sān-sìshí duō kuài Rénmínbì.) Ōuzhōu ne, zài Ōuzhōu yān gèng guì, chōuyān de méiyǒu yǐqián de nàme duō, kěshì kěnéng háishi bǐ Měiguó de duō yìdiǎnr. Wǒ ma, wǒ zìjǐ bù chōuyān, érqiě cónglái méi chōuguo, dànshi biérén yào chōu, nà, wǒ jiù bú huì guǎn tāmen. Wǒ de kànfǎ shì 'biéguǎn-xiánshì', xiǎng chōu jiu chōu ba!

VOCABULARY

dàduōshù	'majority' ('big-many-number')
fǎnzhèng	'in any case, anyhow' ('turned over-upright')
xíguàn	'habit; custom': distinguish from *xǐhuan* 'like' and *xīwàng* 'hope'
fǎnduì	'oppose; object' ('overturn-against')
làngfèi	'waste' [time, money, etc.]
kěxī	'pitiable; unfortunate': cf. *Tài kěxī le* 'That's too bad.'
páizi	'brand name'
jiē shang	'on the street(s)'
Wànbǎolù	'Marlboro' [brand]
Luòtuo	'Camel' [brand]
shíjǐ kuài	'ten yuan and then some'
jìnr [jyer]	'strength; vigor' [coll]: cf. *yǒu lìqi* ('have strength')
fābù	'issue; announce' ('emit-disseminate'): *fābù xīnwéngǎo* 'issue a news bulletin'; *fābù jìnlìng* 'issue a ban on'
jìnyānlìng	'smoking ban' ('ban-smoke-order')
jìnzhǐ	'prohibit, forbit' ('ban-make')
chǎngsuǒ	'venue, place' ('open area-place')
zhèi lèi	'this type of; this kind of' ('this category')
zhìdìng	'formulate; draft' ('make-fix')
xīyānqū	'place for smoking': *Qū* is a bound word meaning 'region'; cf. *jiāoqū* 'suburbs,' *chéngqū* 'city proper,' *yóujīqū* 'guerrilla area,' *shíqū* 'time zone'
bìng	'really not': *bìng bù piányi* 'not at all cheap'

yǎnyuán	'actor' ('perform-person')
zuìjìn èrshí duō nián lái	'over the past twenty plus years'
jièyān	'give up smoking' ('renounce-smoking'): *Nǐ yuè zǎo jièyān yuè hǎo.*
dé áizhèng	'get cancer' ('obtain cancer-illness')
mà	'get mad at; criticize; show displeasure'
bèipò	'be compelled; be forced to': *bèipò tóuxiáng* 'forced to capitulate,' *bèipò gǎibiàn lìchǎng* 'forced to change a position [about something]'
tiē gàoshì	'post a sign; stick on a notice or poster' ('stick notice')
zhǔn	'permit': usually negated; common on signs, such as *bù zhǔn* . . . 'it's forbidden to . . .'
zhèngshì	'formal'
kǒuyǔ	'spoken language': *hěn kǒuyǔ* 'be colloquial'
wǒ ma	'as for me . . .': *ma* is a particle that separates an initial topic from the ensuing comment, rather like English 'as for'; cf. *ne*, which is used for follow up questions, such as *Nǐ ne?*
érqiě	'moreover; in addition'
guǎn	'take care of; deal with; run [an enterprise]'
biéguǎn-xiánshì	'mind one's own business' ('don't-concern leisure-affairs')

NOTES

a. There is a tremendous variety of cigarettes for sale in China, from the very ordinary (cheap local or fake imported) to the very expensive (fine local or genuine imported).

b. *Yǒu jìnr*; Example sentences:

Nèi zhǒng yān hěn yǒu jìnr!	'That kind of tobacco is very strong!'
Zhōngguó de báijiǔ hěn yǒu jìnr.	'Chinese clear liquor is really strong.'
Wǒ jīntiān bù shūfu, méi jìnr.	'I don't feel well today; I have no strength.'

Exercise 8

Explain the following: American beer is more expensive than Chinese beer, but Chinese people still buy it. Budweiser, called *Bǎiwēi* in China, is getting more and more popular (*shòu huānyíng* 'receive welcome'). You don't think it has as much flavor as Chinese brands such as *Qīngdǎo, Shànghǎi*, or *Yànjīng*, so you always tell your Chinese friends they should drink Chinese brands, not imports! The same is true with cigarettes. Chinese pay attention to brands (*zhòngshì* 'heavy-view'), and American brands are well known, so many Chinese buy American brands. They say that, in any case, American cigarettes are stronger than Chinese cigarettes and taste better. I can't believe this is really the case!

Yāntānr 'cigarette stand' (*Běijīng*)

A college-age friend (*Jiǎ*) offers you (*Yǐ*) a cigarette. Most males in China smoke, so offering someone a cigarette is considered a friendly gesture, and it is sometimes difficult to refuse.

Jiǎ:	*Lái (yì) gēn yān ba.*	'Have a cigarette.'
Yǐ:	*Xièxie, wǒ bù chōuyān.*	'No thanks, I don't smoke.'
Jiǎ:	*Zhēnde bù chōu a?*	'You really don't smoke?'
Yǐ:	*Zhēnde!*	'Really!'
Jiǎ:	*Duì a, chōuyān bù hǎo, duì shēntǐ bù hǎo.*	'Right, smoking's not good; it's not good for your body.'
Yǐ:	*Zhōngguórén dōu chōuyān ma?*	'Do all Chinese smoke?'
Jiǎ:	*Chàbuduō le, nánde dōu chōu, nǚde bǐjiào shǎo. Wǒ chōu, xíng ma?*	'More or less. Men all smoke; women less so. Do you mind if I smoke?'
Yǐ:	*Xíng, xíng, méi guānxi.*	'Fine, fine, no problem.'
Jiǎ:	*Hǎo, suīrán duì shēntǐ bù hǎo, kěshì wǒ háishi děi chōu.*	'Good, although it's not good for me, I still have to smoke.'
Yǐ:	*Wèishénme?*	'How come?'
Jiǎ:	*Péngyou gěi nǐ yān, zěnme néng bù chōu?*	'If friends give you cigarettes, how can you not smoke?'

VOCABULARY

lái	'take' ('cause to come'): cf. *lái yì bēi kāfēi*
zhēnde	'really': a variant of *zhēn*

NOTE

Cigarettes can be counted with the measure word *kē*, which is also used for grainlike things (and bullets); with *zhī*, which is used for stubby things; and with *gēn*, which is used for branchlike things.

15.12 Rhymes and rhythms

Because the form of various characters is affected by changes in pronunciation far less than happens in alphabetic orthographies, modern readers of Chinese have relatively easy access to past eras of literature. They can read selections with modern pronunciation (whether it is in Mandarin, Cantonese, or some other regional language) and, if they haven't studied the classical language formally, project meaning from their knowledge of the modern language. Classical poetry, since it is often cast in short, even stanzas with very little grammatical and semantic complexity, is particularly popular and still committed to memory by young and old alike. If it were not for the characters, which are often rare or archaic, learners too could gain some appreciation of the classic poems. In this unit and some subsequent units, a poem is given in pinyin with a word-for-word gloss and minimal annotation. Your Chinese friends will probably regard poems written only in pinyin as aesthetically deprived, which is not an unfair criticism. Nevertheless, as long as you can recite the poems, you will still get the kudos.

The first poem in this unit is by *Cáo Zhí* (192–232), the son of the famous military leader *Cáo Cāo. Cáo Zhí* was a brilliant poet, but he led a dissolute life and fell out with his more wily elder half-brother, *Cáo Pī*, who eventually became emperor of *Wèi*. The poem is cited in the 79th chapter of the *Romance of the Three Kingdoms* (*Sānguó Yǎnyì*). In that version of the tale, *Cáo Pī* condemns his half-brother to death but offers him a reprieve if *Cáo Zhí* can compose a poem on an assigned subject after taking only seven steps. He succeeds brilliantly but is asked to top it off by composing yet another on the spot. The result is the following poem, which has inherited the 'seven pace' title. The last two lines, of course, extend the concrete image of beans cooking to the torment that one brother is inflicting on the other. Of the words in the poem, you are probably familiar with the following: *dòu* 'bean'; *zài* 'be at'; *zhōng* 'middle'; *běn* 'root; original'; *shì* 'be'; *tóng* 'same'; *shēng* 'be born'; and *tài* 'too'. *Hé* (in the last line) is a classical question word, whose meaning overlaps with modern *shénme, wèishénme*, or *zěnme*.

Qī Bù Shī 'A Poem within Seven Steps'

Zhǔ dòu rán dòu qí,	('cook beans char bean stalk')
dòu zài fǔ zhōng qì.	('beans in kettle middle wail')
Běn shì tóng gēn shēng,	('once be same stalk born')
xiāng jiān hé tài jí?	('mutual simmer why too intense')

The second selection shifts away from the classical to a traditional, colloquial rhyme about the lunar new year.

Xīnnián láidào 'The New Year's Arrived'

Xīnnián láidào,	('new-year come-arrive')
rénrén huānxiào,	('people happy-laugh')
gūniang yào huār,	('young-girls want flowers')
xiǎozi yào pào,	('young-boys want firecrackers')
lǎo tàitai yào kuài dà niángāo,	('old ladies want piece big sticky-cake')
lǎotóur yào dǐng xīn zhānmào!	('old men want M new felt hat')

NOTES

a. *Niángāo* is literally 'sticky cake' and named for the glutinous rice flour used to make it. *Nián* 'sticky' is homophonous with *nián* 'year'—drawing the connection to the new year, when the cakes are eaten.

b. Fireworks in general are usually called *yànhuǒ* or *huāhuǒ* ('flower-fire'). Firecrackers, which come in braided strings like whips or lashes and explode like burning bamboo, are *biānpào* ('lash-cannon') or *bàozhú* ('explode-bamboo'). The verb associated with 'setting off' fireworks is *fàng* ('put').

Summary

Qǐngjiào	*Nǐ kě.yǐ qǐngjiào tā.*
Guānyú	*guānyú Měiguó hé Ōuzhōu de shìqing*
Indefinites	*Xiǎng chī shénme jiu chī shénme.*
Duì … yǒu yánjiū	*Tā duì Zhōngguó lìshǐ hěn yǒu yánjiū.*
Xiān … ránhòu	*Wǒmen xiān qù Běijīng, ránhòu qù Shànghǎi.*
Zài 'and then'	*Xiān shàngchē zài mǎi piào.*
Family	*Jiālǐ yǒu xiē shénme rén? / Jiālǐ yǒu jǐ kǒu rén?*
Láizhe	*Tā jiào shénme míngzi láizhe?*
Sequence	*Nǐ lǎo jǐ? / Wǒ <páiháng> lǎo'èr.*
Professions	*Wǒ māma dāng yīshēng.*
V-zhe	*Zhànzhe shūfu. / Mén kāizhe ne.*
	Zài shāfā shang zuòzhe ne.
	Zhuōzi shang fàngzhe jǐ zhāng míngpiàn.
	Tā názhe huàr huíjiā le.

Bǎ	*Wǒ yǐjīng bǎ tā dǎkāi le.*
Objects	*Tā ná qǐ bǐ lái le.*
V-combos	*jìbuzhù; kāibukāi; bānzǒu; zuòxia; mǎibuqǐ; nábuliǎo*
V *qǐlai*	*Shuō qǐlai róngyì, zuò qǐlai nán.*
Do more slowly	*Qǐng shuō màn yìdiǎnr.*
Waiting	*Shāo děngyixiàr, mǎshàng jiu huílai.*
	Nǐ zuò yìhuǐr (~ yíhuìr) ba.
Cigarettes	*Péngyou gěi nǐ yān, zěnme néng bù chōu?*

Xīnliánxīn: Gòngchǎndǎng jìniànbēi 'Heart linked to heart:
CCP memorial' (*Shànghǎi*)

Unit 16

Jǐ suǒ bú yù, wù shī yú rén.
('Self which not want, don't do to others.')
—Chinese version of the Golden Rule

This unit begins with the conversation between *Méi Tàidé* and *Ōuyáng xiānsheng* on the bus to *Miányáng* (from Unit 4), retold as a narrative. There is then an introduction to the rich topic of adverbials (the equivalent of English words such as 'frantically' and 'patiently'). A long interview with a teacher in the following section offers a chance to review typical questions and learn some minor constructions. The topic of indefinite pronouns (words such as 'anywhere' and 'everywhere'), which has been touched upon in earlier units, is taken up again in earnest. Then, we return to a conversational topic: talking about religions. Another set of verb combos is introduced—the fourth—and they are followed by a consideration of *bèi* (and similar words) and the relevance of passive voice in Chinese. The unit winds down with the first part of a very colloquial discussion about cars, driving, and getting around in China, and it ends with a section on banquets and toasts—along with the usual selection of rhymes and rhythms.

A note to the epigraph is located at the end of the unit.

Contents

16.1 *Méi Tàidé:* The story

Méi Tàidé is the student you encountered in Unit 4 of the elementary volume. He was originally from Holland (*shi Hélánrén*), attended the University of Michigan (*Měiguó Mìxīgēn Dàxué*), and took a year off to study Chinese economics (*Zhōngguó jīngjì*) in China. At the time of this retelling, he's a passenger (*chéngkè*) on a long-distance bus (*chángtú qìchē*) going to *Miányáng* in central Sichuan. He's hoping to improve his Chinese conversational skills (*tígāo tā de Zhōngwén tīng-shuō nénglì*), and people on the bus are chatting up a storm (*dōu liáo+de hěn rènao*). Eventually, another passenger (*Ōuyáng xiānsheng*) notices him reading a Chinese newspaper (*kàndào Méi Tàidé zài kàn Zhōngwén bàozhǐ*) and starts to chat with him (*liáole qǐlai*). Ouyang turns out to be from Changchun in northeastern China (*tā shi Dōngběi Chángchūnrén*), and they discover they have lots of interests and hobbies in common (*fāxiàn bǐcǐ yǒu hěn duō gòngtóng de xìngqù, àihào*).

> *Èrlínglíngwǔ nián wǔyuè de yì tiān, zài Chéngdū kāiwǎng Miányáng de chángtú qìchē shang zuòzhe hěn duō rén, yǒude zài kànbào, yǒude zài kàn xiǎoshuōr, yǒude zài liáotiānr, yǒude zài dǎpái, yǒude zài xià xiàngqí, yǒude zài chī dōngxi, hái yǒude rén zài shuìjiào.*

Zài chéngkè zhōng, yǒu yí ge huáng tóufa、lán yǎnjing、dà bízi de wàiguórén. Tā jiào Méi Tàidé, shi Hélánrén, jǐ nián qián cóng Hélán dào Měiguó Mìxīgēn Dàxué qù xuéxí. Tā èrniánjí de shíhou juédìng xuéxí Zhōngguó jīngjì, xiànzài yǐjīng shi sìniánjí de xuésheng le. Tā juéde yánjiū Zhōngguó jīngjì hěn yǒu yìsi, rúguǒ dǒng Zhōngwén jiu gèng hǎo le. Suǒ.yǐ tā liǎng nián yǐqián kāishǐ xuéxí Zhōngwén. Suīrán tā zài Měiguó yǐjīng xuéle liǎng nián de Zhōngwén le, kěshì tā juéde zhǐyǒu qù Zhōngguó cái nénggòu gèng hǎo de tígāo tā de Zhōngwén tīng-shuō nénglì, cái néng gèng hǎo de liǎojiě Zhōngguó wǔ qiān duō nián de wénhuà hé lìshǐ, cái néng gèng hǎo de rènshi Zhōngguó shèhuì, suǒ.yǐ shàng ge xuéqī tā cóng Mìxīgēn Dàxué láidào wèiyú Chéngdū de Sìchuān Dàxué xuéxí Zhōngwén hé Zhōngguó wénhuà. Tā zhèi cì lìyòng shǔjià de jīhuì yí ge rén qù Miányáng lǚxíng.

Tā zài chē shang yě xiǎng gēn biérén liáotiān, liànxí Zhōngwén, kěshì tā kàndào liáotiānr de rén dōu liáo+de hěn rènao, tā yě bù zhīdào yào gēn tāmen shuō shénme, suǒ.yǐ tā zhǐ hǎo yìbiānr tīng biérén shuōhuà, yìbiānr ná chūlai dāngtiān de Zhōngwén bàozhǐ kàn.

Zhè shíhou, yí wèi zuò zai lí Méi Tàidé bù yuǎn de rén kàndào Méi Tàidé zài kàn Zhōngwén bàozhǐ, juéde hěn hǎowánr, yīnwèi yǒude Zhōngguórén xiǎng, Zhōngwén duìyú wàiguórén lái shuō fēicháng nán. Wàiguórén néng shuō yìdiǎnr Zhōngwén yǐjīng hěn búcuò le, néng kàndedǒng Zhōngwén bàozhǐ de wàiguórén jiu gèng liǎobuqǐ le. Tā juédìng yào gēn zhèi ge lǎowài liáoliao. Tā zhàn qǐlai, zǒu guòqu gēn Méi Tàidé zuòle zìwǒ jièshào, ránhòu yòu gěi Méi Tàidé jièshàole tā tàitai. Méi Tàidé yě zuòle zìwǒ jièshào. liǎngge rén jiù zhèyàng liáole qǐlai. Liáotiānr zhōng, Méi Tàidé zhīdaole zhèi wèi Zhōngguórén xìng Ōuyáng, shi ge gōngsī de jīnglǐ. Tā xiànzài hé tàitai yìqǐ qù Déyáng kàn tā de jiějie. Déyáng zài Chéngdū hé Miányáng zhījiān.

Ōuyáng xiānsheng yě hěn gāoxìng rènshi zhèi wèi huì jiǎng Zhōngwén, jiào Tàidé de lǎowài. Liǎngge rén liáo+de hěn kāixīn, cóng Zhōngguó lìshǐ, liáo dào Zhōngguó gǎigé kāifàng; cóng Zhōngguó gǎigé kāifàng liáo dào Zhōngguó jīngjì; cóng Zhōngguó jīngjì liáo dào Zhōngguó wénhuà. Zuì ràng Ōuyáng xiānsheng gāoxìng de shi tāmen liǎng ge dōu xǐhuan chī Sìchuān cài. Tàidé gàosu Ōuyáng, tā lái Zhōngguó yǐhòu tiāntiān dōu chī Zhōngguó fàn, suǒ.yǐ tā xiànzài yǐjīng chīguànle, tèbié shi Sìchuān cài, yòu má yòu là, chīle yǐhòu ràng

rén yǒu yì zhǒng shuō bu chūlai de gǎnjué. Ōuyáng gàosu Méi Tàidé, tā shi
Dōngběi Chángchūnrén, tā de jiāxiāng yě yǒu hěn duō hǎochī de dōngxi, kěshì
tā zuì xǐhuan de háishi Sìchuān cài.

Liǎng ge rén liáozhe liáozhe, Déyáng jiu dào le. Xiàchē yǐqián, Ōuyáng
xiānsheng gàosu Méi Tàidé, dàgài xiàwǔ yì diǎn zuǒyòu dào Miányáng, ràng
tā tíqián zuòhǎo xiàchē de zhǔnbèi. Ōuyáng xiānsheng hé tā tàitai yào xiàchē
le, Ōuyáng xiānsheng hé Méi Tàidé dōu yǒu diǎnr nánguò, yīnwèi tāmen
fāxiàn bǐcǐ yǒu hěnduō gòngtóng de xìngqu, àihào. Yòng Zhōngguóhuà shuō
zhè shi yǒu yuánfèn.

Ōuyáng xiānsheng gěile Méi Tàidé yì zhāng míngpiàn, hái shuō, rènshi tā
zhèi ge wàiguó péngyou hěn gāoxìng, xīwàng néng bǎochí liánxì. Yīnwèi Méi
Tàidé méiyǒu míngpiàn le, tā zhǐhǎo bǎ zìjǐ de diànhuà hàomǎ hé yīmèi'ér
dìzhǐ xiě zai Ōuyáng xiānsheng de běnzi shang. Dào Déyáng le, Méi Tàidé hěn
rèxīn de yào bāng Ōuyáng xiānsheng ná xíngli, sòng Ōuyáng xiānsheng hé tā
tàitai xiàchē, kěshì Ōuyáng xiānsheng shuō tāmen de xíngli bù duō, zhǐ yǒu yí
jiàn, jiù bù máfan le. Ōuyáng xiānsheng gēn Méi Tàidé shuō yàoshi tā yǒu
shíjiān de huà, huānyíng tā dào Chángchūn qù wánr liǎng tiān. Jiù zhèyàngr,
tāmen shuōle zàijiàn, jiù fēnshǒu le.

VOCABULARY

kāiwǎng	'head to; be bound for': often used in reference to buses, planes, and so on
chángtú	'long distance' ('long-route'): often used as a modifier, as in chángtú diànhuà
xiǎoshuō<r>	'novel' ('lesser-discourse')
dǎpái	'play cards, dominoes, mahjong, and so on' ('hit-tiles')
xià xiàngqí	'play Chinese chess' ('place ivory-chess')
chéngkè	'passenger' ('ride-guest'): zài chéngkè zhōng 'among the passengers'
juédìng	'decide' ('decide-fix')

nénggòu	*néng*
tígāo … nénglì	'to improve; raise' ('lift-high') … 'abilities' ('capable-strength')
shèhuì	'society'
wèiyú	'be located or situated at; in' ('place-at'): *wèiyú Zhōngguó de xīběibù* 'located in northwestern China'
lìyòng	'utilize; make use of' ('benefit-use'): *lìyòng tàiyángnéng* 'make use of solar energy'
shǔjià	'summer vacation' ('heat-vacation')
jīhuì	'opportunity': *lìyòng shǔjià de jīhuì* 'take advantage of the summer break to …'; cf. *chèn … jīhuì* 'take the opportunity to …'
yìbiānr … yìbiānr	'on one hand … on the other hand; and; while' ('one-side')
ná chūlai	'take out'
dāngtiān	'that day; the same day'
duì<yú> … lái shuō	'in regard to …; for …' ('face-at … come say'): *duì wǒ lái shuō* 'to me; as far as I'm concerned; from my point of view'
liǎobuqǐ	'remarkable; amazing' ('complete-not-worthy')
zìwǒ	'self; oneself' ('self-me'): *zuò zìwǒ jièshào* 'to introduce oneself'
zhījiān	'among; between': composed of the formal suffix/pronoun *zhī* (as in *sì fēn zhī yī* 'one-fourth') and the bound form *jiān* 'space' (as in *fángjiān* 'room' or *shíjiān* 'time'); cf. *zhīhòu* 'afterward; after'
kāixīn	'be happy; rejoice; make fun of' ('open-heart')
gǎigé kāifàng	'reform' and 'open up; bloom; openness': See note *b* below.
ràng	'[here] to make [someone do something]': See note *d* below.

gǎnjué	'feelings': cf. *gǎn xìngqu*; *gǎnxiè*
jiāxiāng	'native place'
tíqián	'to bring forward; in advance': *bǎ shìqing tíqián zuòhǎo* 'finish everything in plenty of time'; *tíqián ānpáihǎo le* 'prepared in advance'
zhǔnbèi	'preparations; to prepare'
nánguò	'sad' ('hard to pass through')
fāxiàn	'discover' ('to issue forth-appear')
bǐcǐ	'each other; one another; me too' ('that-this'): *bǐcǐ fēnshǒu* 'part from one another'; *Nín xīnkǔ la / Bǐcǐ, bǐcǐ!* 'It wasn't easy for you' ('you bitter le-a') / Nor for you!'
gòngtóng	'shared; common' ('together-same')
àihào	'interests; hobbies'
yuánfèn	'destiny; fate; affinity; the influence that brings people together'
bǎochí liánxì	'keep in touch' ('preserve-links')
rèxīn	'be enthusiastic, warm; enthusiasm' ('hot-heart')
fēnshǒu	'part company; go separate ways; say goodbye' ('part-hands')

NOTES

a. *Liáole qǐlai*: Notice how, in this case of a verb (*liáo*) plus directional complement (*qǐlai*), the postverbal *le* (with the perfective meaning of 'completed') intrudes in the verbal string rather than appearing at the end.

b. *Gǎigé kāifàng* is usually translated into English as 'reform and opening up.' The term was applied to an economic and political campaign initiated in 1978 by Deng Xiaoping and the Communist Party of China. *Gǎigé kāifàng* recalls the Soviet concepts of glasnost and perestroika, which in this context mean 'opening' and 'rebuilding'—policies associated with Mikhail Gorbachev's less successful (and differently implemented) reforms.

c. *Liáozhe liáozhe* 'continued to chat [in this way until …]': cf. *zǒuzhe zǒuzhe* 'they walked on [like this until …]. This can be treated as one of a number of common patterns in which *zhe* appears, and, like the others, this one also serves to set the scene as part of the buildup to an event—in this case, *Déyáng jiu dào le*.

d. *Ràng* 'make; cause [someone] to be': This important word has functions that range from the fully verbal ('to yield') to the prepositional ('by'). Here, though, it functions as a causative verb with the meanings given.

e. *Bǎochí liánxì* 'stay in touch' is one of a number of set phrases that can be used in taking one's leave; another is *duōduō bǎozhòng* 'take care' ('by + much protect-heavy').

Exercise 1

Provide accurate but idiomatic translations of the following excerpts (some of which are full sentences, some of which are not).

1. *Kěshì tā juéde zhǐyǒu qù Zhōngguó cái nénggòu gèng hǎo de tígāo tā de Zhōngwén tīng-shuō nénglì, cái néng gèng hǎo de liǎojiě Zhōngguó wǔ qiān duō nián de wénhuà hé lìshǐ.*

2. *Tā zài chē shang yě xiǎng gēn biérén liáotiān, liànxí Zhōngwén, kěshì tā kàndào liáotiānr de rén dōu liáo+de hěn rènao, tā yě bù zhīdào yào gēn tāmen shuō shénme, suǒ.yǐ tā zhǐhǎo yìbiānr tīng biérén shuōhuà, yìbiānr ná chūlai dāngtiān de Zhōngwén bàozhǐ kàn.*

3. *Liǎngge rén jiù zhèyàng liáole qǐlai.*

4. ... *yòu má yòu là, chīle yǐhòu ràng rén yǒu yì zhǒng shuō bu chūlai de gǎnjué ...*

In groups of two or three, prepare answers to the following questions.

5. *Méi Tàidé hé Ōuyáng xiānsheng shi zěnme rènshi de?*

6. *Qǐng shuō yìdiǎnr guānyú Méi Tàidé de bèijǐng.* ('background')

7. *Shuō yìdiǎnr guānyú Ōuyáng xiānsheng de qíngxing.*

8. *Méi Tàidé Hànyǔ shuō+de zěnmeyàng? Xuéle duōcháng shíjiān le?*

9. *Méi Tàidé hé Ōuyáng xiānsheng liáole xiē shénme?*

10. *Ōuyáng xiānsheng wèishénme juéde Méi Tàidé hěn liǎobuqǐ?*

16.2 Adverbials

In *Méi Tàidé*'s narrative, there were two occurrences of the adverbial phrase *gèng hǎo de*, each of which was signaled by a final *de*. But which *de* is that? The fact that it is not written +*de* rules out, in this book at least, the *de* that introduces comments on action (*shuō+de hěn hǎo*). It is not the *de* of possession (*wǒ de*), the final *de* of the *shì ... de* construction (*shì zìjǐ zuò de*), the *de* of potential verb combos (*kàndedǒng*), or the emphatic *de* seen in expressions such as *tǐng hǎo de*. It is, in fact, a *de* you have not encountered in earlier units. It marks manner adverbials, which generally answer how something is done. In English, manner adverbials may be adverbs ending in *–ly* (*fluently, gradually, awkwardly*); they may be phrases introduced by prepositions such as *with* or *in* (*with effort, in a panic*); or they may be terms such as *well, right away,* or *fast.*

For the sake of providing more interesting examples, you will find that this section introduces more new vocabulary in the examples than is normal for sections that focus on grammar. However, the emphasis is on recognition rather than production. If you can recognize adverbial constructions and retain a few prototypical examples, then that will be a good first step.

In sentence structure, adverbs are positioned directly before verbs (or other adverbs). You have seen common adverbs since the very first units of the elementary level. Many are only a single syllable: *dōu, yě, hái*. Others are disyllabic: *mǎshàng, zǎojiù* ('long ago'), *yìzhí* ('all along; straight'). Here are some mostly familiar examples.

Wǒ xiān zǒu.	'I'll go first.'
Yòu lái le!	'Here she is again!'
Zhēn tǎoyàn!	'How annoying!'
Gāng chīwán le.	'We just finished eating.'
Wǒ dào bù juéde rè!	'I, on the contrary, do not feel hot!'
Míngtiān zài shuō ba.	'Let's talk tomorrow then.'
Wǒ fēicháng mǎnyì.	'I'm quite satisfied.'
Mǎshàng jiu lái.	'I'll be right back.'
Xiāngdāng fùzá.	'It's rather complicated.'
Wǒmen gǎnkuài zǒu ba.	'We'd better be off right away.'

VOCABULARY

tăoyàn	'nasty; disgusting; be fed up with; disgusted with': *zuì tăoyàn de míngxīngmen* 'the most annoying movie stars'; *tăoyàn míngxīngmen* 'be fed up with movie stars'
dào	'actually; on the contrary': The English equivalent is often contrastive stress: *Wŏ dào bù juéde rè!* 'It doesn't feel hot to *me*.'
mănyì	'feel satisfied; pleased' ('fulfill-desire')
măshàng	'right away; at once' ('horse-on')
xiāngdāng	'rather; quite; fairly'
fùzá	'be complicated'
gănkuài	'quickly; hastily' ('make a dash for-fast')
fēng	'be crazy; nuts'

16.2.1 Reduplication and adverbs

One of the most common sources of adverbials is adjectival verbs (SVs) that have undergone various kinds of modification or marking before occupying the adverbial slot. Single-syllable adjectives, with some exceptions (such as those mentioned below), can be reduplicated to form adverbs.

Hăohăo xuéxí, tiāntiān xiàng shàng.	'Study properly and advance daily.'
Mànmàn zŏu.	'Take it easy.'
Qĭng duōduō zhĭjiào.	'Comments welcome.' ('please more advise') [a polite formula, used when asking for comments on your work]
Shèhuì yĭjīng dàdà de găibiàn le.	'Society has undergone major changes.'

For many northern Mandarin speakers, this reduplicated pattern shows an interesting phonetic modification—the second iteration of the adjective is spoken with the *r* suffix, and the tone, if not already so, shifts to level: *hăo* →

hǎohāor; màn → mànmānr; duō → duōduōr. Thus, the rhyme with a northern provenance cited in Chao's grammar is pronounced as follows.

Zǎozāor shuì, wǎnwānr qǐ, yòu	'Early to bed, late to rise, saves you
shěng dēngyóu, yòu shěng mǐ.	lamp oil, saves you rice.'

The shift to level tone may appear even without the *r* suffix, so the following options are all possible.

Wǒ děi hǎohǎo xièxie tā.
Wǒ děi hǎohāo xièxie tā. } 'I must thank him properly.'
Wǒ děi hǎohāor xièxie tā.

Mànmàn zǒu.
Mànmān zǒu. } 'Take it easy.'
Mànmānr zǒu.

Single-syllable adjectives can also be transformed into adverbials if they are modified and marked with a following *de*: *hǎo → gèng hǎo de; kuài → hěn kuài de.*

Tā juéde zhǐyǒu qù Zhōngguó cái	'He felt that only if he went to
nénggòu gèng hǎo de tígāo tā de	China could he raise the level
Zhōngwén tīng-shuō nénglì.	of his Chinese listening and
	speaking abilities.'
Wǒ hěn kuài de pá dào shāndǐng,	'I quickly climbed to the top of
wǎng xià kàn Zhènjiāng.	the hill and looked down at
	Zhenjiang.'

VOCABULARY

shěng	'save on'
pá	'climb'
shāndǐng	'top of the hill or mountain'

Disyllabic and other polysyllabic SVs, however, are more versatile and can appear as adverbials without reduplication and either with or without *de*.

Jīntiān fēicháng \<de\> rè!	'It's extremely hot today!'
Wǒmen zhíjiē \<de\> qù.	'We're going directly there.'
Tā nǔlì \<de\> gōngzuò. ⎫	'She works very hard.'
Tā hěn nǔlì de gōngzuò. ⎭	
Tā nàixīn \<de\> děngle tā hěn duō nián le. ⎫	'He's been waiting patiently for her for many years.'
Tā hěn nàixīn de děngle tā hěn duō nián le. ⎭	
Tā hái yúkuài de huíyìle qùnián 12 yuè duì Zhōngguó de yǒuhǎo fǎngwèn.	'She still fondly recalled her friendly visit to China last December.'

VOCABULARY

nǔlì	'try hard; make a great effort' ('exert-effort')
nàixīn	'be patient' ('endure-heart')
yúkuài	'be happy; cheerful' ('contented-fast')
huíyì	'recall' ('return-bring to mind')
yǒuhǎo	'friendly'
fǎngwèn	'to visit; interview; a visit' ('inquire-ask')

Many, but not all, disyllabic SVs can also be reduplicated. Those that do follow the pattern AB → AABB (with the second syllable often more lightly stressed): *shūfu* → *shūshū-fúfú*; *qīngchu* → *qīngqīng-chǔchǔ*. As the examples show, under reduplication, the neutral tone of the second syllable often gets restored to a full tone. Such reduplicated adverbials are also usually marked with the adverbial particle *de*.

Wǒ cōngcōng-mángmáng de pǎolái-pǎoqù.	'I was running back and forth frantically.'

The four-syllable adverbial is a preferred type, and it appears not just as a result of reduplication but also through other processes of elaboration.

Tā bùzhī-bùjué de shuìzháo le.	'He couldn't help but fall asleep.'
Tāmen liǎng ge liǎng ge de *zǒu jìnqu le.*	'They went in two by two.'
Wǒ mànwú-mùdì de shàngle *gōngjiāo.*	'I got on the bus without knowing quite where I was going.'

VOCABULARY

cōngmáng	'hastily; in a hurry'
bùzhī-bùjué	'without warning; without being aware' ('not-know not-perceive')
mànwú-mùdì	'without direction; aimless' ('all over the place-without goal-place')
gōngjiāo	'public transport; bus'

Onomatopoeic expressions are also frequently found in the adverbial position. One common construction subordinates them to a noun, *yì shēng* 'the sound of': *huālā yì shēng* 'with a whoomp sound'. The phrase may be followed by the adverbial *de* (*huālā yì shēng de*). If *de* appears between the onomatopoeic phrase and *yì shēng*, as in the second example below, then it is the modifying *de* (i.e., 'with the sound of a pop').

Qiáng huālā yì shēng <de> *jiù dǎo le.*	'The wall collapsed with a whoomp (*huālā*) sound.'
Pā de yì shēng píngzi zhà le.	'The bottle exploded with the sound of a bang (*pā*).'
Fēng pāle yì shēng <de> bǎ *chuānghu chuīkāi le.*	'The wind blew the window open with a loud gust (*pā*).'

16.2.2 Manner adverbials versus predicate complements

A source of confusion for English speakers is the fact that some words that are clearly adverbs in English do not show up in the adverbial position in Chinese.

Tā Zhōngwén shuō+de hěn biāozhǔn.	'He speaks Chinese properly.'
Tā yě xiě+de bú cuò.	'He doesn't write badly either.'

In both of these examples, the English adverbs (*properly*, *badly*) correspond to a complement with +*de* in Chinese. In other cases, however, where English has adverbs, so will Chinese.

Wǒ cōngcōng-mángmáng de pǎolái-pǎoqù.	'I was running back and forth frantically.'

In some cases, both options are possible.

Adverbial (*de*):	*Tā qīngqīng-chǔchǔ de bǎ zhèi ge wèntí jiěshìle yíxiàr.*
Predicate complement (+*de*):	*Tā bǎ zhèi ge wèntí jiěshì+de hěn qīngchu.*

The difference is subtle. In the first example, with the adverbial, the focus is on the process: 'Her method of presentation is very systematic and clear.' In the second example, the focus is on the result: 'People were very clear about her presentation.' If you keep the distinction between process and result in mind, then it is not surprising that instructions tend to employ manner adverbials, and evaluations use predicate complements.

Instructions:	*Qǐng hǎohāor bǎ nǐ de míngzi xiě zai hēibǎn shang.*	'Please write your name carefully on the blackboard.'
Evaluation:	*Nǐ xiě+de hěn hǎo.*	'You wrote it very nicely.'

16.2.3 The three functions of *de*

Normally, character issues are left to the units on reading and writing. As far as conversation is concerned, the various meanings and uses of *de* are simply a case of homophony: different words that sound alike. In English, the letter *s* (which can be pronounced /s/ or /z/) is also used for different functions; it can indicate plural nouns (book/books), third-person verbs (hit/hits), and possessive nouns (Dylan's). In fact, fifty years ago, written Mandarin followed the spoken language in writing the several functions of *de* all the same way (with the character 的). Since World War II, however, educators have insisted on

Dàotián 'rice fields' (*Lí Guìlín bù yuǎn.*)

distinguishing the three main functions with three distinct characters: 的, 得, and 地 (the last, the *dì* of *dìfang,* was inspired by regional pronunciations in which the adverbial *de* is pronounced *dì*). The following list includes examples of each.

Zhèi ge cái shi nǐ de.	的
Tǐng hǎo de.	的
Wǒmen shi zài Xiāng Gǎng rènshi de.	的
Tā shuō+de hěn biāozhǔn.	得
Nǐ tīngdedǒng ma?	得
Tā jìngjing de tǎng zai shāfā shang.	地

16.2.4 A vivid event

Here's a short dialogue that incorporates some of the adverbial usage described in the previous sections.

Jiǎ:	*Jīntiān zǎoshang, nèi ge rén zhēn dòu!*	'That guy was really funny this morning!'
Yǐ:	*Shéi a?*	'Who?'
Jiǎ:	*Bú rènshi. Tā jíjí-mángmáng de pǎojìn jiàoshì, bǎ yīfu guà zai mén hòubiānr, bǎ shū fàng zai zhuōzi shang.*	'I don't know him. He hurried into the classroom, hung his coat behind the door, and put his books on the table.'
Yǐ:	*Tā shàngkè lái le.*	'He was coming to class.'
Jiǎ:	*Shì a! Kěshì tā yòu huānghuāng-zhāngzhāng de názhe dōngxi pǎo chūqu le.*	'Yes. But then he frantically grabbed his things again and ran out.'
Yǐ:	*Zěnme yòu pǎo le; bú shi lái shàngkè de ma?*	'How come he ran out again; wasn't he coming to class?'
Jiǎ:	*Tā hūrán fāxiàn zǒucuò jiàoshì le!*	'He suddenly realized he'd walked into the wrong room!'

VOCABULARY

dòu	'be weird; be funny; tease'
jímáng	'be in a hurry; anxious; urgent' ('urgent-busy')
huāngzhāng	'be flustered'
hūrán	'suddenly'

16.2.5 Bits and pieces

Here are a few additional notes on adverbials that cover some special cases you might encounter. *Kuài* 'fast', *màn* 'slow', and a number of other single-syllable words can serve as both adjectives (SVs) and adverbs without any kind of modification.

SV:	*Huŏchē gèng kuài.*	'Trains are even faster.'
	Zìxíngchē hěn màn.	'Bikes are slow.'
ADV:	*Kuài zŏu ba, bù zăo le.*	'Hurry, it's late.'
	Màn zŏu.	'Take it easy.'

Some single-syllable words have developed special meanings as adverbs. *Lăo*, for example, means 'be old' as an SV but 'always; persistently' as an ADV.

| SV: | *Tāmen lăo le.* | 'They're getting old.' |
| ADV: | *Tāmen lăo băochí yídìng de jùlí.* | 'They always keep a set distance between them.' |

Words and phrases other than adverbs can also occupy the adverbial position—where they typically convey something about the manner of the verbal event: the 'how.'

Tā dīzhe tóu zŏulái-zŏuqù.	'He walked back and forth with his head down.'
Dă ge dī qù ba.	'Why don't you take a taxi there?'
Tā shi chēhuò sĭ de.	'He died in a car accident.'
Tā wăn dào shí fēnzhōng.	'She got there ten minutes late.'
Gāi duō fàng yìdiăn yán.	'You should put a little more salt in it.'

VOCABULARY

dī	'to lower'
chēhuò	'automobile accident' ('vehicle-misfortune')
băochí	'preserve; keep'
jùlí	'distance'

16.3 May I ask you some personal questions?

Now for something different: a chance to put aside all the complexities of adverbials and settle back for a review of more familiar structures as you interview a teacher (whose name happens to be *Wèi*—but you can fill in the name of your own teacher). Admittedly, an interview in real life wouldn't normally be as smooth as this one. This one is more like interviews you see on television, where all the false starts, miscues, and extraneous material have been edited out.

Nǐ:	*Wèi lǎoshī, néng bu néng wèn nín jǐ ge gèrén de wèntí?*	'Professor Wei, may I ask you a few personal questions?'
Wèi:	*Gèrén de wèntí? Kě.yǐ, kě.yǐ.*	'Personal questions? Okay, sure.'
Nǐ:	*Wǒ xiǎng wèn nín jǐ ge jiātíng fāngmiàn de wèntí, àihào fāngmiàn de wèntí.*	'I'd like to ask you about your family and about your interests.'
Wèi:	*Hǎo, kě.yǐ. Wèn ba!*	'Fine, fine, go ahead and ask!'
Nǐ:	*Wèi lǎoshī, nín shēng zai Yīngguó ba?*	'Professor Wei, you were born in England, right?'
Wèi:	*Shì a, kěshì wǒ shíwǔ suì jiu lái Měiguó le.*	'Yes, but at 15, I came to the United States.'
Nǐ:	*Shíwǔ suì, kěshì Wèi lǎoshī hái dài diǎnr Yīngguó de kǒuyīn!*	'At 15 … but you still have a bit of an English accent!'
Wèi:	*Yīngguó rén shuō wǒ yǒu Měiguó de kǒuyīn, Měiguó rén shuō wǒ yǒu Yīngguó de kǒuyīn. Kě.yǐ shuō shi'bàn Yīng bàn Měi'.*	'The English say I have an American accent; the Americans say I have an English accent. One could say it's "hahf" English and "haef" American.'
Nǐ:	*Wèi lǎoshī jiéhūn le ma?*	'Professor Wei, are you married?'
Wèi:	*Jiéhūn le, jiéhūn sānshí duō nián le, yǒu sì ge háizi.*	'Yes, I am, I've been married for more than thirty years, and I have four children.'

Nǐ:	*Wèi shīmǔ yě shì Yīngguórén ma?*	'Is Mrs. Wei English too?'
Wèi:	*Bù, tā shi Měiguó Xīn'ǎo'ěrliáng lái de! Wǒmen shi zài Xiāng Gǎng rènshi de!*	'No, she's from New Orleans in the United States! We met in Hong Kong!'
Nǐ:	*O, Xiāng Gǎng rènshi de, zhēn qiǎo!*	'Oh, you met in Hong Kong. How serendipitous!'
Wèi:	*Shì a, nèi ge shíhou wǒ zài Xiāng Gǎng jiāoshū, tā qù Xiāng Gǎng lǚyóu yí ge xīngqī. Wǒmen shi zài chēzhàn pèngdao de.*	'Yes, at that time, I was teaching in Hong Kong, and she traveled to Hong Kong for a week. We met at a bus station.'
Nǐ:	*Wèi lǎoshī háizimen duō dà?*	'How old are your children, Professor Wei?'
Wèi:	*Sān ge yǐjīng chéngnián le, xiǎo de shíqī suì.*	'Three of them are already grown; the small one's 17.'
Nǐ:	*Jǐ ge nánháir, jǐ ge nǚháir?*	'How many boys and how many girls?'
Wèi:	*Dōu shì nǚháir.*	'They're all girls.'
Nǐ:	*Dōu shì nǚháir—wa! Wèi lǎoshī yǒu méiyǒu xiōngdì-jiěmèi?*	'All girls—wow! Do you have any brothers and sisters?'
Wèi:	*Yǒu ge dìdi, qíshí shi ge tóngfù yìmǔ de dìdi.*	'I have a younger brother. Actually, he's a half-brother—same father, different mother.'
Nǐ:	*Chúle Zhōngwén yǐwài, nín hái huì shuō shénme biéde wàiyǔ ma?*	'Professor Wei, do you speak any other languages besides Chinese?'

Wèi:	*Wǒ yě huì shuō diǎnr Miǎndiànyǔ. Nǐ zhīdao, wǒ duì Miǎndiàn hěn gǎn xìngqu.*	'I also speak some Burmese. You know, I'm quite interested in Burma.'
Nǐ:	*Tīngshuō nín qùguo hǎo jǐ cì le.*	'I hear you've been many times.'
Wèi:	*Shì, wǒ chàbuduō měinián dōu qù yí cì. Xīwàng jiānglái yǒu jīhuì qù zhù yī-liǎng nián duō zuò yìdiǎnr yánjiū, bǎ wǒ de jīngyàn xiě chéng yì běn shū.*	'That's right; I go almost every year. In the future, I hope to have a chance to go and live there for a year or two, do some more research, and write a book based on my experiences there.'
Nǐ:	*Nà, Wèi láoshī, nín zài zhèr zhùle jǐ nián le?*	'Well, Professor Wei, how long have you been living here?'
Wèi:	*Yǐjīng bā nián le, zhè shi dì-jiǔ nián.*	'Eight years so far; this is my ninth year.'
Nǐ:	*Chúle jiāoshū zuò yánjiū yǐwài, nín shì bu shì hái yǒu qítā àihào?*	'Apart from teaching and doing research, do you also have some other interests?'
Wèi:	*Wǒ xǐhuan qí zìxíngchē, páshān. Nǐ ne?*	'I like to ride my bike and climb mountains. How about you?'
Nǐ:	*Wǒ xǐhuan tīng liúxíng yīnyuè, tiàowǔ, kàn diànyǐng. Wèi láoshī, gēn nín liáotiānr hěn kāixīn, xièxie.*	'I like to listen to modern music, dance, and go to the movies. Professor Wei, it's been a pleasure talking to you. Thank you.'
Wèi:	*Bú xiè, bú yòng kèqi.*	'You're quite welcome.'

VOCABULARY

gèrén	'individual; personal'
jiātíng	'family; household': *jiātíng fāngmiàn de wèntí*
àihào	'hobby; interest' ('love-like')
dài … kǒuyīn	'have (carry) an … accent': *dài yìdiǎnr nánfāng de kǒuyīn*
shīmǔ	'wife of teacher' [polite]
qiǎo	'be coincidental; opportune': *Qiǎo jíle!* 'What a coincidence!'
lǚyóu	'travel; tour'
chēzhàn	'station'
pèngdao	'bump into; come into contact with' ('bump-to'): *zài chēzhàn pèngdao tā*; *pèngdao qián de wèntí* 'have money problems'
chéngnián	'mature; grown' ('become-year')
qíshí	'actually; in fact' ('its reality')
tóngfù yìmǔ	'half-sibling' [same father, different mother]: cf. *tóngmǔ yìfù*
chúle … yǐwài	'in addition to; besides': cf. §16.3.1
hǎo jǐ cì	'many times': *hǎo jǐ cì le* 'many times [up to now]'
jiānglái	'in the future': *xīwàng jiānglái yǒu jīhuì*
jīhuì	'opportunity'
jīngyàn	'experience': *Nǐ guòqu yǒuguo gōngzuò jīngyàn ma?*
bǎ … xiě chéng	'write … into a book': in other words, 'write a book based on …'
pá	'crawl; climb; scramble': *páshān* 'go climbing, hiking'
liúxíng	'popular': *huì liúxíng hǎo jǐ nián* 'will be popular for many years'; *liúxíng qǐlai* 'suddenly catch on'
yīnyuè	'music'
tiàowǔ	'dance'

NOTE

Duō, in its question sense—'to what degree; how' (*Dūo dà* 'how old'; *duō yuǎn* 'how far away')—is also heard with a rising tone: *duó dà, duó yuǎn*.

16.3.1 *Chúle … yǐwài*

Chúle … yǐwài 'in addition to; besides; except for' literally means 'having removed … and put aside'. The following clause will generally contain an inclusive adverb, such as *dōu, yě,* or *hái*. In more formal contexts, *yǐwài* can be rendered as *zhīwài* (cf. *zhī yī* 'one of', *zhīqián* 'before', *zhīhòu* 'afterward'). Sometimes, either the first part of the expression (*chúle*) or the second (*yǐwài*) will be omitted.

Chúle Zhōngwén yǐwài nǐ hái hui shuō shénme wàiyǔ?	'What foreign languages do you speak other than Chinese?'
Chúle zhōumò <yǐwài>, tā biéde shíhou dōu bú zài jiā.	'Except for the weekends, he's never at home [at other times].'
Míngcháo Zhū Yuánzhāng huángdì jiàn de gōngdiàn, xiànzài chúle dìjī yǐwài, biéde dōu méiyǒu le.	'Except for the foundations, nothing remains of the imperial palace built by Ming Emperor Zhu Yuanzhang.'

VOCABULARY

jiàn	'build; construct': cf. *jiànlì* 'set up; establish'
dìjī	'ground; base; foundation' ('land-base')

16.3.2 *Yuè lái yuè* 'more and more'

Yuè 'exceed' can be repeated to indicate a positive correlation: *yuè duō yuè hǎo* 'the more the merrier'. When only one variable is involved, the default verb is *lái*: *yuè lái yuè hǎo* 'better and better'.

Ài, shìjiè yuè lái yuè luàn.	'Gosh, the world is getting more and more chaotic.'
Dà chéngshì yuè lái yuè wēixiǎn.	'Big cities are becoming more and more dangerous.'

Nà shi yīnwèi rén yuè lái yuè duō.   'That's because there are more and
                                                       more people.'

Wénhuà Dàgémìng gǎo+de yuè   'The Cultural Revolution was
lái yuè jīliè.   carried out more and more
                                                       intensely.'

Lái may be replaced with other verbs, as in the following examples.

Guōtiē, yuè chī yuè xiǎng chī.   'With potstickers, the more you eat,
                                                  the more you want to eat.'

Hànzì xué+de yuè duō,   'With characters, the more you
  wàng+de yuè kuài.   study them, the faster you forget
                                                  them.'

Pá+de yuè gāo, shuāi+de   'The higher you climb, the farther
  yuè cǎn.   you fall.'

VOCABULARY

luàn	'chaotic'
wēixiǎn	'dangerous': *Xiǎoxīn, hěn wēixiǎn!*
gǎo	'to do; make; manage; pick up': This is a verb with a wide range of senses.
jīliè	'intense': of sports—*jīliè de yùndòng, hěn jīliè de bǐsài*; of arguments—*Zhēnglùn jīliè qǐlai le* 'The argument intensified.'
shuāi	'fall down; slip': *Dàjiǎo hǎo, dàjiǎo hǎo, yīntiān xiàyǔ shuāibudǎo.*
cǎn	'tragic; miserable': cf. *bēicǎn* 'tragic', *bēicǎn de shēnghuó* 'a tragic life'

16.3.3 'Ought' and 'must'

There are a number of common verbs that convey notions of obligation and necessity. One, *děi* 'have to', is paired with a different root for the negative: *búbì* 'don't have to'. The other compounds that convey necessity contain *yào* 'want;

need' or one of the bound forms *bì* or *xū*, both of which are associated with 'compulsion': *bìxū; bìyào; xūyào*. Here is a review of them.

a. *<Yīng>gāi* 'ought; should'

> *Nǐ yīnggāi xiūxi xiūxi.*   'You should take a rest.'
> *Míngtiān yǒu kǎoshì, wǒ gāi qù*   'Tomorrow there's a test; I should go
>   *túshūguǎn xuéxí.*   to the library to study.'

b. *Děi* 'must; have to' and *búbì* 'needn't; mustn't' [relatively colloquial]

> *Wǒ děi mǎshàng huíqu.*   'I have to go back right away.'
> *Cóng Guǎngzhōu zuò huǒchē*   'If you go by train from Guangzhou
>   *dào Běijīng yídìng děi jīngguò*   to Beijing, do you have to go
>   *Wǔhàn ma?*   through Wuhan?'
> *Wo xiǎng bù yídìng děi jīngguò*   'I don't think you *have* to go through
>   *Wǔhàn.*   Wuhan.'
> *Búbì dǎochē.*   'There's no need to change buses.'
> *Búbì dōu qù, yí ge rén qù jiù*   'There's no need for you all to go;
>   *xíng le.*   one will do.'

c. *Bìxū* 'must; have to; be necessary' [more formal than *děi*]

> *Yào kāichē bìxū yǒu jiàzhào.*   'If you want to drive, then you have
>   to have a license.'
>
> *Zhèr de xuéshēng rúguǒ yào*   'Students here need to study a
>   *bìyè bìxū xué wàiyǔ.*   language if they want to graduate.'
> *bìxū kào zuǒ*   'must keep to the left'
> *bìxū hǎohāo fùxí*   'need to review it well'
> *rìyòng bìxūpǐn*   'daily necessities' ('daily-use
>   necessary-items')

d. *Bìyào* 'essential; indispensible; obligatory; necessary' [often used as a modifier]

> *Méiyǒu bìyào.*   'No need.'
> *bú bìyào de máfan / shǒuxù*   'unnecessary bother/ procedures'

| *Wǒ kàn méiyǒu bìyào bǎ tā suǒshang.* | 'I don't think it's necessary to lock it.' |

e. *Xūyào* 'need; require; want'

Ài nǐ yě xūyào hěn duō de yǒnggǎn.	'Loving you takes a lot of courage.' [title of a popular song]
Nǐmen xūyào bǐ píngcháng zǎo yìdiǎnr chī zǎofàn.	'You need to eat breakfast a bit earlier than usual.'
Yǒu shénme xūyào bāngmáng de ma?	'Is there anything you need help with?'

Exercise 2

Explain the following situation in Chinese.

Although things are getting more and more expensive, people (*rénmen*) are also earning (*zhuàn*) more and more money. For example, in the past, people used to eat watermelons in the spring and apples in the fall. That was it. Occasionally, there were also bananas or oranges, but except for those, you couldn't find many other fruits. Even if you could, you couldn't afford it. However, the situation (*qíngxing*) now is quite different. You can buy oranges and bananas in the winter, but they are much more expensive than they were in the past. When I was a child, we used to pay about 90 cents for a bunch (*chuàn*) of bananas. Now you pay 4–5 yuan. The more expensive they are, the more people buy them! It's amazing!

16.4 Indefinites

As noted in earlier units, question words in Chinese can also function as indefinites. With this in mind, *nǎr* can mean 'where' or 'anywhere'; *shénme* can mean 'what' or 'anything'; and *jǐ* can mean 'how many' or 'many; several', depending on the context.

Wǒ bú qù nǎr.	'I'm not going anywhere [in particular].'
Wǒ bù zhǎo shéi.	'I'm not looking for anyone [in particular].'
Wǒ bù xiǎng mǎi shénme.	'I don't feel like buying anything [in particular].'
Wǒ méi chī shénme yào.	'I didn't take any medicine [in particular].'
Zhōngwén shū, wǒ méiyǒu jǐ běn.	'I don't have many Chinese books.'
Tāmen méiyǒu duōshao qián.	'They don't have much money.'
Tā bù zěnme gāo.	'She's not that tall.'

16.4.1 Complete exclusion or inclusion

Complete exclusion or inclusion can be conveyed by placing the indefinite phrase before the verb and supporting it with inclusive adverbs such as *dōu* or *yě*. In English, the difference between the plain indefinite (illustrated in the previous section) and the exclusive/inclusive indefinite illustrated in this section can be highlighted by the addition of 'in particular' to the English translation of the plain indefinite or by the addition of 'at all' (or 'else' in some contexts) to the English translation of the exclusive/inclusive indefinite.

Wǒ nǎr yě bú qù.	'I'm not going anywhere [at all].'
Wǒ bú qù nǎr.	'I'm not going anywhere [in particular].'
Wǒ bú dào nǎr qù.	'I'm not going anywhere [in particular].'
Tāmen shéi dōu bú rènshi.	'They don't know anyone [at all].'
Tāmen bú rènshi shéi.	'They don't know anyone [in particular].'
Wǒmen shénme dōu bù xiǎng mǎi.	'We don't want to buy anything [at all].'
Wǒmen bù xiǎng mǎi shénme.	'We don't want to buy anything [in particular].'
Wǒ shénme dōu bú pà.	'I'm not afraid of anything [at all].'
Tā shéi dōu bú pà.	'She's not afraid of anyone [at all].'
Tā bǐ shéi dōu gāo.	'He's taller than anyone [else].'

Něitiān dōu xíng.	'Any day [at all] is fine.'
Tā zěnme shuì yě shuìbuzháo.	'No matter how he tries, he can't sleep [at all].'
Nèi ge biān zì, wǒ zěnme xiě yě xiěbuduì.	'The character for *biān*, no matter how I write it, I can't get it right [at all].'
Jīntiān de zuòyè zěnme zuò yě zuòbuwán.	'No matter how I try, I can't get today's homework done [at all].'

16.4.2 Virtual exclusion or inclusion

Another strategy for indicating near or complete exclusion or inclusion is to cite a small amount and then rule that out.

Wǒ yì fēn qián dōu méiyǒu.	'I don't have a cent [to my name].'
Wǒ yì máo yě méiyǒu.	'I don't have a dime [to my name].'
Tā yì běn yě méi kànguo.	'He's hasn't even read one [of them].'
Tā yì kǒu dōu bù gǎn chī.	'She didn't dare to eat a bite [of it].'

When no particular item suggests itself, *yìdiǎnr* can provide the appropriate amount.

Wǒ yìdiǎnr dōu bú lèi / bú è.	'I'm not the least bit tired / hungry.'
Wǒ yìdiǎnr dōu bú pà.	'I'm not the least bit scared.'
Wǒ yìdiǎnr dōu bù dǒng.	'I don't understand any of it.'

16.4.3 *Lián ... dōu/yě*

Lián has a core meaning of 'join; link; connect', but in certain contexts—in conjunction with inclusive adverbs such as *dōu* or *yě*—it corresponds to English 'even', and as such, it can serve to support virtual exclusion or inclusion of the type cited previously.

Wǒ yí fēn qián dōu méiyǒu.   →   *Wǒ lián yí fēn qián dōu méiyǒu!*

In other examples, *lián ... dōu/yě* indicates 'to a degree that includes even ...'

| *Jīntiān máng+de bùdeliǎo, lián wǔfàn yě méi shíjiān chī!* | 'I'm really busy today; I didn't even have time to eat lunch!' |

Wǒ shénme dōu bú pà! (Dàlián)

Wǒ lèi+de lián zìjǐ de míngzi dōu wàng le!	'I was so tired I forgot my own name!'

In another common constuction, *lián* appears with *bié shuō* 'to say nothing of'.

Nǐ qùguo Hūhéhàotè ma?	'Have you been to Hohhot?'
Hūhéhàotè?! Bié shuō Hūhéhàotè le, wǒ lián Běijīng dōu méi qùguo.	'Hohhot!? I haven't even been to Beijing, to say nothing of Hohhot.'
Nǐ kànguo Hóng Lóu Mèng ma?	'Have you read *Dream of the Red Chamber*?'
Hóng Lóu Mèng a! Bié shuō Hóng Lóu Mèng, wǒ lián Hóngsè Niángzǐjūn yě méi kànguo!	'*Dream of the Red Chamber*! I haven't even read *The Red Detachment of Women*, let alone *Dream of the Red Chamber*!'

NOTE

Hóng Lóu Mèng ('Red-Building Dream'), is usually translated as 'Dream of the Red Chamber'. Written by *Cáo Xuěqín* at the end of the 17th century, it is probably the best known of the Chinese classical vernacular novels. *Hóngsè Niángzǐjūn* 'The Red Detachment of Women' ('red-color woman-troop') is one of the so-called model ballets (which was later made into both a play and a film) from the Cultural Revolution. As a ballet, it was performed for U.S. president Richard Nixon during his 1972 visit to China.

16.4.4 Paired indefinites

Indefinites often come in pairs, and the second refers back to the first.

Xiǎng chī shénme jiu chī shénme.	'Eat whatever you want.'
Xiǎng qù nǎ.lǐ jiu qù nǎ.lǐ.	'Go wherever you want.'
Xiǎng wèn shénme jiu wèn shénme.	'Ask whatever you want.'
Xiǎng gēn shéi liáotiān jiu gēn shéi liáotiān.	'Talk to whomever you want.'

Exercise 3

Provide Chinese for the following conversations.

1. A: It's so hot; I don't feel like going anywhere in particular.
    B: Nor me, I'm just going to stay home and watch the World Cup.

2. A: What did you do over the New Year break?
    B: Absolutely nothing! I got sick and had to stay in bed the whole week.

3. A: Order whatever you like; it's my treat ('I'm inviting') today!
    B: You shouldn't; you treated last time. This time, I'm treating.

4. A: This is a bright little kid; she does things faster and better than anyone!
    B: That's my fourth daughter. Actually (*qíshí*), she's more mischievous than any of them!

5. A: No matter how I try, I can't sleep; it's just too hot.
    B: Don't you have air conditioning?

6. A: Have you been to Burma?
    B: Burma?! I haven't been to Italy, let alone Burma!

16.5 Religion

Though the official line in China is that religion is superstition (*míxìn* 'confused belief'), religious activity is tolerated in modern China, provided it does not show potential for threatening the social order. Chinese people, knowing that formal religion plays a more prominent role in the lives of many foreigners, will often ask about religious affiliation.

Nǐ xìn shénme jiào?	'What's your religion?'
Wǒ shi Fójiàotú.	'I'm Buddhist.' ('Buddhism-follower')
Wǒ bú xìn jiào.	'I don't have a religion.'

Positive answers would generally be expected to come from the following list.

	RELIGION		PRACTITIONER	
Christianity	*Jīdūjiào* ('Christ-religion')		Christian	*Jīdū jiàotú*
Catholicism	*Tiānzhǔjiào* ('heaven-host-religion')		Catholic	*Tiānzhǔ jiàotú*
Protestantism	*Xīnjiào* ('new-religion')		Protestant	*Xīnjiàotú*
Judaisim	*Yóutàijiào*		Jew	*Yóutài jiàotú*
Islam	*Yīsīlánjiào*		Muslim	*Mùsīlín* (*Yīsīlán jiàotú*)
Buddhism	*Fójiào*		Buddhist	*Fójiàotú*
Hinduism	*Yìndùjiào*		Hindu	*Yìndù jiàotú*

NOTES

a. *Jiào* 'teachings': reduced from *zōngjiào* 'religion'

b. *Tú* 'disciple; follower': a bound form

c. Chinese Muslims are considered a minority group (*shǎoshù mínzú*) in China; they are the only minority group defined in terms of religion. They are often labeled *Huímín* 'Muslim people'. Jews are also often treated as an ethnic group: *Yóutàijiào rén*. *Yóutài jiàotú* refers to practicing Jews.

d. Although ordinary people in China know about *Tiānzhǔjiào*, there is often some confusion about the difference between *Jīdujiào* and *Xīnjiào*.

e. It is often argued that Taoism (*Dàojiào*) and Buddhism operate syncretically, or within a single system. In ordinary speech, people often identify themselves—or others—as *Fójiàotú* or *xìn Fójiào de* but not, apparently, as *Dàojiàotú* or *xìn Dàojiào de*.

f. Because of their importance in U.S. history, *Qīnqjiàotú* 'Puritans' ('clear-religion-followers'), are also well known in China.

The following table indicates the names of the practitioners for the three main religions in China, their places of worship, and their methods of worship.

Fójiàotú	*sìmiào* 'temple'	*shāoxiāng* 'burn incense'; *bàifó* 'worship Buddha'
Jīdū jiàotú	*jiàotáng* 'church'	*zuò lǐbài* 'worship'; *qídǎo* 'pray'
Yīsīlán jiàotú	*qīngzhēnsì* 'mosque'	*qídǎo ~ zuò lǐbài* 'pray'

NOTES

Buddhist priests are known as *héshang*, Catholic priests are *shénfu*, Protestant pastors are *mùshi* ('shepherd-teacher'), but nonspecialists would be unlikely to know the comparable terms for the other religions.

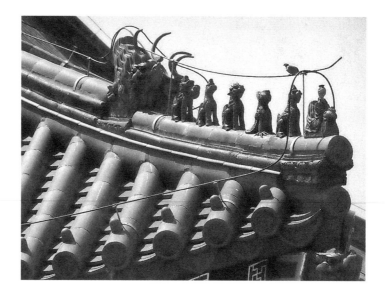

Yōnghégōng. The Lama Temple, Beijing.

16.6 Verb combos (4)

Students of English know the difficulty of dealing with its vast repertoire of phrasal verbs, such as *check in, check out, check up, pick on, pick off, pick up,* and *pick out.* The second element of these combinations is a directional particle, but the meaning of the whole phrase is often not easily deduced from its component parts (e.g., 'fill in a form' and 'fill out a form'). In other words, many phrasal verbs are idiomatic. In Chinese, verb combos present much the same problem. Though some are transparent (*ná guòqu*), others are harder to derive from the elements involved (*mǎibuqǐ*). For this reason, they have been introduced in this program incrementally. This section introduces a few more idiosyncratic sets.

16.6.1 *Xiàlai*

Verbs of recording or notation are completed by the directional complement *xiàlai*, which roughly corresponds to 'down' in 'write it down'. The relevant verbs include the following.

xiě	'write'
jì	'note'
bèi	'memorize'
lù	'record'
zhào	'photograph'
huà	'draw; paint'
miáo	'trace'

1. *Qǐng bǎ tā xiě xiàlai.* — 'Would you mind writing it down?'
2. *Shuō màn yìdiǎnr, wǒ jì bu xiàlai.* — 'Not so fast; I can't get it down.'
3. *Méi tīngqīngchu, nǐ shì bu shì bǎ tā jì xiàlai le?* — 'I didn't hear clearly; did you get it down?'
   Jì xiàlai le, nǐ kàn. — 'Yes, I did, look.'
   Ng, wǒ kànbudǒng. — 'Uh, I can't read it.'
   Wǒ de zì xiě+de bù hǎo. — 'I didn't write the characters very well.'
4. *Tāmen shuō de hěn yǒu yìsi; wǒmen yīnggāi bǎ tā lù xiàlai.* — 'What they're saying is fascinating; we should record it.'

5. *Wǒmen zuì hǎo bǎ nèi zhāng dìtú*   'It would be great if we traced that
   miáo xiàlai.   map.'

16.6.2 *Chūlai*

Chūlai ('come out') combines with verbs of perception to mean 'figure out;
recognize'.

Yīnwèi tā de màozi, wǒ rèn chū tā lái le.	'I recognized him by his hat.'
Nǐ cāi de chūlai wǒ shi shéi ma?	'Can you guess who I am?'
Cāi bu chūlai.	'No, I can't.'
Dǎ diànhuà de shíhou tīng bu chūlai tā shi wàiguó rén.	'On the phone, you can't hear that she's a foreigner.'
Nǐ kàn de chū zhèi ge dìfang yǒu hěn duō biànhuà.	'You can see that this place has a lot of changes.'

16.6.3 Moving out: A dialogue

Here's a short dialogue that illustrates how the selection of particular verb
complements can modify verbal meaning—in this case, the motion verb
bān 'move'. *Hǎi Bó* is trying to get in touch with his friend *Xǔ Chángdé*, but
when he phones *Xǔ*'s apartment, the woman who answers doesn't know where
he is.

Hǎi:	*Wèi, qǐngwèn, zhè shi Xǔ Chángdé jiā ma?*	'Hello, is that Xu Changde's place?'
Nǚde:	*Xǔ Chángdé a, tā bānzǒu le.*	'Xu Changde? He's moved away.'
Hǎi:	*Tā bānjiā le ma?*	'He's moved?'
Nǚde:	*Shì, bānjiā le.*	'Yes.'
Hǎi:	*Bān dào nǎ.lǐ, zhīdao ma?*	'Do you know where he's gone?'
Nǚde:	*Bù zhīdào.*	'I don't know.'
Hǎi:	*Tā shi shénme shíhou bān chūqu de?*	'When did he move out?'

Nǚde:	*Bù zhīdào. Wǒmen běnyuè chū bān jìnlai de.*	'I don't know. We moved in at the beginning of the month.'
Hǎi:	*Hǎo, duōxiè, duōxiè.*	'Okay, thanks.'
Nǚde:	*Bú xiè!*	'You're welcome!'

NOTES

a. *Wèi* is an interjection used to open a telephone conversation or call out to someone.

b. *Běnyuè chū* 'at the beginning of the current month' ('root-month onset'): cf. *běnyuè dǐ* 'at the end of the month'

16.6.4 Peking duck

Here's another conversation that contains a selection of verb combos. This one, though, is done in the style of a *xiàngshēng* 'cross talk' comedy routine. *Jiǎ* is the straightman, and *Yǐ* is the joker.

Jiǎ:	*Nǐ huì zuò Běijīng kǎoyā ma?*	'Can you cook Peking duck?'
Yǐ:	*Bú huì de!*	'Nope!'
Jiǎ:	*Tài hǎo le. Wǒ jiāo nǐ. Xiān zhǎo yì zhī yāzi lai.*	'Great; I'll teach you. First, find a duck.'
Yǐ:	*Zhǎobudào ~ zhǎobuzháo.*	'I won't be able to.'
Jiǎ:	*Nà, nǐ qù mǎi yì zhī ba!*	'In that case, go and buy one, okay?'
Yǐ:	*Mǎibuqǐ.*	'I can't afford to.'
Jiǎ:	*Nà, wǒ sòng <gei> nǐ yì zhī ba.*	'Okay then, I'll give you one.'
Yǐ:	*Duōxiè.*	'Thanks.'
Jiǎ:	*Nǐ xiān bǎ yāzi xǐgānjìng!*	'First, clean the duck!'
Yǐ:	*Hǎo, xǐ yāzi.*	'Okay, clean duck.'
Jiǎ:	*Ránhòu bǎ cōng jiāng fàng jìn yā dùzi li qu.*	'Afterward, put the scallions and ginger in its stomach.'
Yǐ:	*Hǎo, fàng cōng jiāng.*	'Okay, put in scallions and ginger.'

Jiǎ:	*Xiànzài bǎ yāzi fàng jìn kǎoxiāng li qu.*	'Now put the duck in the oven.'
Yǐ:	*Hǎo, kǎo yāzi.*	'Okay, roast the duck.'
Jiǎ:	*Xiǎoxīn, bié kǎohú le.*	'Be careful; don't overcook it.'
Yǐ:	*Fàngxīn, kǎoshì kǎodehú, kǎoyā, kǎobuhú.*	'Don't worry, I only burn out on exams; I don't burn ducks.'

VOCABULARY

xiàngshēng	'cross talk': a popular style of comedy that involves a lot of language play and usually involves two people, one of whom plays straight while the other plays 'dumb' or 'literal'
Běijīng kǎoyā	'Peking duck': one of the cases in which English still uses 'Peking'
zhī	M for ducks, chickens, birds, sheep, and other animals
sòng	'to present; escort': *Sòng*, like *gěi*, can take both person and thing as its object. More often, however, it is followed by *gěi*—*sòng gěi*—cf. *mài gěi* 'sell to someone' (with *mài* 'sell', *gěi* is not optional).
xǐgānjìng	'wash so as to be clean'
cōng jiāng	'scallions and ginger'
dùzi	'stomach'
kǎoxiāng	'oven' ('bake-box'): cf. *bīngxiāng, xìnxiāng*
xiǎoxīn	'careful' ('small-heart')
hú	'be overcooked'
fàngxīn	'take care' ('put-heart')

NOTE

The routine ends in a play on *kǎo* 'to test' and *kǎo* 'to bake'; *hú* is 'to overcook food', but in slang, it also means 'to fail an exam'.

Běijīng kǎoyā

16.7 *Bèi* and the relevance of passive voice

In English, a sentence such as 'the police arrested them' can be recast, for various rhetorical reasons, as 'they were arrested by the police' or 'they got arrested by the police.' In the latter cases, the agent (police) can be stated with the preposition *by*, or it can be omitted: 'They were ~ got arrested.' Sometimes, the agent is unknown; at other times, it may be preferable not to state the agent in order to avoid responsibility (it's not important who did it). In many languages, the changes in word order and consequent change in the form of the verb go under the names of *active* and *passive*.

Chinese verbs, as we have seen, are uncommitted to many of the categories that are taken for granted in English and many European languages, including tense (sing, sang), person (she sings, they sing), and passive voice. In many cases where English has a passive, Chinese is noncommittal and simply lets the context determine how a particular noun relates to the verb. The following Chinese sentences are structurally identical; yet in most contexts, the first is translated into the English passive voice, the second into the active voice.

| *Nín zěnme chēnghu?* | 'How should you be addressed?' |
| *Nín zěnme yòng?* | 'How do you use this?' |

However, there are cases in Chinese that bear a resemblance to passive voice. These involve the word *bèi* (or one of several other words whose function is nearly synonymous with *bèi*). The pair of sentences that follow (utilizing the verb *zhuā* 'arrest; seize') illustrate.

| *Jǐngchá bǎ tāmen zhuā qǐlai le.* | 'The police arrested them.' |
| *Tāmen bèi <jǐngchá> zhuā qǐlai le.* | 'They got arrested <by the police>.' |

In both Chinese and English, the subject (agent) and the object (person or people affected) are rearranged so as to make the object (*tāmen* or 'they') the starting point. In the Chinese, *bèi* cannot be omitted, but the subject, *jǐngchá*, can be. (In the English example, the whole phrase 'by the police'—not just 'the police'—can be omitted.) It is noteworthy, however, that the verb in Chinese undergoes no modification—it is *zhuā* in both cases, contrasting with the English 'arrested' and 'got arrested.' However, under some conditions, the Chinese verb can be modified by the addition of *gěi* ('give' in one of its diverse functions) before the verb.

Tāmen <bèi jǐngchá> gěi zhuā qǐlai le. 'They got arrested <by the police>.'

The addition of *gěi* may add an additional nuance of commiseration or regret. (The use of 'got' in English, rather than the more neutral 'have been,' may serve the same purpose.) The possibility of adding *gěi* to the verb makes the structural comparison between English and Chinese more compelling. Regardless of the structural similarities, *bèi* has certain conditions that make Chinese constructions with it much less common than English passives. In most cases, though not all, *bèi* (and its counterparts) appears with actions that have an adverse effect—with things breaking, getting lost or stolen, being damaged, and so on.

1.	*Tā de zìxíngchē bèi bómǔ mài le.*	'His bike got sold by my aunt.'
	Ou, nà tài kěxī le.	'Oh, what a pity.'
	Tā shuō qí zìxíngchē tài wēixiǎn le.	'She said that riding bikes was too dangerous.'

2. *Wǒmen liù diǎn bèi chǎoxǐng le.* 'We were woken up at 6:00.'
   Bèi háizimen ma? 'By the kids?'
   Bù, bèi lājīchē. 'No, by garbage trucks.'
3. *Xíngli dōu yǐjīng bèi tāmen názǒu le.* 'They've already taken the luggage.'
   Ná dào nǎ.lǐ le? 'Where was it taken to?'
   Wǒ bù qīngchu, yěxǔ ná dào wàitou le. 'I'm not sure; they might have taken it outside.'

VOCABULARY

zhuā	'arrest; seize'
jǐngchá	'police officer'
kěxī	'unfortunately; it's a pity'
chǎoxǐng	'awakened' ('noise-awake')
lājīchē	'garbage truck'

16.7.1 Other options with *jiào*, *ràng*, and *gěi*

It is worth noting that there are alternatives to *bèi*, some of them more colloquial, including *jiào*, *ràng*, and *gěi*. Unlike *bèi*, they all also function as main
verbs: *ràng* 'let'; *jiào* 'call'; *gěi* 'give'. *Ràng* and *jiào* require an object, even if it's
a so-called dummy object such as *rén*; but *gěi*, like *bèi*, does not.

Zìxíngchē bèi <rén> tōu le.
Zìxíngchē jiào rén tōu le. } 'My bike got stolen by someone.'
Zìxíngchē ràng rén tōu le.
Tā chē gěi <rén> zále 'Her car was smashed by someone.'

The last example breaks the pattern only as an excuse to introduce the colloquial verb *zá* 'smash' (as in *zákāi* 'smash open [a lock]') or 'fail; bungle' (as
in a talk or experiment). In that example, *gěi* functions like *bèi*. No doubt you
have marveled at the versatility of the word *gěi*, which occurs as a main verb
('give'), as a preposition or co-verb ('for the benefit of'), as an alternative to *bèi*
('by'), and as a signal of the passive turn in the verb (*gěi zhuā qǐlai le*). Yes, it
is possible to find a single sentence that contains several different functions of

gěi; and yes, at times there is ambiguity. But all this is new, and, for now, we should focus on the options that are the least problematical—the *bèi* options. The following section includes some examples and dialogues that encapsulate what needs to be learned at this point.

16.7.2 I was stopped by the police, and other predicaments
Since sentences with *bèi* tend to comment on misfortunes, questions that express curiosity about events provide a typical lead-in. Here is a list of questions, followed by some possible answers with *bèi*.

Zěnme yì huí shì?	'What happened?'
Zěnme le?	'What's going on?'
Zěnme gǎo de?	'What the heck? / What's going on?'
Wǒ bèi jǐngchá jiàozhù le.	'I was stopped by the police.'
Bú yào bèi wàibiǎo qīpiàn.	'Don't be fooled by appearances.'
Wǒ bèi fá le.	'I was fined.'
Tāmen bèi kòuyāle yì tiān.	'They were detained for a day.'
Tā bèi dàkǎchē zhǎnguò le.	'She was run over by a truck.'
Tā màozi bèi fēng chuīzǒu le.	'His hat was blown away by the wind.'
Tāmen tǔdì bèi mòshōu le.	'Their land was confiscated.'

VOCABULARY

yì huí shì	'an item of business': The expression with *zěnme* is idiomatic and should be learned as such.
gǎo	'do; make; manage'
jiàozhù	'pull over' ('call-stop')
fá	'fine': cf. *fákuǎn* 'pay a fine'
kòuyā	'detain'
zhǎn	'roll over'
chuī	'to blow'
mòshōu	'confiscate' ('conceal-receive')

16.7.3 Arrested!

Jiǎ has just been told about the arrest of an acquaintance; *Yǐ* has the details.

Jiǎ:	*Ài, tīngshuō Lǐ Xīnjié zuótiān zāoyù yí jiàn bù hǎo de shìr.*	'Gosh, I heard that something bad happened to Li Xinjie yesterday.'
Yǐ:	*Shì, tā bèi zhuāzǒu le.*	'Yes, he got taken away.'
Jiǎ:	*Zěnme yì huí shìr?*	'What happened?'
Yǐ:	*Tā qù yóuxíng le, bèi jǐngchá zhuāzǒu le.*	'He was demonstrating and got taken off by the police.'
Jiǎ:	*Yóuxíng? Shénme yóuxíng?*	'Demonstrating? What demonstration?'
Yǐ:	*Shìwēi yóuxíng.*	'A protest demonstration.'
Jiǎ:	*Zhēnde ma?*	'You're kidding!'
Yǐ:	*Zhēnde.*	'I'm serious.'
Jiǎ:	*Qù shìwēi shénme?*	'What was he protesting?'
Yǐ:	*Fǎnduì fǔbài.*	'He was protesting corruption.'
Jiǎ:	*Fǔbài?*	'Corruption?'
Yǐ:	*Fǎnduì dāngdì guānyuán fǔbài.*	'Yes, they were protesting corruption among local officials.'
Jiǎ:	*Tā huì zěnmeyàng ne?*	'What'll happen to him?'
Yǐ:	*Tā kěnéng huì bèi guān jǐ ge yuè ba.*	'He may be locked up for a few months.'
Jiǎ:	*Huì bu huì yǒu ge shěnpàn?*	'Will there be a trial?'
Yǐ:	*Bù, tā huì bèi fákuǎn, ránhòu qiǎnsòng huíjiā.*	'No. He'll be fined and then sent home.'
Jiǎ:	*Wà, zhēn shi yí jiàn hěn yánzhòng de shìr.*	'Gosh, that's serious.'

Gōng'ān 'Public security'

VOCABULARY

zāoyù	'encounter; meet'
zhuā	'seize; catch; arrrest': *zhuāzǒu* 'seize and take off'
yóuxíng	'parade / to parade'
shìwēi	'demonstration/protest; demonstrate'
fǎnduì	'oppose; protest'
fǔbài	'corruption'
dāngdì	'local': cf. *dāngshí* 'at that time'
guānyuán	'officials'
guān	'close': *bèi guān jǐ ge yuè* 'get shut in for several months'
shěnpàn	'trial'
fákuǎn	'fine / to pay a fine' ('assess-fine')
qiǎnsòng	'to send back; expel; deport'
yánzhòng	'serious' ('strict-heavy')

Exercise 4

Provide Chinese paraphrases for the following sentences.

1. We got locked outside and had to call the police to let (*ràng*) us in.
2. May I borrow (*jiè*) your camera (*zhàoxiàngjī*)? / Someone's already borrowed it.
3. My plane tickets and passport got stolen (*tōu*). / Oh, that's too bad!
4. They stole a car and got arrested by the police! The car got smashed up.
5. He was fined $200 for spitting (*tǔtán*). [VO: *fá ... kuǎn*]

Provide an English paraphrase for the following paragraph.

Wǒ dì-yī cì zài Yīngguó lǚxíng de shíhou fāshēng de zuì zāogāo de shìqing shi dāng wǒ zài qù Lìwùpǔ de huǒchē shang shuìzháole de shíhou, hùzhào bèi tōu le. Xìngyùn de shi lǐngshìguǎn tóngyì mǎshàng fā gěi wǒ yì běn xīn de. Chūménr lǚxíng de rén suíshí-suídì dōu yào zhùyì xiǎotōu. Zài nǎr dōu yíyàng.

VOCABULARY

fāshēng	'happen; occur; take place'
zāogāo	'too bad; what a pity'
xìngyùn	'be fortunate'
lǐngshìguǎn	'consulate'
tóngyì	'agree; approve' ('same-intention')
fā	'issue'
suíshí-suídì	'whenever and wherever' ('follow-time follow-place')
xiǎotōu	'crooks; thieves' ('little-thief')

16.8 Driving and owning a car (1)

The following dialogue is a conversation about driving, cars, and other aspects of transportation in China. It is too long and complicated to serve as a model conversation. Rather, like the narratives that appear at the beginning and the end of most units (such as the one on smoking in Unit 15), its purpose is to provide material in context and consolidate grammatical patterns and vocabulary usage—as well as introduce new words. Therefore, no parallel translation is provided. In fact, rather than a long vocabulary list, words, phrases, and even whole sentences are listed after the text with a translation and relevant notes. This way, the focus is on chunks, the building blocks of speech, rather than individual words.

This conversation is quite colloquial, which inevitably means regional. In this case, the language is Mandarin with a mixture of slang, *r*-suffixed words, and northern (or Beijing) usage. My good friend Li Bo, a well-known Chinese author and blogger who moves back and forth between the United States and China, has put his fine ear for Mandarin usage to work to improve the authenticity of this conversation. I've modified it to make it more accessible to a second-year student of the language, so I take the blame for any slight usage problems that might remain.

Liáoliao Zhōngguó qìchē de shìr

A = *Zhù zài Běijīng de Zhōngguórén*
B = *Zhù zài Zhōngguó bù jiǔ, xuéguo Hànyǔ de wàiguórén*

A: *Èrshí nián yǐqián, zài Zhōngguó, chē xiāngdāng guì, juédà duōshù rén mǎibuqǐ, lùshang de chēzi bǐjiào shǎo. Ǒu'ěr yǒu ge chē, nà shi guānchē.*
B: *Méi jiànguo, xiǎngbì yě shì.*
A: *Dàn nín kàn a, zuìjìn shí duō nián lái, qíngkuàng biànle hěn duō.*
B: *Xiànzài dōu zài jiǎng Zhōngguó juéqǐ ma. 'Dìfùtiānfān'.*
A: *Shi tiānfāndìfù! Nín shuōfǎn la.*
B: Okay, *xièxie! Tiānfāndìfù.*
A: *Duì, jiù ná yī-shí-zhù-xíng de "xíng" lái shuō: chē yuè lái yuè piányi. Xiànzài, guóchǎn chē bǐ Měiguó de chē hái piányi, Rénmínbì dàgài qī-bāwàn jiù néng mǎi yí liàng. Jìnkǒu de dāngrán bǐ guóchǎn de guì hěn duō, dàn yě yuè lái yuè piányi. Tóngshí, gàosù gōnglù yě shì yì nián bǐ yì nián duō, nǐ xiǎng qù nǎr dōu xíng! Zài chéngshì li yǒu chē de yuè lái yuè duō; nóngcūn qíngkuàng yǒu suǒ bùtóng, dàn yě zài cháo zhèi ge fāngxiàng fāzhǎn.*
B: *Nín huì kāichē ma?*

A: *Bú huì, kěshì hěn xiǎng xué, xiànzài shàng jiàxiào. Wǒ péngyou shuō kāichē hěn róngyi, dànshi wǒ juéde bìng bú shi nàme huí shìr.*

B: *Nín huì mǎi chē ma?*

A: *Wǒ zhèng zhǔnbèi mǎi, yǒu diǎnr yóuyù. Yǒu shíhou wǒ juéde háishi bù kāichē hǎo. Qìyóufèi, guòlùfèi, wéixiū, bǎoxiǎn měi yí yàng piányi de; nín kàn zhè kōngqì, dōu shì chē duō gěi nào de. Chéng li hái chángchang dǔzhe, dǔ+de nǐ xīnfúqìcào. Zài shuō, hǎo duō rén kāichē bù shǒu jiāotōng guīzé, wánrmìng ne!*

B: *Duì a, wǒ yě juéde zài Zhōngguó háishi bù kāichē hǎo. Méi chē bìng bú àishìr. Zhōngguó jiāotōng xìtǒng sìtōngbādá, dào nǎr dōu piányi, fāngbiàn. Běijīng de gōngjiāo kěnéng shi shìjiè shang dà chéngshì lǐ zuì piányi de, gōng-qì shí zhàn yǐnèi cái sì máo qián, dìtiě yílù liǎng kuài! Jīchǎng dàbā 15 kuài, jīchǎng qīnggui 25 kuài!*

A: *Nín kě zhēn shi ménrqīng a!*

B: *Hēi, wǒ jīngcháng qù Běijīng, zǎojiù qīngchērèlù la!*

A: *Nà, nín zuòguo Zhōngguó de huǒchē ma?*

B: *Dāngrán, Zhōngguó shi dàguó, tiělù xìtǒng shi zuì zhòngyào jiāotōng gōngjù. Jìnnián lái fāzhǎn xùnsù, yǒu dòngchē, gāosù tiělù, jīchǎng kuàigui, děngděng. Hěn fāngbiàn, zhǐ shi bié gǎnshang Chūnyùn … guònián qījiān. Nín zuì hǎo bié gǎn nà rènao.*

A: *Zhōngguó jiāotōng fāzhǎn shì hěn kuài, kěshì gēn nǐmen Měiguó bǐ hái yǒu hěn dà chājù; nǐmen Měiguó bú shi yǒu ge yǎhào, jiào shénme "zhuāng zài qìchē lúnzi shang de guójiā" ma!*

B: *Nà yě shì huánjìng zàochéng de. Měiguó hé Zhōngguó hěn bù yíyàng. Liǎng guó dōu shì dì dà, dàn Zhōngguó rén duō, Měiguó rén shǎo. Zài Měiguó, méi chē hěn bù fāngbiàn, kě.yǐ shuō méi chē děngyú méi tuǐ. Zài Měiguó méi chē jiu bù néng qù kàn péngyou, bù néng qù kàn diànyǐng, yě bù néng qù shàngxué. Chūmén chī ge fàn, chūmén mǎi gēn cōng dōu yào kāichē qù chāoshì. Měiguó méi chē shénme shìr dōu zuòbuliǎo.*

A: *Zài Zhōngguó yǒu chē yě shì wèile xiǎnshì shēnfen. Yǒu chē, rénjiā jiu juéde nǐ chénggōng. Gǎnqíng wèn nín yí jù, nín xiǎng zài Zhōngguó zhǎo xífur ma?*

B: *Nà gǎnqíng hǎo! Zhōngguó měinǚ duōduō.*

A: *Hēhē, yǒu fáng ma?*

B: *Wǒ zū fáng, gōngyù.*

A: *Yǒu chē ma?*

B: *Wǒ yǒu gōngjiāokǎ, piányi.*

A: *Hāhā, nín zuòmèng qǔ xífur ne. … Zám yòu pǎotí le.*

B: *Shì de, yánguīzhèngzhuàn.*

A: *Hǎo. Nín yì xíguàn zìjǐ kāichē le, jiù hěn nán fàngqì le. Wèile*
     miànzi, wèile shūshì, wèile yǐnsī, jiù méi bànfǎ, bù néng fàngqì le.
     Jíshǐ nǐ hái děi wèi tā huā hěn duō qián, shēng-lǎo-bìng-sǐ nín dōu
     děi guǎn, wǒ shuō a, nǐ bú shi qìchē tā yé, dào chéngle tā sūnzi.

B: *Nín shénme yìsi? Yéye, sūnzi? Wǒ hútu le.*

A: *Hēhē, wǒ shi shuō, yídàn nǐ mǎile chē, jiù bú shi chē de zhǔrén le,*
     érshì chē de núlì le.

B: *Hāhā, míngbai le. Nín zhēn yōumò! Dàn yě yǒu diǎnr hǎochù,*
     Běijīng gōngjiāo suīrán piányi, dàn jǐ qǐlai xiàng shādīngyú
     guàntou. Yǒule chē jiù xiàng yǒu yí fù kuījiǎ, kě.yǐ cáng qǐlai, bù
     xūyào miànlín gōngzhòng.

A: *Yě shì tuōlí qúnzhòng.*

B: *Duì a, qǐng gēn wǒ shuōyixiàr Zhōngguó qìchē de páizi. Zài Měiguó*
     yǒu hěn duō Měiguó páizi de chē, xiàng Xuěfúlán, Kǎidílākè,
     Fútè; yě yǒu Ōuzhōu de, xiàng Àodí, Bēnchí; yě yǒu Rìběn de,
     xiàng Fēngtián, Běntián; Hánguó de xiàng Xiàndài, Qǐyà.

NOTES

jué dàduōshù rén	'the vast majority of people': *jué* 'to sever', but also used adverbially to mean 'extremely'
Ǒu'ěr yǒu ge chē, nà shi guānchē.	'And if occasionally, there was a car, it was an official's car.'
Ǒu'ěr	'on occasion; occasionally': *Wǒmen ǒu'ěr xià guǎnzi, dàn yìbān dōu zài jiā chī.* 'We occasionally eat out, but in general, we eat at home.' (*xià guǎnzi* 'go down to a restaurant')
guānchē	'car of an official' ('official-car')
Xiǎngbì yě shì.	'That's probably true.'
xiǎngbì	'presumably; most probably' ('think-necessary')

juéqǐ	'rise; become prominent': The verb *jué* originally referred to peaks towering over other mountains, but nowadays, it is almost a clichéd way to describe China's rapid economic growth. The sentence-final particle *ma* suggests obviousness.
tiānfāndìfù	'earthshaking' ('sky-upset-earth-overturn'): B gets it backward (*Nǐ shuōfǎn la; la = le + a*), starting with *dìfù* instead of *tiānfān*. *Dìfùtiānfān* is an occurring expression, but it is one with a slightly different meaning—one that is not so appropriate in the context. Mistaking the order of elements in a four-character phrase is a common learner error caused by attention to the meaning of the parts rather than the sound of the whole.
Duì, jiù ná yī-shí-zhù-xíng de "xíng" lái shuō.	'Right, so consider transport one of the basic necessities.': *yī-shí-zhù-xíng* 'the necessities' ('clothing-food-housing-getting around'). The Chinese phrase looks strange because of the conjunction of *xíng* in the compound and *xíng* as the item under discussion: *yī-shí-zhù-xíng de "xíng"* 'the *xíng* of *yī-shí-zhù-xíng*'; That phrase is embedded in the construction *ná ... lái shuō* 'when it comes to; talking about; consider'.
gāosù gōnglù	'expressway; highway' ('high-speed public-road')
yì nián bǐ yì nián duō	'more and more each year' ('one year than one year more'): cf. *yì tiān bǐ yì tiān lěng*
yǒusuǒ-bùtóng	'be different in some ways' ('have that-which is-not-same')
cháo zhèi ge fāngxiàng fāzhǎn	'developing in that direction': *cháo* is here used as a preposition with the meaning of 'toward; in'; The whole phrase, *cháo zhèi ge fāngxiàng* 'in this direction', is a complement to the verb *fāzhǎn* 'develop; grow' ('emit-develop').
shàng jiàxiào	'attend driving school': *jià* a specialized verb meaning 'pilot; drive'; cf. *jiàshǐ zhízhào<r>* 'driver's license'
bú shì nàme huí shìr	'it's not quite like that': *yì huí shìr* 'one thing; one and the same thing'; cf. *Zěnme yì huí shì<r>?* 'What's going on?'
zhèng zhǔnbèi mǎi	'just preparing to buy ...': The adverb *zhèng* 'exact' indicates that the preparation (*zhǔnbèi*) is in progress; cf. *zhènghǎo* 'as it happens'.
yǒu diǎnr yóuyù	'be a bit hesitant': *yóuyù* 'hesitate'
Qìyóufèi, guòlùfèi, wéixiū, bǎoxiǎn méi yí yàng piányi de.	'The cost of gasoline, tolls, maintenance, and insurance—none of it's cheap.': *Yí yàng* here is 'one kind' (not *yíyàng* 'the same'), so the verbal phrase reads, literally, 'there's not one kind that is cheap'.

Nǐ kàn zhè kōngqì, dōu shì chē duō gěi nào de.	'Look at this air; it's all caused by the number of cars.': *Nào* is the *nào* of *rènao* 'bustle and noise' and *nàozhōng* 'alarm clock'; as a verb, it can mean 'cause trouble' or 'muck something up', as here. *Gěi* serves the passive function described in §16.7, so *gěi nào* could be translated as 'get mucked up by'.
dǔzhe	'be blocked, clogged': *dǔ+de nǐ xīnfúqìzào* 'clogged to the point of making one edgy'; *xīnfúqìzào* 'impetuous, short-tempered' ('heart-float-temperament-irascible')
bù shǒu jiāotōng guīzé	'not follow the traffic regulations': *guīzé* 'rule; regulation' ('compass-principle')
Wánrmìng ne!	'to risk one's life needlessly; play with danger' ('play-life'): a colloquial (northern) term; The final *ne* conveys a slightly indignant tone.
bú àishìr	'not a hindrance' ('not hinder-things'): cf. *zhàng'ài* 'hinder; obstruct'
jiāotōng xìtǒng	'transportation system': *sìtōngbādá* 'extend in all directions' ('four-through-eight-reach'); cf. the apt name of Hong Kong's versatile transit card, the *Bādátōng* 'Octopus card'
gōng-qì shí zhàn yǐnèi cái sì máo qián	'you can go ten stops on a city bus for 40 cents': *gōng-qì* is short for *gōnggòng qìchē*; *shí zhàn* 'ten stops or stations'; *yǐnèi* 'within; as far as'
dìtiě yīlǜ liǎng kuài	'the subway is uniformly two yuan': *yīlǜ* 'equally; without exception; uniformly' ('one-standard'); The Beijing subway, unlike those in Shanghai and Hong Kong, uses a single price regardless of distance (with some exceptions).
qīngguǐ	'light-rail' ('light-track'): often elevated or on ground level rather than underground
Nín kě zhēn shi ménrqīng a!	'You're quite the expert!': *Ménrqīng* 'well-informed' ('subject-be clear'); a second case of an *r* suffix appearing in the middle of a compound (cf. *wánrmìng*)
Zǎojiù qīngchērèlù la!	'It's become routine for me!': *qīngchērèlù*, also *qīngchēshúlù*, 'second nature; routine task' ('light-vehicle-hot/familiar-route')
tiělù xìtǒng	'the railway system'
jiāotōng gōngjù	'means of transportation'
fāzhǎn xùnsù	'development has been very rapid'
dòngchē, gāosù tiělù, jīchǎng kuàiguǐ	'bullet train' ('move-train'), 'express line', 'airport express'

Bié gǎnshang Chūnyùn . . . guònián qījiān nín zuì hǎo bié gǎn nà rènao.	'Don't find yourself in the Spring Rush; during the New Year period, you'd best stay away from all the hullabaloo.': *Gǎn* can mean 'catch up with,' but here it means 'run into; find oneself in a situation.' The *Chūnyùn* ('spring-transport') period is around the Lunar New Year, when the transportation system is severely strained by the masses of people traveling to and from home for the holiday.
shì hěn kuài, kěshì . . .	The pattern with stressed *shì* followed by *kěshì* acknowledges a truth before mentioning a drawback. For example, 'it has been very fast, but . . .'
yǒu hěn dà chājù	'there's a big difference'
yǎhào	originally 'esteemed title' ('elegant-assumed name') but used ironically: *"Zhuāng zài qìchē lúnzi shang de guójiā"* ma! 'A country that runs on wheels.' The sentence-final particle *ma* here conveys the notion that the statement is not controversial.
huánjìng zàochéng de	'a product of the environment': *huánjìng* 'environment'; *zàochéng* 'give rise to' ('create-become')
děngyú méi tuǐ	'equivalent to not having legs'
chūmén chī ge fàn, chūmén mǎi gēn cōng	'go out to have a meal, go out to buy onions': *chāoshì* 'supermarket'; *cōng* 'onions'; *gēn* is the M
wèile xiǎnshì shēnfen	'in order to display status': The enlarged form, *wèile* 'for the sake of', rather than just *wèi*, is required when the object is verbal; cf. *Wèile wǒmen liǎng guó rénmín de yǒuyì gānbēi. Xiǎnshì* 'display' ('reveal-show')
rénjiā jiù juéde nǐ chénggōng	'people think you're successful'
rénjiā	'other people; he; them': *rénjiā shi láodòng mófàn* 'that guy's a model worker'
gǎnqing wèn nín yí jù	'Say, mind if I ask you something': *Gǎnqing* ('dare-emotion') is a colloquial expression that serves to introduce something pertinent to the argument; cf. English 'say; I dare say; as luck would have it; indeed; of course'. The response is *Nà gǎnqing hǎo!* 'I dare say that would be fine!'
xífur (north), *xífù* (other places)	'wife; young married woman' [coll]
Wǒ zū fáng, gōngyù.	'I rent a place, an apartment.': *zū* 'rent'; *chūzū* 'rent out', as in *chūzūchē*, the formal term for 'taxi'. *Fáng* here is used in a general sense meaning 'a place to live'; cf. *fángzi*.
gōngjiāokǎ	'transportation card': a contactless smart card for use on buses and other forms of transport

Nín zuòmèng qǔ xífur ne.	*zuòmèng* 'dream; daydream; have a pipe dream'; *qǔ* 'marry [a wife]' (cf. *jià* 'to marry [a husband]': *Wǒ mèi jiàle ge Àozhōurén*) The sense is 'dream on if you think you'll find a wife,' or, more idiomatically, 'fat chance you have of finding a wife.'
Zám yòu pǎotí le.	'We're off topic again.' ('we once-again flee-topic LE'): *zám* = *zánmen*; cf. *yánguīzhèngzhuàn* 'getting back to the topic' ('speech-return-proper-commentary')
fàngqì	'give something up'
wèile miànzi, wèile shūshì, wèile yǐnsī	'for face, for comfort, for privacy': *shūshì* ('comfort-fit'); *yǐnsī* ('cover-self')
jíshǐ nǐ hái děi wèi tā huā hěn duō qián	'even if you have to spend lots of money on account of it': *jíshǐ* 'even if'; *Jíshǐ xiàyǔ wǒ yě yào qù.* 'I'm going even if it rains.' *Shēng-lǎo-bìng-sǐ nín dōu děi guǎn.* 'You've got to deal with all the miseries.'
shēng-lǎo-bìng-sǐ	('birth-old age-illness-death'): the four banes of existence—a Buddhist notion
Nǐ bú shì qìchē tā yé, dào chéngle tā sūnzi.	'You're not the master of the car; rather, you become its grandson.': *dào* 'on the contrary'; *Tā yé … tā sūnzi* 'its master … its grandson'; cf. *lǎodàye* 'uncle; grandfather'
Wǒ hútu le.	'I'm confused.': *hútu* 'muddled; foolish'; cf. *húlihútu* 'confused'
yídàn nǐ mǎile	'once you've bought a car': *yídàn* 'once; some time or other; in a very short time'
Bú shì chē de zhǔrén le, érshi chē de núlì le.	'You're not the master of the car; you're its slave.'
Nín zhēn yōumò!	'Quite a sense of humor!': *yōumò* 'be humorous', a rare borrowing from English; cf. *yōumògǎn* 'sense of humor'
jǐ qǐlai xiàng shādīngyú guàntou	'be packed in like a can of sardines': *jǐ* 'to crowd'
yí fù kuījiǎ	'a suit of armor'
kě.yǐ cáng qǐlai	'you can hide'
bù xūyào miànlín gōngzhòng	'no need to face the public'
yě shì tuōlí qúnzhòng	'it also separates you from the masses': *qúnzhòng* ('multitude-mass'); cf. *gōngzhòng* ('public-mass')
Xuěfúlán, Kǎidílākè, Fútè, Àodí, Bēnchí, Fēngtián, Běntián, Xiàndài, Qǐyà	'Chevrolet', 'Cadillac', 'Ford', 'Audi', 'Benz', 'Toyota', 'Honda', 'Hyundai', 'Kia'

Exercise 5

Huídá wèntí.

1. *Zài Zhōngguó wèishénme yǒu rén bù xiǎng mǎi qìchē?*
2. *Xiànzài zài Zhōngguó jiāotōng de qíngkuàng zěnmeyàng?*
3. *Wèishénme shuō zài Zhōngguó méiyǒu chē méiyǒu guānxi?*
4. *Wèishénme shuō zài Měiguó bìxū děi yǒu qìchē?*
5. *Nà, zài Ōuzhōu ne? Shì bu shì méiyǒu qìchē yě hěn bù fāngbiàn?*
6. *"Nín xiǎng zài Zhōngguó zhǎo xífur ma?" Wèn nà ge wèntí tā shì bu shì pǎotí le?*
7. *Zhōngguó de lǎobǎixìng dōu xiǎng mǎi qìchē de huà, nà jiāotōng de qíngkuàng huì zěnmeyàng?*

16.9 Banquets and toasts

Banquets and formal meals in restaurants are almost always served in private rooms. The host generally sits farthest from the door, and guests are arranged to his or her left and right, according to rank. Guests seated in a place of honor may ritually offer the place to someone of about the same rank before falling in line with the host. A useful expression for resisting such social honors is *bùgǎndāng* 'I don't deserve it; you flatter me' ('not-dare-assume-[it]').

Conversation at banquets is usually light and humorous, with anecdotes, personal stories, and often a lot of language play. Foreigners with even quite advanced conversational abilities may find such talk difficult to follow. One subject that can break the ice is the food itself—food names, ingredients, regional dishes, and differences between Chinese and foreign eating habits and cuisines.

At a banquet or formal meal, there may be several drinks served, including mineral water, soft drinks, wines, and liquors. Although soft drinks may be drunk at one's pleasure, wines and liquors are usually drunk only with toasts, which may be made to individuals or to the whole table. Typically, one calls for a toast with *lái* 'come', which in this context has the sense of 'come on', and then follows with the expression *jìng [yí] ge jiǔ* ('show respect [with a cup of] wine'), adding *gānbēi* 'bottoms up' ('dry-glass'). *Gānbēi* ideally only applies to drinks served in small glasses.

Lái, wǒ lái jìng ge jiǔ. Gānbēi.	''Here, a toast. Bottoms up.'
Hǎo, hǎo, gānbēi.	'Good, cheers.'

In principle, toasts are reciprocal, meaning that if someone toasts you, then you can (and should) return the toast.

Lái, wǒ lái jìng ge jiǔ. Wèi xuéyè yǒu chéng gānbēi.	'I'd like to propose a toast. Here's to the success of your studies.'
Xièxie, yě zhù nín ~ dàjiā shēntǐ jiànkāng.	'Thank you, and to your health.'
Zhù dàjiā xīnxiǎngshìchéng.	'May your wishes come true.' ('heart-desire thing-succeed')

Females will find it easier to resist calls to *gānbēi*, since many women in China do not drink in public. Men who do not drink will have to develop ways of resisting calls to drink with a minimum loss of face. The following, rather embarrassing, conversation has a few pointers.

Jiǎ:	*Lái, lái gānbēi, gānbēi!*	'Come on, bottoms up!'
Yǐ:	*Bù hǎo yìsi, wǒ bù néng hē.*	'Sorry to say I don't drink.'
Jiǎ:	*Hē yì bēi mā.*	'Just a glass.' [urging]
Yǐ:	*Shízài bù hǎo yìsi, nín jìnxíng.*	'I'm really sorry; you carry on.'
Jiǎ:	*Hǎo, wǒ gān le, nín suíyì.*	'Okay, I'll drink up; you do what you can.'

NOTES

a. *Mā* as a final particle is associated with pleading or urging (and, in some contexts, obviousness); cf. *Nǐ bié fāhuǒ mā!* 'Don't get angry!' ('don't send forth-fire MA'); You should listen for *mā* and similar tone particles in colloquial discourse.

b. *Jìnxíng* 'carry on; advance' ('enter-go')

c. *Suíyì* ('follow your inclination'): cf. *yìsi* 'meaning'; *yìjiàn* 'opinion'; *Yǐ* is obviously trying to offer *Jiǎ* a way out, but the situation is awkward.

Other toasts may involve health, cooperation, success, and so on. The co-verb *wèi* 'for the sake of' or the verb *zhù* 'wish for' may introduce such toasts. For the actual invitation to drink, *jìng nǐmen yì bēi* ('respect you a cup') may be used instead of *gānbēi*. Here are some samples.

Wèi dàjiā de jiànkāng!	'Here's to everyone's health!'
Zhù nín jiànkāng!	'A glass to your health!'
Wèi zánmen gòngtóng de shìyè gānbēi!	'Here's to our common cause!'
Wèi nǐmen de xuéyè jìnbù gānbēi!	'Here's to progress in your studies!'
Wèi wǒmen de hézuò yúkuài!	'Here's to successful cooperation!'
Zhù nǐmen chénggōng!	'Success to you all!'
Jiāqiáng jiāoliú, zēngjìn yǒuyì!	'Strengthen exchanges and promote friendship!'

In giving toasts, it is important to raise the glass with two hands; extra deference can be shown by raising the glass high (still with two hands). At large gatherings, the host will normally toast first near the beginning of the meal; later, the head of the guest delegation will return the toast. When a number of tables are involved, hosts and guests may walk over to toast other tables. People will often stand to toast. Possible expressions of thanks include the following.

Xièxie nǐmen de kuǎndài.	'Thank you for the hospitality.'
Xièxie nǐmen de rèqíng zhāodài!	'Thanks for your warm reception!'

At banquets or other meals, Chinese often play very rapid games of *huáquán* 'finger guessing' or, more generally, *hējiǔ de yóuxì* 'drinking games', with the loser(s) drinking. Such games come in a number of varieties and require a lot of practice. With foreigners, the simple children's game of 'rock, paper, scissors' often substitutes for the real thing. That game is called *shítou, jiǎnzi, bù* ('stone, scissors, cloth') in Chinese, and participants play by shouting out the phrase *shítou, jiǎnzi, bù*, displaying their choice on the count of *bù*. Another game, *bàngzi lǎohǔ jī* 'club, tiger, chicken', is common and simple enough to learn. In addition to the three items mentioned in the name, there's a fourth: *chóngzi* 'insect'. The rules are: *Chóngzi chī bàngzi, bàngzi dǎ lǎohǔ, lǎohǔ chī jī, jī chī chóngzi.*

The cadence is fast, and participants simply utter their choice in unison, adding up wins and losses until some previously designated number is reached and losers drink. One version of another game, *xíngjiǔlìng* 'ordered to drink a toast', was popular with some of the great poets and literati of earlier times.

Exercise 6

Distinguish the following words by using them in short phrases. You may have to jog your memory by looking some of them up in a dictionary (or in the comprehensive vocabulary files on the *Learning Chinese* Web site).

fāshēng	*huāshēng*	*mǎshàng*	*fákuǎn*	*fādá*
qiǎo	*jiào*	*xiǎo*	*qiáo*	*jiāo*
bìyè	*bìxū*	*bǐjiào*	*búbì*	*liúxíng*
xíguàn	*xǐhuan*	*xīwàng*	*xiūxi*	*xīguā*
kǎolù	*kǎoshì*	*jǐngchá*	*wēixiǎn*	*yóuxíng*

16.10 Rhymes and rhythms

Among his many contributions to students of Chinese, the linguist *Chào Yuánrèn* wrote a three-volume series called *Readings in Sayable Chinese*, which was intended "to supply the advanced student of spoken Chinese with reading matter which he can actually use in his speech" (Chao, 1968, Vol I, p. iv). The series includes fables (such as 'The North Wind and the Sun,' cited in the final unit of this book), autobiographical fragments from his childhood and later life, and several translations of longer works, including a translation (revised and reedited from a translation that he made earlier) of Lewis Carroll's *Through the*

Xīn jiàn de gōngyùlóu (*Shànghǎi*)

Looking Glass. Chao's tour de force includes a Chinese version of the nonsense poem "Jabberwocky", which is unfortunately too long to cite here. Instead, we will cite Humpty Dumpty's song from *Through the Looking Glass* (ibid., Vol II, p. 150).

Hūndì Dūndì zuò de qiáng zhōngjiànr,	('Humpty Dumpty sit on wall middle')
Hūndì Dūndì yì gǔlu shuāi liǎng bànr,	('Humpty Dumpty one rumble fell two halves')
Suǒyǒu Huángdì de mǎ,	('all the emperor's horses')
gēn suǒyǒu Huángdì de rén,	('and all the emperor's men')
yě zài bù néng bǎ Hūndì Dúndì	('also again not able BA Humpty Dumpty')
pīnchéng ge húlúntún.	('join-become a whole lump')

NOTES

a. The *de* after *zuò* in the first line represents an unstressed pronunciation of *zài* 'at': *zuò zài qiáng zhōngjiànr*.

b. *Gǔlu* is onomatopoeic, depicting a rumbling sound of the stomach or, in this case, of a giant egg hitting the ground.

c. *Pīnchéng*, with *pīn* 'join' (as in *pīnyīn* 'join sounds; spell sounds') and *chéng* 'become'.

d. You won't find *húlúntún* in a dictionary. It was created by Chao as a rhyme for *rén* out of *húlún* 'whole' and *tún* 'assemble'.

In Unit 14, you learned a Chinese version of the song 'Red River Valley,' an old standard in the English-speaking world. Now here's a Chinese standard, the *Kāngdìng Qínggē* 'Kangding Love Song'. Kangding is a town in the west-central region of Sichuan Province, about 250 miles west of Chengdu, in what historically has been the Kham region of eastern Tibet. The Tibetan name of Kangding is *Dartsedo* (with various spellings). It lies in a steep valley over 8,000 feet above sea level. Only two of the four verses are given here; most Chinese will know the tune, and many will know the other verses as well. The song makes extensive use of the expressive phrase *liūliū* to provide metrical support. *Liūliū* is left untranslated.

> *Kāngdìng Qínggē*
>
> *Pǎomǎ liūliū de shānshang, yì duǒ liūliū de yún yō,*
> 'On Paoma Mountain, a cloud'
> ('paoma LIULIU DE mountain-on, one M LIULIU DE clouds YO')
>
> *duānduān liūliū de zhào zài, Kāngdìng liūliū de chéng yō,*
> 'perfectly reflects light from the town of Kangding,'
> ('proper LIULIU DE reflect on Kangding LIULIU DE town YO')
>
> *yuèliang wānwān, Kāngdìng liūliū de chéng yō!*
> 'with the rounded moon over Kangding!'
> ('moon rounded, Kangding LIULIU DE town YO')
>
> *Lǐjiā liūliū de dàjiě, réncái liūliū de hǎo yō,*
> 'The oldest girl in the Li family, a good person,'
> ('Li-family LIULIU DE big-sister, human-value LIULIU DE good YO')

Zhāngjiā liūliū de dàgē, kànshang liūliū de tā yō,
'The oldest brother in the Zhang family regards her highly,'
('Zhang-family LIULIU DE big-brother, view-highly LIULIU DE her YO')

yuèliang wānwān, kànshang liūliūde tā yō!
'with the rounded moon, regards her highly!'
('moon rounded, view-highly LIULIU DE her YO')

Summary

Improvement	*Tā juéde zhǐyǒu qù Zhōngguó cái nénggòu gèng hǎo de tígāo tā de Zhōngwén tīng-shuō nénglì.*
V-zhe V-zhe	*Liǎngge rén liáozhe liáozhe, Déyáng jiu dào le.*
Stay in touch	*Xīwàng néng bǎochí liánxì; duōduō bǎozhòng.*
Adverbial *de*	*Tā hěn nǔlì <de> gōngzuò.*
Reduplication	*Wǒ dōu cōngcōng-mángmáng de pǎolái-pǎoqù.*
Onomatopoeia	*Píngzi pā de yì shēng zhà le.*
Accent	*dài yìdiǎnr nánfāng de kǒuyīn*
Besides	*Chúle xīngqīsì yǐwài, měitiān dōu yǒu kè.*
More and more	*Dà chéngshì yuè lái yuè wēixiǎn.*
	Pá+de yuè gāo, shuāi+de yuè cǎn.
No need to	*Búbì huànchē.*
Indefinites	*Wǒ shénme dōu bú pà. / Něitiān dōu xíng.*
Even	*Lián lǎoshī yě bù zhīdào zěnme xiě.*
Paired indefinites	*Xiǎng chī shénme jiù chī shénme.*
What religion?	*Nǐ xìn shénme jiào? / Wǒ xìn Huíjiào.*
Write down	*Qǐng bǎ tā xiě xiàlai.*
Recognize	*Nǐ cāi de chū <lai> wǒ shi shéi ma?*
To move in	*Wǒmen běnyuè chū cái bān jìnlai de.*
By	*Tā bèi jǐngchá zhuāzǒu le.*
Get ... by	*Wǒ de zìxíngchē jiào rén gěi tōu le.*
Driving	*Wǒ juéde kāichē bìng bù róngyì.*

Status	*yě shì wèile xiǎnshì shēnfen*
Toasts	*Lái, wǒ lái jìng ge jiǔ.Gānbēi.*
	Wèi dàjiā de jiànkāng gānbēi!

NOTE TO THE EPIGRAPH

Like the English version that begins 'Do unto others', this version has deep antecedents. In the *Lúnyǔ* ('The Analects'), Confucius answers the question 'Is there one saying that always applies?' with the single word *shù* 'empathy', before going on to elaborate with *jǐ suǒ bú yù*. This saying is, of course, written in literary style, so you can expect a proliferation of single-syllable words. Many of these words survive in the modern language either in compounds or in formal registers: *jǐ* = *zìjǐ*; *yù* = *xiǎngyào*; *wù* = *bú yào*; *yú* 'to' (cf. *guānyú* 'about; dealing with'; *duìyú* 'toward'; *wèiyú* 'located at'); *rén* 'people' [in the sense of 'others'].

Unit 17

Dà jiāng dōng qù, làng táo jìn qiān gǔ fēngliú rénwù.
'The great river flows eastward, its waters having scoured away a thousand years of great men.'
('Great river east goes, waves scour entirely a-millennia-of ancient refined personages.')
—From *Chì Bì Huái Gǔ*, by *Sū Shì*

The theme of this unit is geography: large towns, small towns, rivers and plains, cities and countryside. The opening narrative is a geographical sketch. It is followed by a dialogue on places to visit in Beijing. Then there is a section that deals with requests and complaints, from the mild to the indignant. This is followed by a review of modification (especially *de* patterns) with a number of dialogues that involve identifying things and people by shape, clothing, and other features. We return to shopping with a dialogue about buying a chop—or seal—and then continue with another dialogue about someone who has moved from China to Australia. In 17.8, the discussion of cars and brands that began in the last unit continues, and this unit ends with a provocative dialogue between two people who have had an unpleasant encounter on a busy street. As always, there is a selection of rhymes and rhythms at the end.

A note to the epigraph is located at the end of the unit.

Contents

17.1 A geography lesson

Chinese often characterize their country as 'large in size, rich in resources, and long in history'—reducing the phrasing to four-syllable chunks of the type preferred in formal expressions: *Zhōngguó dìdà wùbó, lìshǐ yōujiǔ.* The colloquial equivalent would be *Dìfang hěn dà, zīyuán hěn duō, lìshǐ cháng jiǔ.* Because so much of the population is concentrated in the eastern half of the country, it is easy to underestimate the vastness of the great northwest, which stretches all the way to that narrow finger of land called the Wakhan Corridor in Afghanistan.

The following—which can be thought of as the record of an oral presentation—deals with Chinese geography (*Zhōngguó dìlǐ*) and includes short comments on the following subjects: China's two great rivers (*liǎng tiáo dà hé*), the *Huáng Hé* 'Yellow River' and *Cháng Jiāng* 'Yangtze River' (and, incidentally, why one is a *hé* and the other is a *jiāng*); the Three Gorges (*Sānxiá*), situated in the middle reaches of the Yangtze; the mountains and deserts (*gāoshān, shāmò*) in the western and northwestern regions of the country; population disparities (*Zhōngguó rénkǒu zuì duō de dìfang dōu zài dōngbù*) and agricultural production; the inland basin of Sichuan (*Sìchuān shi ge péndì*), the most populous province; and, finally, the Five Sacred Mountains (*Wǔ Yuè: wǔ zuò yǒumíng de shān*) that have been pilgrimage destinations for centuries.

Zhōngguó dìdà wùbó

Wǒ jīntiān yào gēn nǐmen shuō yìdiǎnr Zhōngguó dìlǐ. Nǐmen dōu zhīdao, Zhōngguó shi yí ge hěn dà de guójiā, rénkǒu yě hěn duō. Zhōngguórén de shuōfǎ shi: "Zhōngguó dì dà wù bó, lìshǐ yōujiǔ." 'Wù bó' de yìsi shi zīyuán hěn duō, hěn fēngfù'; 'yōujiǔ' de yìsi shi 'hěn cháng shíjiān'. Kànkan dìtú jiù zhīdao Zhōngguó yǒu duō dà le. Cháoxiǎn, Éluósī, Měnggǔ, Āfùhàn, Bājīsītǎn, Níbó'ěr, Yìndù, Miǎndiàn, Lǎowō, hái yǒu Yuènán dōu shì Zhōngguó de línguó.

Huáng Hé gēn Cháng Jiāng

Zhōngguó yǒu liǎng tiáo dà hé, Huáng Hé gēn Cháng Jiāng. Huáng Hé zài běibianr, Cháng Jiāng zài nánbianr. Shànghǎi lí Cháng Jiāng de rùhǎikǒu hěn jìn; Nánjīng, Wǔhàn, Chóngqìng zài Cháng Jiāng biānr shang. Huáng Hé gēn Cháng Jiāng de shuǐ dōu shì cóng Qīng-Zàng Gāoyuán liú xiàlai de. Huáng Hé liúguo Gānsù, Nèiměnggǔ, Shǎnxī hé Shānxī de shíhou, shuǐ biàn+de yuè lái yuè huáng. Yīnwèi zhèi xiē dìfang de tǔ shi huángsè de, jiào huángtǔ, suǒ.yǐ Zhōngguórén jiào zhèi tiáo hé Huáng Hé. Huáng Hé shi huáng de, běifāng nóngcūn de tiān, dì, hé fángzi yě dōu shì huáng de.

    Měinián xiàtiān, běifāng xiàyǔ de shíhou, Huáng Hé de shuǐ bǐjiào duō. Kěshì bú xiàyǔ de shíhou, Huáng Hé de shuǐ jiu hěn shǎo, yǒu shíhou shènzhì huì duànliú. Wǒ tīngshuō chàbuduō sānshí nián yǐqián, zài Shāndōng de Jǐ'nán, kě.yǐ qí zìxíngchē guò Huáng Hé. Yīnwèi shuǐ yǒu shíhou bù duō, suǒ. yǐ zài Huáng Hé shang kànbudào shénme dàchuán, zhǐ kàndedào hěn duō xiǎo de dùchuán. Xiàyǔ xià+de duō de shíhou, Huáng Hé yě yǒu hóngshuǐ de wèntí. Zài 1855 nián, Huáng Hé xiàyóu fànlàn. Jiéguǒ ne, Huáng Hé zài xiàyóu rùhǎikǒu cóng yuánlái de Shāndōng yǐnán gǎidào Shāndōng běibù. Zài nà cì shuǐzāi zhōng hěn duō rén sàngshēng.

Pǔ Jiāng shi Cháng Jiāng de yì tiáo zhīliú.

Cháng Jiāng shi Zhōngguó de lìngwài yì tiáo dà hé. Cháng Jiāng yě jiào
'Yángzǐ Jiāng'. Qíshí, Cháng Jiāng zài bùtóng de dìfang yǒu bùtóng de míngzi.
Bǐrú shuō, zài Shànghǎi, Nánjīng nèi xiē dìfang dàjiā jiào Cháng Jiāng
Yángzǐ Jiāng. Zài Sìchuān, Yúnnán nèi xiē dìfang dàjiā jiào Cháng Jiāng
Jīnshā Jiāng. Yěxǔ yīnwèi yǐqián dào Zhōngguó de wàiguórén dàduōshù dōu
dāi zai Shànghǎi dào Nánjīng nà yí duàn, suǒ.yǐ tāmen dōu yòng Yángzǐ zhèi
ge míngzi.

Hé gēn jiāng

Nǐmen yěxǔ juéde hěn qíguài, wèishénme Zhōngwén yǒu 'hé' yě yǒu 'jiāng',
zhèi liǎng ge cí? Wǒmen shuō Cháng Jiāng, Zhū Jiāng (jīngguò Guǎngzhōu de
nèi tiáo dà hé), hái yǒu Hàn Jiāng (zài Guǎngdōng), Mǐn Jiāng (zài Fújiàn),
hé Lí Jiāng (zài Guǎngxī). Dōu zài nánbianr. (Cháng Jiāng yǐnán de dìfang
yě kě.yǐ jiào Jiāngnán—xiàng Chángshā, Wǔhàn, Nánchāng, Nánjīng nèi xiē
chéngshì.) Hé ne, xiàng Huáng Hé, Huái Hé (zài Jiāngsū, Ānhuī, Húběi)
dàduōshù dōu zài běibù. 'Jiāng' zhèi ge cí bǐjiào lǎo, chúle hé de míngzi yǐwài,
dàjiā píngcháng bú tài yòng le. Píngcháng shuōhuà de shíhou, wǒmen yòng
'hé', bǐfang shuō: 'Zhōngguó yǒu liǎng tiáo dà hé'; 'Měiguó zuì cháng de hé shì
Mìxīxībǐ Hé.'

Sānxiá

'Sānxiá' nǐmen yěxǔ tīngshuōguo ba. Zài Cháng Jiāng zhōngyóu, héshuǐ liúguo yìxiē hěn zhǎi de shānqū. Yǒu yí duàn, Cháng Jiāng zhǐ yǒu chàbuduō yìbǎi mǐ kuān, liǎng biānr dōu shi yòu gāo yòu dǒu de shān, hěn zhuàngguān. Yóukè dōu hěn xǐhuan kàn zhèyàng de fēngjǐng. Kěshì yěxǔ nǐmen yě tīngshuōguo, wèile fāzhǎn diànlì, zài Cháng Jiāng Sānxiá de zhè yí duàn, xiūle yí ge hěn dà de shuǐbà, héshuǐ yānmòle hěn duō cūnzi, nóngmín děi bān dao bǐjiào gāo de dìfang huòzhě děi qù biéde dìfang.

Gāoshān, shāmò

Nǐmen xǐhuan páshān ma? Xǐhuan tànsuǒ dàzìrán ma? Nǐ kànkan Zhōngguó dìtú, nǐ huì kàndào Zhōngguó dàbùfen dōu shì gāoshān huòzhě shāmò. Shìjiè shang zuì gāo de shān, hěn duō zuòluò zai Xīzàng. Zhūmùlángmǎfēng jiu zài Xīzàng hé Níbó'ěr de biānjiè shang. Zhōngguó xīběi yǒu liǎng tiáo dà shānmài: zuì běibianr de shi Tiān Shān; gèng nán yìdiǎnr, zài Xīnjiāng hé Xīzàng zhōngjiān shi Kūnlún shānmài. Xīběi yě yǒu hěn duō shāmò—shuǐ shǎo, shù shǎo, rén shǎo, tàiyáng hěn rè de dìfang. Yào guò shāmò háishi qí luòtuo zuì hǎo, yīnwèi luòtuo kě.yǐ zǒu hěn yuǎn de lù ér bú yòng hē shuǐ.

Rénkǒu

Zhōngguó xībù dōu shì shān, běibù shāmò hěn duō. Nèi xiē dìfang yīnwèi shuǐ bù duō huò tǔrǎng bù hǎo, bù néng zhòng zhuāngjia, suǒ.yǐ rén bù duō. Nǐ dǎkāi yì běn Zhōngguó dìtú kàn yì zhāng dìxíngtú, nǐ jiu huì zhīdao wèishénme Zhōngguó rénkǒu zuì duō de dìfang dōu zài dōngbù. Dōnghù, yóuqí shi Huáběi Píngyuán hé Cháng Jiāng zhōng-xiàyóu píngyuán, dìshì bǐjiào píng, tǔrǎng xiāngduì féiwò, kě.yǐ zhòng xiǎomài gēn shuǐdào. Mín yǐ shí wéi tián; dōngbù zhòngzhíqū jiu jùjīle dàliàng de rénkǒu.

Sìchuān

Sìchuān shi Zhōngguó de rénkǒu dà shěng, dànshi rén duō dì shǎo, suǒ.yǐ hěn duō rén xuǎnzé wàichū dǎgōng. Sìchuān shi ge péndì, sìbiānr dōu shì shān, *zhōngjiān hěn dà de dìfang dōu bǐjiào dī. Sìchuānhuà yě suàn shi Běifāng fāngyán, kěshì Sìchuānrén shuō Pǔtōnghuà dài hěn zhòng de dāngdì kǒuyīn, suǒ.yǐ wàiguó lái de xuéshēng yěxǔ zài nàr zhù yí duàn shíjiān yǐhòu cái néng tīngdeguàn.*

Wǔ Yuè

Zhōngguórén juéde shān suīrán hěn měi hěn zhuàngguān, dànshi duì shān huáiyǒu jìngwèi de xīn. Chuántǒng de Zhōngguórén rènwéi shān shi shén, xiān, móguǐ zhù de dìfang, hěn wēixiǎn. Búguò yǒu xiē shān Zhōngguó rén háishi hěn xǐhuan qù. Wǔ Yuè shi wǔ zuò yǒumíng de shān. (Yuè jiùshi gāodà de shān de yìsi.) Dōngyuè shi Tàishān (zài Shāndōng), Běiyuè shi Héngshān (zài Shānxī), Xīyuè shi Huáshān (zài Shǎnxī), Nányuè shi Héngshān (zài Húnán), Zhōngyuè shi Sōngshān (zài Hénán). Yǒu liǎng zuò jiào Héngshān, duì ma? Liǎng zuò Héngshān dúyīn shi yíyàng, kěshì Hànzì bù yíyàng. Shānxī de Héngshān shi 'shùxīnpáng' de 'héng' zì (恆), Húnán de shi 'shuānglìrén' de 'héng' zì (衡). Zhōngguó yě yǒu sì dà Fójiào míngshān. Sìchuān de Éméi Shān jiùshi qízhōng zhī yī. Zhōngguórén

Yùlóng Xuěshān (Yúnnán)

xǐhuan pá zhèi xiē míngshān, yě chángcháng zài shāndǐng zhù yí ge
wǎnshang kàn rìchū. Yīnwèi zuìjìn jiànle hěn duō lǎnchē, kě.yǐ cóng shān
xia zuò chē dào shānyāo huò shāndǐng, suǒ.yǐ xiànzài jiùshi niánjì dà
yìdiǎnr de yóukè yě kě.yǐ pá míngshān. Kěshì wǒ zìjǐ juéde páshān yīnggāi
shi fèilì de huódòng, bù yīnggāi tài qīngsōng, háishi zǒu shàngqu, pá
shàngqu hǎo, shíjiān cháng yìdiǎnr, nà wúsuǒwèi, zhèi yàng cái kě.yǐ shuō
shi hǎohàn!

SHĒNGCÍ

zīyuán hěn duō, *hěn fēngfù*	'lots of plentiful resources': *zīyuán* 'natural resources'; *fēngfù* 'plentiful; rich'
Zhōngguó de línguó	'China's neighbors': *Jiānádà shi Měiguó línguó zhī yī.*
cóng Qīng-Zàng *Gāoyuán liú xiàlai de*	'flows down from the *Qīnghǎi–Xīzàng* Plateau: *Gāoyuán: hǎibá bǐjiào gāo de dà piàn píngdì*; *liú* 'flow', cf. *liúguò* 'flow through'
yǒu shíhou shènzhì huì *duànliú*	'sometimes the flow can even cease': *shènzhì* 'to the point of; even; so much so that'; *Tā máng+de shènzhì hǎo jǐ yè méi shuìjiào* 'She's been busy to the point of not sleeping for several nights'; *duànliú* 'for the flow to cease' ('break-flow')
dùchuán	'ferry' ('cross a river-boat')
yǒu hóngshuǐ de wèntí	'have flooding problems' ('flood-water')
Huáng Hé xiàyóu *fànlàn*	'the lower reaches of the Yellow River flooded': *xiàyóu, zhōngyóu, shàngyóu* 'the lower reaches, middle reaches, upper reaches [of a river]'; *fànlàn* 'overflow; spread unchecked' ('drift-overflow')
Shāndōng yǐnán	'to the south of Shandong': cf. *Shāndōng nánbianr* 'south of Shandong'

Zài nà cì shuǐzāi zhōng hěn duō rén sàngshēng.	'Lots of people lost their lives in that flood.': The bound form *zāi* 'disaster' combines with whatever causes the disaster to form freestanding compounds. For example, *shuǐzāi* 'floods'; *chóngzāi* 'plague of insects'; *tiānzāi* 'natural disaster'; *huǒzāi* 'fire'; *hànzāi* 'drought'; *sàngshēng* 'lose one's life' ('lose by death-life').
Jīnshā Jiāng	'The River of Golden Sand' ('gold-sand-river'): name of the Yangtze along the Sichuan–Yunnan border
dāi zai Shànghǎi dào Nánjīng nà yí duàn	'lived in the stretch of river between Shanghai and Nanjing': *dāi* = *tíngliú* 'stop and stay'; *yí duàn* 'a section of'
liúguò yìxiē hěn zhǎi de shānqū	'pass through some very narrow mountainous areas': *shānqū* = *shān duō de dìqū*
zhǐyǒu chàbuduō yìbǎi mǐ kuān	'only about 100 meters wide': *kuān de xiāngfǎn shi zhǎi*
yòu gāo yòu dǒu de shān	*dǒu* 'steep': *zhèi ge shānpōr tài dǒu* 'this slope is too steep'
wèile fāzhǎn diànlì	'in order to develop electrical power': *fāzhǎn* 'develop; expand; grow'; *xiūle yí ge hěn dà de shuǐbà* 'built a great dam'; *xiū* can mean repair (*xiū biǎo* 'repair a watch') or build a road or something that requires land clearance (*xiū tiělù* 'build a railway'); *shuǐbà* 'dam' ('water-embankment')
héshuǐ yānmòle hěnduō cūnzi	'The river water inundated a lot of villages': *yānmò* 'inundate' ('drown-sink')

tànsuǒ dàzìrán	'explore nature': *tànsuǒ* 'explore; probe / explorations' ('inquire-search'); *dàzìrán* 'nature' ('big-nature'); *shāmò* 'desert' ('sand-desert')
zuòluò zai Xīzàng	'are located in Tibet': *zuòluò* 'be located; be situated' ('sit-fall')
Zhūmùlángmǎfēng jiu zài Xīzàng hé Níbó'ěr de biānjiè shang.	'Mt. Everest is on the border between Tibet and Nepal.': *fēng* 'peak' [bound form]; *biānjiè* 'border' ('side-limit')
shānmài	'mountain range' ('mountain-vein')
tǔrǎng bù hǎo, bù néng zhòng zhuāngjia	'the soil's not good; you can't plant crops': *zhòng* 'to plant'; *zhuāngjia* 'crops; farming'
dìxíngtú	'relief map' ('land-form-map'): *Huáběi Píngyuán* 'North China Plains'; *Huá* is one of the names of China; cf. *Zhōnghuá Rénmín Gònghéguó, Zhōnghuá Mínguó.*
tǔrǎng xiāngduì féiwò	'the soil is comparatively fertile': *xiāngduì* 'relatively; comparatively' ('reciprocal-facing'): *xiāngduì lái shuō* 'relatively speaking'; *Àiyīnsītǎn de xiāngduìlùn* 'Einstein's Theory of Relativity'; *xiǎomài* 'wheat' ('small-wheat'); *shuǐdào* 'paddy rice' ('water-rice plant')
Mín yǐ shí wéi tiān.	'For the people, food is the only pleasure.' ('people take food to-be sweet')
Dōngbù zhòngzhíqū jiu jùjīle dàliàng de rénkǒu.	'The eastern growing area attracted the greatest number of people.': *zhòngzhí* 'to plant, grow' ('plant-plants'); *jùjī* 'amass; collect' ('gather-accumulate'); *rénmen jùjī qǐlai le* 'people gathered together'; *jùjī zai chūshìr xiànchǎng* 'they gathered at the site of the accident'

Hěn duō rén xuǎnzé wàichū dǎgōng.	'A lot of people choose to work away from home.': *xuǎnzé* 'choose'; *wàichū* 'go out; away from home' ('away-go out'); *dǎgōng* 'have a temporary job; do manual work; do odd jobs' ('hit work')
dài hěn zhòng de dāngdì kǒuyīn	'have a heavy local accent': *dài kǒuyīn* 'have an accent' ('carry mouth-pronunciation')
duì shān huáiyǒu jìngwèi de xīn	'regard mountains with awe': *huáiyǒu* 'cherish; possess; hold'; *huáiyǒu xǔduō xīnlǐ zhàng'ài* 'have a lot of hang-ups' ('heart-in obstacles'); *jìngwèi* 'hold in awe; revere' ('respect-fear'); *jìngwèi de* 'with awe'; *jìngwèi zhī gǎn* 'feelings of awe'
rènwéi shān shi shén, xiān, móguǐ zhù de dìfang	'feel that mountains are places where spirits, immortals, or demons live': *rènwéi* 'think; regard . . . as' ('recognize-to be'); *Wǒ rènwéi tā shi duì de* 'I think she's right'; *xiān* 'celestial beings'; *móguǐ* 'demons'
dúyīn shi yíyàng	'read the same way': *dúyīn* 'reading pronunciation'; Some characters have a reading pronunciation that is different from the ordinary spoken pronunciation (e.g., *le* read as *liǎo*).
jiùshi qízhōng zhī yī	'that's one of them': *qízhōng* 'among them' ('their-midst'); cf. *qíshí* 'actually' ('its-actual'); *Yígòng yǒu èrshíbā ge xuéshēng, qízhōng Rìběn rén zuì duō. Zài Xīnxīlán de shí dà chūkǒu shìchǎng zhōng, yǒu liù ge zài Yàzhōu, qízhōng Rìběn shi Xīnxīlán chǎnpǐn chūkǒu de dì-èr dà shìchǎng* 'Six of New Zealand's ten largest export markets are in Asia, of which Japan is the second largest.'

kàn rìchū	'watch the sunrise': *rìchū* 'sunrise' ('sun-come out'); cf. *rìluò* 'sunset' ('sun-fall')
jiànle hěn duō lǎnchē	'have built a lot of cable cars': *jiàn* 'build; establish; found; set up'; *lǎnchē* 'cable cars' ('basket-vehicles')
dào shānyāo huò shāndǐng	'to the mid-slopes or the peak': *shānyāo* 'mid-slope' ('mountain-waist'); *shāndǐng* 'top of a mountain'
Yīnggāi shi fèilì de huódòng, bù yīnggāi tài qīngsōng.	'It should be a strenuous activity rather than something relaxed.': *fèilì* 'requiring great effort' ('exert-strength'); *huódòng* 'activity' ('live-move'); *qīngsōng* 'be relaxed' ('light-lax')
wúsuǒwèi	'never mind; it doesn't matter' ('nothing-to be-said')
hǎohàn	'man; hero' ('good-Han')

Exercise 1

Translate the following excerpts into English.

1. *Huáng Hé liúguò Gānsù, Nèiměnggǔ Shānxī hé Shǎnxī de shíhou, shuǐ biàn+de yuè lái yuè huáng.*
2. *Yǐqián dào Zhōngguó de wàiguórén dàduōshù dōu dāi zai Shànghǎi dào Nánjīng nà yí duàn.*
3. *Wèile fāzhǎn diànlì, zài Cháng Jiāng Sānxiá de zhè yí duàn, xiūle yí ge hěn dà de shuǐbà, héshuǐ yānmòle hěn duō cūnzi.*
4. *Yào guò shāmò, háishi qí luòtuo zuì hǎo, yīnwèi luòtuo kě.yǐ zǒu hěn yuǎn de lù ér bú yòng hē shuǐ.*

Huídá wèntí.

1. *Línguó shi shénme yìsi? Bǎ Měiguó de línguó liè xiàlai. Fǎguó de ne?*
2. *Huáng Hé cóng nǎ.lǐ liúdào nǎ.lǐ?*

4. *Wèishénme xiàmian de Zhōngguó dìtú yǒu yí ge Shānxī* (Shanxi), *yě yǒu yí ge Shānxī* (Shaanxi)?
5. *Zhōngwén zěnme yǒu 'hé', yě yǒu 'jiāng' nèi liǎng ge cí?*
6. *Zhūmùlángmǎfēng zài nǎr? Yīngwén de míngzi shi shénme?*
7. *Luòtuo Yīngwén zěnme shuō? Luòtuo zài nǎ.lǐ zuì chángjiàn?*

In an essay, describe the Mississippi River (or some other river with which you are familiar) to friends in China.

17.2 Places to see in Beijing

Professor *Kǒng* from *Běi Dà* is visiting *Máo Dàwéi*'s family in *Bōshìdùn* 'Boston'. Professor *Kǒng* is about the same age as *Dàwéi*'s father, so he addresses him as *shūshu* 'uncle'.

Máo:	*Kǒng shūshu, nín shi Běijīng lái de, néng bu néng gàosu wǒ Běijīng yǒu xiē shénme hǎowánr de dìfang?*	'Uncle Kong, you're from Beijing, can you tell me what sort of interesting places there are in Beijing?'
Kǒng:	*Hǎowánr a, āi, hǎowánr de dìfang hěn duō ya: chéng lǐ yǒu Gùgōng—jiùshi yǐqián de Zǐjìnchéng. Yě yǒu Tiān'ānmén Guǎngchǎng, Tiāntán, Běihǎi. Hěn duō ya!*	'Interesting places, huh . . . wow, there are a lot of interesting places: in town, there's the Palace Museum— the former Forbidden City. And there's Tiananmen Square, the Temple of Heaven, and North Lake. Lots!'
Máo:	*Wǒ tīngshuō Běihǎi tèbié měi.*	'I've heard that Beihai is especially attractive.'

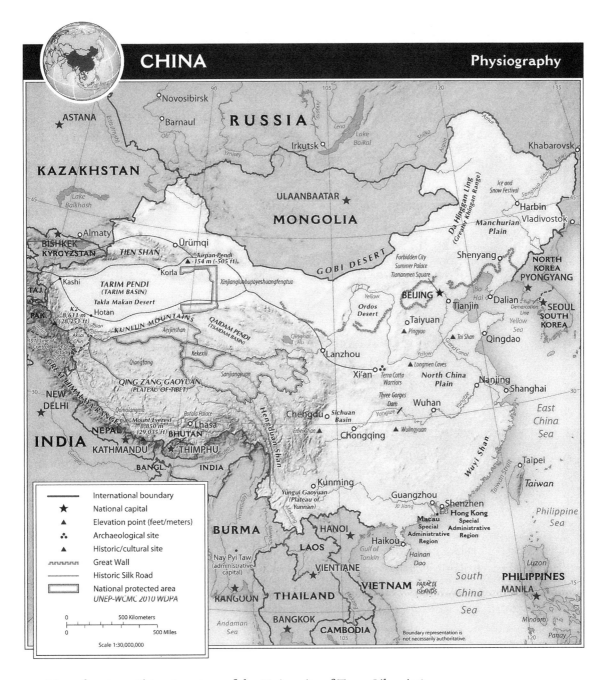

Map of eastern China (courtesy of the University of Texas Libraries)

Kǒng:	*Shì a, nà shi yīnwèi Běihǎi Gōngyuánr yǒu Báitǎ.*	'Yes, that's because Beihai Park has the White Dagoba.'
Máo:	*Wèishénme yǒu Báitǎ jiù měi ne?*	'What's so attractive about the White Dagoba?'
Kǒng:	*Báitǎ hěn piàoliang, yǒu Zàngzú de fēnggé. Fēngjǐng yě hěn měi: zài xiǎoshān shang, qiánbianr yǒu hú, liǎngbianr dōu shi shù.*	'The White Dagoba is very attractive; it's Tibetan style. The scenery is also very beautiful: it's on a small hill with a lake in front and trees all around.'
Máo:	*Nà, chéng wài ne?*	'How about out of town?'
Kǒng:	*Chéng wài a, xīběibianr yǒu Yíhéyuán, Yuánmíngyuán, hái yǒu Běijīng Dàxué gēn Qīnghuá Dàxué. Yǒu rén shuō Qīnghuá shi Zhōngguó de MIT.*	'Out of town, there's the Summer Palace in the northwest, Yuangming Gardens, and Peking and Tsinghua Universities. Some people say that Tsinghua is China's MIT.'
Máo:	*Yīnggāi shuō MIT shi Měiguó de Qīnghuá.*	'They should say that MIT is America's Tsinghua.'

NOTES

a. *Gùgōng* ('old-palace'); *Zǐjìnchéng* ('purple-forbidden-city'); *Tiān'ānmén* ('heaven-peace-gate'); *Tiāntán* ('heaven-altar'); *Báitǎ* ('white-stupa'); *Yuánmíngyuán* ('round-splendor-garden')

b. *Liǎngbianr dōu shi shù*, with *shì* rather than *yǒu*, means not just that 'there are trees on both sides' but that 'both sides are all trees'—'there's a profusion of trees around'.

VOCABULARY

Zàngzú	'Tibetan-ethnic group'
fēnggé	'style' ('wind-pattern')
fēngjǐng	'landscape; scenery' ('wind-scene')

Exercise 2

With yourself as the main character, paraphrase (and, if you like, elaborate on) the narrative below in Chinese. Then, in groups of three or four, compare your responses with classmates, and create a single final version to read aloud (or hand in). Your teacher will provide some guidance if needed.

We got in from Shanghai at ten in the morning. It was a beautiful day with blue, sunny skies. Beijing rarely has such clear skies, so we decided to go and see the Great Wall! There wasn't much time, so we had to hurry. We took a taxi to the hostel (*zhāodàisuǒ*) and dumped our bags. Then we caught the subway to *Dōngzhímén* ('east-direct-gate'), ran to the bus station, and found the bus to *Mì Yún*. The bus pulled out as soon as we got on. It took an hour and a half to get to *Mì Yún*. From *Mì Yún*, we took a minibus to *Sīmǎtái*. We arrived at the parking lot below the wall at 3:00. As soon as we arrived, we climbed up to the wall. The lower parts were covered with tourists, but the higher parts were almost empty. It took about two hours to go all the way (*yìzhí dào*) to the highest point and back. Going back, we got caught in traffic jams (*dǔchē*), so we didn't get back to Beijing until after 11:00. By that time, the only place that was open was the *Dūnhuáng* ('The Den') in *Cháoyáng* District (*qū*), so we had a meal there—hamburgers and beer. What a great day!

17.3 Requests

Recognizing that requests for assistance are impositions on another person's time, speakers can couch their requests in the form of a question that at least gives the potential benefactor a choice. Alternatively, they can begin the request with a covering phrase such as *máfan nǐ* 'may I bother you' or *tuō nǐ yí jiàn shìr* 'mind if I ask a favor' ('entrust you one M thing'). The latter is more common

Báitǎ shi Zàngzú de fēnggé.

when the request involves an item of business rather than just passing help. Because someone—oneself or another—stands to gain from a request, it may also be associated with preverbal phrases such as the following examples.

bāng wǒ	'help me to'
gěi nǐ	'for your benefit'
tì wǒ	'for me' [in my place]
wèi tāmen	'for their sake'

Exercise 3

Combine the previous phrases with the following actions to form requests. There may be more than one option for each. (*Qǐng* can convey a sufficient tone of politeness.)

1. *mǎi yì zhāng fēijīpiào*	'buy a plane ticket'
2. *bǎ biǎo tiánhǎo*	'fill out a form'
3. *jiào ge chūzūchē*	'order a taxi'
4. *bǎ bāoguǒ dǎkāi*	'open the package'
5. *mǎi yí ge xiāngzi*	'buy a trunk'
6. *zuò wǎnfàn*	'make dinner'
7. *zhǎo ge jìniànpǐn*	'find a souvenir'
8. *zhǎo 314 hào de fángjiān*	'find room #314'
9. *shàngwǎng*	'get online'
10. *bǎ píngzi dǎkāi*	'open a bottle'
11. *jiē diànhuà*	'answer the phone'
12. *yòng Hànzì xiě míngzi*	'write a name in characters'
13. *bǎ huāpíng fàng gāo yìdiǎnr*	'put the vase higher up'
14. *jièyān*	'give up smoking' ('prohibit-cigarettes')
15. *tiāo yí gè*	'pick one'

NOTE

The co-verb *wèi* (as in *wèishénme*, contrasted with *wéi* 'be; make', with which it has a historical connection) seems particularly common in titles of songs and stories. Here are some examples.

Wǒ wèi nǐ zhùfú.	'I wish you happiness' ('I for you wish-luck') [song]
Wèi nǐ zhōngqíng.	'Walk the line' ('for you be-deeply-in-love') [film and song]
Wèi nǐ kū.	'I cry for you' [song]
Shéi wèi nǐ zuòzhèng.	'I vouch for you' ('for you give-evidence') [TV drama]
Wèi nǐ chīkuáng.	'I'm crazy about you' ('for you idiotic-crazy') [novel]

17.3.1 Mild requests

Requests can be couched in a way that suggests they require very little effort. One way to do this is with verb reduplication (or V *yíxiàr*).

> *Jièyixiàr nǐ de zìdiǎn, hǎo ma?*   'May I borrow your dictionary for
> a bit?'

Qǐng nǐ gěi wǒmen jièshao yíxiàr Gē Dà de qíngkuàng, hǎo bu hǎo?	'Would you mind saying something about the situation at Columbia University by way of introduction?'
Nǐ néng bu néng gěi wǒ shuōshuo Yīngguó dàxué de biānzhì shi zěnme yàng de?	'Could you tell me a little bit about how English universities are organized?'
Néng bù néng gěi wǒmen jiěshì yíxiàr 'sì' hé 'miào' nèi liǎng ge zì bù yíyàng zài nǎ.lǐ?	'Would you mind explaining to us how the two words *sì* ('temple') and *miào* ('shrine') differ?'

NOTES

a. *Qíngkuàng* and *qíngxíng* are near synonyms.

b. *Biānzhì* is a verb, which literally means 'weave together', but it can also mean 'work out; organize'.

As the previous examples show, the question form gives the appearance of choice by the donor and, provided that only minor assistance is required, offers a conventional way of preempting any possible offense. Tag questions may also serve the same purpose.

Qǐng bǎ làjiàng ná guòlai, hǎo ma?	'Please get the chili paste, okay?'
Qǐng bǎ cù dì guòlai, hǎo bu hǎo?	'Please pass the vinegar, okay?'

NOTE

Dì means 'pass, forward, transmit'. *Dì guòlai* is generally used for passing something at the table rather than going elsewhere to get it (*ná guòlai*). Recall other verbs in the carrying domain: *ná* 'carry in the hands'; *dài* 'bring someone; carry something light'; *káng* 'carry something heavy; lug'; *tái* 'carry by lifting, as a table or trunk', *tí* 'carry in the hand, with arms down, as a briefcase'; and, coming up in §17.3.2, *shāo* 'take something small to somebody'.

17.3.2 More imposing requests

With requests that involve more work by the donor, the imposition can be acknowledged with phrases such as the following.

Máfan nǐ	'May I bother you to . . .'
Bàituō	'Would you mind . . .' ('beg-impose')

Tuō nǐ yí jiàn shìr.	'Can I make a request?' ('impose-on you one M thing')
Láo <nín> jià . . .	'Excuse me; please . . .' ('trouble your progress')
Fán nín . . .	'Can I bother you . . .'
Tuō nǐ yí jiàn shìr: bāng wǒ dìng ge fángjiān, hǎo bu hǎo?	'May I ask you something? Can you help me make a room reservation?'
Tuō nǐ yí jiàn shìr: nǐ qu Kūnmíng de shíhou máfan nǐ bāng wǒ bǎ yí jiàn dàyī shāo huílai.	'Can I make a request? When you go to Kunming, would you mind bringing a coat back for me?'
Máfan nǐ kànyixiàr xíngli, wǒ děi qù <yí>tàng xǐshǒujiān.	'Would you mind watching my luggage? I have to go and find a restroom.'
Láo nín jià bǎ zhèi ge bāoguǒ gěi lǎobǎn.	'Excuse me, would you mind giving this package to the boss?'
Fán nín gěi wǒ bāng ge máng.	'May I bother you for a little help?'
Rúguǒ nǐ míngtiān yǒu kòngr de huà, qǐng bāng wǒ kāi ge hùtóur.	'If you happen to have some time tomorrow, could you help me open an account?'
Máfan nǐ bāng wǒ tiánhǎo zhèi xiē shēnqǐngbiǎo.	'Would you mind helping me fill out these application forms?'

VOCABULARY

dìng	'book; subscribe to'
shāo huílai	*shāo* 'take something small to someone; bring back'; cf. *Bàituō nǐ shāo ge xìn gěi tā* 'Would you mind taking a letter for her?'; *Tì wǒmen gěi nǐ fùmǔ shāo ge hǎo* 'Give our regards to your parents'.
bāoguǒ	'package; parcel'
yǒu kòngr	'have free time': *kòng<r>* is obviously related to *kōng* 'empty; hollow; blank'; the latter is seen in words such as *kōngtiáo* 'air conditioning' and *kōngqì* 'air'.

hùtóur	'bank account': *kāi ge hùtóur* 'open a bank account'
tián	'fill out': *tiánhǎo* 'fill out properly'; *tiánwán* 'finish filling out'
shēnqǐngbiǎo	'application form' ('apply-form')

17.3.3 Complaints

A request for someone to modify his or her behavior—in other words, complaining—is more sensitive. Typically, it takes the form of a request plus a reason for the complaint.

Qǐng nǐ bǎ diànshì kāi xiǎo yìdiǎnr, hǎo bu hǎo? Yǒu diǎnr chǎo.	'Would you mind switching down the TV? It's a bit loud.'
Qǐng bǎ zìxíngchē fàng zài wàitou, hǎo ma? Zhèr tài jǐ le.	'Would you mind putting your bike outside? Space is tight here.' ('too crowded')
Shuōhuà qǐng xiǎoshēng yìdiǎnr, hǎo ma? Wǒ méi fǎ kànshū a.	'Would you mind speaking more softly? I can't concentrate.' ('no way to read')

VOCABULARY

jǐ	'be crowded; pressed'
xiǎoshēng	'less loud': cf. *dàshēng* 'louder'
méi fǎ	= *méiyǒu fǎzi* 'no way'

People cutting in line can be a problem at ticket booths (and other places). Here are some progressively more abrupt complaints, couched in the form of requests. Foreigners probably shouldn't venture past the first example.

Qǐng nǐ páiyíxiàr duì.	'Please line up.'
Bú yào chāduì!	'Don't cut in line!'
Páiduì qù, nǐ jí shénme?	'Go line up—what's your hurry?'

Finally, a miscellaneous collection of responses to annoying situations.

Nǐmen bié chǎo le, fánsǐ le!	'Stop the noise, it's driving me nuts!'
Shénme fúwù tàidu!	'What an attitude to service!'
Zhèi ge rén tài bú kàopǔ!	'This guy's just too unreliable!'

VOCABULARY

páiduì	'line up' ('arrange-line')
chāduì	'cut in linc' ('insert-line')
jí	'be impatient; be urgent': cf. *jíjí-mángmáng* 'be in a rush; in haste'; *jíxìngzi* 'someone with a frenetic personality'; contrast with *jǐ* 'be crowded, pressed'
chǎo	'be noisy; have a fight; quarrel'
fán	'be annoyed': *fánsǐ* 'be a real nuisance' ('annoy to-death')
tàidu	'attitude'
kàopǔ	'be reliable; be regular': usually used in the negative, as in *bú kàopǔ* 'unreliable'; cf. *lípǔr* 'beyond the pale; off the wall; excessive' ('separate-ordinary')

17.4 Modification (with *de*)

Early on in the first volume of *Learning Chinese*, the components of noun phrases, particularly those that involve specification (measure words and the attribute particle *de*), were introduced. We return to them here, first to review and consolidate and then to practice longer and more complex modification phrases. First, consider again the schema of the noun phrase that indicates the relative position of various components.

DEMONSTRATIVE	NUMBER	M	SV<*DE*>	ATTRIBUTE N	NOUN	PREDICATE
nèi ~ nà		*běn*	*dà*		<*zìdiǎn*>	*shi shéi de?*
nèi ~ nà	*liǎng*	*běn*		*Zhōngwén*	*zìdiǎn*	*shi tā de.*
	Liǎng	*ge*	*dà de*			*jiù gòu le!*
zhèi ~ zhè	*xiē*				<*dōngxi*>	*dōu shi nǐ de ma?*

In the above schema, notice where measure words and the possessive marker *de* appear. Measure words only follow numbers (*yí ge; liǎng ge*) or demonstratives (*nèi ge ~ nà ge; zhèi ge*). *De*, on the other hand, follows stative verbs (and other attributes not shown on the chart): *hěn dà de wénzi* 'large mosquitos'. Demonstratives sometimes appear without measure words, in which case the meaning is 'that class of item'. For example, *zhè chá* means 'this type of tea' and not just the sample in front of you (cf. *zhèi zhǒng chá* with the M *zhǒng* 'kind; type'). When several items are indicated, *xiē* is used (cf. §6.3.3).

Zhèi xiē sǎn, něi bǎ shi nǐ de?	'Which of these umbrellas is yours?'
Nǐ gàosu wǒ něi xiē yīfu shi xǐ de, něi xiē shi gānxǐ de.	'Tell me which of these clothes are to be washed and which are to be dry cleaned.'

As noted earlier, *de* is typically a mark of modification: *zuótiān de bàozhǐ* 'yesterday's newspaper'; *wǒmen zuótiān mǎi de nèi xiē huǒchēpiào* 'the train tickets we bought yesterday'; *líkāi de lí* 'the *lí* of *líkāi*'. Such modifying phrases serve to pin down a particular item. In other words, not any *bàozhǐ* but *zuótiān de bàozhǐ*; not just any *lí* but *líkāi de lí*. Definitions are a good source for the modification pattern.

lǎoshī	*zài xuéxiào jiāoshū de <rén>*
gōngrén	*zài gōngchǎng gōngzuò de <rén>*
xuéshēng	*zài xuéxiào dúshū de <rén>*

As noted earlier, such phrases can be problematical for speakers of English (as well as many other European languages), because the order of elements differs strikingly. In Chinese, such modifying phrases consistently precede the noun of interest, whereas in English, they tend to follow the noun, particularly if they are long or complex.

Chúshī shi <zài fànguǎnr zuòfàn de> rén.	A chef is someone <who cooks in a restaurant>.

Exercise 4

Provide items that fit the following definitions.

1. *Zhōngguórén chīfàn de shíhou yòng de gōngjù:* _____
2. *Wèi biérén zhàoxiàng de rén:* _____
3. *Gěi bìngrén kànbìng de rén:* _____
4. *Wèi Zhōngguó rénmín gōngzuò de rén:* _____

Provide Chinese definitions based on the characteristics provided.

5. *nóngmín:*   _____   'cultivate land in the countryside'
6. *jìzhě:*   _____   'write news reports'
7. *fúwùyuán:*   _____   'serve [for the sake of] guests'
8. *wǎngyǒu:*   _____   'friends made online'

   This exercise provides some practice with definitions. It makes reference to the following phrases.

wǎng shang	'on the Internet' ('net on')
jiāo péngyou	'meet friends' ('exchange friends')
zhòngdì	'cultivate the soil' ('plant-ground')
gōngjù	'tool' ('work-tool')
zhàoxiàng	'take photographs' ('reflect likeness')
shèyǐngshī	'photographer' ('shoot-picture-expert')
gànbu	'political-worker'
nóngmín	'farmers' ('agricultural people')
xīnwén bàodǎo	'the news' ('news report')
wòfáng	'bedroom' ('sleep-room')
zhèngfǔ	'government'
fúwù	'to serve'

Like definitions, identifying people (in photographs or other contexts) also generally calls for *de* modification. In the following dialogue, *Máo Dàwéi* is with the mother of one of his friends (whom he calls *bómǔ* 'wife of father's elder brother; auntie'). She is a photographer (*shèyǐngshī*). They are looking at photographs taken in the 1930s when *Máo Zédōng* was in *Yán'ān* (in northern *Shǎnxī*).

Bómǔ:	*Nǐ kàn, zhè shi Máo Zédōng zài Yán'ān.*	'Look, here's Mao Zedong at Yan'an.'
Máo:	*Tā pángbiānr de nèi ge rén shi shéi?*	'Who's that next to him?'
Bómǔ:	*Yòubianr de shi Zhū Dé; zuǒbianr de shi Zhōu Ēnlái. Nǐ kàn, hòubianr de nèi liǎng ge wàiguó rén shi Sīnuò hé Sīnuò fūrén.*	'The one on the right is Zhu De; the one on the left is Zhou Enlai. Look, those two foreigners in the back are Edgar Snow and Mrs. Snow.'
Máo:	*Sīnuò fūfù shi Měiguó jìzhě, shì bu shì?*	'The Snows were American reporters, right?'
Bómǔ:	*Duì, Sīnuò shi ge 'Guójì Yǒurén', xiàng Bái Qiú'ēn dàifu.*	'Right, Edgar Snow was an "International Friend," like Dr. Norman Bethune.'
Máo:	*Zhū Dé ne?*	'And Zhu De?'
Bómǔ:	*Zhū Dé zuòle jiāngjun, cānjiāle Cháng Zhēng.*	'Zhu De was a general who took part in in the Long March.'
Máo:	*Cháng Chéng ne?*	'The Great Wall?'
Bómǔ:	*Bú shì Cháng Chéng, shi Cháng Zhēng; Hóngjūn cóng Jǐnggāng Shān zǒu dào Yán'ān de zhēngtú.*	'Not the Great Wall, the Long March—the journey that the Red Army took from Jingangshan to Yan'an.'
Máo:	*O, Cháng Zhēng, wǒ tīngcuò le. Nǐ shuō de shi 1935*	'Oh, the Long March—I heard it wrong. You're talking

	nián de Cháng Zhēng ba.	about the Long March of
	Wǒ bǎ Cháng Zhēng	1935. Instead of Long March,
	tīngchéng Cháng Chéng le.	I heard Great Wall.'
Bómǔ:	Jiùshi le! Zhū Dé cānjiāle	'Exactly! Zhu De took part in
	Cháng Zhēng.	the Long March.'

VOCABULARY

fūfù	'husband and wife': level-toned *fū* 'man', as in *fūren* 'wife', (presumably 'husband's person'); falling-toned *fù* 'woman', as in *fùkē* 'department of gynecology' ('woman-section')
Guójì Yǒurén	'International Friend': a designation for foreigners who helped China during hard times, especially in the 1950s and 60s, when China was isolated from the rest of the world
jiāngjun	'military officer; general'
cānjiā	'join; participate in; take part in'
Hóngjūn	'Red Army'
zhēngtú	'journey' ('march-journey')

NOTES

a. *Yán'ān* is a city in a remote part of northern *Shǎnxī*. From 1937–1947, it was the capital of the communist-controlled part of China.

b. *Zhū Dé* (1886–1976) was a close associate of Mao who, at the inauguration of the People's Republic of China (PRC), was the commander-in-chief of the People's Liberation Army (PLA).

c. *Zhōu Ēnlái* (1898–1976) was premier of the PRC.

d. *Sīnuò* 'Edgar Snow' (1905–1972) was an American reporter and author of *Red Star over China*, a book based on interviews with Mao and others conducted at Yan'an after the Long March. His first wife, Helen Foster Snow, was also a journalist and accompanied him for part of his stay in Yan'an.

e. *Bái Qiū'ēn* 'Norman Bethune' (1890–1939) was a Canadian physician who died of blood poisoning while serving as a doctor in the communist area of China. Mao wrote an essay on him that was once required reading in China.

f. *Cháng Zhēng* 'The Great March': In 1934, the communist forces retreated from their base areas in rural *Jiāngxī* (known as the Jiangxi Soviet) under military pressure from the Kuomintang

(Nationalist Party). They marched westward at first and then moved in a great arc northward, ending up in Yan'an in 1935, a journey of almost 10,000 kilometers.

g. *Jǐnggāng Shān*: Jinggang Mountains in Jiangxi Province

NOTES ON TAKING PHOTOGRAPHS (CF. §18.3)

zhàoxiàng	'take photographs' ('reflect-likeness'): cf. *zhào ge xiàng*
pāizhào	'take photographs' ('strike-reflection')
Zhèr bù zhǔn pāizhào.	'No taking photos here.'
Wǒ zhào ‹yí› ge xiàng, hǎo bu hǎo?	'Let me take a photo, okay?'
Wǒmen dào Tiān'ānmén Guǎngchǎng zhàoxiàng qu le.	'We went to Tiananmen Square to take some photographs.'
Zuótiān wǒmen zài Shànghǎi zhàole jǐ zhāng xiàng.	'Yesterday, we took some photos in Shanghai.'

17.5 Clothing and shape

Thirty years ago, the predominant color of clothing in the PRC was white for shirts and dark blue or dark gray for most everything else. On occasion, youth wore red scarves to show their political loyalty. Men in those days wore Mao suits, a type of attire originally promoted by Sun Yat-sen earlier in the 20th century to provide a formal dress for civil servants that looked modern but not completely Western. So-called Mao suits are still called *Zhōngshānzhuāng* 'Zhongshan tunics' or *Zhōngshānfú* 'Zhongshan clothes'. In Mandarin, Sun Yat-sen is usually known not by the Mandarin rendition of his name, which is *Sūn Yìxiān*, but by his alternative name *Sūn Zhōngshān*. Zhongshan, on the coast of Guangdong Province, was his birthplace.

Beginning in the late 1980s, clothing styles started to change in China, and, nowadays, there is little in the way of dress to distinguish people in Chengdu from their counterparts in Chicago or Hamburg. However, Chinese-styled garments (actually modern versions of more traditional garments), such as the following, are still occasionally seen.

mián'ǎo	cotton padded jacket
cháng páo‹r›	long scholar's robe
mǎguà‹r›	man's short coat

| qípáo<r> | woman's long gown (with slit skirt), often known by its Cantonese name of *cheongsam* |
| *Zhōngguó chuántǒng de yīfu yǒu mián'ǎo, chángpáor, mǎguàr, qípáor, děngděng.* | 'Chinese traditional clothing includes padded jackets, robes, short coats, and cheongsams.' |

Ordinary types of clothing are listed below. Most types of clothing are counted by way of the measure word *jiàn*; shoes and boots, however, are counted with *shuāng* 'pair' or *zhī* (if singly).

máoyī	'sweater' ('wool-clothing')
chènshān	'shirt' ('lining-shirt')
jiákè	'jacket' [from English]
qúnzi	'skirt'
kùzi	'trousers'
niúzǎikù	'jeans' ('cow-boy-trousers')
duǎn kùzi	'shorts'
chènkù	'underpants' ('lining-trousers')
nèiyī	'underwear' ('inner-clothes')
wàzi	'socks; stockings'
xié ~ xiézi	'shoes'
xuēzi	'boots'
T xù<shān>	'T-shirt' [from English]: by way of Cantonese, where *xù* is pronounced 'xut'—more like 'shirt'. In an etymological sense, then, *shān* is redundant.

Formal types of clothing are listed below.

<yí tào> xīfu	'suit' ('<a set of> Western-clothes')
wǎnlǐfú	'formal evening dress for females' ('evening-ceremony-clothes')
yèlǐfú	'formal attire for men; tuxedo' ('night-ceremony-clothes')

There are two words in Chinese that correspond to English 'wear': *chuān* ('to pass through') is used for clothing and shoes, and *dài* is used for accessories, such as hats, belts, and glasses.

dài	*màozi*	'hat': M *dǐng*
dài	*yǎnjìng*	'glasses' ('eye-mɪrror'): M *fù* 'pair of glasses'
dài	*tàiyángjìng*	'sunglasses' ('sun-mirror'): M *fù*

There is a third word—*jì* 'tie; fasten; do up'—that is used for things such as neckties and seatbelts, which in English also get 'worn'.

jì	*lǐngdài*	'tie' ('neck-belt'): M *tiáo* or *gēn*
	ānquándài	'seatbelt' ('safety-belt'): cf. *jìhǎo ānquándài!*

NOTE

The *dài* of *lǐngdài* is homophonous with *dài* 'wear', but the two words are unrelated (and written with different characters).

Měnggǔrén chuántǒng de yīfu

People can be characterized in terms of the clothes they wear.

Nǐ kàn, chuān niúzǎikù de nèi ge rén—tǐng shímáo de!	'Look at that guy in jeans—such style!'
Chuān hóng máoyī de nèi ge rén shi něi wèi?	'Who's the person in the red sweater?'
Chuān duǎn kùzi de nèi wèi shi shéi?	'Who's that person wearing shorts?'
Dài tàiyángjìng de shi Àobāmǎ.	'The one with the sunglasses is Obama.'
Jì huáng lǐngdài de shì Zhū Róngjī.	'Zhu Rongji's the one with the yellow tie.'

Finally, another common situation that involves selection—and therefore identification by way of the *de* pattern—is buying a seal. Seals, made of stone, jade, and other material are sold from street stands, in specialty shops, and in department stores. When you buy one, you select a blank onto which characters are engraved in either standard script or, more often, in small seal script (*xiǎozhuàn*). In the following dialodue, *Jiǎ* is the buyer, and *Yǐ* is trying to make the sale.

Jiǎ:	*Nèi ge túzhāng, wǒ xiǎng kànkan, kě.yǐ ma?*	'Mind if I take a look at that seal?'
Yǐ:	*Nǐ shuō de shi zhèi ge ma?*	'You mean this one?'
Jiǎ:	*O, bú shì, shi nèi ge fāngfāng de.*	'Um, no, that square one.'
Yǐ:	*Zhèi ge ma?*	'This one?'
Jiǎ:	*Ng, duì, kànyixià xíng ma?*	'Uh-huh, that's it; can I take a look?'
Yǐ:	*Méi wèntí, suíbiàn kàn.*	'Sure, take your time.'
Jiǎ:	*Shi yù zuò de ba.*	'It's jade, I take it.'
Yǐ:	*Bú shì a, yù hěn guì, zhèi ge shi shítou de, dàlǐshí de.*	'Nooo—jade's expensive; this is stone, marble.'
Jia:	*O. Nà duōshao qián?*	'Ah. How much is it?'
Yǐ:	*50 kuài.*	'¥50.'
Jiǎ:	*Nà, jiā zì hái yào qián ma?*	'Well, are characters extra?'

Yǐ: *Kè yí ge zì shíwǔ kuài.*   '¥15 to carve a character.'

Jiǎ: *Zhème guì a! Wǒ dásuàn kè sān*   'So expensive! I'm planning to
        ge zì ne. Piányi diǎnr ba.   have three characters. Can
                                                       you make it a bit cheaper?'

Yǐ: *Nà, zhèyàngr ba. Yí ge zì gěi nǐ*   'Well, how about this. I'll
        piányi liǎng kuài, zài   reduce the cost of each
        jiāshang túzhāng běnshēn, 45,   character by ¥2 for you. Add
        yígòng 84 kuài, xíng ba?   on the seal itself, ¥45, and
                                                       that's ¥84 all together,
                                                       okay?'

Jiǎ: *80 kuài ba. Qǔ ge zhěngshù.*   '¥80. Make it a round
                                                       number.'

Yǐ: *Hǎo, yí jù huà, gěi nín 80 kuài.*   'Okay, in a word then, I'll give
                                                       it to you for ¥80.'

Jiǎ: *Xièxie lǎobǎn. Gěi nín. Wǒ bàn*   'Thanks. Here's the money. I'll
        ge xiǎoshí hòu guòlai qǔ.   come back in half an hour to
                                                       pick it up.'

Yǐ: *Hǎo lei. Zhèi ge bāozhǔn nín*   'Good. I guarantee you'll be
        mǎnyì.   happy with it.'

VOCABULARY

túzhāng	'a seal' ('illustration-seal'): also *yìnzhāng* ('print-seal')
yù	'jade'
dàlǐshí	'marble' ('big-grain-stone')
jiā	'add'
kè	'carve'
běnshēn	'the thing itself' ('root-body'): in this case, the shaped stone
qǔ ge zhěngshù	'pick a round number' ('take a whole-number')
Hǎo lei.	*Lei* is a colloquial sentence-final particle conveying approval.
bāozhǔn	'guarantee; vouch for the fact' ('envelop-assured')
mǎnyì	'be satisfied; be pleased' ('full-intention')

GŌNGYÌ

GŌNGYÌ	'HANDICRAFTS' ('WORK-ART')	M WORD
zìhuà	'scrolls' ('character-picture')	*zhāng*
huāpíng	'vases' ('flower-bottle')	*gè*
shànzi	'fans'	*bǎ* [for hand fans]
ěrhuán	'earrings' ('ear-rings')	*duì* [for a pair]; *zhī* [for one of a pair]
xiàngliàn	'necklace' ('nape-chain')	*tiáo*
màozi	'hat'	*dǐng*
yùdiāo	'jade carving'	*gè*
xiàngyádiāo	'ivory carving'	*gè*

Mài túzhang de. (Tiānjīn)

SHAPES AND TEXTURES

yuán <yuán> de	'round'
cū <cū> de	'rough'
guānghuá de	'smooth'

MATERIALS

sùliào de	'plastic'	*shítou de*	'stone'
mùtou de	'wooden'	*xiàngyá de*	'ivory' ('elephant-tooth')
zhēnsī de	'[real] silk'	*zhǐ de*	'paper'
bù de	'cloth'	*jīnzi de*	'gold'
yínzi de	'silver'	*qīngtóng de*	'bronze' ('green-copper')

17.6 Constructions with *yī* 'one'

Yī + **Verb:** In addition to combining with a measure word to form a quantifying phrase (*yí gè; yì tiáo*), *yī* 'one' can also be found directly before a verb, in conjunction with the adverb *jiù* in the ensuing clause. In such cases, the meaning is 'as soon as' or 'whenever'. You can easily make up a sequence along the following lines to illustrate this usage.

> *Lǎoshī yí jìn jiàoshì, xuéshēng jiu zhàn qǐlai;*
> *xuéshēng yí zhàn qǐlai, jiu gēn lǎoshī shuō: 'Lǎoshī hǎo';*
> *xuéshēng yì shuōwán, lǎoshī jiu qǐng tāmen zuòxia;*
> *tāmen yí zuòxia, lǎoshī jiu kāishǐ diǎnmíng;*
> *lǎoshī yì diǎnwán míng, jiu kāishǐ shàngkè.*

VOCABULARY

jiàoshì	'classroom' ('teaching-room'): *Jiào,* with a falling tone, is generally a noun—*jiàoshòu* 'professor'; *jiàoxué* 'education'. *Jiāo,* with a level tone, is a verb—*jiāoshū* 'teach'.
kāishǐ	'begin; start to'
diǎnmíng	'call roll' ('check-names'): cf. *diǎncài* 'order food'; The core meaning of *diǎn* 'dot; point; bit' can be extended to the

notion of 'check mark' or 'designation', hence 'select; choose; pick out'.

Yī + **Noun:** *Yī* also combines directly with certain nouns to mean 'all of; whole'. The phrase is typically supported by *dōu* 'all'.

Wǒ yì shǒu dōu shi shuǐ.	'My hands are covered in water.'
Wǒ yì shēn dōu shi hàn.	'I'm covered in sweat.'
Yí dì dōu shi fàn!	'There's rice all over the floor!'
Xiǎoxīn, yí dì dōu shi shuǐ.	'Watch out, the floor's covered in water.'
Zhēn kěpà. Tā yì liǎn dōu shi xiě. Hòulái cái zhīdao yuánlái jiùshi liú bíxiě.	'It was terrible. Her face was covered in blood. It turned out she just had a bloody nose—as we found out later.'

NOTES

a. *hàn* 'sweat'; *chūhàn* 'to sweat'

b. There are at least three possible pronunciations of the word for 'blood'. The most colloquial is *xiě* (as above): *bíxiě* 'nose bleed; *liúxiě* 'to bleed' ('flow-blood'); *tùxiě* 'spit blood'; *xiànxiě* 'donate blood' ('contribute-blood'); *chōuxiě* 'draw blood' ('pull-blood'). The more formal pronunciation is *xuè*, but not in all contexts. Thus, *liúxiě* and *liúxuè* are both possible (plus the more regional *liúxuě*), but words such as *xuèyā* 'blood pressure' and *jīngxuè* 'menstruation' are usually *xuè*.

17.7 Dialogue: My younger sister moved to Australia

Now a departure from heavy doses of new material to consolidate patterns and vocabulary you already know. Although, to be sure, there are a few geographic and other terms introduced toward the end of the dialogue in keeping with the geographic theme of this unit. *Jiǎ* is a foreign student attending Nanjing University, and *Yǐ* is a Chinese student there. We start off mid-conversation.

Jiǎ:	*Nǐ yǒu xiōngdì jiěmèi ma?*	'Do you have any siblings?'
Yǐ:	*Yǒu ge jiějie, yǒu ge mèimei.*	'I have an older sister and a younger sister.'
Jiǎ:	*Tāmen yě zhù zai Nánjīng ma?*	'Do they also live in Nanjing?'

Yǐ:	*Jiějie zhù zhèr, wǒ mèi jiàle ge Àozhōurén. Tāmen xiān zài Nánjīng zhùle liǎng nián, ránhòu bāndào Àozhōu qù le.*	'My older sister lives here; my younger sister married an Australian. They first lived in Nanjing for a couple of years, then they moved to Australia.'
Jiǎ:	*O, tāmen zhù zai Àozhōu!*	'Oh, they live in Australia!'
Yǐ:	*Shì a, zài Xīní, yǐjīng zài nàr sān nián le. Kāile yì jiā lǚxíngshè, shēngyì bú cuò.*	'Yes, in Sydney, they've already been there three years. They opened a travel agency, and business isn't bad.'
Jiǎ:	*Fāngbiàn; hǎo mǎi fēijīpiào ya!*	'Convenient; good for buying plane tickets!'
Yǐ:	*Shì a; tāmen jīngcháng lái kàn wǒmen, qǐmǎ, yì nián yí cì.*	'For sure; they regularly come to see us—at least once a year.'
Jiǎ:	*Wǒ yě zài Àozhōu zhùguo, zài nàr shàngguo liǎng nián xué.*	'I also used to live in Australia; I went to school there for a couple years.'
Yǐ:	*Nǐ méi shénme Àozhōu kǒuyīn ya!*	'You don't have much of an Australian accent!'
Jiǎ:	*Yǐqián yǒu, xiànzài méi le.*	'I used to, but I don't anymore.'
Yǐ:	*Àozhōu hěn tèbié, duì ma?*	'Australia's very special, isn't it?'
Jiǎ:	*Shì a. Bǎi fēn zhī bāshí dōu shi shāmò. Dàduōshù de rén zhù zài yì xiē hǎibiānr de dà chéngshì, xiàng Xīní, Bósī, Bùlǐsīběn, Dá'ěrwén. Shǒudū dàoshi zài nèidì de.*	'Yes, it's about 80 percent desert. Most of the people live in the large cities on the coasts—Sydney, Perth, Brisbane, Darwin. But the capital's inland.'
Yǐ:	*Ng, Kānpéilā ba. Wǒ yě tīngshuō Àozhōu hái yǒu*	'Uh huh, Canberra, right? I also read that there are a lot

	hen duō qítè de zhíwù hé dòngwù.	of strange plants and animals in Australia.'
Jiǎ:	*Shì a: xiàng dàishǔ, èyú, kǎolā, yāzuǐshòu, xiàoniǎo, shénme de.*	'Yes, like kangaroos, crocodiles, koalas, platypuses, "laughing birds," and so on.'
Yǐ:	*Nǐ shuō de nèi ge xiàoniǎo shi shénme niǎo?*	'What sort of a bird is the laughing bird you mentioned?'
Jiǎ:	*Shì Àozhōu de yì zhǒng dà cuìniǎo. Jiào de shēngyīn yǒu diǎnr xiàng rén xiào de shēngyīn.*	'It's a kind of large Australian kingfisher. Its call is a little like the sound of human laughter.'
Yǐ:	*Yǒu zhèyàng de niǎo ma?*	'Is there such a bird?'
Jiǎ:	*Yǒu, yídìng yǒu, kěshì bù zhīdao dàodǐ Zhōngwén míngzi shi shénme.*	'Yes, there certainly is, but I haven't a clue what the Chinese name is.'
Yǐ:	*Zhōngguó de zhíwù dòngwù yě tèbié duō. Tīngshuō Zhōngguó xī'nán hé dōngbù de wùzhǒng chàbuduō gēn Yàmǎxùn liúyù yíyàng fēngfù, bǐ shìjiè shang biéde dìfang dōu duō.*	'China also has a tremendous number of plants and animals. I've heard it said that the southwest and east of China have as many species as there are in the Amazon River basin—more than any other place in the world.'
Jiǎ:	*Zhè yěxǔ shi Zhōngguó cài fēngfù de yuányīn. Měi cì yànxí dōu yǒu wǒ cónglái méi chīguo de cài, xiàng shàng cì wǒmen qù Xīníng chī de hóutóugū a, niàngpí a, gǒujiāoniào bǐng a.*	'That must be why Chinese food is so varied. Banquets have dishes I've never eaten. On the last trip we took to Xining, we had "monkey-head mushrooms," "fermented skin," and "dog-sprinkle-urine pancakes."'

VOCABULARY

zhù zhèr	= *zhù zài zhèr*
jià	'to marry' [of a female]: *Wǒ mèi jiàle ge Àozhōurén.*
jiā	'house': here used as an M for certain kinds of establishments; *yì jiā fànguǎn, yì jiā gōngchǎng*
lǚxíngshè	'travel agency'
shēngyi	'business; trade' ('living-significance')
hǎo	'the better to': here used as a conjunction
qǐmǎ	'at least': = *zhìshǎo*
dàoshi	'contrary to expectations; exceptionally; actually'
shǒudū	'capital'
qítè	a blend of *qíguài* and *tèbié*
zhíwù	'plants' ('growing-things'): cf. *dòngwù* 'animals' ('moving-things')
dàishǔ	'kangaroo' ('pocket-rodent'): cf. *sōngshǔ* 'squirrel' ('pine-rodent'); *lǎoshǔ* 'rat; mouse' ('venerable-rodent'); *jiāshǔ* 'domestic rat/mouse' ('house-rodent')
èyú	'crocodile' ('crocodile-fish')
yāzuǐshòu	'platypus' ('duck-snout-wild animal')
cuìniǎo	'kingfisher' ('emerald green-bird'): cf. *cuìyù* 'blue jade', frequently advertised in jewelry shops in China. The large species of kingfisher is, of course, the kookaburra, known as *xiàocuìniǎo* ('laughing-kingfisher') in Chinese.
shēngyīn	'sound': cf. *shēngdiào* 'tones'; *dàshēng* 'loud'
dàodǐ	'in the end; after all' ('reach-bottom'): contrast with *dìdào ~ dàodì* 'authentic'
wùzhǒng	'species' ('thing-kind')
liúyù	'river basin; drainage area' ('flow-region')
de yuányīn	'the reason that; the reason why . . .' ('original-cause')
yànxí	'banquets' ('banquet-mat')
hóutóugū a	The final particle *a* can separate items in a list.

NOTES

a. *Jià* 'to marry' [of a female] is related to *jiā* 'home', having the sense of 'marry into the male household'. It is derived by the fourth tone shift; cf. *hǎo* 'be good' → *hào* 'like'; *jiāo* 'teach' → *jiào* 'instruction'; *zhōng* 'middle' → *zhòng* 'hit a target'. The comparable word for males is *qǔ* 'marry' [of a male], which derives from the verb *qǔ* 'get'; cf. English 'take a wife'.

b. *Gǒujiāoniào* ('dog-sprinkle-urine'): The reference to dog urine comes from the fat that is sprinkled on the pancakes during cooking. The name is local to Xining and probably other parts of Qinghai and the Northwest.

Exercise 5

Explain and give comparable examples of the following uses of *le*.

1. *Wǒ mèi jiàle ge Àozhōurén.*
2. *Tāmen xiān zài Nánjīng zhùle liǎng nián.*
3. *Ránhòu tāmen bāndào Àozhōu qù le.*
4. *Tāmen yǐjīng zài nàr sān nián le.*

In small groups, think of some requests and support them with reasons introduced by *hǎo* in its conjunction function ('so as to').

> *Nǐ liú ge diànhuà, yǒu shìr*   'Leave a phone number so I can get
> *hǎo gēn nǐ liánxì.*   in touch if something happens.'

Complete the following sentences, which all contain *de yuányīn*.

1. *Wǒ jīngcháng gǎnmào de yuányīn* . . .
2. *Kuàicān zài Zhōngguó shòu huānyíng de yuányīn* . . .
3. *Nánren bǐ nǚren gèng xǐhuan hūnwàiliàn de yuányīn* . . .
4. *Tāmen chuīle de yuányīn* . . .

VOCABULARY

hūnwàiliàn	'extramarital affair' ('marriage-outside-love')
chuī	'blow', but here 'break up; fail' [of a relationship]

Kànkan dìtú jiu xíng le.

17.8 Driving and owning a car (2)

A: *Zhōngguó páizi? O, Zhōngguó yě yǒu hěn duō páizi. Bǐjiào pǔbiàn de shi Hóngqí, nà shi Zhōngguó lǎo páizi, guòqu dōu shì dàguānyuán cái néng zuò de. Cháng'ān, Jílì, Qíruì (QQ), Bǐyàdí (BYD). Sāngtǎnà, Jiédá, Wǔlíng, Biékè, Xiàndài, děngděng shi hézī qǐyè de. Jìnkǒu de yě bù shǎo, yě shì yuè lái yuè duō. Jùshuō, zhèngfǔ guānyuán tèbié xǐhuan Àodí; niánqīngrén bǐjiào xǐhuan Bǎomǎ; tuìxiū de xǐhuan Bēnchí; zài Zhōngguó Biékè shi ge hěn shòu huānyíng de háohuá jiàochē. Wǒ tīngshuō Zhōngguó de yǒuqián rén, tāmen mǎi Láosīláisī, Bīnlì, Bǎoshíjié . . .*

B: *Shénme guì mǎi shénme!*

A: *Hāi, mǎi de shi páizi, yào de shi miànzi.*

B: *Rén shǎ, qián duō.*

A: *Hēhē, nǐ yě kuài chéng Zhōngguórén la! Zài Zhōngguó mǎi chē, chúle kàn chē de páizi, chē nèi de kuǎnshì yě hěn zhòngyào. Shēnfen bǐjiào gāo de, jiù nèi xiē yàobu yǒuquán, yàobu yǒuqián, yàobu yǒumíng, tā de zuòwèi yídìng shi zhēn pí zuò de, chēchuāng bōli*

shēnsè de, zhèyàngr, wàibianr kànbujiàn lǐbianr, kěshì lǐbianr
kàndejiàn wàibianr.

B: Niú.

A: Qìchē de páizhào yě hěn zhòngyào.

B: Hái yǒu zhè jiǎngjiu ne?

A: Dāngrán la. Nín zài Měiguó mǎi liàng chē, gěi nǐ ge 13 hào nǐ yào
      ma?

B: Ng—, zhèi ge, bù xǐhuan.

A: Zhè bù jié le ma? Páizhào shang de shùzì yídìng yào jílì, xiàng bā,
      fācái ma; sān, zài Guǎngdōnghuà li tīng qǐlai xiàng chūshēng de
      shēng; liù, yǒu liùliùshùn de yìsi. Bù jílì de shùzi, bǐrú sì, tīng qǐlai
      xiàng sǐdiào de sǐ, méi rén xiǎngyào. Wǒ gēn nǐ shuō a, hái yǒu
      diànhuà hàomǎ, ménpáihào, dōu zhèyàngr.

B: Shéi dōu xiǎngyào 8, 3, 6, nà bu luànle tào ma?

A: Luànbuliǎo, nín yào jílì hào, děi duō tāoqián.

B: Yǒu dàoli. Wù yǒu xī wéi guì.

A: Wù yǐ xī wéi guì! Suǒ.yǐ ma, cóng chēpáihào, shǒujīhào nǐ jiù kě.yǐ
      kàn de chū zhǔrénjia de shēnfen. 0001, 0002 chēpái kěndìng shi
      dāngdì zuì dà de guānyuán, yǒu jǐ ge 6, jǐ ge 8 de, kěndìng shi běndì
      shǔyī-shǔ'èr de dàhēng! Kànjiàn zhè zhǒng chē, nǐ gǎnjǐn duǒ yuǎn
      diǎnr!

B: Qíguài, wǒ wèishénme yào duǒ yuǎn diǎnr? Xíngrén yǒu
      yōuxiānquán.

A: Hāi, nǐ jiù bù zhīdao la, zánmen zhè guīju bù yíyàng. Yàoshi chē li
      zuò de shi Lǐ Gāng de gōngzǐ, dāngxīn nǐ xiǎomìng bù bǎo.

B: Zhēn kěpà! Shéi shi Lǐ Gāng de gōngzǐ? Shéi shi Lǐ Gāng?

A: Zìjǐ dǎting qu. Lǐ Gāng bǐ nǐmen zǒngtǒng Àobāmǎ yǒumíng!

B: Rào wǒ gūlòu-guǎwén!

A: Shi "shù wǒ gūlòu-guǎwén", rào yě shi shù, yí ge yìsi, shuōfǎ shi
      gùdìng de.

B: Xièxie zhǐjiào! Ai, Zhōngguó biànhuà zhēn dà ya! Tiānfān-dìfù!

A: Nà gǎnqing! 20 duō nián yǐqián, Zhōngguó lǎobǎixìng yǒu
      zìxíngchē, jiù hěn zhīzú le. Xiànzài shéi dou xīwàng zìjǐ yǒu yí liàng

qìchē. Búguò rúguǒ Zhōngguó měi ge jiātíng dōu yǒu yí liàng qìchē
de huà, nà Zhōngguó de jiāotōng qíngkuàng huì shi shénme yàngzi
de ne? Nǐ zhīdao Běijīng shi Zhōngguó de shǒudū ma?

B: Dāngrán, shǎguā yě zhīdao.

A: Běijīng hái yǒu yí ge wàihào—shǒudǔ! Zuì zǔsè de chéngshì.

B: Duì a! Gēn Luòshānjī yíyàng, sān fēn zhī yī de tǔdì dōu shì mǎlù
huò tíngchēchǎng, yě shì Měiguó de—shǒudǔ.

VOCABULARY IN PHRASES

dàguānyuán	'important officials'
niánqīngrén	'young people; youth' ('years-light-people')
tuìxiū de	'retirees' ('retreat-to rest DE')
hézī qǐyè	'joint venture' ('share-capital-enterprise')
jùshuō	'it's said that; it's reputed that': cf. tīngshuō 'I've heard it said that; I've heard that'
hěn shòu huānyíng de háohuá jiàochē	'a very popular luxury car': jiàochē 'carriage; sedan'; háohuá often corresponds to English 'deluxe' [of hotel rooms] or 'luxury' [of cars]
Shénme guì mǎi shénme.	'They buy whatever's expensive': with the indefinite sense of shénme—'whatever is expensive, they buy whatever it is'
Rén shǎ, qián duō.	A pithy response to a pithy comment: shǎ 'be stupid; muddleheaded'; cf. shǎguā 'idiot' ('stupid-melon')
chē nèi de kuǎnshì	'design of the inside'
yàobu yǒuquán, yàobu yǒuqián, yàobu yǒumíng	'either they're powerful, or they're rich, or they're famous': with yàobu reduced from yàoburán 'or else; otherwise; or' ('if-not-so')
zuòwèi yídìng shi zhēn pí zuò de	'the seats are bound to be made from real leather'
chēchuāng bōli shēnsè de	'the car windows are darkened glass': shēnsè 'dark colored' ('deep-color')

niú	'cow': also slang, with meanings ranging from 'cool' to 'terrific' to 'bad'. Like English 'bull', the word in this usage has escaped its more abusive and obscene origins to become fairly innocuous—at least in certain contexts.
páizhào	'license plate'
zhòngyào	'important'
jiǎngjiu	'details for consideration / be fussy about'
Zhè bù jié le ma?	'Does that settle it?': *jié* 'tie; join together; conclude / a knot'; cf. *jiéhūn* 'get married' ('tie up-the wedding')
jílì	'auspicious': *Bā* 'eight', for example, sounds quite like the *fā* of *fācái* 'get rich'—even more so in Cantonese, where the syllables are pronounced *baat* and *faat* (still on the same tone). In Cantonese (whose speakers seem particularly attuned to this kind of paranomasia), 'three', pronounced *sāam* is close enough to *sāang* 'give birth' for some of the auspicious associations of 'birth' to rub off onto 'three'. Similarly, *liù* 'six', recalls words having to do with flow and smoothness (such as *liùliù-dàshùn*).
Nà bú luànle tào ma?	'Doesn't that muddle things up?': *luàntào* ('confuse-the set'); In other words, won't everyone want three, six, and eight at the expense of all other numbers? Well, it turns out that you often have to pay to get the auspicious numbers: *tāoqián* 'pay out; fork out' ('scoop-money'); *Wù yǐ* (rather than *yǒu*) *xī wéi guì* 'rare things cost more' ('things take rare be valued')—'scarcity breeds value'.

běndì shǔyī-shǔ'èr de dàhēng	'one of the top local bosses': *shǔyī-shǔ'èr* 'rank high' ('count-one-count-two'); *dàhēng* 'VIP; big shot'
gǎnjǐn duǒ yuǎn diǎnr	'quickly hide yourself far away': *gǎnjǐn* 'as fast as possible; losing no time' ('rush-as much as possible'); *duǒ* 'hide; avoid'
xíngrén yǒu yōuxiānquán	'pedestrians have right of way': *yōuxiān* 'priority' ('superior-first') plus *quán* 'right; authority'
Lǐ Gāng de gōngzǐ.	*Gōngzǐ* was the term given to the son of a feudal prince. Here, the term is used ironically to refer to the playboy son of an official named Li Gang. Suffice it to say that his son gained notoriety by his behavior after a traffic accident in 2010, an incident that is well described online under the heading of the father, Li Gang. *Zìjǐ dǎting qu.* 'Check it out yourself'; *dǎting* 'inquire' ('hit-hear')
Dāngxīn nǐ xiǎomìng bù bǎo.	'Watch out, your life is in danger.' ('take-care your life not safe'): *bǎo*, short for *bǎohù* 'protect'
shù wǒ gūlòu-guǎwén	'excuse my ignorance': The parts of *gūlòu-guǎwén* are themselves compounds: *gūlòu* 'ignorance' ('isolated-poor') and *guǎwén* 'of limited experience' ('scant-knowledge'). Our learner says *ráo* 'spare' [someone from something] rather than *shù* 'forgive', a forgiveable offense considering the proximate meaning of the two words. In fact, they appear together as a compound: *bú huì ráoshù nǐ* 'won't forgive you'.
shuōfǎ shi gùdìng de	'the phrasing is fixed' ('firm-set'): The use of *ráo* (see the previous entry) is not an option. B wisely welcomes the correction: *Xièxie zhǐjiào!* 'Thanks for the instruction!'

zhǐjiào	'advice; instruction' ('indicate-teaching'): appears in a lot of formulaic phrases acknowledging other people's help. *Qǐng duōduō zhǐjiào* 'I welcome your advice', for example, may be written on a paper you've asked someone to read or inscribed in a book you've written. Alternatively, *Méng nín zhǐjiào, wǒ shòuyì-bùqiǎn.* 'I'm grateful for your advice; it helped me a great deal.' *Méng* 'receive' [polite]; *shòuyì-bùqiǎn* 'I got a lot out of it' ('receive-benefit-not-shallow') is often with the more formal negative, *fēi, shòuyì-fēiqiǎn.*
lǎobǎixìng	'ordinary people' ('the hundred surnames of yore'): Hundred is used loosely; there have always been more than a hundred surnames. *Zhīzú* 'be satisfied' ('know-sufficiency').
wàihào<r>	'nickname' ('out-appellation'): Its nickname, *shǒudū*, is a play on the word *shǒudū* 'capital' (cf. the name of Beijing's international airport, *Shǒudū Jīchǎng*). For the *dū* of *shǒudū*, recall the phrase from the narrative in Unit 16: *Chéng lǐ hái chángchang dǔzhe.*
zǔsè	'traffic jam / block up; obstruct' ('block-clog')

NOTE

Hóngqí ('Red Flag'), *Cháng'ān* (named for the city), *Jílì* ('Geely'), *Qírui* ('QQ'), *Bǐyàdí* ('BYD'), *Sāngtǎnà* ('Santana', a type of VW produced in a joint enterprise), *Jiédá* ('Jetta', also a VW product), *Biékè* ('Buick'), *Xiàndài* ('Hyundai'), *Bǎomǎ* ('BMW'). For other brands, the Chinese names are close enough to the English.

17.9 In the convenience store

You can't get too much practice buying things, so here's a relatively uncomplicated transaction that takes place in a convenience store (*biànlìdiàn*).

Lǎobǎn:	*Zǎo. Nǐ xūyào mǎi yìdiǎnr shénme?*	'Morning. How can I help you?'
Gùkè:	*Zǎo. Yǒu miànjīnzhǐ ma?*	'Morning. Do you have tissues?'
Lǎobǎn:	*Yǒu de. Yào bāo de, háishi hé de?*	'Sure. Do you want a box or a pack?'
Gùkè:	*Yào bāo guóchǎn de.*	'I'd like a pack of a domestic brand.'
Lǎobǎn:	*Qítā de hái yào ma?*	'Anything else?'
Gùkè:	*Yǒu diànchí ma? 1.5 fú de.*	'Do you have batteries? 1.5 volt ones.'
Lǎobǎn:	*Yǒu de. Yào něi zhǒng? Jìnliàng pái?*	'Sure. Which kind? Eveready brand?'
Gùkè:	*Jìnliàng? Jìnliàng bú shì jìnkǒu de ma?*	'Eveready? Isn't Eveready imported?'
Lǎobǎn:	*Shi zài Zhōngguó shēngchǎn de, hézī de ba. Nǐ yào Héngbāng ma?*	'They're made in China, a joint venture. Do you want Hengbang?'
Gùkè:	*Héngbāng de piányi diǎnr ma?*	'Are Hengbang a bit cheaper?'
Lǎobǎn:	*Chàbuduō.*	'Not by much.'
Gùkè:	*Nà, jiù mǎi Jìnliàng ba. Hái yào yì píng kuàngquánshuǐ.*	'Okay, I'll take Eveready and a bottle of water as well.'
Lǎobǎn:	*Yào jǐ ge diànchí? Shuǐ yào dàpíng ma?*	'How many batteries? For the water, do you want a large bottle?'
Gùkè:	*Yào dàpíng de. Diànchí yào liǎng ge.*	'A large one. Make that two batteries.'
Lǎobǎn:	*Hǎo de, yì bāo miànjīnzhǐ, liǎng ge diànchí, yì píng shuǐ, yígòng ¥42.70.*	'Okay, a pack of tissues, two batteries, and a bottle of water—that'll be ¥42.70.'

Gùkè:	Gěi ¥50.	'Here's ¥50.'
Lǎobǎn:	Hǎo de, zhǎo nǐ ¥7.30.	'Okay, here's ¥7.30 in change.'
Gùkè:	Hǎo.	'Fine.'
Lǎobǎn:	Nín màn zǒu.	'Take it easy, sir.'

VOCABULARY

yǒu de	'it is the case that we do': with *de* associated with emphasis; cf. *shì de* 'that's so'
bāo / hé	'pack; box': both are possible measure words, but here, they are used as modifiers
qítā	'additional things; else': cf. *biéde* 'the other members of a set'
diànchí	'battery' ('electric-reservoir')
fú	'volt': a loan word from English
Jìnliàng[pái]	'Eveready' ('utmost-amount'): a brand name
shēngchǎn	'produce; manufacture' ('give birth to-product')
hézī	'joint' ('join-capital'): as in 'joint enterprise'
Héngbāng	a Chinese brand
zhǎo	'find': here, in the sense of 'give change'

Other items sold in convenience stores include the following.

wèishēngzhǐ	'toilet paper' ('sanitary-paper')	yì bāo 'pack'
shūzi ~ lǒngzi	'comb' ~ 'fine-toothed comb'	yí ge; yì bǎ
zhǐjiadāo ~ qián ~ jiǎn	'nail clippers' ('finger-nail-knife~clippers~scissors')	yí ge
féizào ~ xiāngzào	'soap ~ scented soap'	yí kuài 'bar'
máojīn	'towel' ('wool-cloth')	yì tiáo
xǐfàshuǐ	'shampoo' ('wash-hair-water')	yì píngr, yí dài
yáshuā	'toothbrush' ('tooth-brush')	yí ge; yì bǎ
yágāo	'toothpaste' ('tooth-paste')	yì tǒng 'tube'
chúngāo ~ kǒuhóng	'lipstick' ('lip-paste') ~ ('mouth-red')	yì zhī 'stick'

chúchòujī ~ fàngchòujī	'deodorant' ('eliminate-smell-compound') ~ ('prevent-smell-compound')	*yìxiē* 'some'
āsīpǐlín	'aspirin'	*yì píng\<r\>* 'bottle'; *yí piàn\<r\>* 'pill'
diàn\<dòng\>tìxūdāo	'electric shaver' ('electric-cut-beard-knife')	*yí ge; yì bǎ*
guāhúdāo ~ guāxūdāo	'razor' ('shave-beard-knife')	*yí ge; yì bǎ*
dāopiànr	'razor blade' ('knife-slice')	*yí ge; yí piàn; yì hé*
kuàngquánshuǐ	'spring water'	*yì píng\<r\>*
bìyùntào ~ ānquántào	'condom' ('prevent-birth-glove') ~ ('safety-glove')	*yí ge; yì bāo; yì hé*
wèishēngmiántiáo ~ wèishēngjīn	'tampons' ('sanitary-cotton-length') ~ ('sanitary-cloth')	*yí ge; yì hé*

Táiwān zhēnzhū nǎichá 'Taiwan pearl milk-tea' (*Chóngqìng*)

17.10 Confrontation (1)

Given the population concentration in China and the daily pressures on people, confrontations seem relatively rare. Nevertheless, not all conversations are genteel, so it is useful to consider the expression of emotional language. Here is a sample involving a confrontation between two women: *Jiǎ*, who seems to have wandered into the bike lane, and *Yǐ*, who runs over her foot. *Jiǎ* grabs the back of the bike and comments about *Yǐ*'s biking skills: *Nǐ huì qíchē ma? Yǐ* takes a while to figure out what's going on: *Zěnme la?*

The exchange gets more heated. *Jiǎ*'s third comment is a colloquial expression that is difficult to translate: *Qiáo nǐ nèi fù déxing. Qiáo* is a synonym for *kàn* 'look at'. *Déxing* (with *dé* 'moral') is, literally, 'moral caliber', but used in this context, it has the sense of 'moral turpitude' or 'shameful; disgusting'. An English translation for the whole phrase might be 'look at the way you're acting' or simply 'just look at you'. *Déxing* is measured by *fù*, a measure word for pairs, (*yí fù shǒutào*), sets of things (*yí fù xiàngqí* 'a chess set'), and facial expressions (*yí fù xiàoliǎn* 'a smiling face'). Therefore, *yí fù déxing* 'your disgusting ~ shameful conduct'.

A few turns later, *Jiǎ* makes further reference to behavior and moral norms, saying that *Yǐ* 'lacks morality': *quē dàdé* ('lack big-morality'). *Bǐng*, the passerby, gets involved in the end. This is quite typical, even though in this case, *Bǐng* finds it difficult to resolve the issue.

You are not likely to find yourself in a comparable situation, so rather than try to reenact the conversation, you should instead look for occasions to make use of some of the colloquialisms and other phrases. This conversation and the notes that follow also serve to illustrate the sort of difficulties that can arise from dealing with colloquial language in a foreign culture at a distance.

Jiǎ:	*Nǐ huì qíchē ma?*	'Where'd you learn to ride?'
Yǐ:	*Zěnme la?*	'What do you mean?'
Jiǎ:	*Nǐ yà wǒ jiǎo le! Zhème kuān de mǎlù, nǐ wǎng nǎr qí bù xíng, fēi wǎng rén jiǎo shang qí!*	'You crushed my foot! Such a wide road, and you can't find anywhere to ride but over someone else's foot!'

Yǐ:	*Nǐ zǒu nǎr bù xíng, fēi wǎng wǒ chē gūlu dǐxia zuān!*	'And you can't walk anywhere else, but you have to get under my wheels!'
Jiǎ:	*Qiáo nǐ nèi fù déxing!*	'Look at you—disgraceful!'
Yǐ.	*Nǐ déxing hǎo?*	'And how about you?'
Jiǎ:	*Nǐ yàoshi bú huì qíchē, huíjiā liànlian zài chūlai!*	'If you can't ride a bike, then go home and practice and come out again!'
Yǐ:	*Nǐ zǒudàor, zhǎng diǎnr yǎnshénr. Zhuàngle wǒ piányi nǐ le, zhuàng qìchē shang jiu méi mìng le.*	'You'd better watch out when you're on the move; if you hit me, it's no big deal, but if you hit a car, you're done for.'
Jiǎ:	*Nǐ quē dàdé de, nǐ zài wǎng qián qí, zhuàngshang diànxiàn gānzi, zhuàngsǐ nǐ bái zhuàng!*	'You're a reprobate; ride on, hit a telegraph pole and kill yourself! Killing yourself won't be any loss!'
Yǐ:	*Nǐ yā cái zhuàngsǐ ne! Chòu bú yàoliǎn de, zuǐ gānjìng diǎnr, gěi nǐmen jiā jí diǎnr dé!*	'It's you who should kill yourself! You stinking shameful person; clean out your mouth; do your family a favor!'
Bǐng:	*Wǒ shuō jiějie suàn le ba! Nǎr name dà huǒqì ya! Shìjiè mòrì a?*	'Say, sister, let it go! Why such a temper? Are we at Judgement Day?'
Yǐ:	*Jiějie jiùshi huǒ dà, zěnme le?*	'I am angry—what of it?'
Bǐng:	*Yo, jiějie jīnr chīle qiāngyào le! Huǒ bù dǎ yí chù lái; zám rěbuqǐ, hái duǒbuqǐ ma? Zǒu le gēr jǐ ge, zám chī huǒguō qu le!*	'Hey, you've really eaten some explosives today, sister! Any spark can start a fire, so we don't want to add fuel to it, but can we avoid doing so? Come on, gals, how about some hot pot instead?'

NOTES

a. *Nǐ wǎng nǎr qí bù xíng, fēi wǎng rén jiǎo shang qí!* *Fēi* 'not' is the reduced form of the double negative *fēi . . . bù kě* 'not to . . . not possible'—'must; have to'. *Nǎr* is used in its indefinite sense: 'You can't ride anywhere else, but . . .'

b. *Nǐ zǒu nǎr bù xíng, fēi wǎng wǒ chē gūlu dǐxia zuān!* *Yǐ* responds in kind, insinuating that *Jiǎ* was actually at fault. *Gūlu* is a word for cylindrical things such as spools, spindles, and winches; it is also colloquial for 'wheels'. *Zuān* is a verb meaning 'bore into; slip into': *zuānle yí ge dòng* 'bored a hole'; *zuān dào shuǐ li qù* 'slip into the water'. Here, the notion is that *Jiǎ*, in her carelessness, somehow got her foot in the way of *Yǐ*'s wheels.

c. *Qiáo nǐ nèi fù déxing. / Nǐ déxing hǎo?* Very colloquially, this means 'Look at you!' / 'And what about you?' *Déxing* 'behavior; conduct', but in this context, the implication is 'disgusting or shameful behavior'.

d. *Nǐ zǒudàor, zhǎng diǎnr yǎnshénr. Zhuàngle wǒ piányi nǐ le, zhuàng qìchē shang jiu méi mìng le!* The key verb is *zhuàng* 'collide; run into'; *zhuàngsǐ* 'collide and die'; *zhuàngshang* 'collide with'. *Piányi* in this context means 'regard as cheap'—'take advantage of; get off lightly': *zhàn biérén de piányi* 'take advantage of others'. Here, the notion is 'if you run into me, then you'll get off lightly—but not so if you run into an automobile'. *Zǒudàor* in this context is equivalent to *zǒulù*. That leaves *zhǎng diǎnr yǎnshénr*, with *zhǎng* 'grow; develop; increase' and *yǎnshénr*, which can mean 'the twinkle or expression in one's eye', or in colloquial speech, simply 'eyesight': *Wǒ yǎnshénr bù hǎo, tiān yì hēi jiù kànbuqīng le.*

e. *Nǐ quē dàdé de, nǐ zài wǎng qián qí, zhuàngshang diànxiàn gānzi, zhuàngsǐ nǐ bái zhuàng!* Tempers are fraying: *Nǐ quē dàdé de*, with *quē* 'lack' and *dàdé* 'great virtue'. So it doesn't matter what happens to you: *zhuàngsǐ nǐ bái zhuàng* has *bái* ('white' in other contexts) used as an adverb meaning 'in vain; for nothing'; cf. *bái pǎo yí tàng* 'a wasted journey' ('pointless run one time').

f. *Nǐ yā cái zhuàngsǐ ne! Chòu bú yàoliǎn de, zuǐ gānjìng diǎnr, gěi nǐmen jiā jí diǎnr dé.* *Yǐ* addresses *Jiǎ* as *yā*, short for *yātou* 'servant girl', and continues with *chòu bú yàoliǎn de*, with *chòu* 'foul; stinking; disgraceful' and *bú yàoliǎn de* 'someone who doesn't care about saving face; shameless' ('not want-face person'). *Yǐ* ends with advice: 'clean out your mouth and *gěi nǐmen jiā jí diǎnr dé*, with *jídé* 'accumulate merit'—or in other words, 'do a favor for your family'.

g. *Wǒ shuō jiějie suàn le ba! Nǎr nàme dà huǒqì ya! Shìjiè mòrì a?* A third party steps in to put things in perspective: 'Why the great anger? Is it the *shìjiè mòrì* ('world last-day')?

h. *Yo, jiějie jīnr chīle qiāngyào le, huǒ bù dǎ yí chù lái. Zám rěbuqǐ, hái duǒbuqǐ ma? Zǒu le, gēr jǐ ge, zám chī huǒguō qu le!* *Bǐng* has the last word. *Chī qiāngyào* 'eating gunpowder' naturally puts a person in an explosive mood, but watch out: *huǒ bù dǎ yí chù lái* ('fire not from one place come') (*dǎ* here has one of its more specialized senses of 'from'). That is, there's no knowing where the spark that will set her off is going to come from, so *zám rěbuqǐ*, with *rě* 'provoke; set someone off': 'it's not worth provoking you'. *Hái duǒbuqǐ ma?* 'Is it even worth hiding from you?' By this time, the argument seems to be getting some traction, and *Bǐng* ends with a play on *huǒ* 'fire / temper': 'Come on, gals, let's go and have some hot pot.'

VOCABULARY

qíchē	'ride a bike': contrast with *qìchē* 'vehicle'
yà jiǎo	'run over; crush my foot'
kuān	'wide': *bù zhǎi* 'not narrow'
qiáo	'look; look at; observe'
liàn	'practice': cf. *liànxí* 'to practice / exercises'
mìng	'life; fate; destiny': cf. *wánrmìng* 'play with fire'
diànxiàn gānzi	'electrical pole' ('electric-line pole')
jīnr	= *jīntiān* 'today'
qiāngyào	'explosives; gunpowder' ('fire-medicine'): *chī qiāngyào* 'speak rudely'
yí chù	'one place': cf. *dàochù ~ chùchù* 'everywhere'; *hǎochù* 'good outcome'
gēr jǐ ge	'you gals ~ guys' ('brother-several')
huǒguō	'hot pot'

17.11 Rhymes and rhythms

Jingles are easy to remember—that's why they are an effective way of spreading a brand. In China, you can hear them on radio and television and see them in print media. A couple of samples are included below. One is a translation of a familiar American jingle—or perhaps it is more of a slogan. The other is for a local Chinese product: a tonic drink called *Jiànlìbǎo*, which has lost sales to foreign soft drinks. A traditional equivalent of the jingle is the call of hawkers who traveled the lanes of Chinese cities announcing their wares.

Zhǐ róng zài kǒu bù róng zài shǒu.	('Only melt-in mouth not melt-in hand.')
Nǐ xiǎng shēntǐ hǎo qǐng hē Jiànlìbǎo.	('You intend body good request drink Jianlibao.')

The next is the call of a traditional Beijing 'deep-fried fritter' peddler (Sai, Wei, & Constant, 2004). *Sài* in line 3 is the verb 'compete' or, in this case, 'rival'. In other words, the fritters (*yóuzháguǐ*) are as big as little boats. The last line would scan better if the *de* or the final *lái* were omitted.

Yóu yòu xiāng, miàn yòu bái,   ('oil also fragrant, flour also white')
rēng dào guō lǐ piāo qǐlai,   ('throw to pot in [and] float')
sàiguò xiǎochuán de   ('rival-pass small-boat DE oil-fry-devil
   yóuzháguǐ lái.   come')

Here is the first verse of a song by Teresa Teng (*Dèng Lìjūn*) (1953–1995), praising the virtues of small-town life. It has been popular since it first came out in the 1970s, so you'll be able to ask almost any Chinese for the tune.

Xiǎochéng gùshi duō, chōngmǎn xǐ hé lè;
'Small towns have lots of stories of joy and happiness;'
('small-town stories many, full + of joy and happiness')

Ruòshi nǐ dào xiǎochéng lái, shōuhuò tèbié duō.
'if you should visit a small town, you'll find it's really worthwhile.'
('should you to small-town come, benefits especially many')

The following is a well-known folk song with ancient roots. It is said to be as old as some of the material in the *Shī Jīng* ('poetry classic'), a collection thought to have been compiled by Confucius from popular songs dating back as far as 1000 BCE. The *Jī rǎng gē* is cited in *Dì Wáng Shìjì* 'The Record of the Lives of Emperors and Kings' from the 3rd century, which contains material from sources since lost. It is, of course, written in classical Chinese. A modern rendering is provided below for comparison.

Jī rǎng gē 'Ram earth song' (original version)

Rì chū ér zuò,   ('sun rise and work')
Rì rù ér xī,   ('sun set and rest')
záo jǐng ér yǐn,   ('dig wells and drink')
gēng tián ér shí.   ('till fields and eat')
Dì lì yǔ wǒ hé yǒu zāi?   ('emperor power to us what have "the
      heck"?')

(modern version)

Tàiyang chūlai jiu gōngzuò,   ('sun come-out then work')
tàiyang xiàshān jiu xiūxi,   ('sun behind-hills then rest')

> *zài dì lǐ wā ge jǐng hē shuǐ,*   ('at earth in dig a well drink water')
> *zài tián lǐ zhòngdì chīfàn.*   ('at fields in till soil eat-meals')
> *Huángdì de wēilì duì wǒmen*   ('emperor's might to us')
> *yǒu shénme guānxi ne?*   ('have what connection?')

Almost all the words in the original version still appear in the modern vocabulary, but they are often in compounds (*yǐn* 'drink' → *yǐnliào* 'beverages'; *xī* 'rest' → *xiūxi* 'rest'; *zuò* → *gōngzuò*) or with different meanings (*rì* 'day' rather than 'sun'). The classical roots of *yǐn* 'drink' and *shí* 'eat' are also reflected in the common words for 'drink' and 'eat' in Cantonese, *yám* and *sihk*, respectively.

Summary

Topic-comment	*Zhōngguó dì dà wù bó, lìshǐ yōujiǔ.*
To the south of	*Cháng Jiāng yǐnán de dìfang*
The conjunction *ér*	*zǒu hěn yuǎn de lù ér bú yòng hē shuǐ*
Of whom	*qízhōng Rìběnrén zuì duō*
Existence with *yǒu / shì.*	*Qiánbianr yǒu hú, liǎngbiānr dōu shi shù.*
Asking a favor	*Tuō nǐ yí jiàn shìr.*
Would you mind . . .	*Máfan nǐ kànyixià xíngli.*
For; on behalf of . . .	*Wǒ wèi nǐ zhùfú.*
Mild requests (*yíxià*)	*Néng bù néng gěi wǒmen jiěshì yíxià.*
Requests → complaints	*Qǐng nǐ bǎ diànshì kāi xiǎo yìdiǎnr.*
Definitions	*zài gōngchǎng gōngzuò de <rén>*
Modification with *de*	*Yòubianr de shi shéi de?*
	Chuān duǎnkùzi de nèi wèi shi shéi?
Round it off.	*Qǔ ge zhěngshù.*
Whenever; as soon as . . .	*Lǎoshī yí jìn jiàoshì, xuéshēng jiu zhàn qǐlai.*
Covered with . . .	*Yì shēn dōu shi hàn.*
The better to	*hǎo mǎi fēijīpiào*
Actually; unexpectedly	*Shǒudū dàoshi zài nèidì de.*
Or else; or; otherwise	*nèi xiē yàobu yǒuquán, yàobu yǒuqián, yàobu yǒumíng de*

Mén shang de mùdiāo 'Wooden carving above a door'
(*Xīnjiāpō*)

NOTE TO THE EPIGRAPH

This is the first few lines of *Chì Bì Huái Gǔ* 'At Red Cliff Contemplating the Past', one of the best known poems of *Sū Shì* (1037–1101), also known as *Sū Dōngpō* 'Su of the Eastern Shore' (where he once built a house). The Red Cliff, on the *Cháng Jiāng* in *Húběi*, was the site of the defeat of General *Cáo Cāo* by *Zhōu Yú* during the Three Kingdoms period.

Unit 18

Zhī bǐ zhī jǐ, bǎi zhàn bú dài,
bù zhī bǐ ér zhī jǐ, yí shèng yí fù,
bù zhī bǐ bù zhī jǐ, měi zhàn bì bài.
('Know others know self, 100 battles without peril'
'not know others and know self, a victory [for every] loss'
'not know others not know self, every battle inevitably lose.')
—From *Art of War*, by *Sūnzi*

Unit 18 begins with a narrative on learning characters (which does not presuppose prior knowledge of them). This is followed by three shorter sections: one that deals with *chéng* 'become', another that deals with taking photographs, and a third that deals with etiquette. The second long narrative is on the extended family and the terms for family members. After that come three shorter subjects: death, illness, and a visit to a temple. A third narrative introduces the Chinese school system, and the unit comes to a close with the second in our series of confrontations, this one between males. The rhymes include a short classical poem and a rousing modern song.

Contents

A note to the epigraph is located at the end of the unit.

18.1 Studying characters

Regardless of whether you have been interleaving the character reading units of *Learning Chinese* with the spoken material up to now—or only focusing on the spoken—you will want to be able to talk about the form of characters: about the number of strokes, the different components, the compounds. Therefore, this presentation, which can be thought of as a record of an informal talk, deals with studying characters.

Yǒurén shuō xué Hànyǔ bù yídìng děi tóngshí xuéxí Hànzì. Yìsi yěxǔ shi gāng kāishǐ xuéxí Hànyǔ de shíhou, bù yídìng děi tóngshí xuéxí Hànzì. Zhèyàng, nǐ kě.yǐ xiān xué dào fāyīn, shuōhuà de shùnxù, cóng'ér tígāo huìhuà de nénglì. Rúguǒ xūyào bǎ huìhuà jì xiàlai, nàme nǐ kě.yǐ yòng Hànyǔ Pīnyīn. Pīnyīn jiùshì kǒuyǔ de jìlù. Rènhé néng tīngdǒng de dōu néng yòng Pīnyīn xiě xiàlai. Yòng Hànzì bǎ tā jì xiàlai bù xíng ma? Xíng shi xíng, dànshi xuéxí Hànzì hé xuéxí huìhuà shi yòng wánquán bù tóng de fāngfǎ. Yòng Hànzì lái jiāo huìhuà, xuéxí yídìng huì màn xiàlai, huì xiànzhì xuéxí de jìndù. Wǒmen xuéxí yǔyán de biǎodá bú yào shòudào Hànzì xuéxí yǒuguān de gè zhǒng yīnsù de búlì yǐngxiǎng. Zǒngzhī, zhè shi wǒ de gèrén kànfǎ.

Děng xué kǒuyǔ guòle yíduàn shíjiān yǐhòu, yǐjīng yǒule yídìng de huìhuà de jīchǔ yǐhòu, nà nǐ zuì hǎo jiu kāishǐ xuéxí Hànzì. Wèishénme ne? Yīnwèi zhǐ néng shuōhuà ér bú rènde zì jiu bù néng zhēnde liǎojiě Zhōngguó. Zhōngguó měi ge dìfang dōu yǒu Hànzì, chéngshì nóngcūn chùchù dōu yǒu. Bú rènshi zì nǐ jiùshi ge wénmáng! Bú rènshi zì nǐ jiu bù néng kànshū, bù néng kànbào, bù néng chàng kǎlāOK, yě kànbudǒng biāoyǔ, kànbudǒng duìlián, chūnlián shénme de. Rénjiā gěi nǐ míngpiàn, nǐ yě shuō bù chū míngzi lái děng.děng. Zài nà huánjìng lǐ, nǐ huì gǎndào hěn kǔnǎo, gēn rén jiāowǎng huì hěn gāngù.

Hànzì yǒu liǎng zhǒng, duì ma, yǒu fántǐzì, yě yǒu jiǎntǐzì. Zhōngguó Dàlù gēn Xīnjiāpō dōu yòng jiǎntǐzì; Xiāng Gǎng, Táiwān hé yìxiē hǎiwài Huáqiáo Huáyì dōu yòng fántǐzì. Yòng fántǐzì de, yóuqí shi niánjì bǐjiào dà de, yǒurén xiǎokàn jiǎntǐzì, shuō chuántǒng de zì cái shi guīfàn de. Dàlù yě yǒurén juéde zài bǐjiào zhèngshì de zhuàngkuàng, háishi yòng fántǐzì bǐjiào héshì. Bǐfāng shuō, shāngdiàn de zhāopái, hūnlǐ de qǐngtiē, shāngrén de míng-piàn yǒu shíhou xiězhe shi fántǐzì. Dàn jǐ nián qián Zhōngguó zhèngfǔ wèile tǒngyī yòng zì, guīdìng bú zài yòng fántǐzì, bāokuò suǒ.yǒu de guǎnggào hé duìwài xuānchuán dōu bú yǔnxǔ yòng le.

Jiǎntǐzì wèishénme jiào jiǎntǐ ne? Shi yīnwèi bǐhuà bǐjiào shǎo, duì ma? Búguò, bǐhuà bǐjiào shǎo, zì shì bu shì yídìng bǐjiào jiǎndān? Nà bù yídìng. Bǐhuà bǐjiào shǎo, xiězì de shíhou huì juéde bǐjiào róngyi, bǐjiào jiǎndān. Dàn bǐhuà shǎo, rènzì yǒu shíhou bǐjiào nán, duì ma? Jǔ ge lìzi: dōngxi de 'dōng', yòng fántǐzì shi zhèyàng xiě: 東; kuàilè de 'lè', yòng fántǐzì shi zhèi yàng xiě: 樂. Liǎng ge zì de xíngzhuàng wánquán bù tóng, duì ma? Bǎ nèi liǎng ge zì xiěchéng jiǎntǐ, nǐ kàn, hěn xiàng (东, 乐). Liǎng ge dōu shì wǔ ge bǐhuàr. Kàn qǐlai, hěn róngyi bǎ 'dōng' nèi ge zì kànchéng 'lè', bǎ 'lè' kànchéng 'dōng'. Suǒ.yǐ jiǎntǐ bù yídìng jiǎndān, duì ma?

Xué Hànzì hěn yǒu yìsi, kěshì yǒu shíhou bù róngyi jìzhù! Zěnme bàn? Nǐ yǒu méiyǒu hǎo bànfǎ? Lǎoshī cháng shuō xué yí ge zì yīnggāi xiān kàn nèi ge zì de piānpáng, nà jiùshi shuō xíngpáng hé shēngpáng. Xíngpáng yě kě.yǐ jiào bùshǒu. Bùshǒu yǒu zìjǐ de míngzi: rénzìpáng (亻); kǒuzìpáng (口); yánzìpáng (言 / 讠); jīnzìpáng (金 / 钅); sāndiǎnshuǐ (氵); cǎozìtóu (艹), děngděng. Nàme, lǎoshī kě.yǐ wèn nǐmen: 'chī' (吃) nèi ge zì de bùshǒu shi shénme? Nà, nǐ kě.yǐ shuō 'chī' de bùshǒu shi kǒuzìpáng (口). Huòzhě, lǎoshī wèn nǐmen 'shuōhuà' de 'huà' nèi ge zì (話/话) de bùshǒu shi shénme, nǐ jiù kě.yǐ shuō, 'huà' de bùshǒu shi yánzìpáng (言 / 讠). Huòzhě, lǎoshī wèn nǐmen, něi xiē zì yǒu 'qǐngkè' de 'qǐng' (請/请) de shēngpáng (青)? Nǐ jiù kě.yǐ shuō qíngtiān de 'qíng' (晴), huòzhě qíngxíng de 'qíng' (情) dōu shì 'qǐngkè' de 'qǐng' zì de shēngpáng.

Zhōngguó xiǎo háizi zěnme xuéxí Hànzì? Wǒ bù zhīdao tāmen xiànzài yòng shénme fāngfǎ, kěshì yǐqián, tāmen yòng yìxiē shū, xiàng Sān Zì Jīng, Qiān Zì Wén. Zhèi xiē shū shi tèbié wèile gěi xiǎoháir jièshào zuì jīběn de Hànzì xiě de. Sān Zì Jīng, měi jù yǒu sān ge zì, Qiān Zì Wén, měi jù yǒu sì ge zì. Qíshí, nèi liǎng běn shū búdàn yǒu shēngzì, érqiě yǒu Zhōngguó lìshǐ, zhéxué, wénhuà de nèiróng. Gěi nǐmen jǔ ge lìzi: Zhè shi Sān Zì Jīng de jǐ jù. Shi yòng Wényánwén xiě de, kěshì nǐmen kànkan Yīngwén de fānyì jiu dǒng le.

養不教	Yǎng bú jiào,	('Raise [a child] not instruct')
父之過	fù zhī guò;	('father's error')
教不嚴	Jiào bù yán,	('Teaching not rigorous')
師之惰	shī zhī duò.	('teacher's laziness')

Yìsi shi shénme? Yìsi jiùshi bù hǎohāor xuéxí jiùshi fùqin de guòcuò, bù yángé yāoqiú shi lǎoshī de lǎnduò. Shuō de yǒu dàolǐ, duì ma? Búguò Zhōngguó xuéshēng xuéxí Hànzì hé wàiguó xuéshēng xuéxí Hànzì qíngkuàng wánquán bù tóng. Zhōngguó xuéshēng shuōhuà shi méi wèntí, kě.yǐ zhuānxīnyú rènzì xiězì. Wàiguó xuéshēng rúguǒ gāng kāishǐ xuéxí Hànyǔ, nà hái děi tóngshí xué kǒuyǔ hé rènzì, ér yǔyán nénglì bù néng bāng tāmen yòng shàngxiàwén rènzì dǒng dúwù. Suǒ.yǐ wàiguó xuéshēng zuìhǎo yǒu kǒuyǔ de jīchǔ cái kāishǐ xuéxí Hànzì. Rènzì ne, nà, yěxǔ xiān fēnxi yíxiàr zì de xíng-zhuàng, zì de piānpáng, bùshǒu, shēngpáng, děngděng. Ránhòu kàn yìxiē bǐjiào jiǎndān de dōngxi, kàn de yuè duō jì de yuè hǎo. Fùxí ne, nǐ kě.yǐ yòng chuántǒng de xuéfǎ, bǎ zì chóngfù xiě; kěshì xiě de shíhou, bú yào kàn nǐ yǐjīng xiěguo de zì, yàoburán nǐ jiùshì xiě yì bǎi cì, nǐ háishi jìbuzhù! Nǐmen tóngyì bu tóngyì?'

NOTES

a. děi tóngshí xuéxí Hànzì: tóngshí = tóng yí ge shíhou

b. gāng 'just; a short time ago': gāng dào 'just arrived'; gāng xuéle yì nián 'just completed a year'; cf. gāngcái 'just a short while ago'; gānghǎo 'just at the right time; just manage to'; Tā gāngcái zài jiā 'She was home a short time ago'; Wǒ gānghǎo jíshí dàohuì 'I made it to the meeting just in time'.

c. *fāyīn* 'pronunciation' ('issue-sound'): *shuōhuà de shùnxù* 'the order of spoken words'; *shùnxù* 'sequence; order / in proper order'; *zìmǔbiǎo* ('initial-table') *de shùnxù* 'alphabetical order'

d. *cóng'ér tígāo huìhuà de nénglì* 'thereby improving my conversational ability': *cóng'ér* 'thus; thereby' ('follow-and'); *cóng'ér tígāole rénmín de shēnghuó shuǐpíng* 'thereby raising the standard of living of the people'

e. *kǒuyǔ de jìlù*; *jìlù* 'record; keep minutes' ('note-record')

f. *rènhé néng tīngdǒng de* 'anything that can be understood'; *rènhé* 'any; anything' ('serve in a position-what'); *méiyǒu rènhé yìyì* 'doesn't make any sense'; *rènhé shíhou dōu xíng* 'any time is fine'

g. *xíng shì xíng, dànshi* 'it's okay, but …': note the emphasis (and full tone) on *shì* to convey the adversative meaning 'sure it's possible …'; typically followed by 'but'

h. *yídìng huì màn xiàlai, huì xiànzhì xuéxí de jìndù* 'it will certainly slow you down and will limit the rate of learning': With verbs of slowing and stopping, the *xiàlai* suffix indicates 'a slowing down'—note the English also has 'down': *màn xiàlai*; *xiànzhì* 'limit; restrict / a limit' ('limit-create'); *jìndù* 'progress' ('go forward-degree').

i. *yǔyán de biǎodá* 'linguistic expression': *biǎodá* 'voice; express / expression' ('express-reach'); *biǎodá gǎnqíng* 'express one's feelings'; *biǎodá sīxiǎng* 'express one's thoughts'

j. *shòudào Hànzì xuéxí yǒuguān de gè zhǒng yīnsù de búlì yǐngxiǎng* 'be negatively affected by all kinds of factors related to the study of characters': *shòudào búlì yǐngxiǎng* ('receive non-beneficial influence'); *búlì* 'unfavorable; detrimental'; *jílì* 'auspicious' ('lucky-benefit'); *yǒuguān de* 'related' ('have-connection'); *gè zhǒng yīnsù* ('every type-of element, factor')

k. *zǒngzhī* 'in a word; in short; anyway' ('generalize-it'); cf. *zǒngshì* 'always'; *gèrén kànfǎ* 'individual opinion'; *gèrén* ('single-person')

l. *huìhuà de jīchǔ* 'foundation in conversation'; *huìhuà* ('meet-speech')

m. *chùchù dōu* … 'everywhere; everyplace …': cf. *gèchù* 'everywhere'; *hǎochù* 'good thing; benefit; advantage'

n. *wénmáng* 'illiterate / an illiterate; illiteracy' ('written language-blind'): *biāoyǔ* 'posters' [with slogans or exhortations written on them]; cf. *kǒuhào* 'slogans'; *duìlián* 'antithetical written sayings, of the sort that adorn entranceways or scrolls' ('opposing-couplet'); *Chūnlián* 'New Year's couplets' [often pasted on doorways] ('spring-couplet'); *shénme de* 'and so on'

o. *zài nà huánjìng lǐ* 'in that environment': *gǎndào hěn kǔnǎo* 'feel rather vexed'; *kǔnǎo* ('bitter-angry'); *zài wǒ kǔnǎo de shíhou* 'in my distress'

p. *gēn rén jiāowǎng huì hěn gāngà* 'feel rather awkward in one's interaction with people': *gāngà* 'be awkward; embarrassed' is not a compound but a true two-syllable word; *gēn … jiāowǎng* '(with … exchange-go)'; *Wǒ bú yuànyi zài gēn tāmen jiāowǎng le* 'I don't want to associate with them anymore'

q. *hǎiwài huáqiáo huáyì*: *huáqiáo* 'overseas Chinese, particularly those born in Southeast Asian countries and retaining certain aspects of Chinese life through the generations'; *huáyì*

('Chinese-hem [of clothing]') are Chinese who were born abroad and are more or less assimilated—Chinese Americans, Franco-Chinese, and so on.

r. *xiǎokàn jiǎntǐzì* 'look down on simplified characters': *xiǎokàn* 'look down on; belittle (take a small view of)'; *bú yào xiǎokàn* 'don't make a joke of it'; *guīfàn* 'normal/norm' ('rule-model')

s. *zhèngshì de zhuàngkuàng* 'formal situation': cf. *fēizhèngshì* 'informal'; *bǐjiào héshì* 'more suitable; more appropriate'

t. *shāngdiàn de zhāopai, hūnlǐ de qǐngtiē* 'shop signs and wedding invitations': *zhāopai* 'shop sign; signboard' ('beckon-tablet'); *hūnlǐ* 'wedding' ('wedding-ceremony'); *qǐngtiē* 'written invitation' ('invite-invitation')

u. *wèile tǒngyī* 'for the sake of unity': *guīdìng* 'rule; regulation / stipulate; set' ('rule-fix'); *yǒu yì tiáo guīdìng* 'there's a clause'; *yào zūnshǒu guīdìng* 'one should obey the rules'; cf. *guīzé*, which are less formal rules or principles—*ānquán jiàshǐ zhī guīzé* 'rules for safe driving'

v. *bāokuò suǒ.yǒu de guǎnggào hé duì wài xuānchuán dōu bù yǔnxǔ yòng le* 'are not allowed to be used anymore even for advertisements and outside publicity': *bāokuò* 'include; even including'; *suǒ.yǒu de* 'all of the [N]' ('what-exists'); *suǒ.yǒu de dōngxi* 'all the things'; *xuānchuán* 'publicity'; *yǔnxǔ* 'permit; allow'

w. *bǐhuà bǐjiào shǎo*; *bǐhuà* 'stroke' ('pen-draw')

x. *jǔ ge lìzi* 'cite an example': *jǔ* 'raise; cite'

y. *xíngzhuàng wánquán bùtóng*; *xíngzhuàng* 'form; shape; appearance' ('form-shape')

z. *zì de piānpáng, nà jiùshi shuō xíngpáng hé shēngpáng* 'the components of a character—that is to say, the radical and the phonetic': Compound characters generally contain two constituents (*piānpáng* ['to one side-beside']), one that was selected for reasons of pronunciation—the phonetic (*shēngpáng* ['sound-beside'])—and the other for reasons of meaning (*xíngpáng* ['form-beside']). The latter is also called the *bùshǒu* 'radical' ('category-head'). (English 'radical' is a misnomer, as it suggests 'root'; in fact, the *bùshǒu* serves to classify characters into types, and it is often the *shēngpáng* that is historically the root element.)

aa. *zuì jīběn de Hànzì* 'the most basic characters': *jīběn* 'basic' ('foundation-root')

bb. *búdàn yǒu shēngzì, érqiě yǒu Zhōngguó lìshǐ, zhéxué, wénhuà de nèiróng* 'contains not only vocabulary but also content about Chinese history, philosophy, and culture': *nèiróng* 'content' ('inner-capacity'); *búdàn ... érqiě* 'not only ... but also'; *Búdàn qìwèi hǎowén, érqiě wèidao hǎochī* 'It not only smells good but also tastes good too'.

cc. *bù yángé yāoqiú shi lǎoshī de lǎnduò* 'not being strict and demanding, that's laziness on the part of the teacher': *yángé* 'strict; rigorous'; *yángé shuō lái* 'strictly speaking'; *yāoqiú* 'demands' ('want-seek'); *lǎnduò* 'be lazy'

dd. *kě.yǐ zhuānxīnyú rènzì xiězì* 'they can concentrate on recognizing and writing characters': *zhuānxīn + yú* 'focus; concentrate + on' ('specialize-heart-in')

ee. *yòng shàngxiàwén rènzì dǒng dúwù* 'read the text by recognizing characters from the context': *shàngxiàwén* 'context' ('above-below-text'); *dúwù* 'text; reading' ('read-thing') ff. *xiān fēnxi yíxiàr* 'first, do a bit of analysis': *fēnxi* 'analyze/analysis' ('divide-analyze')

gg. *fùxí* 'review; revise' ('again-practice'): cf. *xuéxí, liànxí, yùxí* 'prepare for class' [by students] ('prepare-practice'); *bǔxí* 'take lessons after school' ('supplement-practice')

hh. *bǎ zì chóngfù xiě* 'write characters over and over': *chóngfù* 'repeat; duplicate / repetition' ('again-duplicate')

ii. *Yàoburán nǐ jiùshi xiě yì bǎi cì, nǐ háishi jìbuzhù! Jiùshi … háishi/yě* 'even if … still': *Jiùshi xià dàyǔ wǒmen hái huì qù* 'Even if it's raining heavily, we'll still go'; *Nǐ de bàngōngshì jiùshi xiǎo háishi bǐ wǒ de dà duō le* 'Your office may be small, but it's still much bigger than mine'.

jj. *Nǐmen tóngyì bu tóngyì?* 'Do you agree?' ('same-opinion')

Bú rènshi zì nǐ jiùshi ge wénmáng! (*Lìjiāng*)

Exercise 1

Provide English translations that are accurate and natural.

1. *Wǒmen xuéxí yǔyán de biǎodá bú yào shòudào Hànzì xuéxí yǒuguān de gè zhǒng yīnsù de búlì yǐngxiǎng.*
2. *Rénjiā gěi nǐ míngpiàn, nǐ yě shuō bu chū míngzi lái děngděng.*

3. *Zhōngguó zhèngfǔ wèile tǒngyī yòng zì, guīdìng bú zài yòng fántǐzì, bāokuò
suǒ.yǒu de guǎnggào hé duìwài xuānchuán dōu bú yǔnxǔ yòng le.*

4. *Nǐ jiù kě.yǐ shuō qíngtiān de 'qíng' (晴), huòzhě qíngxíng de 'qíng' (情) dōu
shì 'qǐngkè' de 'qǐng' zì de shēngpáng.*

5. *Zhèi xiē shū shi tèbié wèile gěi xiǎoháir jièshào zuì jīběn de Hànzì xiě de.*

6. *Wàiguó xuéshēng rúguǒ gāng kāishǐ xuéxí Hànyǔ, nà hái děi tóngshí xué
kǒuyǔ hé rènzì, ér yǔyán nénglì bù néng bāng tāmen yòng shàngxiàwén rènzì
dǒng dúwù.*

7. *Ránhòu kàn yìxiē bǐjiào jiǎndān de dōngxi, kàn de yuè duō jì de yuè hǎo.*

Define the following words (in Chinese). Definitions may cite synonyms
or opposites; others can be descriptive, beginning with a modifying phrase
with *de*.

1. *wénmáng*	2. *màn xiàlai*
3. *fāyīn*	4. *guǎnggào*
5. *zhāopái*	6. *fántǐzì*
7. *chùchù*	8. *duìlián*
9. *gāngà*	10. *Huáqiáo*

Consider the following questions for group discussion.

1. *Táiwān rén duì jiǎntǐzì yǒu shénme kànfǎ? Nǐ ne?*

2. *Sān Zì Jīng shi shénme yàng de shū?*

3. *Xué Hànzì shénme fāngfǎ zuì hǎo?*

18.2 Transformations with *chéng* 'become', and more on *bǎ*

Since learning a language inevitably involves errors of perception or translation, expressions involving transformations will be useful. Added to compatible
verbs, *chéng* introduces a 'transform'—the product of a transformation. Frequently, the 'thing transformed' is marked by *bǎ*. Here are examples.

Ni bǎ 'xǐhuan' nèi ge cí shuō chéng 'xīwàng' le.	'You pronounced the word *xihuan* as *xiwang*.'
Qǐng bāng wǒ bǎ zhèi jǐ ge jùzi fānyì chéng Yīngwén.	'Please help me translate these sentences into English.'
Tā bǎ 'zhuā' nèi ge zì xiě chéng 'zhǎo' le.	She has written the character for *zhua* as *zhao*. [抓 → 爪]
Tā bǎ 'shuǎi' nèi ge zì kàn chéng 'yòng' le.	He read the character for *shuai* as *yong*. [甩 → 用]

NOTES

a. Combinations of V + *chéng* 'change into' are not verb combos such as *xiěhǎo* 'finish writing' or *kàndǒng* 'understand'. They cannot be made potential like true verb combos (*kàndejiàn; kànbujiàn*), and they require the result to be expressed (which is the reason why *chéng* is separated from the main verb by a space): *bǎ Hànzì xiě chéng Pīnyīn* 'write characters as pinyin'.

b. *jùzi* 'sentence'; *fānyì* 'translate; interpret' ('overturn-meaning')

c. Interestingly, standard transliterations of two hotels (*fàndiàn*), Hilton and Sheraton, can be easily confused, particularly in a noisy street setting. The former is *Xī'ěrdùn*; the latter is *Xīláidēng*. It is easy to hear one as the other: *Wǒ bǎ Xī'ěrdùn nèi ge míngzi tīng chéng Xīláidēng le, suǒ.yǐ dàocuòle dìfang!* '... so I went to the wrong place'.

Nǐ shuō Xī'ěrdùn, wǒ bǎ tā tīng chéng Xīláidēng le.	'When you said Hilton, I heard it as Sheraton.'

Exercise 2

Provide translations for the following.

1. We often translate *duìbuqǐ* as 'sorry', but actually, it's not quite the same.
2. You can't call good 'bad' or bad 'good.'
3. His book has been translated into Chinese.
4. First-year students often read the character 也 (*yě*) as 他 (*tā*) or 找 (*zhǎo*) as 我 (*wǒ*).
5. My driver heard Sheraton as Hilton, so I ended up staying far away from the office.

Recipes are another prototypical context for the use of *bǎ* (or its more formal synonym, *jiāng*) together with a variety of V + complement structures: *fàng zài* 'put on', *fàng dào* 'put in', *fàng jìnqu* 'put into', *qiē chéng* 'cut into'. Here are oral instructions from our own *dàshīfu* 'master chef', *Chén Tōng lǎoshī*, for making *jiācháng dòufu* 'home-cooked tofu'. He has already laid the various ingredients out on the kitchen table for you—here's a list of them.

zhǔliào	'basic ingredients'
dòufu yíkuài	'a slab of tofu'
fùliào	'secondary ingredients'
qīngjiāo	'peppers'
xiānggū	'mushrooms'
mù'ěr	'wood ears'
tiáoliào	'seasonings'
dòubànjiàng	'thick spicy broad-bean sauce' ('bean-segment-sauce')
yóu	'oil'
jiàngyóu	'soy sauce'
jiàng	'sauce'
xiāngyóu	'sesame oil' ('fragrant-oil')
táng	'sugar'
jiǔ	'wine; liquor'
liàojiǔ	'cooking wine'
diànfěn	'starch'
jiāng	'ginger'
mò<r>	'tips; slivers'
jiāngmò	'chopped ginger' ('ginger-tips')
cōng	'onions'
qīngcōng	'green onions' ('green-onions')
tāng	'soup'
gāotāng	'soup stock' ('high-soup')

Instructions (*zuòfǎ*) for the recipe, in steps (*bù*):

Dì-yī bù:	*Xiān bǎ dòufu qiē chéng chángfāng kuài. Bǎ qīngjiāo qiē chéng piànr. Bǎ qīngcōng qiē chéng mòr. [bǎ … qiē chéng kuài/piànr/mòr]*
Dì-èr bù:	*Bǎ guō fàng zai lúzi shang shāorè.*
Dì-sān bù:	*Bǎ yóu fàngjìn guō li, shāo dào jiǔ chéng rè. Bǎ jiāngmò fàng dào guō li chǎoyíxiàr. Ránhòu zài bǎ dòubànjiàng fàng jìnqu chǎoyíxiàr.*
Dì-sì bù:	*Xiànzài bǎ gāotāng, xiānggū, mù'ěr hé dòufu fàng jìn guō li, ránhòu zài bǎ yìdiǎnr jiàngyóu hé táng fàng jìnqu. Bǎ zhèi xiē dōngxi shāokāi yǐhòu, bǎ huǒ tiáoxiǎo.*
Dì-wǔ bù:	*Xiǎohuǒ shāo yì fēn zhōng, bǎ shuǐ diànfěn fàng jìnqu, zài bǎ qīngjiāopiànr hé jiāngmò fàng jìnqù. Zuìhòu zài cài shang fàng yìdiǎnr xiāngyóu hé cōngmò. Jiācháng dòufu jiu zuòhǎo le.*

SHĒNGCÍ

qiē	'cut': *qiē chéng* 'cut into'
chángfāng	'rectangular' ('long-square'): cf. *zhèngfāng* 'square'
shāo	'cook; heat': *shāorè* 'to heat'; *shāokāi* 'heat until boiling'
guō	'wok'
lúzi	'stove; cooker'
jiǔchéng	'90 percent of boiling' ('nine-tenths'): *chéng* 'one-tenth'; *bāchéng bù kěkào* '80 percent unreliable'
tiáoxiǎo / -dà	'turn down / turn up' [flames, radio, etc.]; *tiáo* 'adjust'

Zài bāo jiǎozi.

Exercise 3

Translate the following sentences, being careful to account for all the words.

1. *Bǎ guō fàng zai lúzi shang shāorè.*
2. *Bǎ zhèi xiē dōngxi shāokāi yǐhòu, bǎ huǒ tiáoxiǎo.*
3. *Zài bǎ qīngjiāopiànr hé jiàngmò fàng jìnqu.*
4. *Zuìhòu zài cài shang fàng yìdiǎnr xiāngyóu. Jiācháng dòufu jiu zuòhǎo le.*

18.3 Taking photographs

Like people elsewhere, Chinese people like to take photographs to record and commemorate special occasions such as meetings, gatherings with friends or family, or excursions. At scenic spots (*jǐngdiǎn*), this means, ideally, getting onself photographed either by commercial photographers, who often establish themselves at places that command the best views, or by friends or helpful strangers. Photographing a gathering of colleagues or family will initiate mixing and jostling until people of high status—elders or superiors—accept their proper positions front and center. They in turn are likely to assume fairly serious expressions, which will spread to all but the youngest members of the group.

zhào	'to image; to reflect; take a photo'
zhàoxiàngjī	'camera' ('reflect-image-machine')
shùzì zhàoxiàngjī	'digital camera' ('number-camera')
zhàopiàn ~ zhàopiānr	'photograph; picture': *jǐ zhāng zhàopiàn*
zhào ... xiàng	'take a photograph' ('to image-likeness')
pāi ... zhào	'take a photo' ('pat-image')
pāi ... zhàopiàn ~ zhàopiānr	'take photographs'
zhào xiàlai	'photograph': 'record by photographing'
jìngtóu	'camera lens; shot; scene; photograph' ('mirror-*tóu*')

USAGE

1. Getting someone else to take a photograph

Yào wǒ tì nǐ zhào ma ~ tì nǐ pāi ma?	'Would you like me to take it for you?'
Yào wǒ tì nǐ zhào yì zhāng <xiàng> ma ~ pāi yì zhāng <xiàng> ma?	'Want me to take one for you?'
Yào wǒ lái bāng nǐmen zhào ba.	'Want me to help you take it?'
Máfan nǐ, bāng (~ tì) wǒ zhào ge xiàng.	'Would you mind taking a picture for me?'

2. Requests and permissions

Kě.yǐ zhàoxiàng ma ~ pāizhào ma?	'Is it okay to take photographs?'
Zhàoxiàng kě.yǐ ma ~ pāizhào kě.yǐ ma?	'Any objection to me taking a photo?'
Wǒ pāi ge zhào, nǐmen jièyì bu jièyì?	

*Sījī shīfu, néng bu néng zài zhèli
tíng yìhuǐr? Wǒ yào bǎ fēngjǐng
zhào xiàlai.*

'Driver, could we stop here for a
bit? I'd like to get a picture of
the scenery.'

*Wǒ bǎ nǐmen dōu zhào xiàlai,
xíng ma?*

'Can I take a picture of the whole
group?'

3. Taking the photograph

Qǐng zhànjìn yìdiǎnr.   'Stand a bit closer, please.' [*jìn* 'close']

*Qǐng wǎng hòu/qián zhàn
yìdiǎnr.*

'Further back/forward, please.'

Qǐng zhànjǐn yìdiǎnr.   'Could you bunch in a bit?' [*jǐn* 'tight']

*Fēnchéng liǎng pái, hǎo bu
hǎo?*

'Split up into two rows, okay?'

*Gāo de zài hòubianr, ǎi de zài
qiánbianr.*

'Tall people in the back; short people
in front.'

*Dōu shì zìdòng de, àn shàngtou
de niǔ jiu hǎo.*

'Everything's automatic; just press
the button on top.'

*Kàn jiāodiǎn duìzhǔn bu
duìzhǔn; duìzhe qiánbianr
de.*

'You need to check that it's in focus;
focus on the ones in front.'

Kàn qǐlai tǐng hǎo de!   'It looks great!'

Èi, hǎo jìngtóu!   'Say, nice shot!'

Xiào yìdiǎnr; yī èr, qiézi!   'Smiiiile; one, two, eggplant!'

Zài lái yí ge!   'One more!'

Wǒ huì gěi nǐmen jì jǐ fènr.   'I'll send you some copies.'

*Yǒu yìdiǎnr bèiyīnr; wǎng liàng
chù zhànzhan.*

'It's a bit dark; stand out in the light.'

*Tài liàng le, wǎng biānshang
zhànzhan.*

'It's too bright, stand to the side.'

Shǎnguāngdēng liàng le ma?   'Did the flash go off?'

SHĒNGCÍ

tì   'for; instead of': *Xīngqīwǔ néng bu néng tì ge bān?*
                    'Could you take over my class for me on Friday?'

jièyì   'object to' ('insert-opinion')

tíng	'stop'
pái	'row; line': cf. *páiduì* 'line up' [in a row]; contrast with *pāi* 'take a photo'
zìdòng de	'automatic' ('self-move')
àn niŭ	'press a button' ('push-button'): cf. *àn jiàn* 'hit a key'
jiāodiǎn duìzhŭn	'the focus is adjusted correctly' ('focus-point align-accurate')
bèiyīnr	'dark; shady' ('back-dark')
liàng	'be bright; light / shine; flash'
shǎnguāngdēng	'camera flash' ('lightning-light-lamp')
shèyǐng	'to film' ('assimilate-image')
jiāojuǎnr	'camera film' ('plastic-roll')

Exercise 4

In small groups, compose short interchanges that cover the following situations.

1. You'd like to take a photograph of the Buddha statues (*Fóxiàng*) in the main hall (*dàdiàn*) of the Huating Temple (*Huátíng Chánsì*) on *Xī Shān*, near *Kūnmíng*. Ask if it's all right to do so; then set it up.
2. You've just climbed *Fúbō Shān* in *Guìlín* and a view of the city and surrounding karst hills lies before you. Try to get someone to take a photo of you with the hills in the background; then have the person take another to be sure of a good shot.
3. You and a number of visitors are being given a tour by a group from the host university—*Zhōngguó Kēxué Jìshù Dàxué* (known as USTC, 'The University of Science and Technology of China')—in *Héféi*. At a suitable time, ask if it would be okay to take a picture of everyone—in front of the lake might be a nice place. Make sure the arrangement is appropriate.
4. You're driving from Xining (*Xīníng*) toward Qinghai Lake (*Qīnghǎi Hú*). As the road gets higher, the views get better and better. Ask the driver if he'd mind stopping at some convenient point so you (and your colleagues) can take some photos of the impressive scenery.

Gùgōng (Běijīng)

18.4 Chinese etiquette

From taking photos to taking flowers to your host—it's a jump, but life isn't always smooth. In this dialogue, *Téng Shùlíng*, a teacher from Belgium, calls her Chinese friend, *Chén Shānshān*, to ask a question about Chinese etiquette. *Chén*'s daughter (D) answers the phone.

D:	*Wèi?*	'Hello?'
Téng:	*Wèi, nǐ shi Chén Shānshān ma?*	'Hello, is that Chen Shanshan?'
D:	*Qǐng děngyixià, wǒ qù zhǎo tā. … Mā, nǐ de diànhuà!*	'Just a minute please, I'll go and find her. … Mom, it's for you!'
Chén:	*Hǎo, xièxie. … Wèi, nín (shi) něi wèi?*	'Okay, thanks. … Hello, who's that?'
Téng:	*Wǒ shi Téng Shùlíng.*	'I'm Teng Shuling.'

Chén:	*O, Shùlíng, nǐ hǎo. Shénme shì?*	'Oh, Shuling, hi, what's up?'
Téng:	*Shānshān, wǒ néng bu néng wèn nǐ yí ge Zhōngguó fēngsù xíguàn de wèntí?*	'Shanshan, can I ask you a question about Chinese customs?'
Chén:	*Wèn ba.*	'Sure.'
Téng:	*Shi zhèyàng: yǒu rén qǐng wǒ chīfàn, wǒ shì bu shì yīnggāi sòng ge lǐwù gěi tā?*	'It's like this: someone's invited me for a meal; should I bring a present?'
Chén:	*Nà yào kàn shi shénme qíng-kuàng, shénme dìfang.*	'Now that depends on the situation and the place.'
Téng:	*Shi ge tóngshì, wǒmen xiāngdāng shú. Tā qǐng wǒ dào tā jiā qù.*	'It's a colleague. We're quite close. She's invited me to her house.'
Chén:	*Zhèi yàng, dài yí shù xiānhuā, huòzhě yì xiē shuǐguǒ, jiù kě.yǐ le. Búbì huā hěn duō qián. Biǎoshì ge yìsi.*	'In that case, you can take a bunch of fresh flowers or some fruit. No need to spend a lot of money. It's the thought.'
Téng:	*Hǎo, shi chūntiān, wǒ jiù mǎi yí shù huā ba.*	'Okay, it's spring, so I'll buy a bunch of flowers.'
Chén:	*Huā hěn héshì!*	'Flowers are fine!'
Téng:	*Hěn gǎnxiè!*	'Many thanks!'
Chén:	*Bié kèqi.*	'You're welcome.'
Téng:	*Hǎo, jiù zhèyàng. Zàijiàn.*	'Okay, that's it then. Bye.'

NOTES

a. Instead of *Wèi, nǐ shi Chén Shānshān ma*, Teng could also have asked any of the following.

Wèi, Chén Shānshān?	'Hello, Chen Shanshan?'
Wèi, Chén Shānshān ma?	'Hello, Chen Shanshan, is it?'
Wèi, nǐ shì bu shì Chén Shānshān?	'Hello, is that Chen Shanshan?'
Wèi, Shānshān zài ma?	'Hello, is Shanshan there?'
Wèi, qǐng zhǎo Chén Shānshān jiē diànhuà.	'Hello, please have Chen Shanshan come to the phone.'

b. Notice that in conventional usage, Chinese generally makes use of first- and second-person pronouns in expressions such as *Nǐ shi shéi?* / *Wǒ shi Téng Shùlíng*, whereas English prefers 'it' or 'this': 'Who is it?' / 'This is Teng Shuling.' Similarly, *Qǐng zhǎo Téng Shùlíng jiē diànhuà.* / *Wǒ jiùshi.* 'Please have Teng Shuling come to the phone.' / 'This is she' (or, as some say, 'Speaking').

c. The word *huā* has a number of senses, including 'flowers; blossoms' (*yí shù huā*), 'design' (*huāyàng* 'design; pattern'), and 'spend' (*huā qián*). The semantic course may be from 'flower' to 'ornament', from 'ornament' to 'waste or dissipation', and from there to 'expense'. Contrast with *huà* 'change'.

d. *biǎoshì ge yìsi* 'as a token' [of friendship, affection] ('to express a meaning')

There are a number of conventional remarks associated with the giving and receiving of gifts. For larger gifts, the host might say *Tài pòfèi le* 'You spent too much money', using the expression *pòfèi* 'squander money' ('break-expense'). On presenting such a present, the guest (giver) might say, with modesty, *xiǎo yìsi* 'just a token' ('small meaning'). However, bringing some fruit or flowers as an expression of thanks (just as Americans and Europeans might bring a bottle of wine) usually elicits more perfunctory remarks. Here are some examples.

Gěi nǐ dàilai yí ge xiǎo lǐwù; cóng Xīnjiāpō.	'We brought you a small gift; it's from Singapore.'
Ràng nǐ pòfèi le; xièxie.	'Thanks, but you shouldn't have.'
Méi shénme; yì diǎn xīnyì.	'It's nothing—just a little something.' ('heart-meaning')
Gěi nǐ dàilai yí shù huā.	'I've brought you a bunch of flowers.'
A, zhēn piàoliang! Xièxie nǐ.	'Oh, how pretty! Thanks a lot.'
Dàilai yìdiǎnr shuǐguǒ, dàjiā yìqǐ chī.	'I've brought some fruit for everyone.'
Nǐ tài kèqi le. Yídìng hěn hǎochī.	'You shouldn't have. They look very nice.'

18.5 The extended family

There are two types of kinship terms: those used in direct address ('Hi, Dad')
and those used to refer to the relationship ('father', and informally, 'my dad').
In Chinese, a child may address his or her grandfather on the father's side
(*zǔfù*) as *yéye* and his or her grandfather on the mother's side (*wàigōng* or *wài
zǔfù*) as *gōnggong*. Typically, Chinese address forms show wide variations, as
they do in English (e.g., different people may address their grandmothers as
'grandma', 'granny', 'nana', 'mawmaw', and so on). It is therefore important
to remember that even though the relationships mentioned in the passages
below are all significant in the Chinese kinship system, the particular terms
cited may vary from region to region. It is worthwhile to compare the terms
and usage expressed here with those of your Chinese friends and people you
might meet in various parts of China.

The following can be regarded as the record of an informal chat about
exended families (*dàjiātíng*), with the speaker using his own situation as an
example. Traditionally (*chuántǒng sīxiǎng*), several generations live together (*jǐ
bèi rén zhù zai yìqǐ*)—the oldest members of the older generation (*bèifen zuì dà
de rén*) have the most power (*quánlì zuì dà*), and the younger generation (*xiǎobèir
de rén*) don't have freedom to choose (*méiyǒu shénme zìyóu*). The head of the
household makes all the decisions (*yíqiè dōu děi yóu jiāzhǎng lái juédìng*). Be on
the lookout for *yóu* 'by; through', which occurs several times in this
narrative.

As you read paragraphs 6, 7, and 8, you may want to skip ahead to Exercise
5, which includes several charts you can use to keep track of the various family
relationships mentioned.

1. *DÀJIĀTÍNG*

   *Guòqù de Zhōngguó jiātíng dàduō dōu shi dàjiātíng, yóuqí shi zài nóngcūn.
   Tǐng máfan de. Wèishénme máfan ne? Yīnwèi rén tài duō. Rén duō shìr jiu
   duō. Háizimen suīrán dōu jiéhūn le, yǒule zìjǐ de jiātíng, dànshi hái dōu gēn
   fùmǔ guò. Yí dàjiāzi shí duō kǒu rén, yǒude shènzhì èrshíjǐ kǒu rén, nǐ
   shuōshuo zhème duō rén, měitiān děi yǒu duōshao shìr. Rén duō, shìr jiu duō,
   wèntí yě jiu duō, suǒ.yǐ yǒude shíhou wèile yìdiǎnr jīmáosuànpí de xiǎoshìr,
   nòng+de dàjiā dōu bú tài yúkuài. Nǐ shuō máfan bu máfan?*

NOTES

yóuqí shi zài nóngcūn	'that's especially the case in villages'
yí dàjiāzi	a regional version of standard *dàjiātíng*: *Yí dàjiāzi shí duō kǒu rén, yǒude shènzhì èrshíjǐ kǒu rén* 'an extended family has more than ten people, some even more than twenty'; *shènzhì* 'to the extent of; so much so that; even to the point of'
wèile yìdiǎnr jīmáosuànpí de xiǎoshìr	*Wèi* and *wèile* overlap, but the former is more often followed by a person (*wèi rénmín fúwù*), the latter by a purpose or reason (as here). *Jīmáosuànpí* 'inessential matters; trifles' ('chicken-feather-garlic-skin')
nòng+de dàjiā dōu bú tài yúkuài	*Nòng* is a verb with a very broad application: *nòngcuò* 'make a mistake; goof'; *nònghǎo* 'make good; fix'; *nòngqīngchu* 'clarify'; *yúkuài* 'be cheerful; happy; joyful'; cf. *kuàilè*

2. ZHŌNGGUÓ CHUÁNTǑNG DE SĪXIǍNG

Wèishénme rénmen jiéle hūn hái gēn fùmǔ guò? Zhè shi yīnwèi rénmen shòule Zhōngguó chuántǒng sīxiǎng de yǐngxiǎng. Zhōngguórén de chuántǒng sīxiǎng shi shénme ne? Zhōngguórén de chuántǒng sīxiǎng yǒu hěn duō, qízhōng yí ge shi hěn zhòngshì jiātíng guānniàn. Jǐ bèi rén zhù zài yìqǐ de dàjiātíng zài Zhōngguó cúnzàile jǐ qiān nián, zài zhèyàng de dàjiātíng lǐmian niánlíng zuì dà de rén – yě jiùshi bèifen zuì dà de rén – quánlì zuì dà, tāmen shi jiāzhǎng, tāmen shuō de huà shéi dōu děi tīng, xiǎobèir de rén – yě jiùshi háizimen – méiyǒu shénme zìyóu, jiālǐ de yíqiè dōu děi yóu jiāzhǎng lái juédìng, bāokuò háizimen de hūnshì.

NOTES

Rénmen shòule Zhōngguó chuántǒng sīxiǎng de yǐngxiǎng.	*Yǐngxiǎng* 'influence'; *gèzhǒng-gèyàng de yǐngxiǎng* 'all kinds of influences'; *shòu ... yǐngxiǎng* 'be influenced by ...' ('receive ... influence')
rénmen, nǚrénmen	*Men* is a bound form that is toneless with pronouns (*zámen*); it also occurs, sometimes toned, with personal nouns to indicate a collective (rather than a plural, since it does not occur with numbers); *lǎoshīmen*; *xuéshengmen*; with nouns (as opposed to pronouns), it is optional; *men* never co-occurs with a number, so it's either *sān ge rén* or simply *rénmen*.
hěn zhòngshì jiātíng guānniàn	*zhòngshì* 'value; regard as important' ('heavy-view'); *guānniàn* 'concept; notion; idea'
cúnzàile jǐ qiān nián	'has existed for thousands of years': *cúnzài* 'exist; be' ('exist-be at')
niánlíng zuì dà de rén	*niánlíng* 'age' [on forms] ('year-age')

jiāzhǎng	'head of the family' ('family-elder'): cf. *xiàozhǎng, shìzhǎng; yíqiè dōu děi yóu jiāzhǎng lái juédìng* 'everything has to be decided by the elders'; *yíqiè* 'everything; all' ('one-cut'); *yóu* 'by; owing to; from; via'; *yóu ... juédìng* 'decide ... by'; cf. *yóu fùmǔ fǔyǎng* 'looked after by parents'; *yóu wǒ lái zuò* 'it'll be done by me; I'll do it'
hūnshì	'marriage' ('marriage-business'): cf. *jiéhūn, hūnlǐ*

3. *DUÌYÚ NǙRÉNMEN LÁI SHUŌ*

Duìyú nǚrénmen lái shuō, tāmen zài chuántǒng de jiālǐ méiyǒu shénme dìwèi, tāmen zhǔyào de gōngzuò jiùshi zhàogù háizi, zhàogù zhàngfu, zuòfàn, děngděng. Kěshì rúguǒ tāmen shēng de háizi duō, yóuqí shi shēng de nánháir duō, nàme tā duì zhèi ge dàjiātíng de gòngxiàn yě jiu dà. Yīnwèi ànzhào Zhōngguó chuántǒng de sīxiǎng, yí ge jiātíng li rúguǒ érzi duō, sūnzi duō, nàme, jiāzhǎng jiu huì fēicháng gāoxìng, fēicháng zìháo; yīnwèi érzi sūnzi duō dàibiǎo érsūnmǎntáng, duōzǐduōfú, jiātíng-xīngwàng. Zài Zhōngguó jiātíng li, rénmen hái tèbié zhòngshì jìnglǎo'àiyòu. Shénme shì jìnglǎo'àiyòu? Jìnglǎo jiùshi niánqīngrén yào zūnjìng zhǎngbèi, xiàoshùn fùmǔ; àiyòu jiùshi zhǎngbèi yào téng'ài érnǚ, téng'ài xiǎozìbèir. Háizi xiǎo de shíhou yóu fùmǔ fǔyǎng, fùmǔ lǎole yǐhòu yóu érnǚ fúyǎng, zhè zài Zhōngguórén de sīxiǎng zhōng shi tiānjīngdìyì de. Zhè jiùshi wèishénme yǒu xiē Zhōngguórén lái Měiguó hòu shēngle háizi, hái bǎ fùmǔ cóng Zhōngguó jiēlái bāngzhù zhàogù de yuángù.

NOTES

duìyú nǚrénmen lái shuō	'as for women': *duìyú* 'in connection with; for; to'
zhǔyào de gōngzuò jiùshi zhàogù háizi	*zhǔyào* 'main; principle; main thing' ('main-require'): cf. *zhǔyào mùbiāo* 'main objective'
duì zhèi ge dàjiātíng de gòngxiàn	'the contribution to the family is': *gòngxiàn* 'contribution / contribute; devote'; *duì ... gòngxiàn* 'contribute to ...'
ànzhào Zhōngguó chuántǒng de sīxiǎng	'according to traditional Chinese thought': *ànzhào* 'according to'; *ànzhào zìjǐ de xìnniàn* 'according to one's own beliefs'
fēicháng zìháo	'very proud' [*zìjǐ de zì*]: cf. *zìháo zhī wù* 'a thing of pride'; *gǎndào hěn zìháo* 'feel great pride in'; *zìháo de kànzhe zìjǐ de gōngzuò de chéngguǒ* 'look with pride on the results of her work'
dàibiǎo érsūnmǎntáng, duōzǐduōfú, jiātíng-xīngwàng	*dàibiǎo* 'represent/representative'; *érsūnmǎntáng* ('children-grandchildren-fill-house'); *duōzǐduōfú* ('many-children-much-fortune'); *xīngwàng* 'prosperous; thriving'

tèbié zhòngshì jìnglǎo'àiyòu	*jìnglǎo'àiyòu* ('respect-elders-love-youngsters')
zūnjìng zhǎngbèi, xiàoshùn fùmǔ	*zūnjìng* 'respect' [*jìngjiǔ de jìng*]; *xiàoshùn* 'be filial; respect [one's parents]; be obedient'; *téng'ài* 'be fond of; dearly love' ('pain-love')
yóu érnǚ fúyǎng	'supported by the children': *fúyǎng* 'bring up; raise; support' ('support with the hand-nourish'); *yóu gūmǔ fúyǎngdà de* 'raised to adulthood by her aunt' [father's married sister]
shi tiānjīngdìyì de	*tiānjīngdìyì* 'be a matter of course; take for granted; quite all right; proper' ('heaven-pass-earth-proper')
yuángù	'reason; cause': *bù zhīdào shi shénme yuángù* 'I don't know why'; often found in constructions with *yīnwèi* (*yīnwèi tiānqì de yuángù* 'on account of the weather') or, as here, with *wèishénme* ('the reason why; the reason that')

4. *XIÀNDÀI SHÈHUÌ DE JIĀTÍNG*

Xiàndài shèhuì de jiātíng gēn yǐqián bǐ, yǒule fēicháng dà de biànhuà.
Dàjiātíng yě jīběn bù cúnzài le, jiātíng biàn+de yuè lái yuè xiǎo le, dàduōshù
de jiāzhǎng yě dōu bú zài guǎn háizimen de shìr le. Niánqīngrén jiéle hūn,
yǒu tiáojiàn de huà, jiu dōu bān chūqu zhù, dúlì shēnghuó le, zhǐ shì zhōumò
huòzhě yǒu shíjiān de huà, qù kànkan fùmǔ, bāngzhù fùmǔ gàn diǎnr huór.
Nǚrénmen yě yǒule shèhuì dìwèi, hěn duō nǚrén zài jīngjì shang yě dúlì le.
Jiātíng biànxiǎo le, rénkǒu shǎo le, jiu shǎole hěn duō máfan. Kěshì yóuyú
Zhōngguó zhèngfǔ zài qīshí niándài shíxíng de jìhuà-shēngyù zhèngcè, měi jiā
zhǐ néng yǒu yí ge háizi, 'xiǎo huángdì' de wèntí jiu chūxiàn le.

NOTES

xiàndài shèhuì de jiātíng gēn yǐqián bǐ	'comparing families in present-day society with previous ones': *shèhuì* 'society' [*kāihuì de huì*]
jīběn bù cúnzài le	'basically, does not exist anymore': *jīběn* 'basic; fundamental / on the whole; basically' ('foundation-root')
bú zài guǎn háizimen de shìr le	'no longer deals with the children': *guǎn* 'have charge of; bother about; manage' (*guǎnlǐ de guǎn*)
yǒu tiáojiàn de huà	'if they have issues': *tiáojiàn* 'conditions; factors'
dúlì shēnghuó le	'live independently': *dúlì* 'stand on one's own; be independent' ('single-strength')
bāngzhù fùmǔ gàn diǎnr huór	'help their parents get a few things done': *gànhuór* 'work; do things'

Yóuyú Zhōngguó zhèngfǔ zài qīshí niándài shíxíng de jìhuà-shēngyù zhèngcè.	*yóuyú* 'owing to; on account of': cf. *yóu* mentioned above; *yóuyú tóuzī shǎo* 'owing to low investment'; *shíxíng* 'carry out; put into practice; implement' ('actual-move'); *jìhuà-shēngyù* 'family planning; birth control' ('plan-birth'); *zhèngcè* 'policy' ('government-policy')
'Xiǎo huángdì' de wèntí jiu chūxiàn le.	*Xiǎo huángdì* 'little emperor': in other words, a spoiled child; *chūxiàn* 'emerge; happen' ('out-appear'); *chūxiànle yí ge wèntí* 'there's a problem'

5. WǑ JIĀ DE QÍNGKUÀNG

Nǐmen ràng wǒ shuōshuo wǒ jiā de qíngkuàng? Hǎo, wǒ shuōshuo wǒ jiā de qíngkuàng. Wǒ jiā yǒu sān kǒu rén, wǒ tàitai, wǒ háizi, hái yǒu wǒ. Tàitai yě jiùshì wǒ àiren; zhèngshì de chēnghu shi fūren. Rúguǒ nǐmen xiǎng gěi biérén jièshào nǐ tàitai, nǐ kě.yǐ shuō, "zhè shi wǒ àiren". Kěshì rúguǒ zài péngyou huòzhě hěn shú de rén miànqián tíqǐ zìjǐ de tàitai de shíhou, wǒmen yě chángchang shuō 'wǒ nèiwèi', 'wǒ nèi kǒuzi', 'wǒ lǎopo'. Xiànzài rénmen gèng xǐhuan yòng 'tàitai' lái chēnghu zìjǐ de àiren le. Ào, nǐ wèn wǒ tàitai zěnme chēnghu wǒ? Yíyàng, yǐqián tā jièshào wǒ de shíhou yě yòng 'àiren' zhèi ge cí, xiànzài gǎn shímáo, zài bú tài zhèngshì de chǎnghé tā chángcháng yòng 'lǎogōng' zhèi ge chēnghu, zài péngyou, shúrén miànqián yě yòng 'wǒ nèiwèi', 'wǒ nèi kǒuzi', zhèngshì yìdiǎnr de chǎnghé tā chángcháng yòng 'xiānsheng' zhèi ge chēnghu.

NOTES

zhèngshì de chēnghu shi fūren	'the formal term of address is *fūren*': *zhèngshì* 'formal'; cf. *fēizhèngshì* 'informal'
zài hěn shú de rén miànqián	'in front of someone you know well': *shú ~ shóu* 'familiar; close'; *miànqián* 'before; to one's face' ('face-before')
tíqǐ zìjǐ de tàitai	'bring up one's own wife': *tí* 'carry [with arm extended]; raise; to bring up a subject'; cf. *bié tí le* 'don't bring it up'
xiànzài gǎn shímáo	'currently very much in fashion': *gǎn shímáo* 'follow fashion; be with the times' ('chase contemporary-style'); *Tā shi ge gǎn shímáo de rén!*
zài bú tài zhèngshì de chǎnghé	'in an informal setting': *chǎnghé* 'setting; situation; occasion' ('open space-come together')

6. QĪNQI GUĀNXI

Nǐmen xiànzài xiǎng ràng wǒ shuōshuo Zhōngguórén de qīnqi guānxi. Hǎo ba, wǒ jiu lái shuōshuo, búguò, zhè duì nǐmen lái shuō kě shì yí ge tǐng fùzá de

*wèntí, bú tài róngyì jìzhu. Jiù ná wǒ de jiārén lái shuō ba: wǒ bàba shi wǒ
tàitai de gōngong, shi wǒ háizi de yéye; wǒ māma shi wǒ tàitai de pópo, shi wǒ
háizi de nǎinai. Wǒ zài jiā páiháng lǎosān, shàngbianr yǒu yí ge gēge, yí ge
jiějie; xiàbianr yǒu yí ge dìdi, yí ge mèimei. Wǒ háizi jiào wǒ gēge dàye; yǒude
dìfang yě jiào bóbo; jiào wǒ dìdi shūshu, jiào wǒ jiějie dàgū, jiào wǒ mèimei
èrgū.*

NOTE

Wǒ zài jiā páiháng lǎosān.   'I'm the third-oldest child in the family': *páiháng* ('row-column');
cf. *Wǒ páiháng lǎodà.* 'I'm the oldest child in my family.'

7. *ZÌJǏ DE QĪNQI*

*Wǒ de gēge, dìdi, jiějie, mèimei dōu jiéhūn le, tāmen yě dōu yǒule háizi. Wǒ
gēge de tàitai shi wǒ de sǎozi, wǒ háizi jiào tā dàniáng; wǒ dìdi de tàitai shi
wǒ de dìmèi, wǒ háizi jiào tā shěnr; wǒ jiějie de xiānsheng shi wǒ de jiěfū, wǒ
háizi jiào tā dàgūfu; wǒ mèimei de xiānsheng shi wǒ de mèifu, wǒ háizi jiào tā
èrgūfu. Wǒ gēge hé dìdi de érzi jiùshi wǒ de zhízi, tāmen de nǚ'ér shi wǒ de
zhínǚ; wǒ shi wǒ gēge háizi de shūshu, shi wǒ dìdi háizi de dàye; wǒ tàitai shi
wǒ gēge háizi de shěnr, shi wǒ dìdi háizi de dàniáng. Wǒ jiějie hé mèimei de
érzi shi wǒ de wàisheng, tāmen de nǚ'ér shi wǒ de wàishēngnǚ, wǒ shi tāmen
de jiùjiu, wǒ tàitai shi tāmen de jiùmā, yǒude dìfang yě jiào jiùmǔ; wǒ gēge,
dìdi de nánhái shi wǒ háizi de tánggē huòzhě tángdì, tāmen de nǚ'ér shi tā de
tángjiě huòzhě tángmèi; wǒ jiějie, mèimei de nánhái shi wǒ háizi de biǎogē
huòzhě biǎodì, nǚ' ér shi tā de biǎojiě huòzhě biǎomèi.*

8. *YĪNQĪN GUĀNXI: YÓU HŪNYĪN ÉR JIÉ CHÉNG DE QĪNQI*

*Wǒ tàitai de māmu shi wǒ de yuèmǔ, shi wǒ háizi de lǎolao; wǒ tàitai de bàba
shì wǒ de yuèfù, shi wǒ háizi de lǎoye. Wǒ tàitai yě yǒu yí ge gēge, yí ge dìdi, yí
ge jiějie, yí ge mèimei, tāmen yě dōu jiéhūn le, yě dōu yǒule háizi. Wǒ tàitai de
gēge hé dìdi dōu shi wǒ háizi de jiùjiu, tāmen de tàitai shi wǒ háizi de jiùmā,
yě jiào jiùmǔ; wǒ tàitai de jiějie hé mèimei shi wǒ háizi de dàyí hé èryí. Wǒ
tàitai de gēge hé dìdi de érzi dōu shì wǒ háizi de biǎogē huòzhě biǎodì, tāmen
de nǚ'ér shi wǒ háizi de biǎojiě huòzhě biǎomèi; wǒ tàitai de jiějie hé mèimei
de érzi shi wǒ háizi de yígē huòzhě yídì; tāmen de nǚ'ér shi wǒ háizi de yíjiě
huòzhě yímèi.*

9. *TÀI FÙZÁ LE!*

Nà, nǐmen kànkan, Zhōngguó jiātíng de qīnqi guānxi shì bu shì tài fùzá le?
Zài chéngshì shi zhèyàngr, zài nóngcūn jiu gèng fùzá le, yǒude rén shuō
Zhōngguórén de qīnqi guānxi shi qīnqi de qīnqi yě shì qīnqi, suǒ.yǐ yǒude
shíhou jiù lián wǒmen zìjǐ yě gǎobuqīngchu zìjǐ de qīnqi guānxi. Hǎo le, wǒ
shuōle bàntiān, bù zhī nǐmen shìfǒu dōu nòngqīngchule Zhōngguó jiātíng hé
Zhōngguó qīnqi de guānxi. Nǐmen xiànzài kě.yǐ bǎ shàngmian de nèi xiē
Zhōngguó qīnqi guānxi de cíhuì fānyì chéng Yīngwén, zhèyàngr nǐmen jiu néng
duì zhèi liǎng ge xìtǒng de bùtóng de dìfang kàn+de gèng qīngchu.

NOTES

bù zhī nǐmen shìfǒu dōu nòngqīngchu le	'not sure whether you've got it straight or not now': *Shìfǒu* is a formal version of *shì bu shì*, used here to impart a more serious tone to the summing up.
cíhuì fānyì chéng Yīngwén	'translate the words into English': *cíhuì* 'words and phrases'
zhèi liǎng ge xìtǒng	'these two systems of …': *xìtǒng* 'system'; cf. *jiāotōng xìtǒng*

Modified after an original by Chen Tong.

Exercise 5

Translate the following excerpts into English.

1. *Háizimen suīrán dōu jiéhūn le, yǒule zìjǐ de jiātíng, dànshi hái dōu gēn fùmǔ guò.*

2. *Zhōngguórén de chuántǒng sīxiǎng yǒu hěn duō, qízhōng yí ge shi hěn zhòngshì jiātíng guānniàn.*

3. *Kěshì rúguǒ tāmen shēng de háizi duō, yóuqí shi shēng de nánháir duō, nàme tā duì zhèi ge dàjiātíng de gòngxiàn yě jiu dà.*

4. *Niánqīngrén jiéle hūn, yǒu tiáojiàn de huà, jiu dōu bān chūqu zhù, dúlì shēnghuó le, zhǐ shì zhōumò huòzhě yǒu shíjiān de huà, qù kànkan fùmǔ, bāngzhù fùmǔ gàn diǎnr huór.*

5. *Wǒ gēge, dìdi de nánháir shi wǒ háizi de tánggē huòzhě tángdì, tāmen de nǚ'ér shi tā de tángjiě huòzhě tángmèi.*

With one or two classmates, relisten to or reread the kinship passage. As you do so, fill in the Chinese terms in the charts below; then go back and fill in the English terms where applicable. Be prepared to talk about how the two systems differ (in terms of distinctions, ambiguity, overlap, and so on).

	DESCRIPTION	CHINESE TERM(S)	ENGLISH TERM(S) *(IF ANY)*
THROUGH HUSBAND OR WIFE	1. husband's father		
	2. husband's mother	*pópo*	'mother-in-law'
	3. wife's father		
	4. wife's mother		'mother-in-law'

	DESCRIPTION	CHINESE TERM(S)	ENGLISH TERM(S) *(IF ANY)*
THROUGH SIBLINGS	5. older brother's wife		
	6. younger brother's wife		
	7. brother's son		
	8. brother's daughter		
	9. older sister's husband		
	10. younger sister's husband		
	11. sister's son		
	12. sister's daughter	*wàishēngnǚ*	'niece'

	DESCRIPTION	CHINESE TERM(S)	ENGLISH TERM(S) (IF ANY)
	13. mother's father		
	14. mother's mother		
	15. mother's brother		
	16. mother's brother's wife		
	17. mother's older sister	*dàyí*	'aunt'
	18. mother's younger sister	*xiǎoyí*	'aunt'
THROUGH MOTHER	19. mother's brother's older son	*biǎogē*	
	20. mother's brother's younger son		
	21. mother's brother's older daughter		
	22. mother's brother's younger daughter		
	23. mother's sister's older son		
	24. mother's sister's younger son	*yídì*	'cousin'

	DESCRIPTION	CHINESE TERM(S)	ENGLISH TERM(S) *(IF ANY)*
THROUGH MOTHER	25. mother's sister's older daughter		
	26. mother's sister's younger daughter		

	DESCRIPTION	CHINESE TERM(S)	ENGLISH TERM(S) *(IF ANY)*
THROUGH FATHER	27. father's father		
	28. father's mother		
	29. father's older brother		'uncle'
	30. father's older brother's wife		
	31. father's younger brother		
	32. father's younger brother's wife	*shěnr*	'aunt'
	33. father's older sister		
	34. father's older sister's husband		

	DESCRIPTION	CHINESE TERM(S)	ENGLISH TERM(S) (IF ANY)
	35. father's younger sister		
	36. father's younger sister's husband		
THROUGH FATHER	37. father's brother's older son		
	38. father's brother's younger son	*tángdì*	'cousin'
	39. father's brother's older daughter		
	40. father's brother's younger daughter		
	41. father's sister's older son	*biǎogē*	
	42. father's sister's younger son		
	43. father's sister's older daughter		
	44. father's sister's younger daughter		

Create sentences or phrases to illustrate the usage of the following expressions.

1. *shòu ... yǐngxiǎng*
2. *wèishénme ... de yuángù*
3. *duì ... gòngxiàn*
4. *lián ... yě/dōu*

Tuìxiūzhě 'retirees' (*Xiàmén*)

18.6 Death

We haven't had much to say about death so far. Confucius wrote, *Wèi zhī shēng, yān zhī sǐ*? This means, literally, 'Not yet know life, wherein know death?' He was admonishing followers to attend to the rites and rituals of this world—the basis of social stability—rather than follow the prescriptions of those who claimed esoteric knowledge about the hereafter. Although we do not want to dwell upon death, we do want to be able to talk about it from time to time. With that in mind, here are the basics.

Someone's death can be presented in direct, unadorned fashion using *sǐ* 'die'.

Tā sǐ le.	'He's dead; he died'
Tā sǐdiào le.	'He's dead; he died' ('die-fall')

However, Chinese, just like speakers of many other languages, prefer euphemisms, particularly when the death involves a friend or family member. Examples include *bú zài le* 'no longer with us'; *qùshì* 'departed the world' (*shì* being the *shì* of *shìjiè* 'world'); *guòshì* 'pass [from the world]'.

Wǒ bà bú zài le.	'My father's no longer living.'
Mǔqin qùshì shí, wǒ shí suì.	'I was ten when my mother passed on.'
Tā qiánnián jiu guòshì le.	'He passed away the year before last.'

Written and formal language has other options, including *shìshì* 'depart the world' (with a formal word *shì* 'pass' plus the *shì* of *shìjiè* 'world').

Zhōu Ēnlái tóngzhì shìshì èrshíbā zhōunián	'the 28th anniversary of the passing of comrade Zhou Enlai'

18.6.1 Causes

People may die of natural causes, or they may die of disease or by accident. Here are some options.

àizībìng	'AIDS' ('love-spurt-illness')
xīnzàngbìng	'heart attack' ('heart-organ-illness')
chēhuò	'automobile accident' ('auto-disaster')
áizhèng	'cancer' ('cancer-disease')
zhòngfēng	'stroke / have a stroke' ('middle-wind')
zìshā	'suicide; commit suicide' ('self-kill')
xīdú	'take drugs' ('inhale-poison')
yānsǐ	'drown' ('drown-die')
bèi dǎsǐ de	'be killed; be shot' ('by [someone] hit-kill DE')
zài zhànzhēng zhōng	'in the war' ('at war in')
dǎzhàng	'fighting' ('hit-weapons')
fēijī shīshì	'plane crash' ('plane loss-event')
Wénhuà Dàgémìng zhōng	'in the Cultural Revolution'

NOTE

Zhòngfēng 'stroke / have a stroke': cf. *fáng zhòngfēng* 'prevent stroke'; *zhòngfēng de wēixiǎn* 'danger of stroke'; *tā zhòngfēng le* 'she's had a stroke'. With the more formal word *huàn* 'contract; suffer [an illness]': *tā huàn zhòngfēng le* 'she's suffered a stroke'. The more scientific word for stroke, 'cerebral hemorrhage', is the graphic *nǎoyìxuè ~ xiě* ('brain-overflow-blood').

In colloquial speech, the illness phrase can be treated as an adverbial and placed before the verb, often with the *shì … de* pattern shifting focus to the cause of death—the adverbial; cf. English 'He died of natural causes', with the stress on 'natural causes'.

Tā <shi> zěnme sǐ de?	'How did (s)he die?'
Tā lǎo sǐ de.	'She died of natural causes.' ('old-age die')
Tā shi áizhèng sǐ de.	'He died of cancer.'
Tā àizībìng sǐ de.	'She died of AIDS.'
Tā shi xīnzàngbìng sǐ de.	'He died of a heart attack.'
Tā dǎzhàng sǐ de.	'He died fighting.'
Tā shi dìzhèn yàsǐ de.	'He was crushed to death in an earthquake.'
Tā zài Dì-èr cì Shìjiè Dàzhàn zhōng sǐ de.	'She died in World War II.'
Tā shi zìshā sǐ de.	'He committed suicide.'
Tā bèi dǎsǐ de.	'He was killed/shot.'
Tāmen chēhuò sǐ de.	'They died in a traffic accident.'

A more formal version, making use of the versatile literary preposition *yú* 'at; from; of; by' and classical Chinese word order, is also sometimes spoken.

Tā sǐ yú zhòngfēng.	'She died of a stroke.'
Tā sǐ yú fēijī shīshì.	'He died in a plane crash.'

Exercise 6

Report on the date and cause of death of some well-known people. Alternatively, report on people killed in disasters, such as airplane crashes, earthquakes, or wars. Two examples are included below as a guideline; you add six more.

Máo Wáng shi xīdú sǐ de, zài 1977 nián; tā zhǐyǒu 42 suì.

Zài 2005 nián, hěn duō rén shi dìzhèn sǐ de.

Cheung Chao Island, Hong Kong

18.6.2 Consolation

Even in one's native language, it can be hard to know what to say to someone who has suffered bereavement or loss. For this reason, many languages have fixed expressions that can form the basis of a consolatory remark. Before you get to actual condolences, though, you might first want to comment on the situation.

Āiyā!	'My gosh!'
Tiān na!	'Heavens!'
Zhēn kěxī.	'What a shame.'
Zhēn zāogāo.	'How unfortunate.'

If the loss is relatively minor or vague, then you might simply want to say how sorry you are, using the word *nánguò* 'be sad' ('hard-to get through').

Tīngshuō nǐ de māo sǐle, wǒ juéde hěn nánguò.	'I am so sorry to hear that your cat died.'

| *Tīngdào dìzhèn de xiāoxi, wǒ fēicháng nánguò. Xīwàng jiārén dōu ānránwúyàng.* | 'I was very sorry to hear about the earthquake; I hope your family is safe and sound.' |

If the loss is more substantial, then you will need to express condolences. Chinese equivalents are *wèiwèn* 'convey sympathy' ('sympathy-inquire') and *āidào* 'condolences'.

| *Wǒ xiǎng xiàng nín hé nín jiāshǔ biǎoshì shēnqiè de āidào.* | 'I'd like to express heartfelt condolences to you and your family.' |
| *Qǐng jiēshòu wǒ zuì chéngzhì de wèiwèn.* | 'My deepest condolences for your loss.' |

18.7 Feeling ill

While we are dealing with life's misfortunes, let's step back from death and consider illness. In earlier lessons, you encountered the verb *juéde* 'feel'. Here, we expand possible answers to the question *Nǐ juéde zěnmeyàng?* 'How do you feel; how are you feeling?' The context here is casual rather than the formal answers one might hear in a doctor's office, for example.

USAGE

Wǒ jīntiān yǒu yìdiǎnr bù shūfu.	'I don't feel very well today.'
Wǒ yǒu yìdiǎnr gǎnmào.	'I've got a bit of a cold.'
Tā déle gǎnmào.	'She's caught a cold.'
Wǒ yǒu diǎnr késou.	'I've got a bit of a cough.'
Tā gǎnmào le, ké+de hěn lìhai.	'He's got a cold and is coughing terribly.'
Tā fāshāo le, 39 dù.	'He's got a 102-degree fever.'
Tā fāle liǎng tiān shāo le.	'She's had a fever for two days.'
Yǒu diǎnr bù shūfu, tóuténg.	'I'm not feeling well; my head aches.'
Tóu/wèi/jiǎo/bèi téng ~ tòng.	'My head/stomach/foot/back hurts.'

Bù shūfu, tùxiě!	'Not too good; I'm spitting up blood!'
Bù shūfu, tóuyūn.	'I'm not well; I'm dizzy.'
Bù shūfu, guòmǐn le!	'I'm not well—allergies!'
Wǒ hěn xiǎngjiā.	'I'm homesick.'

SHORT DIALOGUES

Wǒmen zǒule hěn yuǎn le, jiǎo shang yǒu shuǐpào!	'We've walked a long way; I've got blisters on my feet!'
Yào yí ge bāngdí ma?	'Do you want a Band-Aid?'
Bǐ bāngdí hái dà.	'It's bigger than a Band-Aid.'
Nà, fàng yì zhāng bēngdài ba.	'So, you'd better put a bandage on it.'
Chīyào le ma?	'Have you taken medicine for it?'
Hái méi. Bù xiǎng chī. Pà kǔ.	'Not yet. I don't want to. I'm afraid it'll taste bad.'
Āi, yá hěn téng. Néng bu néng gěi wǒ jièshào yí ge yáyī?	'Ouch, my tooth hurts. Can you recommend a dentist for me?'
Kě.yǐ, wǒ shūshu shi yáyī.	'Sure, my uncle's a dentist.'

SHĒNGCÍ

dàifu ~ yīshēng	'doctor' [coll] ~ 'doctor' [more formal]
kàn dàifu ~ yīshēng	'visit a doctor'
yáyī	'dentist' ('tooth-doctor')
guòmǐn	'have allergies; allergies' ('excess-sensitivity')
gǎnmào	'have a cold' ('feel-stuffed up')
fāshāo	'have a fever' ('emit-heat')
késou	'have a cough; a cough'
tóuténg	'have a headache; a headache' ('head-hurt')
bèiténg	'have a sore back' ('back-hurt')
yǒu shuǐpào	'get blisters' ('have water-blisters')
xièdù<zi>	'have diarrhea' ('flow-stomach')
tùxiě	'spit up blood'
xiǎngjiā	'be homesick' ('miss-home')

hóulong téng	'have a sore throat'
liúhàn	'sweat' ('flow-sweat')
tóuyūn	'be dizzy' ('head-dizzy')
chīyào	'take medicine'
yīyuàn	'hospital'
dǎzhēn	'get a shot; get an injection'
yàodiàn	'pharmacy'
Zhōngyào/Xīyào	'Chinese/Western medicine' [what you take for illness]
Zhōngyī/Xīyī	'Chinese/Western medicine' [as a subject of study]

NOTES

a. Southern Chinese tend to say *tòng* rather than *téng*: *tóu/wèi/jiǎo/bèi tòng*.

b. Related to *tù* with a falling tone is *tǔ* with a low tone, whose core meaning is 'spit' (with an extended meaning of 'enunciate'—as in 'spit out' words). *Qǐng wù suídì tǔtán* 'please do not randomly spit' is a common public health notice. *Tù*, on the other hand, suggests an unintentional evacuation from the mouth, typically vomiting, but also, as in this case, spitting up blood.

c. Chinese medicines come in many tastes, but if the taste isn't nice, then it's not unusual to try to disguise it by adding sweet ingredients.

Here is a sample exchange that uses terminology from traditional Chinese medicine (*Zhōngyī*).

Zhèi liǎng tiān méi shíyù,
    zuǐ lǐ kǔ, ěrmíng!
	'For the past couple of days I've lost my
	    appetite, and my ears are ringing!'

Nǐ kěnéng shi nèi rè, xūyào
    chī diǎnr qùhuǒyào, xièxie
    huǒ.
	'You might have internal heat; you
	    should take some reduce internal heat
	    medicine and discharge some heat.'

Hǎo, nǐ shuō de yǒu dàolǐ;
    wǒ shìshi kàn.
	'Okay, what you say makes sense;
	    I'll try it.'

SHĒNGCÍ

shíyù	'appetite' ('food-desire')
zuǐ	'mouth'
kǔ	'bitter'

ěrmíng	'ringing ears' ('ear-sound')
nèi	'internal'
xūyào	'need to'
qùhuǒyào	'reduce internal heat medicine' ('eliminate-fire-medicine')
xiè	'discharge'
shì\<shi\>	'try'

Exercise 7

Paraphrase the following paragraph in Chinese.

When I got up this morning, I didn't feel very well. At first, I thought it was because I drank too much the previous night. So I had a cup of coffee and then lay down (*tǎng*) on the sofa for a couple hours. At noon, I ate a bit, but I didn't have an appetite; my stomach was upset, and I had diarrhea. By the afternoon, I realized I had a cold; my head ached, and I didn't have any energy. I took a cab to the hospital, but it was more than an hour before I could see a doctor. She gave me some medicine for reducing internal heat and told me to rest for a few days. So I did. I'm feeling a lot better now, but I still feel a bit dizzy. I guess I need to eat more and drink more water.

18.8 At the temple

Lǎo Wèi is visiting the *Qìngfúgōng* in the Chinese quarter of Yangon (*Yángguāng*) in Burma/Myanmar (*Miǎndiàn*). *Qìngfúgōng* means, literally, 'palace celebrating good fortune'. In China and Southeast Asia, temples are often considered palaces of the gods, hence the use of the term *gōng* 'palace' in the name. In the dialogue below, *Sū xiānsheng* is based on a real person, a Sino-Burmese whose ancestors immigrated to Burma by way of Singapore early in the 20th century. Typical of Sino-Burmese, he speaks Hokkien (*Mǐnnányǔ*), Burmese (*Miǎndiànyǔ*), and some Mandarin.

Yángguāng: Qìngfú Gōng (Miǎndiàn)

Wèi:	*Sū xiānsheng, zhè shi Qìngfúgōng—gōngdiàn de gōng, duì ma? Wèishénme jiào gōng?*	'Mr. Su, this is Qingfu Gong—the 'gong' of 'palace,' right? How come it's called a palace?'
Sū:	*Zài Dōngnányà, gōng yě shì sìmiào de yìsi.*	'In Southeast Asia, 'palace' also means 'temple'.'
Wèi:	*Nà, zhèi ge sìmiào hěn yǒu yìsi. Nǐ kàn, ménshang de ménshén—zhēn wēiwǔ!*	'Well, this temple is interesting. Look at the door guardians on the door—they're quite impressive!'
Sū:	*Zhè shi Yángguāng zuì lǎo de sìmiào, 1898 nián jiànlì de.*	'This is Yangon's oldest temple; it was established in 1898.'

Wèi:	*Sū xiānsheng, qǐngwèn, zhè shi shénme shén?*	'Mr. Su, can I ask you what god this is?'
Sū:	*Guān Dì; huòzhě Guān Lǎoye. Běnlái shi ge jiāngjun, shi Sānguó shídài de yīngxióng. Sǐdiào yǐhòu chéngle ge shén.*	'It's Guan Di, or Lord Guan. He was originally a general, a hero from the time of the Three Kingdoms. After he died, he became a god.'
Wèi:	*Nǐ zěnme zhīdao shi Guān Dì?*	'How do you know it's Guan Di?'
Sū:	*Nǐ kàn, gèzi hěn gāo, yǒu cháng húzi, hóng liǎn, tóu shang dàizhe<yí> ge tèsè de màozi, shǒu lǐ názhe yì běn shū.*	'Look—he's tall, he has a long beard and a red face, he's got a special hat on his head, and he has a book in his hand.'
Wèi:	*Liǎn hěn kěpà! Tā shǒu lǐ názhe de shi shénme shū ne?*	'What a frightening face! What's the book he's holding?'
Sū:	*Hǎoxiàng shi Kǒngfūzǐ de Chūnqiū. Guān Dì yě shì yǒu xuéwen de.*	'Looks like it's Confucius's *Spring and Autumn Annals.* Guan Di is learned as well.'

SHĒNGCÍ

Qìngfúgōng	'The Temple of Blessed Happiness'
sìmiào	'temple' [generic term]
shén	'god; divinity'
yīngxióng	'hero': one of *Zhāng Yìmóu*'s films is called *Yīngxióng*
húzi	'beard'
tèsè	'special, unusual qualities': here referring to an unusual hat
kěpà	'frightening' ('able-fear'): cf. *kě'ài*
yǒu xuéwen de	'one who has ~ shows learning, scholarship'

NOTES

a. *Shén* are often deified historical figures whose spiritual power can be called on for protection or assistance. *Guān Dì* was *Guān Yǔ*, the third of the heroes who swore brotherhood in the famous 'peach garden oath' that opens *Sānguó Yǎnyì* 'The Romance of the Three Kingdoms'. He has many other names, including *Guān Lǎoye* 'Grandpa Guan', which in this context is probably better translated 'Lord Guan'.

b. *Chūnqiū* 'The Spring and Autumn Annals' ('spring-autumn'): a chronicle of the State of *Lǔ* (that covered parts of modern Shandong Province) from 722–481 BCE. It is considered to have been edited by Confucius in such a way as to illustrate his political philosophy.

18.9 The Chinese school system

Xī Mèng mǔ, zé lín chù, zǐ bù xué, duàn jī zhù 'In ancient times, Mencius's mother selected a neighborhood, and if her son didn't learn, then she broke the shuttle of her loom'. Those are four lines from the *Sān Zì Jīng* 'The Three Character Classic', which come a few lines before the lines cited in the first narrative of this unit. The story is well known to Chinese. When left a widow, the mother of Mencius—the Confucian philosopher who lived in the 4th and 3rd centuries BCE—moved around trying to find an environment conducive to her son's education. They lived first near a cemetery and then near a marketplace before finally settling in a district near an academy where the young Mencius learned correct ritual. Each time Mencius failed to learn appropriately, his mother tore the shuttle from the loom, showing him what happens to the cloth—and, by extention, education—when continuity is lost. The story is one of many that illustrate the high regard Chinese have for learning and knowledge.

That's a long buildup to our topic: the Chinese school system (*Zhōngguó jiàoyù zhìdù*). The school system is divided into (*fēn chéng*) elementary (*xiǎoxué*), middle (*zhōngxué*), upper middle (*gāozhōng*), and upper (*dàxué*). There are other refinements, such as curricula for gifted (*zhòngdiǎn*) or regular (*fēizhòngdiǎn*) students, technical schools (*jìshù xuéxiào*), and professional high schools (*zhíyè gāozhōng*).

Zhōngguó jiàoyù zhìdù jīběnshang fēn chéng xiǎoxué liù nián, zhōngxué sān nián, gāozhōng sān nián, dàxué sì nián. Xiǎoxué, zhōngxué, gāozhōng hé dàxué yǒu zhòngdiǎn hé fēizhòngdiǎn. Zhòngdiǎn xiǎoxué, zhōngxué, gāozhōng hé dàxué gè fāngmiàn de tiáojiàn dōu bǐ fēizhòngdiǎn hǎo.

Zhōngguó de háizi yìbān dōu shì qī suì kāishǐ shàng xiǎoxué. Yīnwèi Zhōngguó de xuéxiào bǐ Měiguó de shǎo, lìngwài, Zhōngguó rénkǒu tài duō, zài jiāshang Zhōngguó hěn duō jiātíng dōu zhǐyǒu yí ge háizi, suǒ.yǐ, hěn duō fùmǔ dōu yǒu 'wàng zǐ chéng lóng', 'wàng nǚ chéng fèng' de sīxiǎng. Dàduōshù fùmǔ dōu xīwàng tāmen de háizi yǐhòu bǐ tāmen qiáng, suǒ.yǐ dōu xiǎng bànfǎ ràng zìjǐ de háizi dào zhòngdiǎn xiǎoxué qù dúshū. Dànshi jìn zhòngdiǎn xuéxiào hěn bù róngyì. Chúle xuéshēng zìjǐ xuéxíhǎo yǐwài, fùmǔ hái děi yǒu qián, huòzhě yǒu guānxi cái xíng. Bùguǎn shi shàng zhòngdiǎn xiǎoxué háishi fēizhòngdiǎn xiǎoxué de xuéshēng, tāmen de fùmǔ hé lǎoshī dōu yào xiǎng bànfǎ ràng tāmen shàng zhòngdiǎn zhōngxué hé zhòngdiǎn gāozhōng, yīnwèi zhǐyǒu shàngle zhòngdiǎn zhōngxué, tèbié shi zhòngdiǎn gāozhōng, shàng dàxué de jīhuì cái néng gèng dà. Suǒ.yǐ, jué dàduōshù Zhōngguó de xuéshēng cóng xiǎo xuéxí jiu fēicháng nǔlì, fùmǔ hé lǎoshī yě dōu bī+de hěn jǐn, mùdì jiùshi yǐhòu néng ràng zhèi xiē xuéshēng shàng ge hǎo gāozhōng, yǐhòu hǎo kǎo ge dàxué. Xiànzài hěn duō Zhōngguórén dōu rènwéi zhīshi hěn zhòngyào, méiyǒu zhīshi jiu méiyǒu yíqiè. Érqiě hěn duō fùmǔ dōu bǎ xīwàng jìtuō zài tāmen zhèi ge wéiyī de háizi shēn shang, xīwàng tāmen de háizi néng dédào zuì hǎo de jiàoyù.

Zhōngguó de xuéshēng cóng xiǎo jiu fēicháng xīnkǔ. Tāmen měitiān zǎoshang qī diǎn duō jiu yào dào xuéxiào. Xiàwǔ wǔ-liù diǎn cái néng huíjiā. Xiǎo xuéshēng zhōumò yě xiūxibùliǎo, tāmen de fùmǔ hái yào sòng tāmen qù cānjiā yìxiē xìngqù huódòng, pìrú shuō, qù liàn yuèqì, huìhuà, děngděng. Tāmen de fùmǔ xīwàng tāmen chúle yào xuéxíhǎo yǐwài, hái yào yǒu yíjìzhīcháng, zhèiyàng yěxǔ yǐhòu huì duì háizi de chéngzhǎng yǒu bāngzhù. Xuéshēng dàole gāozhōng jiu gèng máng le. Wèile kǎo dàxué, tāmen měitiān chúle shàngkè yǐwài, kèyú shíjiān jīběnshang dōu yòng zài dàliàng zuò liànxítí shang le. Kǎobushàng dàxué de xuéshēng, dàduōshù dōu shàngle jìshù xuéxiào huòzhě zhíyè gāozhōng le. Zài zhèiyàng de xuéxiào lǐ xuéxí liǎng-sān nián yǐhòu, yǒule yíjìzhīcháng, bìyè hòu dào gōngchǎng qù dāng jìshù gōngrén huòzhě zuò qítā de gōngzuò.

Suízhe gǎigé kāifàng, Zhōngguó de jīngjì yuè lái yuè hǎo. Xiànzài Zhōngguó de xuéxiào dōu shōufèi le. Xuéxiào bù yíyàng, shōufèi de duōshǎo yě bù yíyàng. Zhèyàng, méiyǒu qián de háizi shàngxué hěn kùnnan. Suǒ.yǐ hěn duō xuéxiào yě dōu yǒu jiǎngxuéjīn zhìdù, tèbié shi dàxué. Zhōngguó hái yǒu yí ge "Xīwàng Gōngchéng". "Xīwàng Gōngchéng" zhǔyào shi bāngzhù hěn qióng de dìfang de háizi shàngxué de, yě bāngzhù nèi xiē jiātíng shēnghuó yǒu kùnnan, dàn xuéxí fēicháng hǎo de xuéshēng de. Xiànzài Zhōngguó zhèngfǔ yě ràng yǒu qián rén ná chū yìxiē qián lai bāngzhù Zhōngguó de jiàoyù, ràng tāmen bàn xuéxiào. Suǒ.yǐ Zhōngguó xiànzài yě yǒu sīlì xiǎoxué, sīlì zhōngxué, sīlì gāozhōng hé sīlì dàxué. Zhōngguó xiànzài de jiàoyù bǐ yǐqián hǎo duōle, néng shàng dàxué de rén yě yuè lái yuè duō le.

Modified from an earlier script by Chen Tong.

NOTES

a. *jiàoyù zhìdù* 'system of education': *zhìdù* 'system; rules'; *shèhuìzhǔyì zhìdù* 'socialist system'; *xìtǒng* is a system in the sense of a network (*jiāotōng xìtǒng*); *zhìdù* is a system in the sense of an economic or political organization

b. *jīběnshang* 'basically' ('foundation-root-on'): *wǒ jīběnshang tóngyì nǐ de jiànyì* 'basically I agree with your proposals'

c. *fēi* (as in *fēizhòngdiǎn*) 'non-; un-': cf. *fēicháng* 'unusual'; *fēizhèngshì* 'informal'; *fēijūnshìqū* 'demilitarized zone' ('not-army-business-region'); *fēibàolì* 'nonviolence'

d. *Gè fāngmiàn de tiáojiàn dōu bǐ fēizhòngdiǎn hǎo*: *Gè fāngmiàn* 'each aspect'; cf. *gè guó* 'every country'; *tiáojiàn* 'conditions'; *zhòngdiǎn* 'emphasis; key; priority'

e. *yīnwèi ... , lìngwài ... zài jiāshang* 'because ... and moreover ... as well as': *lìngwài* 'besides; moreover' ('extra-outside'); *zài jiāshang* 'as well as' ('again add-on')

f. *lóng* 'dragon', *fèng* 'phoenix': *wàng zǐ chéng lóng* 'hope their sons become dragons', *wàng nǚ chéng fèng* 'hope their daughters become phoenixes'—a colorful way of saying that 'one hopes one's children have a bright future'

g. *bǐ tāmen qiáng*: *qiáng* 'strong'

h. *bùguǎn* 'no matter [+ question]': The following pair of examples are cited from the very useful Mandarin language Web site of the Center for Chinese Linguistics at Beijing University (ccl.pku.edu.cn). Notice that the phrase immediately following *bùguǎn* always has the form of a question: *qù nǎ.lǐ?*; *shénme shì?* (1) *Bù guǎn qù nǎ.lǐ, yào liú ge huà yǐbiàn liánxì.* ('no matter go where, need leave a note so-as-to-facilitate contact') (2) *Bùguǎn tiānxià fāshēng shénme shìr, zhǐyào rénmen chībǎo dùzi, yíqiè jiu hǎobàn le.* ('no matter under heaven happens what thing, as long as people eat-full stomach, all then easy-manage LE')

i. *jué dàduōshù* 'far and away the majority of': *jué* [short for *juéduì*] 'absolute; complete'

j. *bī+de hěn jǐn* 'push them hard' [*jǐnzhāng de jǐn*]; *bī* 'force; push'

k. *mùdì* 'goal' ('eye-goal'): cf. *mùbiāo* 'objective'

l. *yǐhòu hǎo kǎo ge dàxué* 'so as to better get into university (by exam) later': *hǎo* 'better to; so as to'

m. *rènwéi zhīshi hěn zhòngyào* 'regard knowledge as important': *rènwéi* 'think that; reckon that' [*rènshi de rèn; yǐwéi de wéi*]; *zhīshi* 'knowledge' [*zhīdao de zhī, rènshi de shi*]

n. *bǎ xīwàng jìtuō zài tāmen zhèi ge wéiyī de háizi shēn shang*: *jìtuō zài* 'entrust to the care of; place hope in' [*jì yì fēng xìn de jì; tuō nǐ yí jiàn shì de tuō*]; *wéiyī de* 'sole; only' ('only-one'); *dédào* 'obtain' ('get-reach')

o. *xīnkǔ* 'be laborious; be hard work / work hard'

p. *cānjiā yìxiē xìngqù huódòng*: *cānjiā* 'attend; take part in; join'; *huódòng* 'activities' ('live-move'); *pìrú shuō* 'for example; such as'; cf. *bǐrú shuō*

q. *liàn yuèqì, huìhuà* 'learn to play musical instruments; draw': *liàn* 'practice'; cf. *liànxí; yuèqì* 'musical instrument' ('music-implement'); *huìhuà* 'draw; paint / painting', homophonous with *huìhuà* 'conversation' ('meet-speech')

r. *yìjìzhīcháng* 'professional skill; technical specialization' ('one-skill-*zhī*-long')

s. *duì háizi de chéngzhǎng yǒu bāngzhù*: *duì . . . yǒu bāngzhù* 'assist someone to/with'; *chéngzhǎng* 'grow up; mature' ('become-grown')

t. *kèyú shíjiān jīběnshang dōu yòng zài dàliàng zuò liànxítí shang le*: *kèyú shíjiān* 'after-school time'; cf. *yèyú* 'after work', *yèyú-xuéxiào* 'part-time school'; *zài . . . shang* 'in . . .'; *dàliàng* 'a large amount of; a lot' ('great-amount'); *liànxítí* 'exercises; problems' ('practice-subjects')

u. *dāng jìshù gōngrén* 'be a skilled worker'; *jìshù* 'technology; skill; technique'; *zhíyè gāozhōng* 'professional schools'; *zhíyè* 'occupation; profession'; *wǒ de zhíyè shi . . .*

v. *Suízhe gǎigé kāifàng*; *suízhe* 'following the; along with'; *dōu shōufèi le*; *shōufèi* 'collect fees; charge' [*shōuyīnjī de shōu, diànhuàfèi de fèi*]

w. *shàngxué hěn kùnnan*: *kùnnan* 'difficult; hard; be in dire straits / difficulties'

x. *yǒu jiǎngxuéjīn zhìdù*: *jiǎngxuéjīn* 'scholarship' ('award-study-money'); also *zhùxuéjīn* ('help-study-money')

y. *Xīwàng-Gōngchéng*: 'Project Hope' ('hope-engineering project'); *zhǔyào shi* 'is mainly about / main; fundamental; chief' ('main-need'); cf. *zhǔyào yuányīn* 'main cause'; *zhǔyào de wèntí* 'main problem'; *qióng* 'be poor'

z. *sīlì xiǎoxué* 'private elementary school': *sīlì* 'private' ('private-establish'); cf. *zhōulì* 'state'; *gōnglì* 'public; government established'

Exercise 8

Translate these excerpts into English.

1. *Yīnwèi zhǐyǒu shàngle zhòngdiǎn zhōngxué, tèbié shi zhòngdiǎn gāozhōng, shàng dàxué de jīhuì cái néng gèng dà.*

2. *Suǒ.yǐ, jué dàduōshù Zhōngguó de xuéshēng cóng xiǎo xuéxí jiu fēicháng nǔlì, fùmǔ hé lǎoshī yě dōu bī+de hěn jǐn, mùdì jiùshi yǐhòu néng ràng zhèi xiē xuéshēng shàng ge hǎo gāozhōng, yǐhòu hǎo kǎo ge dàxué.*

3. *Xiǎo xuéshēng zhōumò yě xiūxibùliǎo, tāmen de fùmǔ hái yào sòng tāmen qù cānjiā yìxiē xìngqù huódòng, pìrú shuō, qù liàn yuèqì, huìhuà, děngděng.*

4. *... yě bāngzhù nèi xiē jiātíng shēnghuó yǒu kùnnan, dàn xuéxí fēicháng hǎo de xuéshēng de.*

Answer the following questions in Chinese.

1. *Zhòngdiǎn xuéxiào hé fēizhòngdiǎn xuéxiào zěnme bù yíyàng?*

2. *Qǐng jiěshì yíxià 'wàng zǐ chéng lóng' hé 'wàng nǚ chéng fèng' shi shénme yìyì ('significance')?*

3. *Jùshuō Zhōngguó xuéshēng cóng xiǎo shēnghuó hěn xīnkǔ; wèishénme zhèyàngr shuō?*

4. *'Xīwàng-Gōngchéng' shi shénme?*

Qiānmíng shèjì 'Signature design'

18.10 Confrontation (2)

While you are still coming to grips with basic conversational material, it is appropriate to try to speak a standard form of the language and adopt a fairly formal level of usage. However, if you live in a typical Chinese neighborhood, then you will quickly realize that the Mandarin you hear on the street (rather than in an institutional setting) is likely to be quite regional and informal in its usage. It is larded with colorful language, slang, obscenities, and obscure references. The conversation below, though still idealized compared to real life, provides a glimpse of what you might observe. First, though, allow a digression to introduce some language of mild abuse.

18.10.1 Expletives and swear words

Expletives are phrases along the lines of 'you idiot' or 'you fool' (or worse), which are used to express intense emotions—particularly disgust, anger, or contempt—but also surprise or wonder. Chinese has as many varieties as English. Here is a sampling of words that fall under the general headings of 'nonsense' and 'idiot/bastard'.

Nonsense

gǒupì	'bullshit; nonsense' ('dog-fart')
húshuō	'nonsense'
fèihuà	'rubbish' ('waste-words')
xiāchě	'talk rubbish' ('blind-gossip')
chědàn	'talk nonsense' ('gossip-shallow')

Stupidity

shǎzi	'idiot'
shǎguā	'idiot' ('stupid melon')
shǎmàor	'fool; idiot' ('stupid-hat')
báichī	'idiot' ('white-silly idiot')
nǎozi-yǒubìng	'moron' ('brain have-disease')
shénjīngbìng	'crazy; nuts' ('mental-illness')

Yokel

èrbǎiwǔ	'dope; idiot'
xiāngbalǎor	'hick' ('village-hick')
tǔbiē	'country bumpkin' ('soil-turtle')

Disparaging, cursing

liúmáng	'bum; hooligan'
wúlài	'rascal; good-for-nothing' ('not-rely on')
pǐzi ~ dìpǐ	'riffraff; trash; ruffian' ~ 'local thug' ('tumor')
biēsānr	'bum': by way of Shanghai dialect, possibly from a pidgin English word related to standard English 'beg'
hùnhùnr	'bum; rascal' ('confuse; mix')
hùnzi	'quack; imposter' ('confuse')
wángbādàn	'son of a bitch; bastard': *wángbā* 'turtle; tortoise', with an extended meaning of 'cuckold'; *dàn* 'egg', so 'child of a cuckold' = 'bastard'
zázhǒng	'bastard' ('mixed-race')
gǒuniáng yǎng de	'son of a bitch' ('dog-girl raised')
gǒuzǎizi	'bastard' ('dog-whelp')
<chòu>gǒushǐ	'piece of shit' ('smelly-dog-shit')
tā mā <de>	'damn; damned'

An expression that should be pulled out for special mention in this context is *tā mā <de>* ('his/her mother's'). In its crudest form, the object is provided and the English translation would have to make use of the *f* word. As is, it corresponds to 'damn; damned; bloody', a signal of emotional intensity. It tends to be used adverbially (and mostly by men). In the first of the two examples below, it reinforces an emotion of wonder or delight; in the second, of anger or contempt.

Nǐ tāmā de zhēn xíng a! Jǐ tiān zài gǔshì shang zhuànle shíwàn yuán!	'You're really something! A few days on the stock market and you've earned ¥100,000!' ('you bloody really okay, few days at stockmarket on earn-LE ¥100,000')
Nǐ tāmā de háishi rén ma? Dàjiēshang dàochù luànlā!	'What sort of a person are you? Crapping anywhere you feel like!' ('you damn still-be person? Street everywhere random-pull')

Of course, as an informal ambassador, anxious to show a friendly face to your host country, you will want to keep your emotions under control and learn what you can simply by eavesdropping.

Kūnmíng

18.10.2 Talking tough
This conversation takes place under conditions similar to those in the earlier confrontation, which involved two women involved in a bicycle accident. In this case, the protagonists are men, and their language is concomitantly cruder (though still toned down for this textbook). *Jiǎ* and *Yǐ*, riding bikes on a busy street in Beijing, collide with each other.

Jiǎ:	*Ài, xiāle, wǎng nǎr qí a?*	'Hey, you're blind, where are you going?'
Yǐ:	*Zuǐba gānjing diǎnr, nǐ tāma cái xiā le ne!*	'Clean out your mouth; it's you who's so damned blind!'
Jiǎ:	*Ài, nǐ zěnme chūménr zǒng bǎ nǐ mā dàizhe?*	'Hey, how come you bring your mother with you every time you leave the house?'
Yǐ:	*Zěnme la?*	'How's that?'
Jiǎ:	*Chòu zuǐ, wūrǎn kōngqì! Méi shùkǒu jiu chūlai le?*	'You filthy gob, polluting the air! You came out without gargling?'
Yǐ:	*Shǎo fèihuà! Wǒ zìxíngchē huài le, gěi wǒ xiūchē qu.*	'Cut the nonsense! My bike's damaged; you're going to fix it for me.'
Jiǎ:	*Gěi nǐ xiūchē? Zuòmèng qǔ xífur—xiǎng+de měi ne! Wǒ hái méi ràng nǐ gěi wǒ xiūchē ne.*	'Fix it for you? You're dreaming—dream on! I haven't made you fix mine yet.'
Yǐ:	*Wǒ gěi nǐ xiū ge pì!*	'I'll fix a fart for you!
Jiǎ:	*Nǐ tāma zhǎo chōu a!*	'You're bloody well looking for a thrashing!'
Yǐ:	*Zěnmezhe, xiǎng bǐhua bǐhua? Nǐ hái bú shì gèr. Wǒ kàn nǐ háishi xiān liàn jǐ nián zài lái zhǎo wǒ.*	'How's that; you wanna make gestures? You're not up to it yet. Look, you come and find me after you practice for a couple years.'
Bǐng:	*Suàn le, suàn le, chē méi huài, rén yě méi shāng, zǎ zhème dà huǒr ne?*	'Forget it! Your bikes are fine and no one's hurt; why are you so riled up?'
Jiǎ:	*Bú shì wǒ huǒr dà; tā zhuànglè wǒ hái mà rén.*	'I'm not riled up; he's cursing me out after colliding with me.'

Yǐ:	Nǐ yào bù xiān mà rén ne?	'And if you hadn't cursed first?'
Bǐng:	Déle, déle, shēngqì shāng shēnzi; dàqīngzǎo de.	'Okay, okay already; anger harms the body; it's early in the morning.'
Jiǎ:	Tā yào tàidu hǎo yìdiǎnr, dào ge qiàn, jiu suàn le. Nǐ kàn tā nàyàngr, jiu gēn chīle zhàyào sì de!	'He needs to have a better attitude and apologize, then I'd forget it. Look at him—like he's eaten some dynamite!'
Bǐng:	Sàn le, sàn le, yàoburán shàngbān dōu wǎn le.	'Break it up, break it up, or else you'll be late for work.'
Jiǎ:	Yàobushì kàn zài dàhuǒr de miànr shang, wǒ jīntiān fēi ràng nǐ shūfu shūfu bù kě!	'If I wasn't thinking of your face, I'd sure make you nice and comfortable today!'
Yǐ:	Bié zuǐ yìng le! Xíng le, gāi gànmá gànmá qù ba!	'Don't talk tough! Go ahead; do what you need to do!'
Bǐng:	Sàn le, sàn le!	'Break it up now, break it up!'

With help from friends who wish to remain anonymous.

SHĒNGCÍ

xiā	'be blind'
chòu	'stinking'
zuǐba	'mouth'
shùkǒur	'gargle' ('wash-mouth')
pì	'flatulance; fart': cf. *pìgu* 'buttocks' and *fàngpì* 'fart' ('put-fart')
chōu	'draw forth; take': cf. *chōuyān*, but here 'thrash, lash'
bǐhua	'gestures'
gèr	'stature; height': cf. *tā gèr hěn gāo*
liàn	'train; drill'
zǎ	= *zěnme*
mà	'curse; criticize'

déle	'enough; stop' ('get-LE')
shāng	'harm': *shāng shēnzi* 'harm the body'
tàidu	'attitude'
dào … qiàn	'apologize' ('express-apology')
zhàyào	'dynamite' ('explode-drug')
gēn … sì de	'similar to; like' ('with … like DE')
sàn	'disperse; scatter'
yàoburán	'otherwise; or else' ('if-not-thus'): also *bùrán* or *yàobu*
dàhuǒr	'temper' ('big-fire')
miànr	'face': literal and figurative
fēi … bù kě	'have to; must' ('not to … not be possible')
zuǐ yìng	'talk tough' ('mouth hard')

NOTE

Zuòmèng qǔ xífur—xiǎng+de měi ne: *qǔ xífur* 'take a wife', so 'dream you've taken a wife', often implying a pipe dream; hence *xiǎng+de měi ne* 'a beautiful idea', but it's not going to happen!

18.11 Rhymes and rhythms

18.11.1 Aspirations

Before we close with the usual rhymes, here's a short interlude—a chance to wind down. Mao Zedong, late in his life, used to talk about the *sì yǒu* 'the four musts' ('the four haves'): a bicycle, radio, watch, and sewing machine. Later, Deng Xiaoping added the *bā dà* 'the eight bigs' (the rest of the list follows). During the 1990s, people spoke humorously about the *xīn de sì yǒu* 'the new four musts': *chē*, *fáng*, *kuǎn*, and *xíng*, which make abbreviated reference to a 'car', 'house', 'money', and 'fashion'. The three sets listed below can be roughly associated with particular eras (e.g., *qīshí niándài* 'the 1970s'), as indicated.

qīshí niándài

shǒubiǎo	'watch' ('hand-watch')
féngrènjī	'sewing machine' ('sewing-machine')
zìxíngchē	'bicycle' ('self-power-vehicle')
shōuyīnjī	'radio' ('receive-sound-machine')

bāshí niándài
    xǐyījī   'washing machine' ('wash-clothes-machine')
    diànbīngxiāng   'refrigerator' ('electric-ice-box')
    diànshàn   'electric fan' ('electric-fan')
    móluōchē   'motorcycle' ('motor-vehicle')

jiǔshí niándài
    cǎidiàn   'color TV' ('*cǎisè diànshì*')
    yīnxiǎng   'stereo' ('sound-resound')
    yí tào jiājù   'set of furniture' ('a suite [of] furniture')
    zhàoxiàngjī   'camera' ('reflect-image-machine')

18.11.2 Rhymes

Dà fēng gē 'The song of the great wind' was composed by *Liú Bāng* (256–195 BCE), a general and the founder of the Han Dynasty (who is therefore also referred to as *Hàn Gāozǔ* 'the Great Founder of Han' or *Hàn Gāodì* 'the Great Emperor of Han'). The syllable *xī* in the middle of each line of the poem signals a pause (marked by the ellipsis). The first line has only three syllables before the pause, so you might find it easier to read the *qǐ* (before *xī*) in that line with a 'double mora'—*qì-í*—to balance the lines.

Dà fēng qǐ xī … yún fēiyáng,   ('great wind rise XI … clouds tumble')
wēi jiā hǎi nèi xī … guī   ('[with] awe increased seas in XI …
    gùxiāng.   return home')
Ān dé měngshì xī … shǒu sì   ('how to-obtain warriors XI … to
    fāng?   guard the four frontiers')

Of all the patriotic songs from the 1950s and 60s in China, *Sailing the Seas Depends on the Helmsman* has the most rousing tune and, even though it is a paean to a man who now occupies cultural space between demagogue and demigod, we thought it worthwhile to include here. You can hear many versions online. The refrain is much easier to sing than the verses.

Dàhǎi hángxíng kào duòshǒu
'Sailing the Seas Depends on the Helmsman'

Dàhǎi hángxíng kào duòshǒu,
'Sailing the seas depends on the helmsman,'
('seas navigate depend + on helmsman')

wànwù shēngzhǎng kào tàiyang,
'all things depend on the sun for growth,'
('all-things growth depend-on sun')

yǔ lù zīrùn hémiáo zhuàng,
'water and dew moisten the seedlings and make them strong,'
('rain dew moisten seedlings strong')

gàn gémìng kào de shì Máo Zédōng sīxiǎng.
'people who engage in revolution depend on Mao Zedong Thought.'
('do revolution depend-on DE is Mao Zedong thought.')

Yú líbukāi shuǐ ya,
'Fish can't be separated from water,'
('fish separate-not-away [from] water YA')

guār líbukāi yāng,
'gourds can't be separated from the stalk,'
('gourds separate-not-away [from] stalk')

gémìng qúnzhòng líbukāi Gòngchǎndǎng,
'revolutionary masses can't be separated from the Communist Party,'
('revolution masses separate-not-away [from] Communist Party)

Máo Zédōng sīxiǎng shi bú luò de tàiyang.
'Mao Zedong Thought is a never setting sun.'
('Mao Zedong thought is not falling DE sun')

Summary

Whatever; anything that	*Rènhé néng tīngdǒng de dōu néng yòng Pīnyīn xiě xiàlai.*
Character components	*piānpáng, xíngpáng, bùshǒu, shēngpáng*
	'Chī' de bùshǒu shi kǒuzìpáng.
V-into	*Ni bǎ xǐhuan nèi ge cí shuō chéng xīwàng le.*
Bǎ ... fàng zai ...	*Bǎ guō fàng zai lúzi shang shāorè.*
Photos	*Máfan nǐ, bāng ~ tì wǒ zhào ge xiàng.*
	bǎ fēngjǐng zhào xiàlai
Gifts	*Búbì huā hěn duō qián. Biǎoshì ge yìsi.*
	Ràng nǐ pòfèi le; xièxie. / Méi shénme; yì diǎnr xīnyì.
Be influenced	*shòule Zhōngguó chuántǒng sīxiǎng de yǐng.xiǎng*
According to	*ànzhào Zhōngguó chuántǒng de sīxiǎng*
The reason that (~why)	*Zhè jiùshi wèishénme yǒu xiē Zhōngguórén lái Měiguó hòu shēngle háizi, hái bǎ fùmǔ cóng Zhōngguó jiēlái bāngzhù zhàogù de yuángù.*
Even if (*jiùshi*)	*Yàoburán nǐ jiùshi xiě yì bǎi cì, nǐ háishi jìbuzhù!*
To die of ...	*Tā lǎo sǐ de. / Tā shi áizhèng sǐ de.*
Consolations	*Tīngshuō nǐ de māo sǐle, wǒ juéde hěn nánguò.*
Illnesses	*Tā gǎnmào le, ké+de hěn lìhai.*
Descriptions	*tóu shang dàizhe ge tèsè de màozi*
Basically agree	*Wǒ jīběnshang tóngyì nǐ de jiànyì.*
No matter; regardless of	*bù guǎn qù nǎ.lǐ*

Méiyǒu bù kěnéng!

Appendix: body parts

Core body parts, as opposed to figurative extensions (e.g., 'He's the brains of the operation'), might seem to be well-demarcated notions that would translate easily from language to language. In fact, although their core meanings correspond fairly well, their connotations may be quite different. This is particularly true of the internal organs. In Chinese, for example, *xīngānr* 'heart and liver' is a term of affection (*fùmǔ de xīngān bǎobèi* 'parents' darling treasure'); *xīncháng* 'heart and intestine' is, roughly, 'in the mood for' (*méiyǒu xīncháng qù kàn diànyǐngr*); and *fèifǔ* 'lungs and bowels' means 'from the bottom of one's heart' (*fèifǔ zhī yán* 'words from the bottom of one's heart').

The following is not exhaustive. You will want to add to these words with specialized terms such as 'temple', 'forehead', and 'calf'. In addition, you should check regional and local variations (pronunciation as well as word selection), analyze written and spoken usage, and observe metaphorical extensions.

Names for internal organs often contain the bound form *zàng*: *nèizàng* 'internal organs; viscera' ('inside-viscera'); *xīnzàng* 'heart' (or in less clinical settings, just *xīn*); *shènzàng*, often just *shèn* 'kidney'; *yízàng* 'pancreas'.

The brain as an organ—the cerebrum—rather than as the mind is *nǎojiāng* ('brain-thick liquid'), but as the mind, it is *nǎo, nǎozi,* or even *nǎohǎi* ('brain-sea'). *Nǎodai* 'brain-bag' is a colloquial way of referring to the head.

The liver is *gān* (cf. *gānbìng* 'hepatitis'). The gall is *pí* (*píqi* refers to one's temperament or disposition; *fā píqi* is 'to vent one's spleen; to get angry'). The lungs are *fèi* (cf. *fèibìng* 'tuberculosis').

The stomach is *wèi;* the intestines *cháng* or *chángzi.* The stomach and intestines form the compound *chángwèi,* which refers to the digestive system as a whole (cf. *chángwèibìng*). *Pángguāng* is bladder; *dǎnnáng* is gall bladder ('gall-bag'); the uterus has the evocative name of *zǐgōng* ('child-temple').

Nerves are *shénjīng,* which should not be confused with the reverse *jīngshén* 'spirits; energy'. *Xiě* (~ *xuè*) is blood; *xuèguǎn<r>* ~ *xiěguǎn* ('blood-pipes') are blood vessels. *Jīròu* are muscles. Bones are *gútou* (pronounced *gǔtou* by some). The colloquial word for tendons or sinewy things in general (including muscles) is *jīn* (as in the dish, *hóngshāo-niújīn* 'braised beef tendons'); the more formal word is *jījiàn.*

On the outside, beginning with the head, *tóu, tóufa* is hair, and the forehead is *étóu* (with *tóu* 'head' obviously) and also *qián'é* (*tā qián'é hěn dà*). Ears are *ěrduo,* and eyes are *yǎnjing.* The nose is *bízi.* The mouth is *zuǐ;* teeth in general are *yáchǐ;* and *méimao* are eyebrows. The chin or lower jaw is *xiàba* (*dǎle xiàba yíxiàr*), whereas the word for cheeks is *liǎnjiá* or, more colloquially, *liǎndàn<r>* or *liǎndànzi* ('face-eggs'). The tongue is *shétou;* the throat is *hóulong* (and the inner throat or larynx is *sǎngzi*); and the neck is *bózi.*

Continuing with the outer parts: *pífū* is skin, *máo* is body hair, *jiānbǎng* is the shoulder, and *bèi* is the back, as in *bèi huì tòng de* 'your back will hurt'. The chest is *xiōng,* and breasts are *rǔfáng* ('milk-houses'). The belly or abdomen is *dùzi,* and the navel is *dùqí.* The waist is *yāobù* (e.g., *tóufa chuīdào yāobu* 'her hair hangs down to her waist'). *Shènbù* is the kidney area (*dào shènbù, bú dào yāobù* 'to the hips, not the waist'), and *pìgu* are the buttocks. The vagina is *yīndào* ('yin-passage'); the penis is the *yīnjìng* ('yin-stem'); and *gāowán* are the testicles ('testicle-ball'). The anus is *gāngmén* ('bowel-door').

That leaves the extremities. The arms are *gēbei;* the hands are *shǒu;* and the fingers are *shǒuzhǐ* or, more colloquially, *zhǐtour* (the latter also refers to toes).

The thumb is *dàmǔzhǐ* ('big-mother-finger') or 'the mother of all fingers', and the fingernails are *zhǐjia*. *Tuǐ* are the legs and *dàtuǐ* is the thigh ('big-leg'). The foot and, in some cases, the lower leg is *jiǎo*. The ankle is *jiǎohuái* (cf. *niǔshāngle jiǎohuái* 'twisted an ankle') or *jiǎowànzi* (*wànzi* 'wrist', so 'foot-wrist'). Toes are *jiǎozhǐ* or *jiǎozhǐtou* (*Wǒ de jiǎozhǐ pèngdàole shítou shang le* 'I stubbed my toe on a rock').

NOTE TO THE EPIGRAPH

Sūnzi's *Art of War* is difficult to date but is said to have achieved its current form at least by the early Han period, which dates from 206 BCE. This excerpt shows, again, the succinct style of classical Chinese usage. *Zhī* is, of course, the *zhī* of *zhīdao*. The key contrast is between *bǐ* 'that; other' and *jǐ* 'self'. The *ér* of the second line is the conjunction, already seen in a number of quotes and roughly translated as 'and' (or 'but'); *bì* in the last line is the *bì* of *búbì* or *bìxū*.

Unit 19

Zǐ yuē:
Wú shí -yǒu-wǔ ér zhì yú xué;
Sānshí ér lì; sìshí ér bú huò;
Wǔshí ér zhī tiān mìng;
Liùshí ér ěr shùn;
Qíshí ér cóng xīn suǒ yù, bù yú jǔ.
'The Master said: At fifteen I was determined on learning; at thirty I was established; at forty I had no doubts; at fifty I understood the commands of Heaven; at sixty my ears were obedient; at seventy I may follow what my heart desires without transgressing the limits.'
('The Master said: I ten-have-five and set-sights on learning; thirty and stood-up; forty and had no doubts; fifty and knew heaven's will; sixty and ears were obedient; seventy and follow heart what desires, not crossing limits.')
—*Lúnyǔ* 2.4 (*Analects* 2.4), nonliteral translation from *The Original Analects: Sayings of Confucius and His Successors*, by E. Bruce Brooks and A. Taeko Brooks

We try to end with a bang and not a whimper by saving some interesting subjects for this final conversational unit. The unit starts off conventionally enough, though, with a narrative about Tianjin, a city that is often overshadowed by its neighbor, Beijing, to which it is now virtually joined. That narrative is followed by sections on apologies, current events, and sports. Then there is a narrative about telecommunications in China—from

A note to the epigraph is located at the end of the unit.

telephones to texting—which is followed by a number of dialogues that involve telephoning and bargaining (but this time, as the Chinese might do it). The third of our major narratives in this unit finds us wandering around the second-tier city of Zhenjiang (on the lower Yangtze), uncovering some historical sites and other places of interest. Finally, some odd points and a fable involving bluster and intrigue.

Contents

19.1 Tianjin memories

Tianjin lies about 120 kilometers to the south of Beijing (city center to city center), extending to the *Bó Hǎi* (the name of the sea). Tianjin was the northern terminus of the Grand Canal (*Dàyùnhé*) and the port of entry to Beijing. In fact, it was only named Tianjin ('heaven-ford')—leading to the capital—at the beginning of the 15th century, when the *Yǒnglè* Emperor moved the capital from Nanjing to Beijing. Like Beijing, it is a *zhíxiáshì*; in fact, its borders meet those of the Beijing *zhíxiáshì*, so in many respects, Beijing and Tianjin are becoming twin cities. Like other *zhíxiáshì*, Tianjin includes rural and urban counties in its jurisdiction, so the total population figures are deceptive. The urban population of Tianjin is about six million. On the new fast trains (on the *Jīng-Jīn Chéngjì Tiělù* 'Beijing-Tianjin Intercity Railway'), travel between Tianjin and Beijing takes only thirty minutes. Tianjin is known for its architectural legacy, dating from the concessions granted to European powers and to the Japanese after the Opium Wars of the 19th century. It is also known for the variety of Mandarin spoken there, with its distinctive tonal contours, for *xiàngshēng* comedy routines, for food dishes such as the famous *gǒubùlǐ* dumplings, and for *Chén Tōng*, teacher extraordinaire, who contributed so much to the dialogues and narratives in this intermediate volume of *Learning Chinese.*

The following narrative can be thought of as an informal interview with a longtime resident of Tianjin.

Wǒmen zài Tiānjīn de jiā shi yí ge Rìběnshì de xiǎo lóufáng, yǒu liǎng céng. Dì-yī céng zhùzhe yí hù rénjiā, wǒmen zhù èr céng. Nǐmen kěnéng huì wèn, wèishénme nèi ge xiǎo èrlóu shi Rìběnshì de ne? Yīnwèi 1900 nián, Bāguó Liánjūn rùqīn Zhōngguó yǐhòu, nèi ge dìfang shi Rìběnrén de zūjièdì, yǒu hěn duō Rìběnrén zài nàr zhù, suǒ.yǐ nèi yí dài yǒu hěn duō fángzi dōu shì Rìběnrén gài de, dāngrán yě jiùshì Rìběnshì de le. 1976 nián Tángshān dà dìzhèn de shíhou, fángzi huài le. Wèile bǎochí yuánlái de yàngzi, zhèngfǔ yòu ànzhào yuánlái de shìyàng chóngxīn fān'gài le. Dànshi zhǐ shì wàimiàn gēn yǐqián chàbuduō yíyàng, dìbǎn, mén hé chuānghu dōu hé yǐqián bù yíyàng le.

Wǒmen zhù de nèi ge xiǎo èrlóu zài Tiānjīnshì zhōngxīn, yě jiùshì Tiānjīn zuì rènao de dìfang. Fùjìn yǒu hěn duō dà shāngchǎng, dà fàndiàn, yīyuàn, diànyǐngyuàn, děngděng, suǒ.yǐ huā qián hěn fāngbiàn. Wǒmen zhù de xiǎo èrlóu duìmian shi Tiānjīnshì Diànbào Dàlóu, hòumian shi Tiānjīn Rìbàoshè, zuǒmian shi Tiānjīn Jiàoyù Xuéyuàn, yòumian shi Tiānjīn Gǔpiào Jiāoyì Zhōngxīn. Gǔpiào Jiāoyì Zhōngxīn jiùshì chǎogǔ de dìfang. Suīrán wǒmen zhù de dìfang lí Gǔpiào Jiāoyì Zhōngxīn hěn jìn, chǎogǔ hěn fāngbiàn, dànshi wǒmen méiyǒu qián qù chǎogǔ. Lóuxia shi Tiānjīn hěn yǒumíng de, yě shì hěn zhòngyào de yì tiáo mǎlù jiào Nánjīng Lù. Lóuxia bù yuǎnchù jiùshì dìtiězhàn, qìchēzhàn. Cóng wǒmen zhù de dìfang zǒu shíwǔ fēn zhōng jiùshì Tiānjīn 'Gǒubùlǐ Bāozipù', nèi shi yí ge zài Zhōngguó hěn yǒumíng de bāozipù. Měitiān dōu yǒu hěn duō rén qù nàr chī bāozi, dāngrán yě yǒu hěn duō wàiguórén qù nàr chī. Zǒu èrshí duō fēn zhōng jiùshì Hǎi Hé. Hǎi Hé shi chuānguo Tiānjīn Shì zhōngxīn de yì tiáo hé, shi Zhōngguó hěn yǒumíng de héliú zhī yī. Xiàtiān de shíhou, wǒmen sān kǒur chángcháng chīle wǎnfàn yǐhòu, dào hé biānr qù wánr, qu chéngliáng.

Yīnwèi shi Rìběnshì de xiǎo lóufáng, suǒ.yǐ wǒmen de fángzi bú tài dà.
Wǒmen yǒu liǎng ge fángjiān, yí ge xiǎo wèishēngjiān, hé yí ge xiǎo chúfáng.
Suīrán hé Měiguórén de fángzi bǐ, wǒmen de xiǎole yìdiǎnr, dànshi sānkǒu
zhī jiā zhùzhe hěn shūfu. Fángjiān suīrán bú tài dà, dànshi bèi wǒ tàitai
shōushi+de zhěngqí, hěn gānjìng. Fángjiān lǐ yǒu yí ge hěn dà de diànshì,
yí ge dà bīngxiāng, dōu shì wǒ 1993 nián mǎi de, dōu shì 'Sōngxià' pái de.
Wèishénme mǎi Sōngxià pái de? Dàjiā dōu shuō Sōngxià pái de diànqì bǐjiào
hǎo, suǒ.yǐ wǒ jiu mǎile.

Cóng wàimian de wūzi wǎng wài kàn jiùshì Diànbào Dàlóu de dàzhōng.
Zhèi ge dàzhōng měi yí ge xiǎoshí xiǎng yí cì, shi jǐ diǎn tā jiu xiǎng jǐ xià,
suǒ.yǐ wǒmen nèi ge shíhou bù xūyào biǎo, yào zhīdao shíjiān, wǎng wài
kànkan huò tīngyixiàr jiu zhīdao shi jǐ diǎn le. Suǒ.yǐ yǒude shíhou, wǒmen
péngyou de biǎo bù zhǔn huòzhě tíng le, tāmen jiu huì gěi wǒmen dǎ ge
diànhuà, wèn wǒmen Diànbào Dàlóu de zhōng jǐ diǎn le, yīnwèi rénmen xiǎng
nèi ge dàzhōng yīnggāi shi zuì zhǔn de.

Wǒmen zài Tiānjīn zhù de dìfang suīrán gàn shénme dōu hěn fāngbiàn,
dànshi hěn chǎo. Měitiān cóngzǎo-dàowǎn, láilái-wǎngwǎng de rén hé qìchē
búduàn, yìdiǎnr yě bù ānjìng. Shuōhuà shēng, qìchē shēng, dàzhōng shēng,
chǎo+de nǐ hěn fán. Měitiān yě jiù yǒu sì-wǔ ge xiǎoshí ānjìng yìdiǎnr, nà
jiùshì yè lǐ yì diǎn dào qīngchén sì diǎn. Nǐ rúguǒ yǒu shīmián de wèntí, nǐ bù
néng zhù zài nàr, děi kǎolǜ bānjiā. Nǐmen rúguǒ yǒu jīhuì hé wǒmen yìqǐ qù
Tiānjīn, wǒmen yídìng dài nǐmen qù cānguān cānguān wǒmen yuánlái zhù de
dìfang.

SHĒNGCÍ

-shì	'type': cf. *Yīngguóshì de Yīngwén* 'British English'
lóufáng	'a building of more than one story' ('high rise-house')
rénjiā<r>	'someone else's house; a family' ('person-family')
hù	M for households: *yí hù rénjiār* 'one family'; cf. *kǒu*
Bāguó Liánjūn	'Eight Nation Alliance' ('eight-country united-army'): see note

rùqīn	'invade' ('enter-invade')
zūjièdì	'concession; settlement' ('rent-borrow-place')
yí dài	'belt; band; zone'
gài	'to cover; to build [houses]'
dìzhèn	'earthquake' ('ground-shake')
bǎochí	'preserve' ('hold-support')
ànzhào	'according to; on the basis of; along the lines of'
shìyàng	'style; type; model' ('type-kind')
chóngxīn	'again; anew' ('again-new')
fān'gài	'rebuild [a house]' ('overturn-build'): cf. *fānxiū* 'renovate'
dìbǎn	'floor' ('ground-planking')
shāngchǎng	'bazaar; market' ('business-space')
huāqián	'spend money; cost money'
diànbào	'telegraph' ('electric-report')
rìbàoshè	'newspaper agency'
xuéyuàn	'college'
gǔpiào	'stocks' ('share-ticket')
jiāoyì	'trade; transaction' ('exchange-trade')
chǎogǔ<piào>	'speculate on stocks; play the stock market' ('fry-stocks'): [coll]
mǎlù	'main road' ('horse-road')
yuǎnchù	'distant place' ('far-place'): cf. *dàochù ~ chùchù* 'everywhere'
pù	'shop': the full form is *pùzi*; cf. *diàn, shāngdiàn*
chuānguo	'pass through': *chuān yīfu de chuān*
héliú	'river' ('river-flow')
chéngliáng	'enjoy the breeze' ('ride-coolness')
wèishēngjiān	'bathroom; lavatory; toilet' ('hygiene-room')
shōushi	'tidy up; put in order; pack': *shōushi xíngli*
zhěngqí	'neat; tidy' ('entire-even'): *bǎ dōngxi fàng+de hěn zhěngqí* 'put things in good order'
diànqì	'appliance' ('electric-appliance')

dàzhōng	'large bell'
xiǎng	'ring out': *xiǎng jǐ xiàr* 'ring out a few times'
zhǔn	'accurate': cf. *biāozhǔn* 'standard'; *zhǔnshí* 'punctual / punctually'
láiwǎng	'come and go / comings and goings' ('come-go toward')
duàn	'break; cut off': *búduàn* 'without a break'
fán	'irritating; obnoxious': cf. *máfan*
qīngchén	'early morning' ('clear-morning')
shīmián	'have problems sleeping' ('lose-sleep')
kǎolǜ	'consider; think about': contrast with *shāngliang* 'talk over'
dài	'lead; take by the hand; accompany'
cānguān	'visit; tour': *zhídé cānguān de chéngshì* 'a city worth visiting'; *cānguān Gùgōng Bówùyuàn*

NOTES

a. The *Bāguó Liánjūn* was a foreign expeditionary force sent to China in 1900 to punish the Manchu government for events linked to the Boxer Uprising. In China, this army is remembered for its violent reprisals, including the destruction of the Old Summer Palace (*Yuánmíng Yuán*).

b. *Tángshān* is a city in Hebei Province, northeastern China, not far from Tianjin. In July of 1976, it suffered the most devastating (though not the strongest) earthquake of modern times, with an estimated 250,000 people killed. The city has been entirely rebuilt since.

c. *Gǒubùlǐ*, the name of Tianjin's famous dumplings, literally means 'dogs not obey', presumably because dogs are so smitten with them that they go berserk.

Exercise 1

Translate the following excerpts.

1. *Zhèi ge dàzhōng měi yí ge xiǎoshí xiǎng yí cì, shi jǐ diǎn tā jiu xiǎng jǐ xià, suǒ.yǐ wǒmen nèi ge shíhou bù xūyào biǎo, yào zhīdao shíjiān, wǎng wài kànkan huò tīngyixiàr jiu zhīdao shi jǐ diǎn le.*

2. *Wǒmen zài Tiānjīn zhù de dìfang suīrán gàn shénme dōu hěn fāngbiàn,*
   dànshi hěn chǎo. Měitiān cóngzǎo-dàowǎn, láilái-wǎngwǎng de rén hé qìchē
   búduàn, yìdiǎnr yě bù ānjìng.

Answer the following questions in Chinese.

1. *Wèishénme zài Tiānjīn yǒude fángzi shì Rìběnshì de fángzi?*
2. *Shuōyixiàr Tángshān dàdìzhèn de shìr.*
3. *Wèishénme shuō tā zhù de fángzi hěn fāngbiàn?*
4. *Shuōyixiàr nèi suǒ fángzi de yàngzi.*

Shànghǎi

19.2 Apologies and excuses

When you live in a foreign country or learn a foreign language, you are entitled to make a few mistakes. If you can apologize and explain what happened, then people will generally give you the benefit of the doubt. With that in mind, let's begin with a list of *dàoqiàn* 'apologies' ('declare-deficiency').

<Hěn> duìbuqǐ.	'I'm <so> sorry.' ('face-not-worthy')
Hěn bàoqiàn.	'My apologies.' ('embrace-deficiency')
Nǐ děngle hěn jiǔ le; hěn bàoqiàn.	'You've been waiting a long time; I'm so sorry.'
Wǒ láiwǎn le, hěn duìbuqǐ.	'I'm sorry to be so late.'
Zhēn bù hǎo yìsi, wǒ wánquán wàngle.	'I'm so embarrassed, I completely forgot.'

For an apology to sound sincere, you usually need to give reasons—or excuses. Here is a selection. You arrive late, see the person who's waiting for you, and give as your excuse one of the following.

Wǒmen de fēijī ~ huǒchē wùdiǎn le.	'Our plane ~ train was delayed.'
Wǒ wùle chē.	'I missed my bus/train.'
Gōnggòng qìchē zài lùshang pāomáo le.	'The bus broke down en route.'
Wǒ de shǒujī méi diàn le, bù néng dǎ diànhuà.	'My cell phone ran out of power; I couldn't phone.'
Wǒ mílù le.	'I lost my way.'
Wǒ zǒucuòle lù le.	'I took the wrong road.'
Wǒ shì bu shì jìcuòle shíjiān?	'Did I get the time wrong?'
Ei? Méiyǒu kàndao nǐ. Nǐ děngle duōjiǔ le?	'Huh? I didn't see you. How long have you been waiting?'

Wǎn dào le – yīnwèi jiāotōng gāofēng.	'I'm late—it's because it's rush hour.'
Jiāotōng jíwéi hùnluàn.	'The traffic was terrible.'
Wǒ shuìguo tóu le.	'I overslept.'
Wǒmen xiàcuòle zhàn.	'We got off at the wrong station.'
Méi xiǎngdào yòngdeliǎo nàme jiǔ.	'I didn't think it would take so long.'
Wǒ diūle dìzhǐbù, bù néng gēn nǐ liánxì.	'I lost my address book, so I couldn't get in touch with you.'

SHĒNGCÍ

wùdiǎn	'be late; be behind schedule' ('miss-hour'): *huǒchē wùdiǎn shí fēn zhōng* 'the train is ten minutes late'
wùchē	'miss the train/bus' ('miss-vehicle')
pāomáo	'break down; lie at anchor' ('drop-anchor'): *pāole sān cì máo*
mílù	'lose one's way'
gāofēng	'peak; height' ('high-peak'): *jiāotōng gāofēng* 'rush hour'
jíwéi	'extremely' ('utmost-be'): *hǎo jíle de jí*
hùnluàn	'in disorder; chaotic; bad' [of traffic]
shuìguo tóu	'oversleep' ('sleep-past end')
dìzhǐbù	'address book'

In 2001, a U.S. spy plane, flying off the coast of China, was involved in a collision with a Chinese jet that was shadowing it. The Chinese pilot was killed, and the U.S. plane was badly damaged and had to land on Hainan Island. A poorly planned response from the U.S. side led Chinese leaders to demand a formal apology. The Americans were only willing to express regret. A short article on the issue of the apology was printed in the *Boston Globe*. It is reproduced in part here (with tones added to the pinyin).

Two days ago, U.S. Secretary of State Colin L. Powell said the United States was 'sorry' for the apparent loss of a Chinese pilot's life following the April 1 collision between a U.S. spy plane and a Chinese fighter jet, but Powell said the United States would not apologize for the accident, because it believes it is not at fault. . . . The Chinese language has several words for *apology*, noted Leo Ou-fan Lee, a professor of Chinese literature at Harvard University. China is demanding that the United States give '*zhèngshì dàoqiàn*', 'a formal apology' that acknowledges that the speaker is extremely sorry for having done something wrong that harmed the listener. A softer alternative is '*bàoqiàn*', which means 'deep and sincere regret' or 'to be apologetic'. Bush's expression of 'regret' last week for the loss of the pilot translates as the milder '*yíhàn*', which implies that the speaker is not at fault. [Indira A. R. Lakshmanan, in the *Boston Globe*, April 11, 2001, page A24]

The side panel to the article listed six degrees of 'sorry', with the first as most sorry; the word-for-word glosses have been added to the original.

dàoqiàn	'apologize' ('declare-deficiency')
bàoqiàn	'feel sorry; deplore' ('embrace-deficiency')
yíhàn	'feel regret; be sorry'
nánguò	'feel grieved' ('difficult-pass over')
duìbuqǐ	'have failed you' ('face-not-worthy')
bù hǎoyìsi	'be embarrassed' ('not good-sense')

USAGE

Duìbuqǐ, xiàng nín dàoqiàn.	'Sorry; I apologize to you.'
Hěn bàoqiàn!	'I'm very sorry!'
Duì zhèi jiàn shìqing, wǒ juéde hěn/tèbié yíhàn.	'I have great regrets about this business.'
Hěn nánguò.	'I'm very sad ~ upset about it.'
Duìbuqǐ.	'Sorry ~ excuse me.'
Bù hǎo yìsi.	'I'm very sorry ~ embarrassed.'

19.3 Current events

The Chinese urban classes tend to be well informed—and quite opinionated—about the rest of the world. For example, a taxi driver is as likely to express his views on American elections or European economic problems as he (or less often, she) is about problems that accompany rapid urbanization and growth in China. Given your disadvantages, and the fact that he is going to be facing away from you and speaking a regional version of Mandarin in a noisy setting, the best you can do to hold your own is offer an occasional vague comment and build up a rapport (or, alternatively, knock him off his argument). This section provides no model dialogues—just a selection of utterances you can try out in the safe environment of the classroom and then try to apply to the sometimes harsh world outside. It begins with some names, which can be used as the focus of questions and comments.

Máo Zédōng	
Jiǎng Jièshí	Chiang Kai-shek
Lǐ Guāngyào	Lee Kuan Yew of Singapore
Gāndì	Mahatma Ghandi
Sāqiē'ěr	Margaret Thatcher
Níkèsōng	Richard Nixon
(Lǎo) Bùshí	George H. W. Bush
(Xiǎo) Bùshí	George W. Bush
Xīlālǐ	Hillary Clinton
Àobāmǎ	Barack Obama
Áng Shān Sù Jì	Aung San Suu Kyi: *Miǎndiàn de Nuòbèi'ěr Jiǎng huòdézhě* ('Burmese Nobel Prize receive-er')
Chén Shuǐbiǎn	*Táiwān de zǒngtǒng*: elected in 2000, reelected in 2004, now in jail
Dálài Lǎma	*Xīzàng Lǎmajiào (Huángjiào) de liǎng ge huó Fó zhī yī* ('Tibet Lamaism (Yellow Sect) two living-Buddhas one of ')

ASKING QUESTIONS

Ni duì . . . yǒu shénme kànfǎ?   'How do you feel about . . . ?'

Zhōngguórén duì Níkèsōng   'What do Chinese think of
   zǒngtǒng yǒu shénme kànfǎ?   President Nixon?'

Zhōngguórén zuìjìn duì Cháoxiǎn   'How do Chinese feel about North
   yǒu shénme kànfǎ?   Korea these days?'

Qǐngwèn, Yuènán de qíngkuàng   'May I ask you, what's the situation
   zuìjìn zěnmeyàng?   in Vietnam like these days?'

SOME RESPONSES

Hěn nán shuō.   'Hard to say.'

Zhèi ge wèntí hěn fùzá.   'That question's quite complicated.'

Wǒ yìdiǎnr dōu gǎobumíngbai.   'I can't follow [the argument] at all.'

Zhèi ge wèntí hěn fùzá, kěshì   'That question's quite complicated;
   yěxǔ zuìhòu tāmen hái děi   I guess in the end they're going to
   zìjǐ juédìng.   have to deal with it themselves.'

Zhè jiàn shì shi yǒu zhēngyì de.   'That's very controversial.'

Yìbān lái shuō, hěn xǐhuan tā.   'In general, they quite like him.'

Hěn nán shuō. Zài Měiguó   'It's difficult to say. In America,
   zhèngzhì guāndiǎn xiāngdāng   political opinion runs rather high;
   jíduān; yǒurén hěn xǐhuan tā,   some like him a lot, others detest
   yǒurén yànwù tā.   him.'

Nà dōu shi guòqu de shìr le.   'That's all in the past.'

Xūyào hěn cháng shíjiān cái   'It'll be a long time before we can
   nénggòu jiějué nèi xiē wèntí.   solve those problems.'

Wǒmen de kànfǎ bù yíyàng.   'We see it differently.'

Zhōngguó de jīngjì yǐ zhìzàoyè   'The Chinese economy is based on
   wéi jīchǔ, suǒ.yǐ bǐjiào   manufacturing, so it's more stable;
   wěndìng; wǒmen yǐ cáizhèng   ours is based on finance, so it's up
   wéi jīchǔ, hūshànghūxià de.   and down.'

SHĒNGCÍ

zhēnglùn   'argument; controversy / to debate': *yǒu zhēnglùn de*
        wèntí 'a controversial issue' ('an issue which has

	argument'); *tāmen zhēnglùnle yì fān* 'they argued for a while'; *fān* 'a time'
guāndiǎn	'point of view; standpoint': *guāndiǎn bú shòu huānyíng* 'views haven't caught on'
jíduān	'extreme': *jíduānzhǔyì* 'extremism'; *jíduān fènzǐ* 'extremists'
yànwù	'detest; be disgusted with' ('loathe-hate'): *yànwù zǎo qǐ* 'have an aversion to getting up early'
jiějué	'solve': *wúfǎ jiějué de wèntí* 'a problem without a solution'
zhìzàoyè	'manufacturing industry' ('manufacture-industry'): *zhìzào qǐyè* 'manufacturing firm'
cáizhèng	'finance; financial administration' ('wealth-administration')
hūshànghūxià	'undergo sharp fluctuations' ('sudden-rise-sudden-fall')

NOTE

Yǐ . . . wéi jīchǔ (with *jīchǔ* 'foundation') 'be based on; founded on' ('take . . . to be foundation'); cf. *yǐ . . . wéi zhǔ* (with *zhǔ* 'main') 'based mainly on' ('take . . . to be main').

Issues: Some phrases and vocabulary:

qíngkuàng	'situation' ('emotion-situation'): also *qíngxing* 'situation' ('emotion-form')
fùyǒu de guójiā	'wealthy country'
hěn fādá	'developed': *fādá guójiā zhī yī* 'one of the developed countries'
kējì hěn xiānjìn	'technologically advanced' ('science-technology very first-enter')
qióngrén	'poor people'
hěn luòhòu	'backward' ('fall-back'): often applied to countries as the opposite of *fādá*
rénquán	'human rights' ('people-rights')

zhǒngzú qíshì	'racial prejudice' ('race-prejudice')
gōnggòng wèishēng	'public health; hygiene; sanitation'
yǐnshí	'diet' ('drink-food')
jiāotōng	'transportation; communications; traffic'
tōnghuò péngzhàng	'inflation' ('currency inflation')
huánjìng	'environment'
kōngqì wūrǎn	'air pollution': cf. *shuǐ wūrǎn; huánjìng wūrǎn*
jiàoyù	'education': *shòu jiàoyù de jīhuì* 'access to education' ('receive education DE opportunities')
qìhòu	'climate': literal or metaphorical; *qìhòu biànhuà* 'climate change'; *quánqiú biànnuǎn* 'global warming' ('whole-world change-warm')
zhèngfǔ	'government'
fǔbài	'corruption': *fǔbài de guānliáo* 'corrupt officials ~ bureaucrats'
fànzuì	'crime' ('commit-crime'): *móushālǜ* 'murder rate' ('plot-kill-rate')
huìlù tānwū	'graft' ('bribery') and 'corruption' ('avaricious-stagnant')
xīdú	'taking drugs' ('inhale-poison')
rénkǒu tài duō	'too many people'
shīyè wèntí	'problems with unemployment' ('lose-job'): cf. *xiàgǎng* 'layoffs'
wújiākěguī	'homelessness' ('no-home can-return')
nànmín	'refugees' ('calamity-people'): *bìnànzhě* 'refugees' ('avoid-calamity-ers')
kǒngbùzhǔyì	'terrorism' ('terror-ism'): *kǒngbù fènzǐ* 'terrorists' ('terror-elements')

USAGE

Tīngshuō jīngjì bú cuò, dànshi rénquán yǒu diǎnr wèntí.	'I hear the economy's okay, but there are some problems with human rights.'

Shīyè wèntí hěn yánzhòng,   'Unemployment's a serious
  péngzhàng yě hěn gāo.   problem, and so is inflation.'

19.4 Sports

The Chinese government has long promoted sports and exercise as a means
to health. Many urban dwellers participate in morning exercises, timed to
music over loudspeakers in public squares—*yīnyuè bànzòu de chénliàn* ('music-
accompanied morning-exercise'). More recently, exercise courses have been
constructed in public parks. The following is a slogan from the late 1990s.

Fāzhǎn tǐyù yùndòng, zēngqiáng   ('Develop physical education [and]
  rénmín tǐzhì!   sports, strengthen the people's
                                                 constitutions!')

Although the traditional sports of ping pong, badminton, and martial arts
remain popular in China, a vast range of other sports, such as football (soccer),
basketball, rock climbing, and motor racing, now attract participants or viewers.
This section provides some conversational material and a list of sports and
sportlike activities from which you can select.

USAGE

Nǐ xǐhuan shénme yàng de   'What sort of sports do you like
  yùndòng?   to do?'
Wǒ xǐhuan dǎ wǎngqiú, yóuyǒng.   'I like to play tennis and swim.'

Nǐ zuò shénme yòngdòng ma?   'Do you play any sports?'
Bù, bù xǐhuan yùndòng, dàn wǒ   'No, no sports, but I walk my dog.'
  měitiān liùgǒu.
Sànbù yě shì yì zhǒng yùndòng, bú   'Walking's a kind of sport, no?'
  duì ma?

Wǒ hěn xǐhuan kàn yùndònghuì.   'I like to watch sporting events.'
Qù tǐyùchǎng kàn ma?   'Do you go to stadiums to see
                                              them?

*Yǒu shíhou; yǒu shíhou kàn
    diànshì.*

'Sometimes; and sometimes I
    watch TV.'

Nǐ chángcháng duànliàn ma?

'Do you often work out?'

*Wǒ hěn xiǎng duànliàn, kěshì
    chángcháng méiyǒu shíjiān.*

'I try, but I often don't have time.'

*Zhèr fùjìn yǒu méiyǒu dìfang kě.yǐ
    pǎobù?*

'Is there anyplace in the vicinity
    where I can jog?'

Zài gōngyuán, xíng bu xíng?

'How about the park?'

*Kě.yǐ, huòzhě zài hébiānr de
    xiǎojìng shang.*

'That's possible, or along the path
    by the river.'

Wǒ shi ge zúqiúmí.

'I'm a football fan.'

Wǒ yě shì!

'Me too!'

Wǒ zuì xǐhuan dǎ májiàng.

'I like playing mahjong best.'

Dǎ májiàng? Nà bú shì yùndòng!

'Mahjong? That's not a sport!'

*Nǎr de huà? Dǎ májiàng yǒu
    shíhou yě hěn fèijìn!*

'What do you mean? Playing
    mahjong is sometimes quite
    strenuous!'

*2012 nián de Àoyùnhuì zài
    Lúndūn jǔxíngguo, duì ma?*

'The 2012 Olympics were held in
    London, right?'

*Zài Běijīng Àoyùnhuì, Zhōngguó
    yíngle 100 méi jiǎngpái (jīnpái,
    yínpái, tóngpái).*

'At the Beijing Olympics, China
    won 100 medals (gold, silver,
    bronze medals).'

*Zuì liúxíng de yùndòng yǐqián shi
    pīngpāngqiú, yǔmáoqiú,
    tàijíquán; xiànzài pānyán,
    zúqiú yě hěn liúxíng.*

'The most popular sports used to
    be ping pong, badminton, and
    tai chi; now rock climbing and
    football are popular too.'

Zhèr de yòngdòng shèshī shi yīliú de.

'The sports facilities here are first
    rate.'

SHĒNGCÍ

zuò yùndòng	'do sports': *yùndònghuì* 'sporting event; meet'; *yùndòngchǎng* 'athletic field; playground'
liùgǒu	'walk a dog'
duànliàn	'exercise; work out'
xiǎojìng	'path' ('small-path')
tǐyùchǎng	'stadium': cf. *tǐyùguǎn* 'gymnasium'
qiúmí	'sports fan' ('ball-fanatic'): *mí* 'be enchanted'; cf. *zúqiúmí* ('foot-ball-fan'); *yǐngmí* 'film buff'
nǎr de huà	'whence the words': an expression of disbelief; also used like *nǎ.lǐ*
fèijìn	'be strenuous' ('use energy')
jǔxíng	'to hold [an event]' ('hold-go'): *měinián jǔxíng yí cì* 'held once a year'
méi	M for medals and badges, among other things
jiǎngpái	'medal' ('prize-tablet'): *jīnpái* 'gold medal'
liúxíng	'be popular' ('flow-go')
shèshī	'facilities; installation'
yīliú de	'first-rate; top-notch' ('one-grade')

Zài jiē shang dǎ táiqiú. (*Hūhéhàotè*)

LIST OF SPORTS, WITH ATTACHED VERBS

dǎ bīngqiú	'play hockey' ('hit ice-ball')
dǎ lánqiú	'play basketball'
dǎ májiàng	'play mahjong'
dǎpái	'play cards'
dǎ páiqiú	'play volleyball'
dǎ pīngpāngqiú	'play ping pong'
dǎ qiáopái	'play bridge'
dǎ qūgùnqiú	'play field hockey' ('curved-club-ball')
dǎ wǎngqiú	'play tennis' ('hit net-ball')
dǎ yǔmáoqiú	'play badminton' ('hit feather-hair-ball')
diàoyú	'fish' ('hook-fish')
fàng fēngzheng	'fly a kite' ('put kite')
huáchuán	'row' ('row-boats')
huá gūluxié	'roller skate' ('glide wheel-shoes')
huá hànbīng	'roller skate' ('glide dry-ice')
huáxuě	'ski' ('glide-snow')
jǔzhòng	'lift weights' ('raise-heavy')
liūbīng	'skate' ('skate-ice')
pānyán	'rock climb' ('clamber on-rock')
pǎobù	'jog' ('run-foot')
páshān	'climb mountains; hike'
qímǎ	'ride horses'
qí zìxíngchē	'ride a bike'
sàichē	'motor racing' ('race-auto')
sàimǎ	'horse racing' ('race-horses')
tī zúqiú	'play football – soccer' ('kick foot-ball')
yóuyǒng	'swim'

Exercise 2

Do what is asked, either speaking your answers or writing them.

1. Explain what sports you like, whether you work out, and where you do such activity.
2. Explain where the next summer and winter Olympics will be held.
3. Explain who is the best basketball player, football (soccer) player, and so on.
4. Recall the number of medals that the United States (or some other country) won in the most recent Olympics.

Sports can keep your body in shape. Reciting Chinese sayings that pertain to eating and health can keep your mind in shape—and if you take the advice, all the better. Figure out the meaning of each of the following rhymed couplets, based on the literal glosses provided.

Dōng chī luóbo, xià chī jiāng, bù láo yīshēng kāi yàofāng.
('Winter eat turnips summer eat ginger, not bother doctor write prescription.')

Rén xiǎng cháng shòu ān, yào jiǎn yè lái cān.
('[If] people want long life peaceful, need reduce night bring food.')

Zǎo chībǎo, wǔ chīhǎo, wǎn chīshǎo.
('Early eat-full, noon eat well, evening eat little.')

Yào xiǎng shēntǐ hǎo, zǎocān yào chībǎo.
('Need want body good, breakfast need eat-full.')

Fàn hòu bǎi bù zǒu, huódào jiǔshíjiǔ.
('Food after one hundred steps go, live to ninety-nine.')

Néng jìyān héjiǔ, huódào jiǔshíjiǔ.
('Can forbid tobacco and liquor, live to ninety-nine.')

Yùfáng chángwèibìng, yǐnshí yào gānjìng.
('Prevent intestine-stomach-illness, drink-food must be-clean.')

MORE ON HEALTH

Below is an excerpt, transcribed from characters into pinyin (with a literal gloss), from a longer rhyme containing advice for healthy living. This version was found at the *Qìngfúgōng* temple on the waterfront in Yangon's Chinatown.

Qǐ+de zǎo,	('rise+de early')
Shuì+de hǎo,	('sleep+de well')
Qī fēn bǎo,	('seven parts [70 percent] full')
Cháng pǎopao;	('frequently run')
Duō xiàoxiao,	('a lot laugh')
Mò fánnǎo,	('don't worry')
Tiāntiān máng,	('every-day be-busy')
Yǒng bù lǎo.	('forever not age')
Rì xíng wǔqiān bù,	('day walk five thousand paces')
Yè mián qī xiǎoshí,	('night sleep seven hours')
Yǐnshí bù yú liàng,	('drink-food not exceed amount')
Zuò xī yào jūnhéng,	('do rest need proper-amount')
Xīn zhōng cháng xǐlè,	('heart within always happy')
Kǒutóu wú yuàn shēng,	('in-words not complain tone')
Ài rén rú ài jǐ,	('love others as love self')
Zhù rén jìn zhōngchéng.	('help people utmost sincerely')

The rhyme seems to have been inspired by a genre represented best by the so-called household maxims (*Zhìjiā Géyán*) of *Zhū Yòngchún* (traditionally Romanized as Chu Yongshun [*sic*]), 1617–1689, which are often found in editions of the Chinese farmers' almanac (*Tōngshū*).

19.5 From telephones to texting

It's a rare person who is younger than forty years old and can remember sending a telegram (*fā diànbào*); yet only a few decades ago, it was a common means of long-distance telecommunication (*chángtú-tōngxùn*) in China. To send a message in characters, each character would be transformed into a unique four-digit code (*Zhōngwén diànmǎ*). For example, 中 (the *zhōng* of *Zhōngguó*) was assigned 0022. A good operator would have memorized the code numbers of all the common characters. After transmission, the process would, obviously, have to be reversed.

A few decades ago, even communicating by means of a telephone (*dǎ diànhuà liánxì*) was an ordeal, and few people had phones in their homes. People often wrote and sent letters (*xiěxìn; jìxìn*). Today, of course, it's a rare person who doesn't have a mobile phone (*shǒujī*). Recent figures give nine hundred million accounts in China (*yǒu jiǔyì shǒujī yònghùr*), many of which have Internet functions (*yǒu shàngwǎng de gōngnéng*). People text (*fā duǎnxìn*) far more than they phone, however—even more than they e-mail (*fā diànzǐ yóujiàn = fā yīmèi'er*). There are various character input methods, including pinyin (*yòng pīnyīn de shūrùfǎ*). To go online, many younger people go to Internet bars (*wǎngbā*) where they play video games (*wánr diànzǐ yóuxì*), download music (*xiàzài yīnyuè*), browse the Web (*liúlǎn*), look at news sites (*kàn xīnwén*), and visit chat rooms (*liáotiānshì*).

The following selection is awash with new words and phrases, but the subject is good, the grammar is straightforward, and with enough listenings and readings, many of those words and phrases will stick.

Tōngxùn fāngfǎ

Èrshí nián qián, Zhōngguórén rúguǒ yào gēn yuǎnfāng de qīnqi huò péngyou liánxì, huòzhě gēn liànrén jiāoliú qínggǎn, kě.yǐ xiěxìn. Rúguǒ yǒu jíshìr kě.yǐ fā diànbào. Bǐjiào fùyǒu de jiātíng huòshi zhèngfǔ guānyuán, jiālǐ kě.yǐ zhuāng diànhuà, tāmen jiù kě.yǐ dǎ diànhuà liánxì. Dàn dāngshí néng shǐyòng diànhuà de hěn shǎo, érqiě diànhuàfèi yě hěn guì, suǒ.yǐ jìxìn shi zuì cháng yòng de tōngxùn fāngfǎ.

Xiànzài qíngkuàng wánquán bùtóng le. Shǒuxiān hěn duō rén dōu shǐyòng diànhuà le, cóng chéngshì dào nóngcūn, jiājiā dōu yǒu. Jiā lǐ yǒu, bàngōngshì yǒu, jiēshang yě yǒu. Dàn xiànzài zuì pǔbiàn de dāngrán shi shǒujī. Zài èrshíyī shìjì de dì-èr ge shínián, Zhōngguó shi shìjièshang yǒu shǒujī shǐyòng zuì duō de guójiā. Zài 2011 nián, gūjì zài Zhōngguó yǒu jiǔyì (jiǔwànwàn) shǒujī yònghùr, nà shi zhàn rénkǒu zǒngshù de sìfēn zhī sān zuǒyòu, qízhōng yǒu sān dào sìyì ge shǒujī yǒu shàngwǎng de gōngnéng. (Shùnbiàn shuō, Yìndù jǐnsuíqíhòu; zài Yìndù, shǒujī de yònghù yǐjīng yǒu bāyì rén zuǒyòu, érqiě Yìndù de zēngzhǎnglǜ bǐ Zhōngguó de hái dà.)

Xiànzài, qù Zhōngguó lǚyóu méiyǒu shǒujī huì hěn kùnnan. Rúguǒ nǐ de shi yí ge guójì de shǒujī, nà nǐ kě.yǐ jìxù yòng nǐ zìjǐ de; dànshi diànhuàfèi huì shǐ nǐ zhènjīng. Zài jīchǎng zū ge tīngtǒng, qiān ge hétong, nǐ hái děi àn fēn fùqián, fèiyòng háishi hěn duō. Nǐ zuìhǎo zhèyàngr, wǒ gàosu nǐmen: xiān mǎi ge Zhōngguó shǒujī, hěn piányi – dàgài liǎng-sānbǎi kuài qián jiù kě.yǐ mǎi ge pǔtōng de shǒujī – tóngshí mǎi ge Zhōngguó SIM-kǎ. SIM-kǎ shi yùfùfèi yòng de, yòngwán kě.yǐ mǎi zhāng xùfèikǎ, guāqù kǎ shang PIN de bǎohùcéng, shūrùkǎ shang de mìmǎ, àn xùfèi tíshì shùnxù shūrù jiù kě.yǐ yòng le. Diànhuàfèi gēn Zhōngguórén de yíyàng piányi, yì fēn zhōng dàgài liù máo qián, dǎ dào wàiguó, huòzhě cóng wàiguó shōudào de dōu bù zěnme guì. Nà shi zuì fāngbiàn de, nǐ juéde hǎo ma? Chúle zài piānyuǎn shānqū méiyǒu jīzhàn de dìfang, yìbān qiángdù hěn hǎo, shēngyīn yě hěn qīngchu.

Yào gèng shěngqián, nǐ yě kě.yǐ fā duǎnxìn, yì tiáo dàgài yì máo éryǐ, kě.yǐ shūrù liùshí ge zì zuǒyòu. Qíshí Zhōngguó de niánqīngrén fā duǎnxìn bǐ dǎ diànhuà hái duō. Yòu piányi yòu kuài. Fā Hànzì yě méi wèntí, kě.yǐ yòng Pīnyīn de shūrùfǎ; yǒu 3G gōngnéng de, nǐ yě kě.yǐ yòng shǒuxiě shūrùfǎ, yòng shǒu huòshi péi de bǐ bǎ tóu jǐ ge bǐhuà xiě zai yínmù shang, jiu huì chūxiàn yíxìliè xiāngxiàng de Hànzì, ránhòu xuǎnzhòng héshì de, jiù xíng le, hěn fāngbiàn. Jiùshì lājī duǎnxìn tài duō, dōushòu gè zhǒng xìnxī.

Zhōngguó xiànzài shàngwǎng de rén yě shì yuè lái yuè duō le. Wǎngluò yě yǒu rén jiào Yīntèwǎng – Yīngwén jièlái de cí. Zài 2011 nián zài Zhōngguó, shǐyòng Yīntèwǎng de rén dádào sìyì wǔqiānwàn, nà shi rénkǒu de bǎifēn zhī sān-sìshí zuǒyòu. Zài jiālǐ shàngwǎng de, zài bàngōngshì shàngwǎng de dōu hěn duō, dànshi niánqīngrén zuì xǐhuan de háishi zài wǎngbā shàngwǎng, zhèi yàng fùmǔ huò lǎobǎn bù néng jiāndū tāmen, kě.yǐ suíbiàn wánr diànzǐ yóuxì, xiàzài yīnyuè, liúlǎn kàn xīnwén, zài liáotiānshì hé lùntán tán guójiā de dàshì, tán gèrén de wèntí, hěn yǒu yìsi.

Fā diànzǐ yóujiàn dāngrán yě hěn cháng jiàn. Diànzǐ yóujiàn yǒu shíhou yě yǒu rén yòng Yīngwén de jiècí, yīmèi'er. Xiànzài de Zhōngguó niánqīngrén *juéde háishi yòng liáotiān duìhuà chuándì xìnxī hǎo, bǐ yīmèi'er fāngbiàn, bǐ yīmèi'er qīnmì. Zuì liúxíng zhī yī de shi QQ (quánmíng shi TencentQQ), shi miǎnfèi de, chúle dǎzì-liáotiān, shìpín-liáotiān wài, hái kě.yǐ chuán túpiàn, fā yóujiàn, xiě wēibó, zhìzuò gèrén kōngjiān, cún yìxiē zìjǐ xǐhuan de rìzhì, zhàopiàn děng. Tīngshuō háiyǒu yīyì duō rén tóngshí yòng tāmen de QQ zhànghào, zhǐ shì yǒu yì diǎnr bù ānquán. Zhǐ yào zài diànnǎo shang xiàzài ge ruǎnjiàn, zài guówài yě kě.yǐ yòng.*

Duǎnxìn hé liáotiān xìnxī yòng de xiěfǎ hěn yǒuyìsi. Lüèzì hěn duō. Yǒude shi cūsú de, xiàliú de, bù néng zài zhèr shuō, búguò kě.yǐ jǔ jǐ ge bǐjiào hǎotīng de lìzi: yǒude yòng Yīngwén zìmǔ de fāyīn, xiàng Q = 'kě-ài' (<< 'cute'); yǒude yòng Yīngwén de shǒu zìmǔ, xiàng PK (<< 'player kill'), yìsi jiùshi táotàisài, huò bèi táotàile de yí ge xuǎnshǒu; yǒu de yòng Zhōngwén de Pīnyīn shǒu zìmǔ, xiàng GG 'gēge' huò MM 'mèimei'; ér yǒude yòng shùzi lái dàibiǎo yìsi de. Yìbān lái shuō yòng shùzi de lüèzì shi ànzhào Zhōngwén de shuōfǎ, xiàng 88 (bā-bā) 'bye-bye', 987 (jiǔ-bā-qī) 'duìbuqǐ'. Yòu shěng jījiàn dòngzuò, yòu yǒu chuàngzàoxìng. Xiànzài wǎngzhàn wèi xīyǐn gèng duō rén yòng, zài búduàn chuàngxīn, hái yǒu hěn duō gǎoxiào-túpiàn, kě.yǐ chuānchā zài duìhuà zhōng, zēngjiā liáotiān de lèqù.

Yěxǔ nǐmen yǐjīng zài yòng yìxiē Zhōngwén wǎngzhàn le. Bù shǎo xué Zhōngwén de xuéshēng dōu yòng Zhōngwén.com; kě.yǐ chá shēngcí, liǎojiě Hànzì de láiyuán, dú Zhōngwén wénzhāng, yě kě.yǐ zài Pīnyīn liáotiānshì liáotiān. Yě yǒu Xiè Tiānwéi lǎoshī de wǎngyè yǒu hěn duō gēn xué Zhōngwén yǒuguān de liánjiē; (www.csulb.edu/~txie). Zhōngguó zuì cháng yòng de sōusuǒ-yǐnqíng shi Xīnlàng (Sina) hé Bǎidù. Xīnlàng yě shì ge ménhù wǎngzhàn, hé Sōuhú (Sohu) shi Zhōngguó zuì cháng yòng de liǎng ge. Nàr de xīnwén bàodào nǐmen háishi kànbudǒng, kěshì tiānqì yùgào yěxǔ néng kàndǒng yìdiǎnr. Shìshi kàn ba. Yīngguó Guǎngbō-gōngsī de wǎngzhàn yě yǒuyòng, xīnwén bàodào kě.yǐ fānyì chéng sìshí duō ge yǔyán, qízhōng Hànyǔ shi yí gè (http://bbc.co.uk/worldservice).

Zuìhòu yì diǎn: kàn Zhōngwén wǎngyè, nǐmen huì fāxiàn suīrán nèiróng shi Zhōngwén de (chúle yìxiē guǎnggào), wǎngzhàn de míngzi yě shi Zhōngwén de, kěshì wǎngzhǐ (yùmíng) háishi yòng Yīngwén xiě de, xiàng: http://news .xinhuanet.com; http://www.sina.com. Suǒ.yǐ sōusuǒ yǐnqíng zhǎo wǎngyè bùguǎn shi Zhōngwén de nèiróng háishi Yīngwén de nèiróng dōu méiyǒu wèntí, néng zhǎodào. Dàn xiànzài, yòng Hànzì xiě yùmíng, jìshù wèntí dǒu yǐjīng jiějué le, ér yǒu yìxiē wǎngzhàn yǐjīng shǐyòng Zhōngwén xiě de. Xiànzài bù duō, dàn jiānglái ne? Huì bú huì zhōngyú yǒu liǎng ge dúlì de xìtǒng, liǎng ge dúlì de Yīntèwǎng? Nǐmen juéde ne?

Tǐng Q de! (Q, used in texting instead of *kě'ài*; from Eng. 'cute')

NOTES

a. *tōngxùn fāngfǎ* 'communication' ('through-announce'): cf. *tōngxùnchù* 'mailing address'; *tōngxùn wèixīng* 'communications satellite'; *chángtú-tōngxùn* 'telecommunications'

b. *gēn yuǎnfāng de qīnqi huò péngyou liánxì*: *yuǎnfāng* 'faraway' ('far-place'); *gēn . . . liánxì* 'be in contact with' ('connect-tie')

c. *gēn liànrén jiāoliú qínggǎn*: *liànrén* 'sweetheart' ('long for-person'); cf. *liàn'ài* 'have a romantic attachment / love'; *gēn . . . jiāoliú* 'have an exchange with' ('associate with-flow'); *qínggǎn* 'emotion; feeling' ('emotion-feeling')

d. *yǒu jíshìr*: *jíshì<r>* 'urgent matters' ('urgent-matter')

e. *fùyǒu de jiātíng*: *fùyǒu* 'be wealthy; be rich' ('wealth possess')

f. *huòshì = huòzhě = huò*

g. *zhèngfǔ guānyuán*: *guānyuán* 'officials' ('official-personnel'); cf. *fǎguān* 'judge'; *fúwùyuán*

h. *zhuāng diànhuà*: *zhuāng* 'install'; *yǐjīng bǎ tā zhuāngshang le* 'already installed it'

i. *Néng shǐyòng diànhuà de hěn shǎo, érqiě diànhuàfèi yě hěn guì*: *shǐyòng* 'have access to; use; apply' ('cause to-use'); *érqiě* 'and; moreover'

j. *shǒuxiān* 'first of all' ('head-first')

k. *zài èrshíyī shìjì de dì-èr ge shínián*: *shínián* 'decade' ('ten-year')

l. *gūjì zài Zhōngguó yǒu jiǔyì shǒujī yònghùr*: *gūjì* 'estimate; reckon; look as if' ('estimate-compute'); *yònghù<r>* 'consumer; user' ('use-person')

m. *Zhàn rénkǒu zǒngshù de sìfēn zhī sān zuǒyòu*: *zhàn* 'occupy; constitute; make up'; *zhàn jué dàduōshù* 'occupy the absolute majority'; *zǒngshù* 'total' ('general-figure')

n. *shàngwǎng de gōngnéng*: *shàngwǎng* 'go online; access the Internet' ('go on-net'); *gōngnéng* 'function' ('skill-ability')

o. *Shùnbiàn shuō, Yìndù jǐnsuíqíhòu*: *shùnbiàn* 'in passing' ('accord with-convenience'); *jǐnsuíqíhòu* 'following closely behind' ('tight-follow-its-back')

p. *Yìndù de zēngzhǎnglǜ*: *zēngzhǎnglǜ* 'rate of increase' ('add-grow-rate'); cf. *chūshēnglǜ*

q. *nǐ kě.yǐ jìxù yòng nǐ zìjǐ de*: *jìxù* 'continue'

r. *shǐ nǐ zhènjīng*: *shǐ* 'make; cause'; *zhènjīng* 'shock; astonish' ('shake-surprise'); *shǐ wǒmen hěn zhènjīng* 'shocked us all' ('cause us quite to-be-shocked')

s. *zū ge tīngtǒng, qiān ge hétong*: *zū* 'rent; lease'; cf. *chūzū-qìchē*; *tīngtǒng* 'phone receiver' ('listen-tube'); [M: *gè*]; *qiān* 'to sign'; *hétong* 'contract; agreement' ('join-with') [M: *fèn*]

t. *Àn fēn fùqián, fèiyòng háishi hěn duō*: *àn fēn* 'by the minute'; *àn* 'according to; by'; cf. *ànzhào*; *fùqián* 'pay money'; *fèiyòng* 'cost; expenses' ('expend-use')

u. *SIM-kǎ shi yùfùfèi yòng de*: *yùfù* 'pay in advance' ('advance-pay')

v. *Yòngwán kě.yǐ mǎi zhāng xùfèikǎ, guāqù kǎ shang PIN de bǎohùcéng, shūrù kǎ shang de mìmǎ, àn xùfèi tíshì shùnxù shūrù jiù kě.yǐ yòng le*: A *xùfèikǎ* 'recharging card' ('continue-charge-card') is the card you use to add minutes to your mobile phone; cf. *jìxù* 'continue'; To use it, first you have to *guāqù* 'shave off' [with *guā* 'shave; scrape off'] the *bǎohùcéng* 'protective strip' ('protect-layer'), then you have to *shūrù* 'input' ('transport-in') the *kǎ shang de mìmǎ*, 'password' ('secret-code') that is on the card, and finally you have to *àn xùfèi tíshì* 'according to the directions for recharging', *shùnxù shūrù* 'enter in sequence' the password.

w. *cóng wàiguó shōudào de*: *shōudào* 'receive; get' ('receive-arrive'); *shōudàole hěn duō láixìn* 'receive a lot of letters in response'; contrast with *shòudào* [with falling toned *shòu*] 'be given' ('accept-arrive'), as in *shòudào rèliè de huānyíng* 'be given a warm welcome'

x. *Chúle zài piānyuǎn shānqū měiyǒu jīzhàn de dìfang, yìbān qiángdù hěn hǎo, shēngyīn yě hěn qīngchu*: *piānyuǎn* 'far off; remote' ('inclined-far'); *shānqū* 'mountainous region' ('mountain-region'); *jīzhàn* 'base tower'; *qiángdù* 'strength' ('strength-degree'); *shēngyīn* 'sound'

y. *yào gèng shěngqián*: *shěngqián* 'save money'; cf. *wèi shěng máfan* 'in order to save trouble'

z. *fā duǎnxìn* 'send a text message' ('send short-letter')

aa. *yì tiáo dàgài yì máo éryǐ*: *éryǐ* is a final particle (often paired with *búguò* 'no more than') with the sense of finality: 'and that's it; and that's all; only' ('and-complete'); *búguò shi ge xiàohua éryǐ* 'it's just a joke'

bb. *yòng shǒuxiě shūrùfǎ* 'handwriting input method'; *shǒuxiě* 'write by hand'

cc. *Yòng shǒu huòshi péi de bǐ bǎ tóu jǐ ge bǐhuà xiě zai yínmù shang*: *péi* 'accompany'; *tóu jǐ ge* 'the first few' ('head several M'); *yínmù* 'screen' ('silver-screen')

dd. *chūxiàn yíxìliè xiāngxiàng de Hànzì*: *chūxiàn* 'appear' ('out-appear'); *yíxìliè* 'a series of; a string of'; cf. *yīnwèi yíxìliè de yuányīn* 'for a slew of reasons'; *xiāngxiàng* 'resemble, be similar' ('mutual-similar')

ee. *ránhòu xuǎnzhòng héshì de*: *xuǎnzhòng* 'select [from a group]' ('choose-hit center'); *héshì* 'appropriate; suitable'

ff. *Jiùshì lājī duǎnxìn tài duō, dōushòu gèzhǒng xìnxī*: *lājī duǎnxìn* 'spam' ('trash short-message')

gg. *dōushòu* 'peddle' ('solicit-sell'); *xìnxī* 'message; information'

hh. *wǎngluò* 'network, the net' ('net-mesh'); *jièlái de cí* 'borrowed word' ('borrow-come DE word')

ii. *dádào sìyì wǔqiānwàn*: *dádào* 'reach; attain' ('reach-arrive')

jj. *bù néng jiāndū tāmen*: *jiāndū* 'supervise; keep an eye on'

kk. *zài liáotiānshì hé lùntán tán guójiā de dàshì*: *liáotiānshì* 'chat rooms' ('chat-the day through-room'); *lùntán* 'forum' ('discuss-arena')

ll. *háishi yòng liáotiān duìhuà chuándì xìnxī hǎo*: *háishi . . . hǎo* 'better to . . .'; *duìhuà* 'conversation' ('oppose-words'); *chuándì-xìnxī* 'text message' ('transmit-information')

mm. *bǐ yīmèi'er qīnmì*: *qīnmì* 'intimate; close'; cf. *qīnqi* 'relatives', *mìmǎ<r>* 'password'

nn. *shi miǎnfèi de*: *miǎnfèi* 'free of charge' ('avoid-fee')

oo. *chúle dǎzì-liáotiān, shìpín-liáotiān wài*: *chúle . . . wài* 'besides, in addition to'; *dǎzì* 'type' ('do-words'); *shìpín* 'video' ('view-frequency')

pp. *chuán túpiàn, fā yóujiàn, xiě wēibó, zhìzuò gèrén kōngjiān, cún yìxiē zìjǐ xǐhuan de rìzhì, zhàopiàn děng*: *chuán túpiàn* 'send images' ('transmit image'); *xiě wēibó* ('write tiny-transmission'); Weibo is a Chinese microblogging and social networking service, similar to Twitter; *zhìzuò* 'create; make'; *kōngjiān* 'space' ('empty-space'); *cún* 'exist; store; deposit'; *rìzhì* 'daily record' ('day-record')

qq. *QQ zhànghào*: 'QQ account number'

rr. *zhǐ shì yǒu yì diǎnr bù ānquán*: *ānquán* 'be safe' ('peace-complete')

ss. *xiàzài ge ruǎnjiàn*: *xiàzài* 'download' ('down-transport'); *ruǎnjiàn* 'software' ('soft-item')

tt. *lüèzì hěn duo*: *lüèzì* 'abbreviation' ('abbreviate-word') uu. *yǒude shi cūsú de, xiàliú de*: *cūsú* 'crude'; *xiàliú* 'obscene; dirty' ('low-flow')

vv. *Yīngwén zìmǔ de fāyīn*: *fāyīn* 'pronunciation' ('issue-sound'); The symbols that represent individual speech sounds, such as the letters of the Roman alphabet, are called *zìmǔ* ('character [or letter]-mother'); add a specialized word for 'head', and the meaning is 'initial sound': *shǒu zìmǔ*.

ww. *táotàisài, huò bèi tàotàile de yī ge xuǎnshǒu*: *xuǎnshǒu*, with *xuǎn* 'select' and *shǒu* 'hand' standing in for the whole person (cf. English 'deckhands') are 'contestants'; *Táotài* is a pleasant sounding word, built on *táo* 'rinse; dredge'; here it has the sense of 'eliminate'; *táotàisài*, with the bound root *sài* 'competition', means 'sudden-death elimination'.

xx. *Yòu shěng jījiàn dòngzuò, yòu yǒu chuàngzàoxìng*: *yòu . . . yòu . . .* 'both . . . and . . .'; *shěng* 'save; omit'; *dòngzuò* 'movement' ('move-do'); *jījiàn* 'strike a key; a key stroke'; cf. *jī rènhé jiàn* 'strike any key'; *chuàngzàoxìng* 'creativity' ('create-ness')

yy. *wǎngzhàn* 'Web site' ('net-station')

zz. *wèi xīyǐn gèng duō rén yòng*: *xīyǐn* 'attract'

aaa. *búduàn* 'without a break'

bbb. *chuàngxīn* 'innovate' ('create-new'); in other words, 'continuously innovate'

ccc. *gǎoxiào-túpiàn* 'emoticon' ('make-laugh illustration'); *kě.yǐ chuānchā zài duìhuà zhōng, zēngjiā liáotiān de lèqù*; *chuānchā* 'insert' ('pass through-insert'); *zēngjiā* 'increase'; *lèqù* 'pleasure, fun' ('happy-interest')

ddd. *chá shēngcí* 'look up vocabulary'; *liǎojiě Hànzì de láiyuán* 'learn about the origin of Chinese characters'; *dú Zhōngwén wénzhāng* 'read Chinese articles'

eee. *wǎngyè* 'Web pages'; *gēn xué Zhōngwén yǒuguān de liánjiē* 'links that are related to the study of Chinese'; *gēn . . . yǒuguān de* 'related to'

fff. *sōusuǒ-yǐnqíng* 'search engine'; a translation of the English term, with *yǐnqíng* (originally a loan word from English) applied to engines in general; *ménhù wǎngzhàn* 'Web portal' combines 'gateway' and 'Web site'

ggg. *tiānqì yùgào*: *yùgào* 'weather report' ('predict-report')

hhh. *guǎngbō-gōngsī*: *guǎngbō* 'broadcast'

iii. *suīrán nèiróng shi Zhōngwén de (chúle yìxiē guǎnggào)*: *nèiróng* 'contents' ('internal-contain'); *guǎnggào* 'advertisement' ('broad-report')

jjj. *wǎngzhǐ* 'Web address'; *yùmíng* 'domain name'

kkk. *Bùguǎn shi Zhōngwén de nèiróng háishi Yīngwén de nèiróng dōu méiyǒu wèntí*: *bùguǎn . . . dōu* 'regardless of whether; no matter whether'

lll. *Jìshù wèntí dōu yǐjīng jiějué le*: *jìshù* 'technology'; *jiějué* 'solve'

mmm. *jiānglái* 'future' ('will-come'): *Huì bu huì zhōngyú yǒu liǎng ge dúlì de xìtǒng?*; *zhōngyú* 'in the end; eventually' ('end-at'); *dúlì* 'independent' ('alone-stand')

Exercise 3

Provide a Chinese paraphrase of the following paragraph.

What you say about the situation in China is very interesting. Here in the United States, telephone calls also used to be quite expensive—especially long-distance ones (*chángtú*)—but not anymore. I still often write letters to my relatives, but that's because they're older and they still like to read letters. Sending a letter is still pretty inexpensive. It's only about 50 cents within the country; a letter to China is about 90 cents airmail. Students nowadays all have computers, so we prefer to send e-mail. Often, I don't know enough characters to write what I want to say in Chinese. In any case, I have trouble sending characters, so I write pinyin. As long as I write words, my Chinese friends seem to be able to read it. I don't write the tones (*sìshēng*) either, since that takes too long, and what's more, it makes it too messy to read. Almost all my friends have mobile phones. With the new ones, you can surf the Web, take photos, or listen to music. They're kind of expensive, but we can't live without them. My mobile phone bill is more than my food bill sometimes!

19.6 Making a telephone call

The language used when making a telephone call has changed a lot during the last few decades in China, as it has in the rest of the world. With the rise of personal telephones—especially mobile phones—it is no longer common to have to go off and find someone to deal with an incoming phone call. People also don't deal so much with operators. However, there is still a certain amount of conventional language at the beginning and end of phone conversations. Here are some vocabulary words and phrases (some of them familiar) for reference.

dǎ chángtú diànhuà	'make a long-distance call'
dǎ diànhuà	'telephone; make a phone call'

dǎ guójì diànhuà	'make an international call'
diànhuàfèi	'phone charges'
diànhuà hàomǎ	'phone number'
diànhuàjī	'a telephone' [the instrument]
diànhuàkǎ	'phonc card'
diànhuàtíng	'phone kiosk'
diànhuà zhànxiàn	'the line is busy' ('telephone occupy-line')
jiē diànhuà	'answer the phone'
miǎnfèi	'free' ('avoid-fee')
xiān bō ge yāo	'first dial a one'
xiān bō hàomǎ	'first dial the number'
zhuǎn fēnjī	'connect to an extension' ('turn; revolve')
Shì dìqū yòng de ma?	'Is this for local calls?'
Quánguó yòng de.	'It's used throughout the country.'
Dǎ dào nǎ.lǐ?	'Where are you calling?'
Dǎ gěi shéi?	'Who are you calling?'
Yǒu shìr, dǎ ge diànhuà gěi wǒ.	'If you have a problem, give me a call.'
Nǐ de diànhuà.	'It's for you.'
Qǐng zhuǎn èrshíwǔ (fēnjī).	'Please connect me to extension 25.'
Néng dǎ chángtú ma?	'Can you dial long distance?'
Néng zìjǐ dǎ ma?	'Can we dial it ourselves?'
Zhǐ néng dǎ dào shìnèi.	'You can only call in town.'
Néng dǎ dào guówài ma?	'Can we call abroad?'

NOTE

As in most parts of the world, a variety of discount telephone cards can be bought from news agents and other small shops in China. They are usually sold below face value; a ¥100 card might go for ¥30. Some are local (*dìqū yòng de*); others can be used throughout China (*quánguó yòng de*) or even internationally (*guójì de*).

Wèi.	'Hello.'
<Nín> něi wèi?	'Who is it?'
Wèi, nǐ shi Zhōu Yǔ ma?	'Hello, is that Zhou Yu?'
Wǒ jiùshì.	'This is he; it's me; speaking.'
Qǐng zhǎo Máo Xiān'ān jiē diànhuà.	'Can I speak to Mao Xian'an please?' ('Please ask Mao Xian'an to come to the phone.')
Wǒ gěi nǐ qù zhǎo tā.	'I'll go find her for you.' ('I for you go find her')
Yào liú ge huà gěi tā ma?	'Do you want to leave a message for her?'
Nǐ yào liúyán ma?	'Do you want to leave a voice message?'
Wǒ shi Léi Nuò, qǐng liúyán.	'This is Lei Nuo; please leave a message.'

Leaving a message

Lù Jìngsī, a foreign scholar, is trying to reach *Wáng Xuéyīng* in his office.

Wáng:	*Wèi?*	'Hello?'
Lù:	*Wèi, qǐng zhǎo Wáng lǎoshī jiē diànhuà.*	'Hi, I'm trying to get Professor Wang.'
Wáng:	*O, tā xiànzài bú zài zhèr, kěnéng zài lóushang. Qǐng děngyixiàr, wǒ gěi nǐ qù zhǎo tā.*	'Oh, he's not here right now; he may be upstairs. Just a minute, I'll go and look for him for you.'
Lù:	*Hǎo, máfan nǐ la!* (le a > la)	'Okay, sorry for the trouble!'
Wáng:	*Tā yě bú zài lóushang. Yào bu yào liú ge huà?*	'He's not upstairs. Do you want to leave a message?'
Lù:	*Hǎo, xièxie. Wǒ shi Lù Jìngsī. Qǐng tā huílai yǐhòu gěi wǒ dǎ ge diànhuà. Wǒ zài jiālǐ.*	'Okay, thanks. This is Lu Jingsi. Ask him to call me when he gets home. I'm at home.'

Wáng:	*Tā zhīdao nǐ de diànhuà hàomǎ ma?*	'Does he know your phone number?'
Lù:	*Diànhuà hàomǎ shi 245-1209.*	'My number is 245-1209.'
Wáng:	*Hǎo, wǒ huì gàosu tā.*	'Fine, I'll tell him.'

Jūmínlóu 'residential building' (*Shànghǎi*)

NOTES

a. *Wèi* is an exclamation used to hail people at a distance or confirm a telephone connection. Though its tone is marked as falling in dictionaries, its actual pitch varies.

b. *Qǐng zhǎo . . . jiē diànhuà* 'please get . . . to come to the phone' is a request to speak to a person (~ 'may I speak to . . .') and reflects the fact that before mobile phones, telephones were often outside of residences, and people had to be hailed or fetched from some distance away.

19.7 Bargaining: The way Chinese might do it

Recall the earlier material (especially in Unit 14) on shopping and bargaining. Here is a more sophisticated dialogue that is envisioned as taking place between locals, so the only likely role for a foreign learner of Chinese is as a bystander, listening in. Because it takes place between Chinese people, it is colloquial and incorporates a number of idiomatic expressions, which are explained in the notes. You might try first reenacting this dialogue with a partner, reading the Chinese from the script so you can sustain a convincing level of fluency. Then you can incorporate some of the usage in your own bargaining. This dialogue is set in Beijing. *Yǐ* runs a shop selling leather coats in a street market, and *Jiǎ* is a female customer.

Jiǎ:	*Lǎobǎn, zhèi jiàn pídàyī duōshao qián?*	'Laoban, how much is this leather coat?'
Yǐ:	*Yìqiānwǔ.*	'¥1,500.'
Jiǎ:	*Jiu zhèyàngr de pídàyī yìqiānwǔ?! Tài hēi le ba! Biéde dìfang gēn zhèi jiàn chàbuduō yíyàng de, cái wǔbǎi duō kuài! Nǐ gěi yí ge gōngdaojià!*	'A jacket like this is ¥1,500?! That's a rip-off! At other places, coats almost exactly the same as this one are only ¥500! Give me a decent price!'
Yǐ:	*Nǐ kāi shénme guójì wánxiào! Zhè shi zhēn pí de! Nǐ mōmo, shǒugǎn duō hǎo! Nǐ zài biéde dìfang kàndao de yídìng shi jiǎhuò! Nèi yàng de yīfu, nǐ chuānbuliǎo duō cháng shíjiān jiu huài le. Wǒ zhèi jiàn, bǎo nín chuān tā ge jǐshí nián méiyǒu wèntí!*	'What sort of an international joke are you pulling? This is real leather! Feel it; the texture's so nice! Those you saw elsewhere must be fakes! That sort of clothing—you can't wear it for any length of time before it's worn out. This one—it's a sure thing you can wear it for several decades without a problem!'
Jiǎ:	*Lǎobǎn, nǐ jiu chuī ba! Fǎnzhèng chuīniú yě bú shàngshuì!*	'Laoban, you're putting me on! Still, bragging's not taxed!'

Yǐ: *Zhèyàng ba, dàjiě, wǒ kàn nín*   'How about this, sister—I see
        shi zhēnxīn yào mǎi. Wǒ   you're serious about buying it,
        jiu fàng yìdiǎnr xiě. Nǐ gěi   so I'll take a hit. How about
        yìqiānsān zěnmeyàng?   you pay ¥1,300?'

Jiǎ: *1300 bù xíng. 500, nǐ mài bu*   '¥1,300's no good. ¥500—you
        mài?   selling?'

Yǐ: *Aiya, dàjiě, nín zǒngděi ràng*   'Gosh, sister, you have to let me
        wǒ zhuàn yìdiǎnr ba! Wǒ   earn a little something. My
        jìnjià jiu bābǎi. Nǐ duō gěi   buying price was ¥800. Give
        yìdiǎnr. Nèi diǎnr qián,   me a bit more. That bit of
        duì nín lái shuō, jiùshi jǐ   money, for you, is just money
        dùn fàn qián, dànshi duì   for a couple meals, but for me,
        wǒ lái shuō, hěn zhòngyào.   it's crucial. I need to earn
        Wǒ yào zhuàn yìdiǎnr qián   some money to pay for my
        gěi wǒ háizi jiāo xuéfèi.   kid's tuition.'

Jiǎ: *Bābǎi zěnmeyàng?*   '¥800 then?'

Yǐ: *Bābǎi tài shǎo le; zài duō gěi*   '¥800's too little; make it a little
        yìdiǎnr. Yìqiān'èr.   more. ¥1,200.'

Jiǎ: *Jiǔbǎi.*   '¥900.'

Yǐ: *Yìqiānyī. Yàobu, zám gè ràng*   '¥1,100. Or else we split the
        yí bù: nín gěi yìqiān, wǒ   difference: give ¥1000—I earn
        shǎo zhuàn yìdiǎnr, nín   a little less; you give a little
        duō gěi diǎnr.   more.'

Jiǎ: *Bù xíng, jiǔ bǎi, nín mài bu*   'Nope. ¥900—take it or leave it. If
        mài? Nǐ bú mài wǒ jiù zǒu le.   you don't take it, then I'm leaving.'

Yǐ: *Hǎo, hǎo, jiǔbǎi jiu jiǔbǎi. Ai,*   'Okay, okay, ¥900 then. Gosh,
        dàjiě, nín kě zhēn néng   sister, you can really bargain!
        tǎojiàhuánjià. Wǒ kě zhēn   I've got to hand it to you! So,
        fúle nín le. Hǎo le, dàjiě, jiù   let's be friends, sister. From
        suàn zám jiāo ge péngyou.   now on, come by and help me
        Nín wǎng hòu duō lái zhàogu   out with this business, won't
        wǒ de shēngyi bei? . . . Hǎo,   you? . . . Okay, this is your
        zhè shi nín de pídàyī. Náhǎo.   leather jacket. Got it?'

Jiǎ: *Zhè shi jiǔbǎi zhěng. Nǐ shǔshu.*   'Here's ¥900 exactly. Count it.'

Yǐ: *Méi cuò, zhènghǎo jiǔbǎi.*   'Correct, exactly ¥900. Take
       Nín màn zǒu. Huānyíng   care. Please come back again.'
       nín zài lái.

Based on Chen Tong, 09/05

ANNOTATIONS

Tài hēi le ba!	'too black': suggests 'extortion'; 'rip-off' has the right level of informality but may be too offensive.
Nǐ gěi yí ge gōngdaojià	*gōngdao* 'just; fair; reasonable': *Nà shi fēicháng gōngdao de jiàgé* 'that's a very fair price'; *hédào* in southern Mandarin
Nǐ kāi shénme guójì wánxiào	*guójì wánxiào* 'international joke': in other words, 'out of the realm of possibilities; outlandish; off the wall'
Zhēn pí de	'a real leather one': *Nǐ mōmo, shǒugǎn duō hǎo*; *mō* 'feel'; *shǒugǎn* 'the feel of it' ('hand-feel')
Yídìng shi jiǎhuò	*jiǎhuò* 'fake' ('false-goods'): cf. *shuǐhuò* 'smuggled goods' ('water-goods')
Nǐ chuānbuliǎo duō cháng shíjiān jiù huài le.	*huài le* 'go bad; be ruined; be useless'
Bǎo nín chuān tā ge jǐshí nián méiyǒu wèntí.	*bǎo* 'keep; ensure; guarantee'; *chuān tā* is a case where *tā* refers to a thing, not a person; *jǐshí nián* 'for several decades'; The addition of *gè* to measure the phrase *jǐshí nián* (as if to say, 'you can wear it an age without it wearing out') gives a sense of approximation.
Lǎobǎn, nǐ jiu chuī ba! Fǎnzhèng chuīniú yě bú shàngshuì.	*chuī* 'blow': here, it is short for *chuīniú ~ chuī niúpí* ('inflate the skin of an ox')—a metaphor for bragging or

	talking big (presumably because it makes the ox look bigger than it really is). Since it (an inflated ox or inflated language) isn't substantial, you don't have to pay additional tax on it; *bú shàngshuì* ('charge-tax').
Nín shi zhēnxīn yào mǎi	*zhēnxīn* 'sincere' ('real-heart')
Wǒ jiù fàng yìdiǎnr xiě	*fàng xiě* 'bleed' ('put-blood'): the alternate pronunciation, *xuè*, is less likely in this context; here in the sense of 'make a sacrifice'
Nín zǒngděi ràng wǒ zhuàn yìdiǎnr ba	*zǒngděi* 'must; have to' ('always-must'); here, *ràng* 'let [someone do something]'
Wǒ jìnjià jiu bābǎi	*jìnjià* 'best price' ('best-price')
Jiāo xuéfèi	'pay tuition' ('deliver study-expenses'): cf. *jiāo zuòyè* 'hand in assignments'; *jiāo péngyou* 'make friends'
Zài duō gěi yìdiǎnr	'again more give by a bit': in other words, 'give a bit more again'
Yàobu, zán gè ràng yí bù	*yàobu* 'if not; otherwise': cf. *yàoburán* ('if-not-so') and *bùrán* 'not so'; *zám* is a colloquial elision of *zánmen*; *gè ràng yí bù* 'each yield one step'; cf. *gèguó* 'each and every country'; *gè wèi péngyou* 'my friends' [addressing people]; *ràng*, in addition to its other meanings such as 'allow; let' and 'by', can also function as a full verb meaning 'yield'
Nín kě zhēn néng tǎojiàhuánjià	*tǎojiàhuánjià* 'bargain' ('ask-price return-price'); *kě*, here, is an adverb; cf. *nín kě zhēn néng* 'you sure can' and *kě bú shì ma* 'you said it'

Wǒ kě zhēn fúle nín le	*fú* 'be convinced; submit; be impressed'
Hǎo le, dàjiě, jiù suàn zám jiāo ge péngyou	*suàn* 'calculate; reckon'
Nín wǎng hòu duō lái zhàogu wǒ de shēngyi bei	*wǎnghòu* 'henceforth' ('go-after'); *zhàogu* 'patronize' (elsewhere: 'look after; attend to'); *bei* is a sentence final particle that conveys a sense of 'grudgingly coming around'
Zhè shi jiǔbǎi zhěng. Nǐ shǔshu. / Méi cuò, zhènghǎo jiǔbǎi.	This excerpt contains several examples of related—at least, relatable—words differing in tone. *Jiǔbǎi zhěng* (also *zhěng jiǔbǎi*) has *zhěng* 'whole; entire; fully', with low tone. *Zhènghǎo jiǔbǎi* 'exactly nine hundred' ('precisely-good nine hundred') has *zhèng* 'just; exactly', with falling tone. Similarly, the verb *shǔ* 'count', with low tone, is obviously related to nominal forms with falling tone, such as *shùzi* 'number', *shùxué*, and so on.

NOTES

a. Distinguish *zhěng*, with low tone, 'whole; entire; fully' from *zhèng* 'punctual; exact', with falling tone. The latter occurs in the compound *zhènghǎo* 'just right; just enough'. Keep in mind the phrases *sān diǎn zhěng* or *zhěng sān diǎn* '3:00 sharp' and *zhěng jiǔbǎi* or *jiǔbǎi zhěng* '¥900 precisely' versus *zhènghǎo jiǔbǎi* 'exactly nine hundred'.

b. *Huānyíng nín zài lái*: In China, this phrase is often translated literally into English as 'Welcome to come again!'

19.8 Exploring the city of Zhenjiang (*Zhènjiāng*)

In this, the last of the long narratives in *Learning Chinese* (there's a short one at the very end of this unit), the narrator takes you on a ramble through the city of Zhenjiang ('Garrison of the River'), which lies on the Yangtze between Nanjing and Shanghai. Nowadays, Zhenjiang is overshadowed by its illustrious neighbors, such as Nanjing, Suzhou, and Shanghai, but it was once the provincial capital. In recent years, the city has made substantial efforts to restore some of its historical neighborhoods, providing pockets of calm amid the factories of its booming industries (chemicals, manufacturing, biotechnology, construction) and the glitz of its commercial districts.

Yàoshi cóng Shànghǎi zuò huǒchē dào Nánjīng qù, nǐ huì jīngguo Sūzhōu, Wúxī, Chángzhōu, hé Zhènjiāng nèi jǐ ge chéngshì. Zuìhòu nèi ge shi yīnwèi cù ér yǒumíng: Zhènjiāng xiāngcù, "jùyǒu sè, xiāng, suān, chún de tèdiǎn, suān ér bú sè, xiāng ér wēi tián, sènóng-wèixiān". Kěshì kěnéng shi yīnwèi fùjìn de míngshèng tǐng duō, huòzhě fùjìn de dàchéng, xiàng Nánjīng, Sūzhōu gèng yǒumíng, qù Zhènjiāng de yóukè bù duō. Zhènjiāng zài Cháng Jiāng nán'àn, lí Nánjīng dàgài yǒu 65 gōnglǐ. Zài Zhènjiāng duìmiàn, zài Cháng Jiāng de běi'àn, yě yǒu yí ge lìshǐ bǐjiào yōujiǔ de chéngshì: Yángzhōu. Yángzhōu běnlái shi Cháng Jiāng biān shang de yí ge gǎngkǒu, kěshì zǎojiù bèi yūní sāizhùle, jiéguǒ ne, xiànzài Yángzhōu lí hé biānr yǒu diǎn jùlí.

Zài jiǔshí niándài, wǒ zhù zai Nánjīng de shíhou, tīngshuō Yángzhōu nèi ge chéngshì dàgài yìqiān nián yǐqián shi quán shìjiè bǐjiào yǒumíng de dàgǎng zhī yī, juéde yīnggāi chèn jīhuì qù kànyixiàr. Yángzhōu lí Nánjīng bù yuǎn. Zuì zhíjiē de lùxiàn shi xiān zǒu 1968 nián xiū de Nánjīng Chángjiāng Dàqiáo, ránhòu zài gāosù-gōnglù shang kāi chàbuduō jiǔshí fēn zhōng jiù dào le. Kěshì wǒ juéde zhème zǒu méi shénme yìsi, suǒ.yǐ juédìng zuò huǒchē xiān dào Chángjiāng nán'àn de Zhènjiāng, ránhòu zhǎo ge dùchuán guòhé qù Yángzhōu. Kànle dǎoyóushū, wǒ fāxiàn Zhènjiāng xiàng Yángzhōu yíyàng, lìshǐ yě xiāngdāng cháng. Yǐqián jiào Jīngkǒu. Zài Běi Sòng, Dà Yùnhé xiūhǎo de shíhou, Jīngkǒu shi ge zhòngyào de hégǎng.

Gàosu fángdōng wǒ dǎsuàn dāngtiān yí ge rén yòng gōngjiāo qù Zhènjiāng hé Yángzhōu, tā yǒu diǎnr dānxīn, pà wǒ huì mílù huò wù zuìhòu yì bān chē, shuō gǎi tiān tā kě.yǐ péi wǒ qù. Bù hǎo yìsi, wǒ shuō, "bù xiǎng gěi nǐ tiān máfan". Dào hòulai, tā fàngxīn le, shuō wànyī pèngdao yìwài de shìr, tā zài Zhènjiāng yǒu lǎo péngyou, kě.yǐ hé tā liánxì. Wǒ bǎ dìzhǐ jì xiàlaile, shuō wǒ yídìng huì xiǎoxīn.

Nà, zǎoshang bā diǎn huǒchē líkāile Nánjīng, bú dào shí diǎn jiu dàole Zhènjiāng. Yí lù shang, wǒmen jīngguo bù shǎo xiǎo shāngǔ, liǎngmiàn dōu shi lǜlǜ de dàotián. Wǒ zài huǒchēzhàn xiàle chē, tízhe bāo, zǒu dào wàitou, xiǎng suíbiàn zǒu yi zǒu. Zhènjiāng suàn shi ge zhìzàoyè chéngshì, rénkǒu dàgài yǒu sānbǎiwàn. Nà shíhou shi xiàtiān, suǒ.yǐ tiānqì yòu rè yòu cháo, zǒule yǐhuǐr, wǒ jiu yì shēn dōu shi hàn le. Lù liǎngbiānr yǒu hěn duō xiǎo tānzi, xiǎo gōngchǎng, hái yǒu hěn duō shāngdiàn – lóuxia shi shāngdiàn, lóushang shi zhù de dìfang. Jiē shang dàochù dōu shì gōnggòng-qìchē, kǎchē, xiǎo qìchē hé zìxíngchē. Hòulái, wǒ yánzhe yì tiáo yòu hēi yòu chòu de yùnhé zǒule yǐhuǐr. Nà bú shì Dà Yùnhé; qíshí shi ge bǐjiào dà de shuǐgōur. Fǎnzhèng, wǒ yǐwéi yánzhe shuǐ zǒu, yídìng huì dào hébiānr, kěshì zuìhòu wǒ zǒu dàole yì jiā dà gōngchǎng, guòbuqù le. Hěn máfan!

Zǒuzhe zhǒuzhe, láile yí liàng gōnggòng qìchē, wǒ jiù zhíjiē shàngle. Chē hěn jiù, mào de dōu shì hēi yān. Shòupiàoyuán wèn wǒ qù nǎr, wǒ jiù shuō yào dào chéng li qù. Zuòle yǐhuǐr chē yǐhòu, wǒ kànjiàn yì páipái de lǎo fángzi, jiù zài nàli xiàle chē. Yǒu yì tiáo xiǎojiē, hěn zhǎi, zǒu guòqu yǐhòu wǒ fāxiàn chàbuduō yì gōnglǐ cháng, liǎngbiānr dōu shì shítou zuò de fángzi. Nèi tiáo jiē jiào Xī Jīndù Gǔjiē. Jīndù jiùshì yǒu dùchuán de mǎtóu de yìsi. Wǒ de lǚyóu zhǐnán shang shuō, dàgài yìqiān nián yǐqián, zài Sòngcháo nèi ge shíhou, zhèi tiáo jiē shi hěn rènào de shāngyè jiē. Jiù xiàng míngzi shuō de yíyàng, yǐqián zài jiē de yì tóu shi yí ge xiǎo mǎtou. Jùshuō, zài Yuáncháo de shíhou, Mǎkě Bōluó qù Zhènjiāng jiùshì zài nèi ge mǎtou shàng'àn de. Nǐ xiāngxìn ma? Fǎnzhèng, xiànzài, hé'àn lí nèi tiáo jiē yǐjīng hěn yuǎn le.

Wǒ gēn yìxiē zhù zai Xī Jīndù Gǔjiē de rén liáole liáotiān. Tāmen dōu huì shuō Pǔtōnghuà, kěshì kǒuyīn hěn zhòng, hěn nán tīngdǒng. Tāmen shuō méiyǒu cóng Zhènjiāng zhíjiē dào Yángzhōu de dùchuán; dùchuán zài chéng wài, zài Zhènjiāng de xī bianr, bú suàn tài yuǎn. Tāmen yě shuō líkāi Zhènjiāng yǐqián, yīnggāi qù kànkan Zhènjiāng shìjiè wénmíng de sān zuò shān: Jīn Shān, Jiāo Shān, hái yǒu Běigù Shān. Měi zuò shān shang dōu yǒu yí zuò miào. Hěn yǒu yìsi.

Zhènjiāng, Xī Jīndù Gǔjiē

Hòulái wǒ jiàole yí liàng sānlúnchē. (Sānlúnchē zài dà chéngshì yòng de bù duō, kěshì zài xiǎo chéngshì, hái yǒu.) Yīnwèi yǒu ge huì shuō Zhōngwén de wàiguó rén zuò tā de chē, dēngchē shīfu xiāngdāng gāoxìng. Tā shi ge zúqiúmí, wènle wǒ hěn duō zúqiú de wèntí, yě xiǎng zhīdao wǒ shi něi ge qiúduì de qiúmí. Tā yě xǐhuan lánqiú. Wǒ wèn tā shì bu shì Wáng Zhìzhì de qiúmí, tā shuō gèng xǐhuan Yáo Míng. Zuìhòu tā bǎ wǒ dài dàole yì jiā Màidāngláo. Màidāngláo, Kěndéjī, Bìshèngkè zhèyàng de kuàicāndiàn zài Zhōngguó hěn shòu huānyíng, yīnwèi zhèi xiē kuàicāndiàn dōu yǒu kōngtiáo, yíngyè shíjiān hěn cháng, shèbèi yě hěn fāngbiàn.

Wo xiūxile yìhuǐr yǐhòu, jiù qù zhǎo Zhènjiāng Sān Shān, nèi sān ge jǐngdiǎn. Dì-yī zuò, Jīn Shān, zài Zhènjiāng chéng běi, zài hébiān. Jīn Shān yǐqián shi hé lǐ de yí zuò xiǎo dǎo, xiànzài yǐjīng shi nán'àn de yí bùfen. Jīnshān shang yǒu yí zuò miào, shi hòulái xiū de, niándài bù jiǔ, dànshi háishi hěn piàoliang de. Zhōngguó yǒu yí ge hěn yǒumíng de chuántǒng gùshi, míngzi jiào Báishé Zhuàn. (Báishé jiùshì báisè de shé, zhuàn jiùshì gùshi de yìsi.) Gùshi de yí bùfen jiùshì zài Jīn Shān Sì fāshēng de. Zhīdao nèi ge gùshi ma? Bái Sùzhēn běnlái shi yì tiáo shé, hòulái biàn chéngle yí ge hěn piàoliang de nǚde. Yǒu yí cì, zài Hángzhōu xià dà yǔ de shíhou, Bái Sùzhēn bǎ zìjǐ de sǎn jiè gěile yí ge jiào Xǔ Xiān de nánren.

Tāmen yíjiànzhōngqíng, hòulái jiéhūn le. Kěshì yǒu ge jiào Fǎhǎi de lǎo héshang gàosu Xǔ Xiān tā de qīzi bú shì rén, ér shi yì tiáo shé, shi ge yāojing. Xǔ Xiān jiù pǎo dàole wǒmen shuō de nèi ge Jīn Shān Sì. Bái Sùzhēn yě gēnzhe tā qùle nàli, gēn Fǎhǎi dǎle yí zhàng. Zài Jīn Shān Sì lǐ, xiànzài háishi yǒu yí ge dòng, jùshuō Fǎhǎi yǐqián jiu zhù zai nàli, zài nàr dǎzuò.

Kànwánle Jīn Shān Sì hái yǒu liǎng ge jǐng.diǎn yào qù kàn. Běigù Shān zài Jīn Shān hé Jiāo Shān zhōngjiānr, zǒulù tài yuǎn, fùjìn yě méiyǒu sānlúnchē, suǒ.yǐ wǒ zuòle yí liàng chūzūchē. Běigù Shān hǎoxiàng zhǐyǒu wǒ yí ge yóukè, yěxǔ shi yīnwèi tiānqì tài rè le. Fǎnzhèng, wǒ hěn kuài de pá dào shāndǐng, wǎng xià kàn Zhènjiāng, kànjiàn hěn duō gōngchǎng hé tíng zai ànbiān de hǎo jǐ zhī huòchuán hé kèchuán. Běigù Shān de sìmiào hòumian, yǒu yí zuò xiǎo tíngzi. Nèi ge tíngzi zài lìshǐ shang hěn yǒumíng. Jùshuō, yìqiān qībǎi nián yǐqián, zài Sānguó shídài, Shǔguó de Liú Bèi, gēn tā hòulái de yuèmǔ zài nàr jiànguo miàn.

Yǐjīng xiāngdāng wǎn le, ànzhào wǒ běnlái de jìhuà yīnggāi guòhé qù Yángzhōu, suǒ.yǐ méi shíjiān zài qù kàn Jiāo Shān le. Wǒ zhǐhǎo qù shì zhōngxīn de gōnggòng qìchēzhàn qu, shàng yì bān zhíjiē qu Yángzhōu de chē. Qíshí, lián zhíjiē qù hái děi guò hé; Zhènjiāng xībianr yì tiáo hěn dà de dùchuán bǎ qìchē dài dàole hé de duì'àn. Tiān hēi yǐqián, wǒ dàole Yángzhōu, hái yǒu diǎnr shíjiān qù kànkan Xīhú Gōngyuán. Tángcháo de shīrén, Dù Mù, suīrán zhǎng zai běifāng de Cháng'ān, kěshì tā xiěguo yì shǒu shī shi guānyú Yángzhōu de Xīhú Gōngyuán de. Zhè shi zuì hòu liǎng háng:

Èrshísì qiáo míngyuè yè,   ('twenty-four bridges, bright moon night,
yùrén héchù jiào chuī xiāo?   jade-people what-place instruct blow flute?')

Dì-èr háng nǐmen yěxǔ huì juéde yǒu diǎnr mòmíngqímiào. Nà, nǐ zuìhǎo xiàng lǎoshī qǐngjiào yi xiàr. Yùrén shi shénme rén? Yùrén zěnme néng chuī xiāo?

Suīrán yì zhěngtiān wǒ dōu cōngcōng-mángmáng de pǎolài-pǎoqù, dànshi zhè yì tiān háishi hěn yǒu chéngjiùgǎn, gěi wǒ liúxiàle hěn shēn de yìnxiàng! Wǒ dédàole yí ge jīngyàn, jiùshì: Zhōngguó lìshǐ hěn yōujiǔ: měi ge dìfang dōu zhídé yòngxīn tǐhuì, búbì cōngcōng-mángmáng de zǒumǎguānhuā.

ANNOTATIONS

a. *jīngguo Sūzhōu*: *jīngguo* 'pass through; experience'; 'by way of; via'

b. *yīnwèi cù ér yǒumíng*: *cù* 'vinegar'; *xiāngcù* 'fragrant vinegar'; *ér* 'and then; and as a result'

c. *Jùyǒu sè, xiāng, suan, chún de tèdiǎn, suān ér bú sè, xiāng ér wēi tián, sènóng-wèixiān*: This is a description taken off a bottle of *Zhènjiāng xiāngcù*. Its style is not colloquial and so is more difficult to understand in spoken form. 'It possesses (*jùyǒu*) the special qualities *(tèdiǎn)* of *sè* 'tartness; astringency', *xiāng* 'flavor or scent', *suān* 'sourness', and *chún* 'mellow-ness'. *wēi tián* 'slightly sweet'; cf. *wēimiào* 'subtle; delicate'; *sènóng-wèixiān* ('color-concentrated flavor-fresh'); *chún* is typically used to describe wine.

d. *fùjìn de míngshèng tǐng duō*: *míngshèng* 'scenic spot; historical site'

e. *zài Cháng Jiāng nán'àn*: *nán'àn* 'southern bank'; cf. *shàng'àn* 'go ashore'

f. *Cháng Jiāng biān shang de yí ge gǎngkǒu*: *gǎngkǒu* 'port'; cf. *dàgǎng* 'large port' and *hégǎng* 'river port', both of which appear later in the text

g. *kěshì zǎojiù bèi yūní sāizhùle*: *zǎojiù* 'long ago; early on' ('early-then'); *yūní* 'silt; sludge' ('silt; mud'); *sāizhù* 'block-up; stop up'; cf. *názhù* 'catch', *jìzhù* 'remember'

h. *Jiéguǒ ne, xiànzài Yángzhōu lí hé biān yǒu diǎnr jùlí*: *jiéguǒ ne* 'as a result'; *jùlí* 'distance', incorporating *lí* 'away from'

i. *chèn jīhuì qù kànyíxià*: *chèn . . . jīhuì* 'take the opportunity to . . .'

j. *zuì zhíjiē de lùxiàn*: *zhíjiē* 'direct'; cf. *yìzhí zǒu*

k. *dǎoyóushū* 'guidebook' ('guide-traveler-book'): *lùxiàn* 'route' ('road-thread'); *xiū* 'build, construct; repair, mend'; *dùchuán* 'ferry' ('cross-boat'); *zhòngyào* 'important' ('heavy-crucial') *yào* = 'want'

l. *fángdōng* 'landlord' ('house-east = host'): *Tā yǒu diǎnr dānxīn, pà wǒ huì mílù huò wù zuìhòu yì bān chē*; *dānxīn* 'be worried; worry about' ('bear-heart = concern'); *mílù* 'get lost' ('lose-way'); *wùchē* 'miss the bus'

m. *shuō gǎi tiān tā kě.yǐ péi wǒ qù*: *gǎi tiān* 'change the day; on another day'; *péi* 'accompany'; *péi wǒ de shi . . .* 'the person accompanying me is . . .'

n. *bù xiǎng gěi nǐ tiān máfan*: a conventional phrase meaning 'I don't want to put you to any more trouble'; *tiān* 'add to'; *fàngxīn* 'put your heart at ease; don't worry' ('put-heart'); cf. *dānxīn, xiǎoxīn*

o. *wànyī pèngdao yìwài de shìr*: *wànyī* 'were you to; if by any chance; supposing' ('ten thousand [against] one'); *yìwài* 'unexpected' ('expect-outside')

p. *Shāngǔ, liǎngmiàn dōu shì lùlù de dàotián*: *shāngǔ* 'mountain valley'; *dàotián* 'rice field'; *dào* 'rice plant' or 'unhusked grain'

q. *tízhe bāo*: *tí* 'carry [with the arm down]; hold'; also 'raise questions, issues, concerns'

r. *zhìzàoyè chéngshì*: *zhìzàoyè* 'manufacturing industry'; cf. *zài Zhōngguó zhìzào de* 'made in China'

s. *tānzi* 'market stalls'; *gōngchǎng* 'factories' (M is *jiā*); *kǎchē* 'trucks; lorries' (M is *liàng* and *bù*)

t. *Wǒ yánzhe yì tiáo yòu hēi yòu chòu de yùnhé*: *yánzhe* 'along; following'; *yùnhé* 'canal' ('transport-river'); *bǐjiào dà de shuǐgōur* 'ditch; drain; gutter' (also *shuǐgōuzi*)

u. *Chē hěn jiù, mào de dōu shì hēi yān*: *jiù* 'old; worn'; *mào* 'emit; belch forth'; cf. *màoxiǎn* 'take risks; go on adventures' ('emit-danger'); *gǎnmào* 'have a cold' ('feel-oozy')

v. *yì páipái de lǎo fángzi*: *páipái* 'row upon row'; cf *páiduì* 'line up' ('line-in ranks')

w. *lǚyóu zhǐnán shang shuō*: *zhǐnán* 'guide; guidebook' ('point-south'); *yì tóu* 'one extreme; one end' ('head'); *mǎtóu* 'wharf; jetty'; *shāngyè* 'business; commerce'

x. *shìjiè wénmíng de sān zuò shān*: *shìjiè-wénmíng* is a fixed phrase meaning, literally, 'world-renowned'. Note the measure word for mountains and other large objects, natural or man-made: *zuò* (ultimately related to the word for 'sit' or 'seat'); cf. *yí zuò dǎo* 'an island' and *yí zuò miào* 'a temple'

y. *sānlúnchē* 'three-wheeled bicycle; trishaw': *dēngchē shīfu* 'peddle-bike master'

z. *zúqiúmí* 'football fan'; *qiúduì* 'ball team'; *qiúmí* 'sports fan' ('ball-fan')

aa. *Bìshèngkè* 'Pizza Hut'; *kuàicāndiàn* 'fast-food restaurant'; The Pizza Hut chain is widely represented in China; it also sells a greater variety of non-pizza dishes and tends to be more upscale than in the United States.

bb. *Yǒu kōngtiáo, yíngyè shíjiān hěn cháng, shèbèi yě hěn fāngbiàn*: the compound *kōngtiáo* 'air' + 'adjust' is a loan translation from English 'air conditioning'; *yíngyè shíjiān* 'business hours'; *shèbèi* 'facilities'

cc. *jǐngdiǎn* 'points of interest; scenic spots' ('view-points'); *yí zuò xiǎo dǎo* 'a small island'; cf. *Hǎinán Dǎo* 'Hainan Island'

dd. *hòulái xiū de, niándài bù jiǔ*: for *xiū* 'build', see note below; *niándài bù jiǔ* 'it's not old' ('age not long')

ee. *Báishé Zhuàn* 'The Legend of the White Snake': a story from oral tradition that was probably first put into writing in the Ming Dynasty; more recently it has been adapted to film; *shé* 'snake' (M *tiáo*)

ff. *tāmen yíjiànzhōngqíng* 'fall in love at first sight' ('one-sight-cherish-feeling')

gg. *Héshang* 'Buddhist priest'; *yāojing* 'demon; siren'

hh. *gēnzhe tā qùle nàlǐ*: *gēnzhe* 'with; following'; cf. *gēnzhe wǒ shuō* 'say it after me'

ii. *gēn Fǎhǎi dǎle yí zhàng*: *dǎ . . . zhàng* 'fight' ('hit-cudgel')

jj. *yǒu yí ge dòng, zài nàr dǎzuò*: *dòng* 'hole; cave'; *dǎzuò* 'sit in meditation; meditate' ('hit-sit')

kk. *Pá dào shān dǐng, wǎng xià kàn Zhènjiāng*: *shān dǐng* 'top of the hill; peak'; *wǎng xià kàn* 'look down on'

ll. *Tíng zài ànbiān de hǎo jǐ zhī huòchuán hé kèchuán*: *huòchuán* 'cargo ship' ('goods-boat'); *kèchuán* 'passenger boats' [M for boats: *zhī, sōu*]

mm. *xiǎo tíngzi* 'small pavilion'; *gēn tā hòulái de yuèmǔ* 'with the person who was to become his mother-in-law'

nn. *shīrén* 'poet'; *guānyú* 'about; concerning'; *háng* 'a row; a line [of verse]'

oo. *yǒu diǎnr mómíngqímiào* 'kind of strange; a little weird; puzzling' ('not-name-its-subtlety')

pp. *yì zhěngtiān* 'for the whole day'; *cōngcōng-mángmáng*, from *cōngmáng* 'hastily; in a hurry'

qq. *hěn yǒu chéngjiùgǎn* 'have a sense of accomplishment' ('accomplish-feeling')

rr. *gěi wǒ liúxiàle hěn shēn de yìnxiàng*: *liú* 'stay; keep; remain'; *shēn* 'deep'; *yìnxiàng* 'impression' ('print-likeness'); cf. *Nǐ duì Běijīng zuì chū yìnxiàng zěnmeyàng?* 'What were your first impressions of Beijing like?'

ss. *Wǒ dédàole yí ge jīngyàn, jiùshì . . . měi ge dìfang dōu zhídé yòngxīn tǐhuì . . . zǒumǎguānhuā*: *jīngyàn* 'experience'; *zhídé* 'worthwhile'; *yòngxīn* 'be attentive / motive' ('use-heart = mind'); *tǐhùi* 'learn from experience; get to know' ('body-encounter'); *zǒumǎguānhuā* 'look at the flowers while riding a horse', in other words, a superficial look or cursory examination

NOTES

a. *Běi Sòng* 'Northern Song Dynasty' (960–1127)

b. *Xī Jīndù Gǔjiē* 'Old West Ferry-crossing Street'

c. *Shǔguó* 'Kingdom of Shu': one of the Three Kingdoms (220–265) in the region of what is now Sichuan

d. *Dù Mù* (803–852) was a poet of the late Tang Dynasty (though well enough known to have inspired the line 'lotuses lean on each other in yearning' in Pink Floyd's "Set the Controls for the Heart of the Sun"). The poem excerpted here is called *Jì Yángzhōu Hán Chuò Pànguān* 'Sent to Judge Han Chuo of Yangzhou'. In all, it consists of four lines, each with seven characters; the lines cited are the last two. *Yùrén* 'jade people' in the last line suggests ladies of great delicacy. It is the line about the twenty-four bridges that is most strongly associated with West Lake Park in Yangzhou; there is a pavilion there said to command views of all twenty-four.

e. You have encountered a number of words that can, in the right contexts, be translated 'build'. There is a lot of overlap between them, but here, for reference, is a table that tries to draw some broad distinctions. The four single-syllable words are the most common and general.

	CORE MEANING	POSSIBLE OBJECTS	COMMENT
zào	'make; manufacture'	*fēijī; fángzi; jīqì; jùzi*	not just buildings
xiū	'repair; mend; build'	*jīchǎng; tiělù; shuǐbà*	involves clearing
xiūjiàn	'build'	*jīchǎng; tiělù*	
gài	'cover; build'	*fángzi; sùshè, miào*	buildings with roofs
jiàn	'build; construct'	*shuǐbà; diànzhàn*	large-scale buildings
jiànlì	'set up; found'	*yīyuàn; wàijiāo guānxi*	concrete or abstract
jiànshè	'establish'	*shèhuìzhǔyì; xīn Zhōngguó*	usually abstract
jiànzhù	'build; erect'	*gāolóu*	also the noun 'building'

jīqì 'machines'; *jùzi* 'sentences'; *tiělù* 'railways' ('iron-road'); *diànzhàn* 'power station' ('electric-station'); *wàijiāo guānxi* 'foreign affairs'; *shèhuìzhǔyì* 'socialism'

f. You have also encountered several words that have the general meaning of 'inclusion' (or in the negative, 'exclusion'). As with the 'build' set, there are areas of overlap (such as *quán* and *zhěnggèr*).

	CONTEXT	EXAMPLE
dōu	before verbs	*Dōu bú duì.* 'They're all wrong.'
suǒyǒude	before nouns 'all of'	*suǒyǒude shū* 'all the books'
		suǒyǒude jìnr 'all one's strength'
quán	before nouns 'the whole of'	*quán jiā* 'your whole family'
		quán Zhōngguó 'the whole of China'
zhěng	before M words	*zhěngtiān* 'the whole day'
zhěnggèr	before nouns	*zhěnggèr Zhōngguó* 'the whole of China'
yíqiè	can stand alone	*Yíqiè dōu hěn hǎo.* 'Everything's fine.'

The best way to deal with such sets is to remember typical phrases: *xiūle ge shuǐbà* and *gàile yì suǒ fángzi* in the first set; *quán jiā* and *suǒyǒude dōngxi* in the second.

Exercise 4

Translate the following excerpts into English.

1. *Kěshì kěnéng shi yīnwèi fùjìn de míngshèng tǐng duō, huòzhě fùjìn de dàchéng, xiàng Nánjīng, Sūzhōu gèng yǒumíng, qù Zhènjiāng de yóukè bù duō.*

2. *Yǐjīng xiāngdāng wǎn le, ànzhào wǒ běnlái de jìhuà yīnggāi guò hé qu Yángzhōu, suǒ.yǐ méi shíjiān zài qù kàn Jiāo Shān le.*

3. *Yǒu yì tiáo xiǎojiē, hěn zhǎi, zǒu guòqu yǐhòu wǒ fāxiàn chàbuduō yì gōnglǐ cháng, liǎngbiānr dōu shì shítou zuò de fángzi.*

19.9 Interjections, vivid adjectives, and word-forming affixes

This unit draws to a close with a trio of miscellaneous subjects: interjections, which are characteristic of informal conversation; a type of vivid adjective that contains a reduplicated segment; and a survey of common word-forming affixes. Though examples of these topics have been encountered in earlier material, they deserve a more systematic introduction.

19.9.1 Interjections

Interjections are conventionalized carriers of emotion, typically providing context for a following sentence. Consider these examples from English: aha (recognition), yikes (surprise and fear), whoopee (happiness), yuck (disgust). Interjections sometimes employ sounds outside the regular linguistic system, such as the English alveolar clicks, which are conventionally spelled *tsk tsk* or *tut tut* (disapproval).

Āiyō, Jīn Gāng lái la!

Interjections are quite frequent in informal speech, and they need to be considered. A good place to look for them in written form is comics and advertisements (though you will have to conduct a survey of native speakers to see how the interjections are actually pronounced). Here is an example from the label of a popular brand of fruit drink.

水晶葡萄 – 嗯，好喝
Shuǐjīng Pútao – ng, hǎo hē! } 'Crystal Grape — mmm, delicious!'

The character 嗯 contains the phonetic element 恩 *ēn*, but the interjection is probably pronounced *ng* on low tone in this context.

Though they may occur elsewhere, interjections in Chinese are more frequent in initial position—or rather, prior position. Though they often have a fixed intonation, it is not quite the same as the pitch and contour of the regular tones. The following list is only a beginning; you should add to it or amend it as you observe Chinese speaking.

Ā	Mild interest: *Ā, hěn yǒu yìsi.* 'Ah, interesting.'
Á	Surprise: *Á, yòu lái le!* 'What—you again?'
Āi	Resignation; regret: 'darn; alas'; *Āi, zhēn kěxī.* 'Gosh, what a pity.'
Āiyā	Amazement: 'wow; goodness me'; *Āiyā, yǔ xià+de zhēn dà ya!* "Wow, it's pouring!'
Āiyō ~ yō	Surprise; discomfort: 'yikes'; a stronger form of *āiyā*
È	Agreement: 'yeah; uh-huh'
Éi	Puzzled surprise; remembering something: *Éi, zěnme huí shìr?* 'Huh, what's going on?'
Hà	Satisfaction: 'Ha!'; *Hà, wǒ yíng le!* 'Hah, I win!'
Hài	Disapproval: *Hài, bié zhāi huā!* 'Hey, don't pick the flowers!'
Hǎojiāhuo	Surprise, feigned disbelief: 'Good heavens; crikey' ('good-man, good-fellow'); *Hǎojiāhuo, zuòyè yǐjīng gànwán le!* 'Gosh, you've finished your homework already!'
Hēng	Disapproval, contempt: 'Humph; snort'; *Hēng, shéi xìn nǐ de!* 'Humph, I don't believe it!
Ng ~ M	Weak assent; acknowledgement: 'uh-huh'; *Wèi, nín shi Zhōu lǎoshī ma?* / *Ng, wǒ jiùshì.*

Ō	Understanding: *Ō, wǒ dǒng le.* 'Oh, I get it.'
Ó	Surprise: 'huh?'; *Ó, nǐ rènshi tā?* 'Oh, you know her?'
Ōyō	Surprise, disbelief: 'oops; wow'; *Ōyō, zhèi ge háizi tóu zhème rè! Fāshāo le ma?* 'Wow, this child's head is really hot! Does she have a fever?'
Pēi	Contempt: 'bosh; tut'; *Pēi, xiūxiu liǎn!* 'Fie, for shame!'
Wèi (~wài)	Telephoning; calling out to someone: 'hello; say; hey'

NOTES

a. *Jiāhuo* is a colloquial word with meanings ranging from 'fellow; guy' to 'tool' (hence, 'penis') and 'watchamacalit' (hence, 'son-of-a-bitch'). Although it originates as a noun—or noun phrase—and can still be used as such (in fact, it is the Chinese name of the gangster film *Goodfellas*), *hǎojiāhuo* has also become specialized as an interjection. Its meaning is along the lines of English 'goodness me' or 'heavens to Betsy'.

b. *Xiūxiu liǎn*, composed of *xiū* 'to shame / be shy', corresponds to English 'for shame'; cf. *tā xiū + de liǎn dōu hóng le* 'He blushed with shame'.

19.9.2 Vivid adjectives

In earlier units, you saw vivid adjectives formed from adjectival roots and repeated syllables: *huáliūliū*, based on *huá* 'slippery', or *huīmēngmēng*, based on *huī* 'gray'. Such forms have a long history in Chinese. Here is an example from the *Analects* of Confucius, which contrasts the qualities of the *jūnzǐ*, the man of refinement, and the *xiǎorén*, a base person.

| *Jūnzǐ tǎndàngdàng, xiǎorén chángqīqī.* | 'The gentleman is magnanimous; the base man is resentful.' |

Such compounds have an adjective (stative verb) base, but the repeated syllables vary in type.

Lěngbīngbīng 'icy cold' is probably 'cold' plus 'ice', and the characters confirm as much. In other cases, the identity of the repeated syllable is not so certain. The stem of *làsīsī* 'hot; peppery' is *là* 'hot; spicy', but is *sī* really 'silk', as the characters suggest? What about *làsūsū* also 'hot; spicy', with *sū* 'crisp' (according to the character)? In many cases, the repeated syllable seems to fill out the pattern rather than contribute to the meaning.

As the examples indicate, repeated syllables favor level tone, even when the character used to represent the repeated syllable is not level in citation. Thus, some dictionaries (possibly representing Taiwan or older usage) give *rèténgténg* for 'piping hot', following the character that is, in other contexts, pronounced with rising tone. However, it is generally pronounced with level tone, and most modern dictionaries list it that way: *rètēngtēng*. There are also cases where the repeated syllable is clearly non-level tone: *kōngdàngdàng* 'empty; deserted', with the stem *kōng* 'empty; void' and extension *dàng*.

Vivid adjectives of this type have certain grammatical properties that set them apart from their unaugmented stems. They cannot be modified by adverbs of degree such as *hěn* or *tài*, for example. Typically, they act as modifiers connected to nouns by a following *de*, or they stand alone (still with a following *de*) as commentaries. Here are some examples.

USAGE

Nǐmen niánqīngrén jiu xiàng zǎoshang bā-jiǔ diǎn zhōng hóngtōngtōng de tàiyáng yíyàng.
'You young people look like the glowing red sun at 8 or 9 in the morning.' [Mao Zedong]

Nǐ kàn, tāmen dōu zài kàng shang zuòzhe ne, nuǎnhōnghōng de.
'Look at them all sitting on the stove, all cozy and warm.'

Lái le, rètēngtēng de jiǎozi!
'Here they come! Piping-hot dumplings!'

The following example is cited in its entirety because it contains fine examples of both vivid adjectives and onomatopoeic adverbials.

Guònián de biānpào pīlā-pālā de xiǎng le; tuányuán de zhuō shang bǎimǎnle rètēngtēng, xiāngpēnpēn de niánfàn.
'The New Year's firecrackers went off with a bim-bim-bam-bam; and the delegates' table was spread with the piping-hot, savory New Year's feast.'

Though not onomatopoeic, expressions in the form *x-y-y* are also common in the adverbial position.

Tā xiàomīmī de diǎnle diǎntóu.   'He smiled and nodded his head.'

SHĒNGCÍ

kàng	In houses in the cold northern parts of China, families sleep on a large brick platform heated from within, known as a *kàng*.
tuányuán	'delegate' ('group-member'): cf. *fúwùyuán*
bǎimǎn	'be spread with' ('lay out-full'): cf. *jǐmǎn* 'filled to overflowing'; *kèmǎn* 'full' [with guests or patrons]
niánfàn	'New Year's feast

To give you a feel for their range, here is a selection of vivid adjectives, with the meaning of the stem given in the center column.

cháohūhū	*cháo* 'damp'	'damp; clammy'
hēiyōuyōu	*hēi* 'black'	'jet black' [of hair, soil]
hóngtōngtōng	*hóng* 'red'	'glowing red; brilliant red'
hóngpūpū	*hóng* 'red'	'reddish'
huáliūliū	*huá* 'slippery'	'slimy; slippery' [of roads]; 'slick' [of foods]
kōngdàngdàng	*kōng* 'empty'	'empty; deserted' [of station, mall]
làsīsī	*là* 'peppery hot'	'hot; peppery' [of food]
lètáotáo	*lè*: cf. *kuàilè* 'happy'	'happy' [of children; life]
lěngbīngbīng	*lěng* + *bīng* 'ice'	'icy cold' [of iron, facial expressions]
liàngjīngjīng	*liàng* 'bright'	'glimmering; sparkling'
luànhōnghōng	*luàn* 'chaotic'	'tumultuous'
mínghuānghuāng	*míng* 'luminous'	'gleaming' [of metal]
nuǎnhōnghōng	*nuǎn* 'warm'	'cozy and warm'
rèhūhū	*rè*	'piping hot' [of a stove, heater]

rèhōnghōng	*rè*	'very warm; boiling' [of weather]
rètēngtēng	*rè*	'steaming hot' [of buns, noodles]
wùméngméng ~ *mēng*	*wù* 'fog'	'hazy, misty'
xiāngpēnpēn	*xiāng* 'fragrant'	'sweet-smelling; savory; appetizing'

Kōngdàngdàng de Niǎocháo 'Empty nest'

19.9.3 Word-forming affixes

After encountering so many words, it's appropriate that we end with a note on word formation in Chinese. As you have no doubt observed, the primary source of new words is compounding—putting two roots together in a descriptive relationship. Citing examples from this unit, *chéngjiùgǎn* 'have a sense of accomplishment' is formed by combining *chéngjiù* 'achievement' with *gǎn* 'feeling'. *Gǎn* can be added to other disyllablic nouns to give the meaning 'a sense of': *ānquángǎn* 'sense of security' ('safety-feeling'); *zérèngǎn* 'sense of responsibility'; *róngyùgǎn* 'sense of honor'; and so on. The variable may be trailing, as with the *gǎn* examples, or leading, so that to find all combinations for a particular root syllable, one needs a regular dictionary and a reverse one.

For example, if you are interested in compounds with *mó* 'evil spirit', then you can find *móguǐ* 'demon' and *mówáng* 'king of the demons' in a regular dictionary that is organized by first syllable. However, you would find *èmó* and *yāomó*, types of evil spirits, in a reverse dictionary that is organized by final syllable. A few Chinese-to-English dictionaries give both kinds of compounds under the entry *mó*, but that is not a traditional practice.

Some syllables are particularly versatile, combining with large classes of words to form predictable compounds. Several have been amply illustrated in earlier units. For example, *jiā*, in addition to its 'household' sense, combines with fields of learning to mean 'expert' or 'specialist': *měishùjiā* 'artist'; *dìzhìxuéjiā* 'geologist' ('earth-matter'). As that last example illustrates, *xué* 'study' combines with specializations to form fields of study: *liúxíngbìngxué* 'epidemiology' ('infectious-disease'); *tiānwénxué* 'astronomy' ('sky-signs').

In modern Chinese, some elements have become so abstract that they function like the English affixes '-ism' (capitalism, socialism), '-ity' (productivity, absurdity), or '-less' (aimless, clueless). Here are some examples with both prefixes and suffixes.

1. *Fēi* 'non-' is added to nouns or adjectives (stative verbs) to produce a negation. The process is fairly productive, just as the prefix 'non-' is in English (nonnative, nonfat, nonviolent). Chinese language programs, for example, often refer to students of Chinese heritage as *huáyì* and students not of Chinese heritage as *fēihuáyì*, though the latter is unlikely to be listed in a dictionary. However, certain negations with *fēi* have become so institutionalized that they are listed in dictionaries: *zhèngshì* 'formal' → *fēizhèngshì* 'informal'. The following list includes a selection of relevant examples.

bàolìde (*bàolì* 'violence; force')	→	*fēibàolìde* 'nonviolent'
mǔyǔ ('mother-language')	→	*fēimǔyǔ* 'nonnative language'
guānfāng ('official circles')	→	*fēiguānfāng* 'unofficial'
jīnshǔ ('metal-belong')	→	*fēijīnshǔ* 'nonmetal'
zhòngdú yīnjié 'stressed syllable'	→	*fēizhòngdú yīnjié* 'unstressed syllable'

zhàndòu rényuán   →   *fēizhàndòu rényuán*
   ('combat-personnel')   'noncombatants'

2. *Huà* 'transform' is added to certain classes of nouns and adjectives to give what in Chinese are usually abstract nouns: *zìyóu* 'freedom; be free' → *zìyóuhuà* 'liberalization'; *yǒu zìyóuhuà de dòngxiàng* 'have a liberalization tendancy'. Other examples include the following.

guójì 'international'	→	*guójìhuà* 'internationalization'
quánqiú 'global; whole world'	→	*quánqiúhuà* 'globalization'
mínzhǔ 'democracy; democratic'	→	*mínzhǔhuà* 'democratization'
zìdòng 'automatic'	→	*zìdònghuà* 'automatization'
guīfàn 'be regular'	→	*guīfànhuà* 'regularization'
xiàndài 'modern'	→	*xiàndàihuà* 'modernization'
ér 'the r suffix'	→	*érhuà* 'be suffixed with r'

3. *Xìng* 'property; quality' (cf. *xìnggé* 'personality'; *xìngbié* 'gender') is added to verbal roots to form abstract nouns.

chuàngzào 'create'	→	*chuàngzàoxìng* 'creativity'
kěnéng 'possible'	→	*kěnéngxìng* 'possibility'
tán 'be flexible'	→	*tánxìng* 'flexibility'
pǔtōng 'common'	→	*pǔtōngxìng* 'universality'
zhàndòu 'fight; combat'	→	*zhàndòuxìng* 'militancy'
duìkàng 'resist; antagonism'	→	*duìkàngxìng* 'antagonistic'; cf. *fēiduìkàngxìng* 'nonantagonistic'
rěnnài 'patient/patience'	→	*rěnnàixìng* 'endurance'

4. *Zhǔyì* 'doctrine; policy' ('main-doctrine') is added to nouns to form '-isms'. Almost all *zhǔyì* forms have been inspired by English (or possibly other European language) forms with '-ism'.

yìnxiàngzhǔyì	'Impressionism'
àiguózhǔyì	'patriotism'
kǒngbùzhǔyì	'terrorism'

xiāngduìzhǔyì	'relativism'
shíyòngzhǔyì	'pragmatism
dàmínzúzhǔyì	'big nation chauvinism'
zīběnzhǔyì	'capitalism'
gòngchǎnzhǔyì	'communism'
bēiguānzhǔyì	'pessimism'
fēngjiànzhǔyì	'feudalism'
Sānmínzhǔyì	'the doctrine of the three people's principles' (of Sun Yat-sen)
quǎnrúzhǔyì	'cynicism': The English word 'cynic' is thought to derive, by way of Latin, from the Greek root meaning 'dog' (cf. Latin *canis*); hence the Chinese *quǎnrú* 'cynic' ('dog-scholar').

5. *Yán* 'burning/inflammation' is added to the names of body parts to give medical conditions involving inflammation (most of which, in English, end in '-itis').

wèicháng 'digestive system' ('stomach-intestines')	→	*wèichángyán* 'gastroenteritis'
gān 'liver'	→	*gānyán* 'hepatitis'
ěr 'ear'	→	*ěryán* 'irritation of the ear; otitis'
nǎomó 'brain membrane'	→	*nǎomóyán* 'meningitis'
fèi 'lung'	→	*fèiyán* 'pneumonia'
hóu 'throat'	→	*hóuyán* 'laryngitis'
yíxiàn 'pancreas	→	*yíxiànyán* 'pancreatitis'
biǎntáotǐ 'tonsils' ('flat-peach-body')	→	*biǎntáotǐyán* 'tonsillitis'
guānjié 'joints'	→	*guānjiéyán* 'arthritis'
pí 'skin'	→	*píyán* 'dermatitis'

19.10 The North Wind and the Sun

The following is unlike the material that has been placed at the end of previous units. It is not a rhyme but a tale—in fact, it is one of Aesop's fables. Though some of Aesop's fables are thought to have North Indian sources and could have been transmitted to China along with Buddhism, this version of the fable "The North Wind and the Sun" has a more mundane and recent source. Translations of the fable in different languages were used to demonstrate the International Phonetic Alphabet in various publications, and linguists collected versions of the story for comparative purposes. In that tradition, Yuen Ren Chao, the Chinese linguist frequently cited in this book, composed the following version in the style of a storyteller. It is published in the first volume of his *Readings in Sayable Chinese* (Chao, 1968, p. 3); however, according to a note following the text there, his version was first published in *Le Maître Phonétique* in 1928. Chao, incidentally, was born in Tianjin in 1892, educated at both Cornell and Harvard, taught at U.C. Berkeley for many years, and died in Berkeley in 1982 at the age of 90.

You would do well to memorize the fable and be able to retell it with gestures and emotions. The short tale also provides some fine examples of some of the important grammatical patterns you have encountered in this course.

Běifēng gēn Tàiyang

(1) Yǒu yì huí Běifēng gēn Tàiyang zhèng dāi nàr zhēnglùn shéi de běnshì dà. (2) Shuōzhe shuōzhe, láile yí ge zǒudàor de, shēn shang chuānzhe yí jiàn hòu páozi. (3) Tāmen liǎ jiu shāngliang hǎole shuō, shéi néng xiān jiào nèi ge zǒudàor de bǎ tā de páozi tuōle xiàlai a, jiù suàn shéi de běnshì dà. (4) Hǎo, Běifēng jiu shǐ qí dàjìn lai jìnguā-jìnguā, kěshì tā guā+de yuè lìhai, nèi rén bǎ páozi guǒ+de yuè jǐn; dào mòliǎor Běifēng méile fázi, zhǐhǎo jiù suàn le. (5) Yìhuǐr Tàiyang jiu chūlai rèrēr de yí shài, nèi zǒudàor de mǎshang jiu bǎ páozi tuōle xiàlai. (6) Suǒ. yǐ Běifēng bù néng bù chéngrèn dàodǐ háishi Tàiyang bǐ tā běnshì dà.

Word-for-word:

1. ('Have one time North-Wind and Sun just-then stay there dispute whose talent bigger.')
2. ('Talking on and on, [when] come-LE a walker, body on wear-ing a M thick cloak.')
3. ('They two then consider ready-LE say, whoever can first make that M walker BA his cloak remove-LE off a, then reckon whoever's talent bigger.')

4. ('Okay, North-Wind so apply begin big-strength come exhaust-blow, but he blow+de more strong, that person BA cloak wrap+de more tight; arrive-at end North-Wind not have means, only-good then give-up LE.')

5. ('In a while, Sun then out-come hot-ly once shine, that walker immediately then BA cloak remove-LE off.')

6. ('So North-Wind not able not admit in-the-end still Sun than him talent bigger.')

SHĒNGCÍ

yǒu yì huí	'once upon a time': recall *huí* 'occasion; time'; cf. *yí cì*
běnshì	'resources' ('main-thing')
zǒudàor de	'pedestrian' ('walk-road one')
tāmen liǎ	= *tāmen liǎng ge rén*
shāngliang	'consult; talk over'
shǐ	'make; cause; apply': *shǐ qǐlai*, with *dàjìn* 'effort' as object inserted between *qǐ* and *lái*
dàjìn	'big effort'
jìnguā-jìnguā	*jìn* 'to the utmost; with the greatest of effort' + *guā* 'blow' [of wind]; cf. *guāfēng* 'be windy' ('blows-wind)
guǒ	'wrap up': cf. *bāoguǒ* 'package'
mòliǎor	= *zuìhòu* (*mò* 'end' + *liǎo* 'complete')
méile fǎzi	= *méi fǎzi*: One doesn't expect *méi* and *le* in the same phrase, but here, *méile* can be regarded as a unit, meaning 'lacking' or 'be without'; cf. *méile húnr* 'bewitched' ('lacking a soul')
shài	'dry in the sun; sunbathe; shine': *shài tàiyang* 'bask in the sun; sunbathe'
chéngrèn	'admit; recognize that'

Exercise 5

With one or two other classmates, compose a Chinese version of the following paragraph, and provide an ending.

He rode up on a bike, holding an umbrella in his hand. He was wearing a white shirt (*chènshān*) and jeans (*niúzǎikù*), and he had a black beret (*bèiléimào*) on his head. He was covered in mud (*ní*) and looked tired. It had been raining for three days, and there was water all over. As soon as I saw him, I knew he wasn't well. I was preparing dinner. I gave him a towel (*máojīn*) and told him to hang his pants up to dry. By the time I returned with a cup of tea, he was lying down (*tǎng*) on the sofa. I noticed a small silver box (*yínsè de hézi*) sitting on the table next to him. "I've missed you," he said. We sat for a while, then suddenly (*hūrán*). . . .

Summary

Compared with	*hé Měiguórén de fángzi bǐ, wǒmen de xiǎole yìdiǎnr*
Tidy up; neat; clean	*bèi wǒ tàitai shōushi+de zhěngqí, hěn gānjìng*
Indefinites	*Shí jǐ diǎn tā jiu xiǎng jǐ xià.* [of the clock]
Apologies	*Hěn bàoqiàn. / Zhēn bù hǎoyìsi.*
Opinions	*Zhōngguórén duì Àobāmǎ zǒngtǒng yǒu shénme kànfǎ?*
	Qǐngwèn, Yuènán de qíngkuàng zuìjìn zěnmeyàng?
Reponses	*Zhèi ge wèntí hěn fùzá. / Hěn nán shuō. / Wǒmen de kànfǎ bù yíyàng.*
Sports	*Nǐ xǐhuan shénme yàng de yùndòng?*
E-mail	*fā duǎnxìn / shǒuxiě shūrùfǎ / fā diànzǐ yóujiàn / chuándì-xìnxī*

Abbreviations	*yòng shùzi de lüèzi shi ànzhào Zhōngwén de shuōfǎ*
Telephoning	*Wèi, nǐ shi Zhōu Yǔ ma? / Wǒ jiùshi. / Nǐ yào liúyán ma?*
Bargaining	*Nǐ gěi yí ge gōngdaojià! / Bābǎi tài shǎo le; zài duō gěi yìdiǎnr.*
Cannot not . . .	*Suǒ.yǐ Běifēng bù néng bù chéngrèn dàodǐ háishi tàiyang bǐ tā běnshì dà.*

NOTE TO THE EPIGRAPH

Wú functions like modern Chinese *wǒ*; *ér*, which occurs in every line with the same function, is the classical Chinese conjunction 'and' or 'having reached [age]'.

THE CHARACTER UNITS

With the exception of Unit 21, which in part anticipates material to come, the character units of *Learning Chinese* presuppose vocabulary and grammatical patterns presented in prior spoken units so the focus of learning can be on character recognition and reading. Each unit begins with some review of earlier material and then proceeds to introduce new characters. These are given in large format in sets of about a dozen each, with traditional graphs written above simplified (where both forms exist), and features such as the number of strokes, radical and phonetic elements, possible confusions, and useful hints presented along with each character (or in notes that follow).

Learning Chinese is unusual in presenting both the traditional and simplified sets simultaneously (though it focuses more on the Mainland standard—simplified—in the actual readings). There are good reasons for doing this. Though the simplified set has been the standard for the Mainland and Singapore for more than half a century, the traditional forms were standard in print and formal writing for at least 1,500 years before, and they continue to be the norm in Hong Kong, Taiwan, and many overseas Chinese communities. Showing the relationship between traditional and simplified characters belies the notion that the two sets are entirely distinct. For the majority of characters, in fact, the two sets make either no distinction at all or only a very slight distinction (e.g., 事/事; 谢/謝). The more extreme differences between the two sets involve common characters (个/個 *gè* 'general classifier', 头/頭 *tóu* 'head; noun suffix', 过/過 *guò* 'pass; verb suffix'), which represent words that tend to be the most highly predictable from context. Even these so-called worst cases still show points of commonality that link the two characters together, so reading in both sets is practicable. Handwriting both sets, however, is obviously less so. For *Learning Chinese*, the recommendation is that both sets be practiced, but that the simplified forms be the main medium, as is so on the Mainland. In any case, practical writing (that is not for aesthetic purposes) is now usually done electronically, which involves reading skills (selection among characters triggered by method of input) rather than writing.

The first step in learning to read a character script is to associate a particular character with a syllable sound and, in a more complicated way, with a meaning or range of meanings. Thus, the character 东/東 is associated with the sound *dōng* and the meaning 'east'. If it appears before a following 西 (*xī* 'west'), then the combination *dōngxi* is recognized as 'thing' (and the meanings 'east-west' are not relevant). Many textbooks simply provide pinyin as a diacritic under each character in the hope that the association will eventually lead to recognition. *Learning Chinese*, instead, offers an analysis of the character with emphasis on the phonetic associations (红/紅 *hóng*; 工 *gōng*) and (in most cases) a mnemonic hint that emphasizes meaning. For example, for the graphs 风/風 *fēng* 'wind', the hint (labeled 'mnemonic') is provided as follows: 'the graphs look like kites floating in the *wind*'. Some of the hints reflect probable historical origins of the character, but most are ad hoc with no etymological validity.

Once there is sufficient recognition of individual characters, actual reading begins simply, with compounds or short phrases (with a pinyin check provided at a discreet distance), then comment and response (which provides context), and, in some cases, additional continuous reading and exercises. It is hoped that by the end of each lesson, characters will have been encountered in enough contexts to leave an indelible mark in your memory.

The writing of characters by hand (or brush) plays an important role in drawing attention to detail and learning to distinguish one character from another. Students of Chinese generally enjoy the writing of characters as an aesthetic experience—one that incidentally earns them the awe of friends and the respect of Chinese acquaintances. However, composition (rather than the reproduction of characters for learning or other purposes) is better done by computer, which allows entry by pinyin (among other methods) rather than by character/syllable. In addition, writing becomes a process of 'top-down' selection of characters from a limited choice rather than a 'bottom-up' production of each character, stroke by stroke.

Conventions

Characters are introduced in sets of approximately twenty, with four to five sets in each unit. Each set begins with characters introduced in large font. Those characters that have two forms are listed with traditional above simplified.

The numbers written directly beneath the large characters introduced in each set are a device to indicate the number of strokes and the radical. The first number is the number of strokes in the radical (regardless of its position in the character). The second number is the number of strokes that remain after the radical is accounted for. The total of these two numbers, then, is the total number of strokes in the character. Thus, 知 is labeled 5+3 to indicate that 矢 is the radical with five strokes, leaving three strokes for the rest (口). When the second number is 0, the graph is itself a radical: 竹 6+0. When the two numbers coincide, the abbreviations L ('left'), R ('right'), T ('top'), and B ('bottom') are added to the first number to indicate the position of the radical: 向 3B+3 indicates 口 as the radical. For a few characters, even though there is no distinction between traditional and simplified, the assignment of radical varies. For example, 夜 (yè 'night') has only one form, but the traditional set assigns 夕 (three strokes) as the radical; the simplified set assigns the top two strokes as radical. Thus, the large character 夜 appears with 3+5 below it; below that, where the simplified version would be placed if there were one, 2+6 appears.

The simplified set is standard on the Mainland. Therefore, in cases where traditional and simplified versions of a character are shown in pairs separated by a slash, the order is simplified followed by traditional: 个/個, 东/東, etc. When relevant, sections written in the simplified set are marked SC ('simplified characters'); those written in the traditional set are marked TC ('traditional characters'). The occasional new character (or word) introduced in the readings is underlined (不准吸烟) and glossed at the end of the section: *zhǔn* 'allow'; but where possible, guessing new characters from context is encouraged.

Unit 20 第二十课/課 DÌ-ÈRSHÍ KÈ

入国问禁，入乡问俗，入门问讳。/入國問禁，入鄉問俗，入門問諱。
Rù guó wèn jìn, rù xiāng wèn sú, rù mén wèn huì.
'When you enter a kingdom, you should inquire of its prohibitions; when you enter a district, you should inquire of its customs; when you enter a home, you should inquire of its taboos.'
('Enter country ask-about prohibitions; enter district, ask-about customs; enter home, ask-about taboos.')
—From *Lǐ Jì,* on the importance of adapting to the place and being sensitive to cultural differences

20.0 复习/復習 *Fùxí* 'Review'

Section 20.0 constitutes a review of characters from the first volume of *Learning Chinese.* 20.0.1 is a dialogue written in familiar (simplified) characters which is ideally read out by pairs of people each taking a part. 20.0.2 consists of two columns of questions, one written in traditional characters and the other written in simplified. The section concludes with an exercise focused on tonal sets.

A note to the epigraph is located at the end of the unit.

20.0.1 [SC] Dialogue

甲： 请问，你是哪国人？

乙： 我是法(fǎ)国人。

甲： 可是你像个中国人。

乙： 我爸爸是中国人，妈妈是法国人。我爸爸十八岁到巴黎(Bālí)去留学，在巴黎认识 (rènshi)我妈妈的。

甲： 哦，那你就生在那儿吧？

乙： 是的。你去过法国吗？

甲： 没去过，可是很想去。我会说一点儿法语。

乙： 那，你呢，你是北京人吧？

甲： 不，我生在西安，也长在西安，但是现在住在北京。

乙： 你是哪年来的北京？

甲： 我是1990年来的。父母还住在西安。

乙： 那，你喜不喜欢北京？

甲： 北京不错，但是我很想西安。

乙： 我去过西安，西安很好玩儿。

甲： 你是什么时候去的？

乙： 我是去年六月去的，跟两个中国朋友一块儿去的。一个是西安人所以我们吃的，玩儿的都很好。

甲： 对啊，西安饺子和羊肉比较有名。下次去，请到父母家玩玩儿。

20.0.2 Reading

Answer the questions. Questions on the left are written in full characters, those on the right, in simplified. As you read the questions, circle those characters that have two forms, then answer the questions briefly—you will probably want to write the simplified set for all answers.

1. 个人问题   **個人問題**

a. 第一次来这儿吗？   你是從哪個國家來的？

b. 你是学什么的？   你是本科生還是研究生？

c. 毕业以后要做什么？   你哪年畢業？

d. 你是 哪年去[中国...] 的？   你去過哪些別的國家？

e. 你在哪里生的？   跟誰一起去的？

f. 你最喜欢哪个国家的菜？   在什麼地方上的高中？

g. 当医生的吸烟你觉得怎么样？   朋友吸煙你覺得怎麼樣？

h. 一百块钱，十二个人，
一个人有几块？   你的大學每個學生是否一定得學外語？

2. 跟中国<u>有关</u>的问题   **跟中國<u>有關</u>的問題**

a. 现在一块美金是多少块人民币？   坐飛機去中國，來回<u>票</u>大概多少錢？

b. 哪边的中国人比较喜欢吃面条？   你說麵條好吃還是白飯好吃？

c. 中国人就<u>油</u>条吃粥吗？   吃魚喝白酒行不行？

d. 吃肉一定得喝白酒吗？   中國女孩子是否都不喝牛奶？

e. 中国人吃饭的时候是先喝汤后
吃菜，还是先吃菜后喝汤？   中國最有名的<u>啤</u>酒是哪個？

f. 中国哪个城市人口最多？
第二呢？   "不<u>准</u>吸煙"那四個字是什麼意思？

g. 中国人过生日吃面条，
过年吃鱼；为什么？   中國人常說住在外國生病是因為水土
不服；什麼意思？

3. 跟别的地方有关的问题   跟別的地方有關的問題

a. 用手吃饭应该用左手还是   哪些國家用手吃飯？
   用右手？

b. 你们上大学的时候每天有几个   你說中國人吃飯的時候一碗白飯
   小时的作业？   <u>吃得飽</u>嗎？

c. 中国和美国时差是多少，   現在在中國是否只可以生一個孩子？
   知道吗？

d. <u>世界</u>上最大的城市是不是上海？   中國最大的城市是哪個，你知道嗎？

Běijīng dìtiě: Yīhào xiàn wǎng Àotǐ Zhōngxīn '#1 line to
Olympic Stadium Center'.

NOTES

跟......有关/關	'be connected to'
票	*piào* 'ticket'
油	*yóu* 'oil'
就[油条/條]	*jiù [yóutiáo]* 'go with'
牛	*niú* 'cow'
啤	*pí*
准	*zhǔn* 'allowed'
吃得饱/飽	*chīdebǎo* 'able to eat one's fill'
世界	*shìjiè* 'world'

Exercise 1

[SC] Read the following tonal sets aloud (down, then across).

手机	用手	米饭	应该	洗澡	鸡蛋
广东	厕所	炒面	听说	水饺	医院
每天	路口	考试	飞机	也许	功课
紧张	父母	海菜	清汤	很远	开会
好听	地铁	请问	公司	孔子	音乐
面条	好玩儿	大家	大概	学期	白菜
不同	以前	汽车	再见	茶杯	城市
问题	五楼	大街	汉字	国家	鱼片
外国	每年	看书	睡觉	长安	牛肉
姓陈	女孩儿	面包	看病	河边	不对

20.0.3 New characters

The more than three hundred characters introduced in the first six character units of *Learning Chinese (I)*, together with your knowledge of a much larger vocabulary of compounds that make use of these characters, now make it feasible to introduce new characters in more diverse and interesting ways. Therefore, Unit 20 is organized around a narrative (in the first and second sets), a traditional tale (third set), and several weather reports (fourth set). The total number of characters explicitly introduced is about the same as in previous character units, but the number presented only in glossaries is larger. A feasible goal would be to be able to read aloud (and comprehend!) all of the main texts without reference to the vocabulary lists and to recognize those characters introduced in large format (with notes)—but not those provided only in the glossaries—in novel combinations and new contexts. In other words, the focus should be, as always, on learning to recognize the core sets of characters in a variety of contexts.

20.1 First set

朝	知道	祖	搬	竹	算
4+8	5+3 3+9	4+5	3+10	6+0	6+8
cháo	*zhī* *dào*	*zǔ*	*ban*	*zhú*	*suàn*
'dynasty; facing; toward'	'know' 'way' ('know-speak')	'ancestor'	'move'	'bamboo'	'calculate'

縣	農	養	豬	種	雖然
6+10	7+6	9+6	7+8	5+9	8+9 4+8
县	农	养	猪	种	虽
2+5	2+4	2+7	3+8	5+4	3+6
xiàn	*nóng*	*yǎng*	*zhū*	*zhǒng / zhòng*	*suī* *rán*
'county'	'agriculture'	'nourish'	'pig'	'seed / to plant'	'although'

簡單	屋	具	死	紅	直
6+12 3+9	3+6	2+6	4+2	6+3	5+3
简单				红	
6+7 2+6			1+5	3L+3	
jiǎn *dān*	*wū*	*jù*	*sǐ*	*hóng*	*zhí*
('simple-single')	'room'	'tool'	'die'	'red'	'straight'

NOTES

a. 朝 *cháo* 'dynasty / facing; toward': Contrast the left side of 朝 with 车 / 車 *chē* 'car'; the former contains 早 *zǎo* 'morning' topped with 十 *shí* 'ten', which represents the simplification of what was originally a more complex element. The element on the right, now identical to 月 *yuè* 'moon', also represents a simplification. Although change has obscured the historical source of the character, 朝 itself shows phonetic contact with 潮 *cháo* 'tide' and the traditional graph 廟 *miào* 'temple' (whose simplified version is 庙). (Mnemonic: The *dynasty* holds court in the early morning, 早.)

b. 知 *zhī* 'know; be aware of' contains 矢 *shǐ* 'arrow' (assigned as a radical) to the left of 口 *kǒu* 'mouth'. (Mnemonic: *Knowledge* makes the mouth 口 sharp as an arrow 矢.) The second syllable of 知道, *dào*, means 'way; route' as well as 'speak'. 道 consists of 辶, the 'travel' radical and 首 *shǒu* 'head' (also a measure word for poems). (Mnemonic: to go 辶 ahead 首 along the *route*; *speaking* can also be viewed as following a *route*.) *Dào* is the source of the word that has entered English as 'Tao'. The notion, obviously, has great import in Chinese philosophical thought. To cite one example, the 道德经/道德經 *Dào Dé Jīng* (often Romanized as 'Tao Te Ching'), *The Classic of Tao and Virtue*, attributed to 老子 *Lǎozǐ* around the 4th or 3rd centuries BCE, opens (in the written Chinese of two and a half millennia ago) with the following cryptic and economical comment: 道可道, 非常道 *Dào kě dào, fēi cháng dào* 'The Tao that can be spoken is not the proper Tao'.

c. The radical assigned to 祖 *zǔ* 'ancestor' is 礻 (as in the 视/視 of 电视/電視 'TV'), whose noncombining form is 示 *shì* 'show; indicate'. (礻 should be distinguished from 衤, the combining form of 衣 *yī* 'clothes', which appears in both graphs of 衬衫/襯衫 *chènshān* 'shirt'.) The right-hand constituent of 祖—且 *qiě*—which clearly has a phonetic role in 姐 *jiě*, has no apparent phonetic role in 祖. (Mnemonic: 且 resembles an *ancestor* tablet—or a gravestone marking the *ancestors*.)

d. 搬 *bān* 'move' is composed of 扌 *tíshǒupáng*, the combining form of 手 and phonetic 般 *bān*, itself a combination of elements 舟 (cf. 船 *chuán* 'boat') and 殳 (cf. 没). (Mnemonic: Lifting 扌 things onto a boat 舟 to *move* or transport them.)

e. 竹 *zhú* 'bamboo' (originally a representation of a bamboo segment) appears in its reduced form in characters such as 算 *suàn* 'calculate; plan', 简/簡 *jiǎn* (see note below), and in graphs for words connected with bamboo, segmentation, and calculation.

f. 算 *suàn* is said to have originally represented an abacus (目 in the modern character) constructed of bamboo (竹). The three lines at the bottom of the character, 廾, are a reduction of what were originally two hands. (Mnemonic: hands *calculating* on a bamboo abacus.)

g. 县/縣 *xiàn* 'county; district': The right-hand side of 縣 consists of 糸 (as a radical) plus an additional stroke on top; the left-hand side is often handwritten with 目 connected to a horizontal base line so it has three internal strokes, such as 具 *jù* 'tool'. The graph 縣 represents a loan or extension of a graph that represented a word of similar pronunciation (now pronounced *xuán*), meaning 'hang up; suspend' (which may account for the silk radical). Later, the two meanings (or senses) were differentiated by the addition of the heart radical to give it its present form 悬/懸. The simplified graph, 县, is based on the left-hand portion of 縣.

h. 农/農 *nóng* 'agriculture/agricultural': The traditional graph contains 辰 *chén*, which is assigned as a radical, and 曲 *qǔ* (cf. 晨 *chén* 'early morning', where 辰 is clearly phonetic). The simplified graph keeps the general shape of the traditional graph, elevating the lower portion and reducing the complex top, which is assigned as the radical. (Mnemonic: The traditional graph resembles a field with implements, hence *agriculture*; the simplified graph resembles a *plow*.)

i. 养/養 *yǎng* 'raise; nourish': Both forms contain adaptations of 羊 *yáng* 'goat; sheep' (originally a representation of a goat, face on, with horns as the defining feature). In the traditional graph, 羊 is simply truncated (cf. 美 *měi*, where it is the radical, and 样/樣 *yàng*, where it is not). In the simplified graph, the original vertical (*shù*) stroke is sloped to the left to become a *piě* stroke (cf. 差 *chà*), leaving only three remaining strokes. The 羊 element provides a phonetic cue in both graphs, though in the simplified version—even with the loss of the traditional 'food' radical, 食 *shí*—羊 does not get the radical assignment. (Mnemonic: In the traditional graph, 食 'food' suggests *nourishment* or *raising* the young; the simplified graph shows lambs below the mother sheep, being *nourished*.)

j. 猪/豬 *zhū* 'pig' combines the element 者 *zhě* (cf. 或者) with either 豕 *shǐ* in the traditional graph, representing an older word for pig, or 犭 in the simplified—the combining form of 犬 *quǎn* 'dog', seen in characters that represent words for doglike animals, such as 狗 *gǒu* 'dog' and 狐 *hú* 'fox', or doglike behavior, such as 狂 *kuáng* 'deranged; violent' and 狡 *jiǎo* 'crafty; sly'. The set of characters with 者 *zhě* exhibit two distinct, though still closely related, points of articulation, illustrated by 都 *dōu* on the one hand and 猪/豬 *zhū* on the other (cf. 赌/賭 *dǔ* 'gamble' and 诸/諸 *zhū* 'all'). (Mnemonic: 豕 in the traditional graph looks like a vertical representation of a *pig*; in the simplified graph, 犭, which is associated with doglike animals, is the hint.)

k. 种/種 *zhǒng* 'seed; type; kind' (as well as *zhòng* 'to plant') combines 禾 *hé* 'grain' (as a radical) with phonetically motivated elements—either 重 *zhòng* 'heavy' (cf. 踵 and 肿/腫 *zhǒng*) or 中 *zhōng* 'middle' (cf. 冲 *chōng*; 忠 *zhōng*). (Mnemonic: The *type* or *kind* demarcated by the box at the center of both 重 and 中.)

l. 虽/雖然 *suīrán* 'although': The traditional graph, 雖, contains the element 隹 *zhuī*, which is assigned radical status despite its apparent phonetic motivation (cf. 谁/誰 *shéi ~ shuí*). The simplified graph, 虽, omits 隹 and assigns 口 as the radical. The four dots at the base of 然 is a version of the fire radical (火), which originally represented a word meaning 'burn'. Like 县/縣, 然 was borrowed to write a similarly sounding word, with an extra *huǒzìpáng* added to 燃 ('burn') to differentiate it from 然.

m. 简/簡 *jiǎn* 'a slip of bamboo' (original) was presumably used for note taking and then extended to 'simple; crude' and other meanings. The graph combines the bamboo radical with the phonetic 间/間 *jiān* 'space' (cf. 时间 'time-space' and 一间屋子 'a space of room'). 简/簡 combines with 单/單 *dān* 'odd; single' (also 'a note or bill') to form the compound 简单/簡單 *jiǎndān* 'simple'. Note that the lower part of 单/單 is distinct from 早.

n. 屋 *wū* 'room; house': Distinguish 尸 *shī* 'body', without the top stroke, from 户 *hù* 'door', with it. The latter (户) appears in 房 and in a slightly different form in 所 (whose core meaning of 'place' is confirmed by words such as 厕/廁所). The former (尸) appears in 尿 *niào* 'urine' and 屎 *shǐ* 'excrement', as well as in 屋. The lower component of 屋 is 至 *zhì* 'arrive; reach' (cf. 到 *dào* with a similar meaning). (Mnemonic: a person 尸 arriving 至 at a *room* for the night.)

o. 具 *jù* is one of many characters whose modern form represents considerable reinterpretation of its earlier components. Like 直 *zhí* and 真 *zhēn*, the character (in its modern form) shows three medial horizontals rather than the two of 目. *Jù* is a bound form. In compounds such as 文具 *wénjù* 'stationery' and 家具 *jiājù* 'furniture', where it is the second element, it can be glossed as 'implement' or 'tool'. In compounds such as 具体/體 *jùtǐ* 'actual; concrete' [as opposed to abstract], it reflects earlier meanings, such as 'complete; prepare'. 具 is phonetic in words such as 俱, 飓/颶 ('typhoon'), and simplified 惧 (but not its traditional counterpart 懼), all of which are pronounced *jù*. (Mnemonic: looks like a storage chest (or item of *furniture*) for *implements*, *tools* or other collection of items.)

p. 死 *sǐ* 'die': Although 死 has no distinct simplified form, it is assigned different radicals in the two sets. In the traditional set, the radical is 歹 'evil; vicious' (coincidentally pronounced *dǎi*); in the simplified, it is the horizontal first stroke. The bottom-right element is 匕 *bǐ* (distinct from 七). (Mnemonic: The graph shows a *dead* person, in a seated position under a slab.)

q. 红/紅 *hóng* 'red' combines the silk radical 纟/糸 ('red' is also associated with good fortune and wealth) with the phonetic 工 *gōng* (cf. 功 *gōng*; 攻 *gōng*; 江 *jiāng*).

r. 直 *zhí* shows 十 above 目, with the sides of 目 extended to meet a line across the bottom. Thus, 'eying a cross to makes sure it is *straight, vertical,* and *proper*'. Note that the extension of the sides of 目 to the horizontal base gives the graph three internal horizontal lines rather than two. 直 is the basis of a reliable phonetic set that includes 置, 植, 殖, and 值, all of which are pronounced *zhí*. Contrast with 真 *zhēn* 'true' (Mnemonic: Displayed on a pedestal and found straight and *true*.)

20.1.1 [SC] Compounds and phrases

元朝以前		清朝的时候		明朝以后呢？	
Yuáncháo yǐqián		*Qīngcháo de shíhou*		*Míngcháo yǐhòu ne?*	

知道吗？	不知道。	有道理。	道可道，非常道。		
Zhīdao ma?	*Bù zhīdào.*	*Yǒu dàolǐ*	*Dào kě dào fēi cháng dào.*		
		'be reasonable'	(from the *Dàodéjīng* of *Lǎozǐ*)		

祖父	祖母	祖先	祖籍	太祖	高祖
zǔfù	*zǔmǔ*	*zǔxiān*	*zǔjí*	*tàizǔ*	*gāozǔ*
'grandfather'	'grandmother'	'ancestors'	'family seat'	'first emperor of dynasty'	'great-great-grandfather'

搬家 *bānjiā*	搬走 *bānzǒu*	搬到哪儿？ *Bān dào nǎr?*	搬进来 *bān jìnlai*	搬出去 *bān chūqu*	汉朝 *Hàncháo*
竹子 *zhúzi*	竹字头 *zhúzìtóu*	打算 *dǎsuàn*	算法 *suànfǎ* 'algorithm'	算了！ *Suàn le!* 'Forget about it!'	

元江县在云南。 *Yuánjiāngxiàn zài* *Yúnnán.*	三水县在广东。 *Sānshuǐxiàn zài* *Guǎngdōng.*	县长 *xiànzhǎng*	清河县在河北。 *Qīnghéxiàn zài Héběi.*

农民 *nóngmín* 'farm laborers'	农场 *nóngchǎng*	农学 *nóngxué*	农工 *nónggōng*	农业 *nóngyè*

养猪 *yǎng zhū*	养老金 *yǎnglǎojīn* 'pension'	养父 *yǎngfù* 'foster father'	养母 *yǎngmǔ*	养鸡 *yǎng jī*	养羊 *yǎng yáng*

猪肉 *zhūròu*	种米 *zhòng mǐ*	种花 *zhòng huā*	种地 *zhòng dì*	虽然很累 *suīrán hěn lèi*

虽然没钱 *suīrán méi* *qián*	虽然可爱 *suīrán kě'ài*	虽然很渴 *suīrán hěn kě*	不简单 *bù jiǎndān*	单位 *dānwèi*	几种？ *Jǐ zhǒng?*

单日 *dānrì* 'odd days'	屋子 *wūzi*	房屋 *fángwū*	里屋 *lǐwū* 'inner room'	家具 *jiājù* 'furniture'

工具 *gōngjù*	茶具 *chájù*	教具 *jiàojù*	文具 *wénjù*	农具 *nóngjù*

死了 *sǐle*	饿死了 *èsǐle*	该死 *Gāi sǐ!* 'Damnation!'	找死 *zhǎo sǐ* 'seek danger'	红茶 *hóngchá*

红人	红十字会	红河	口红	一直走
hóngrén	*Hóng Shízì Huì*	*Hóng Hé*	*kǒuhóng*	*yìzhí zǒu*
'up-and-coming person'			'lipstick'	

一直到现在		直飞北京	直心眼儿
yìzhí dào xiànzài		*zhífēi Běijīng*	*zhíxīnyǎnr*
			'a very frank person'

20.1.2 [SC] Comment and response

1. 虽然妈妈是中国人可是她中国话说得不好。/那是因为她从来没有去过中国吧！

2. 她是中国人吧？/不，虽然中文说得很不错，但是她不是中国人，也没去过中国。

3. 明朝以后是清朝，对吗？那，清朝以后呢？/清朝以后是中华民国。<u>中华民国</u>是从1912年起。中华人民共和国是从1949年起。

4. 也许大家都知道明朝的时候，中国的<u>国都</u>从南京搬到北京，一直到现在都在北京。/但是1927到1949年又搬到了南部，对吗？先到南京然后到了<u>重庆</u>。

5. 我祖父七十五岁，已经不工作了，但是以前是很有名的<u>大师傅</u>，在北京饭店工作过二十多年。/六七十<u>年代</u>，我祖母也在北京饭店工作，是个经理。

6. 毛泽东的祖先都是农民吧？/是，元朝的时候，毛家的祖先从江西搬到<u>韶山</u>去了。

7. 打算的算为什么是竹字头？/不知道；是否因为<u>算盘</u>是用竹子做的？

8. 你打算几点走？/还不知道，也许中午，可是我得先洗一点儿衣服，做一点儿饭。晚一点儿离开这儿也没有什么关系！

9. 他们虽然是农民，天天都在外头种地，可是他们晚上还有时间学习英语！/对啊，他们很了不起！他们的房子也不错，屋子里的家具也好看。

10. 她是县长，白天在城市里开会，晚上都在农场工作。/嗯，她真不简单。还有时间养鸡养鱼！

11. 他在哪个单位工作，知道吗？/他是老师，以前在冷水江市的一个小学教书，但是听说最近他搬家了，搬到江西去了。

12. 现在好像有两个中国：一个是东北三省和东边儿的大城市，像北京、天津、上海、广州；一个是北边儿、西边儿的农民。/那，是不是也有两个美国？北边和南边不同，西边和东边不同，中部和海边不同。

13. 周恩来是哪年生的，哪年死的，知道吗？/他大概是1899年生的，出生的地方是江苏省的淮阳。他是1976年去世的；1976年一月八号—中国人都知道他死的那个日子。

14. 在中国大家都喜欢红的东西，红衣服、红包。/那是因为红在中国文化里是高兴、好、吉祥的意思。

15. 在中国养羊的，吃羊肉的很多都在北边儿或者西北边儿。/那，养鸡养鱼的是不是最多都在南边儿？

NOTES

中华/中華	*Zhōnghuá* 'China'
国都/國都	*guódū* 'capital'
重庆/重慶	*Chóngqìng*
大师傅/大師傅	*dàshīfu* 'chef'
年代	*niándài*
韶山	*Sháoshān*
算盘/算盤	*suànpán* 'abacus'
周恩来/周恩來	*Zhōu Ēnlái*
江苏/江蘇	*Jiāngsū*
淮阳/淮陽	*Huáiyáng*
去世	*qùshì* 'pass away'
高兴/高興	*gāoxìng*
吉祥	*jíxiáng* 'auspicious; lucky'

Exercise 2

[TC] Questions: Prepare to read aloud and then answer the following questions.

1. 祖父祖母是父親的父母還是母親的父母，知道嗎？

2. 聽說你要搬家，搬到廣州。什麼時候搬走？

3. 算是竹字頭，節也是竹字頭；那，哪些字是草字頭？

4. 這個地方很美，你看，前邊有湖，後邊有山，左右兩邊都是竹子。這不是跟<u>天堂</u>一樣嗎？

5. 中國，農民多農場小；美國農民少，農場大。英國呢？

6. 雖然沒有課，但是因為天氣很冷，我不想出去；你呢？你打算去哪裏？

7. 一直走，過兩個路口，火車站就到了；你行李多不多？

8. 書多，不過家具不多，所以我們搬家比較簡單。你呢？

9. 你在哪個單位工作？

10. 中國農民用的農具多不多？

11. 這間屋子為什麼都是紅色的？

12. 在現在的中國農民可以養自己的豬，種自己的地嗎？

13. <u>孔夫子</u>說不知道生活，那，當然更不知道死了以後的<u>事情</u>。

14. 漢朝是哪年到哪年，知道嗎？

15. 是縣大還是省大？

NOTES

天堂	*tiāntáng* 'heaven'
孔夫子	*Kǒngfūzǐ*
事情	*shìqing*

Exercise 3

Compose characters from the constituents listed—best to work in teams!

sāndiǎnshuǐ	*qīngkè de qīng de yòubianr*
sāndiǎnshuǐ	*měitiān de měi*
zhúzìtóu	*máobǐ de máo*
mùzìpáng	*bú duì de bù*
huǒzìpáng	*yīnwèi de yīn*
tǔzìpáng	*hē tāng de tāng de yòubiānr*
sāndiǎnshuǐ	*kěyǐ de kě*
shàng yǒu shǎo	*xià yǒu mù (yǎnjīng de yìsi)*
shàng yǒu mù (mùtou de mù)	*xià you zǐ*
sāndiǎnshuǐ	*xiānsheng de xiān*
kǒuzìpáng	*suǒ.yǐ de suǒ de zuǒbian*
wángzìpáng	*sān lǐ lù de lǐ zì*
xiàng dìfang de fāng	*shǎole dì-yí ge bǐhuà*
sāndiǎnshuǐ	*hēchá de hē de yòubianr*
shàng yǒu máng de yòubianr	*xià yǒu ge xīn zì*
zuǒbian yǒu ge yuè zì	*kànbào de bào de yòubianr*
yánzìpáng	*xiǎoháizi de hái de yòubianr*
huǒzìpáng	*duōshao de shǎo*
shàng yǒu ge dōngxi de xī zì	*xià yǒu ge nǚ zì*
xiàng dōu yíyàng	*shǎo le ge yòu ěrduō*
shàng yǒu ge yángròu de yáng	*xià yǒu ge gōngzuò de gōng zì*
shàng yǒu ge bù zì	*xià yǒu ge kǒu*
shàng yǒu ge rén zì	*xià yǒu ge mǔqin de mǔ*
shàng yǒu ge yáng zì	*xià yǒu ge dà*

20.2 Second set

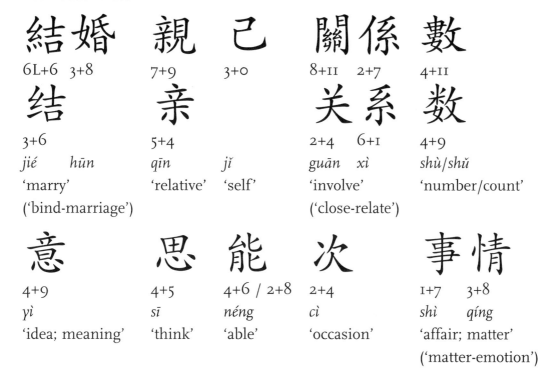

結婚 親 己 關係 數
6L+6 3+8   7+9   3+0   8+11 2+7   4+11

结 亲 关系 数
3+6   5+4   2+4 6+1   4+9

jié   hūn   qīn   jǐ   guān   xì   shù/shǔ
'marry'   'relative' 'self'   'involve'   'number/count'
('bind-marriage')   ('close-relate')

意 思 能 次 事情
4+9   4+5   4+6 / 2+8   2+4   1+7 3+8

yì   sī   néng   cì   shì   qíng
'idea; meaning'   'think' 'able'   'occasion'   'affair; matter'
                          ('matter-emotion')

NOTES

a. 结/結婚 *jiéhūn* is a V+O compound. Both graphs are phonosemantic, with the silk radical 纟/糹, associated with gifts, combined with the phonetic elements 吉 *jí* and 昏 *hūn*. (Mnemonic: Silk 纟/糹 is presented to or by the bride 女 to help *bind the marriage*.)

b. 亲/親 *qīn* 'relative; intimate; self': The simplified form omits the traditional radical (見), a strategy seen in 雖→虽, 號→号, and 電→电. (Mnemonic: For the traditional graph, *relatives* or *intimates* are those seen habitually 見; for the simplified, 木 suggests the *family* tree.)

c. 己 *jǐ* 'oneself' combines with 自 'self; source' to form 自己. 己 is itself assigned as a radical in a few graphs, including the 已 of 已经/已經 (with the third stroke slightly overlapping the second). It also forms a common phonetic set that includes 记/記, 纪/紀, and 忌—all *jì*.

d. 关/關 *guān* 'close': Traditional 關 is part of 開, 問, 間, which are formed with 門. However, only some of the graphs in that set are simplified with 门 (cf. 问 and 间; others focus on the central component, such as 关*guān*, 开 *kāi*). 關 also means 'gate', which is something through which people and things have to pass, hence *hǎiguān* 'customs house; customs' ('sea-pass') and *guānxi* 'connections'. The 係 of 關係, distinct from 系 *xì* 'system; department' in the traditional set, merges with the latter in the simplified (关系). Therefore, traditional 係 and 系 → simplfied 系. (Mnemonic: The traditional graph, 關, looks like a gate *closed* with bolts; the simplified, 关, shows the way *closed* by a trestle; in each case, you need *guānxi* to get through.)

e. 系 *xì* in the simplified set is one of a handful of characters that corresponds to two different characters in the traditional set: 系 and 係 (both *xì*). Thus: 系／系 *xì* 'department; faculty' (as in 中文系); and 关系／關係 *guānxi* 'relationship; connections'. The simplified graph, 系, reverts to the original form, which represented the range of senses now covered in the traditional set by both 系 and 係. 系 shows 糸 'silk thread' (the assigned radical) with a stroke above (originally a hand). (Mnemonic: silk thread represents *connections*; connections suggest *relationships*. A *department* is at the center of a system of relationships.) 系 appears as a component (not phonetic) in a number of characters in the traditional set, such as 縣 *xiàn* 'district' (simplified 县) and 孫 *sūn* 'grandchild' (simplified 孙).

f. 数／數 *shù / shǔ* 'number / count': The right-hand element is assigned as the radical (cf. 教 and 政). The left-hand element, 婁 *lóu* (reduced to 米 above 女 in the simplified 娄), though it does not seem to play a phonetic role in 数／數, forms an extensive phonetic set that includes 楼／樓 *lóu* 'building' and 搂／摟 *lōu*, 篓／簍 *lǒu*, and 缕／縷 *lǚ*.

g. 意 *yì* 'idea; meaning' combines with 思 *sī* 'think; thought' to form the compound *yìsi* 'meaning'. The first graph consists of 音 *yīn* 'sound' above 心 (*xīn* 'heart'); the second consists of 田 above 心 (cf. 想 *xiǎng* 'think', with 相 *xiāng* above 心 which forms the compound 思想 *sīxiǎng* 'thought; thinking; idea'). The upper part of 思 was originally a representation of the head (rather than what it is now—田 *tián* 'field'). (Mnemonic: For 意, *intentions* 心 externalized by speech sounds 音; for 思, head over heart representing *thought*.)

h. 能 *néng* 'able; ability; energy' is said to have originally been a drawing of a bear (head, body, claws), a meaning now restricted to 熊 *xióng*, which at some point in history became differentiated from the former by the addition of the four dots. In the traditional graph, 月 (=肉 'flesh') is selected as the radical; in the simplified, it is the top-left segment. (Mnemonic: The two ヒ components on the right look like *bear* claws, suggesting *power* and *ability*.)

i. 次 *cì* 'time; occasion' is formed with the 'ice' radical (cf. 冷) and 欠 (*qiàn*), the element seen in 欢／歡 *huān* 'pleasure' and 吹 *chuī* 'blow'. It forms a phonetic set that includes 资 *zī*, 姿 *zī*, 茨 *cí*, and 瓷 *cí*. (Mnemonic: The dots on the left mark first *time*, second *time*.)

j. 事 *shì* 'affair; matter' has its lower part in common with the upper part of 書. The graph was apparently formed for an altogether different meaning and then borrowed to represent the current word. (Mnemonic: a hand—the lower three horizontal strokes—grasping an item, suggesting a managing of *affairs*.) 情 *qíng* 'emotion; situation' consists of the heart radical, written vertically, and the phonetic element 青 *qīng* 'colors of nature', also seen in 請 *qīng*, 清 *qīng*, and 晴 *qíng* (cf. fourth set later in this unit).

Qǐng jiǎng Pǔtōnghuà; shǐyòng guīfàn zì. 'Please speak
Mandarin and use standard characters.' (*Hángzhōu Dàxué*
2006)

20.2.1 [SC] Compounds and phrases

结婚	结过婚	结婚三年了	父亲	母亲	亲戚
jiéhūn	*jiéguo hūn*	*jiéhūn sān nián le*	*fùqin*	*mǔqin*	*qīnqi*
自己	知己	已经关上了	自己做的	没关系	关门
zìjǐ	*zhījǐ*	*yǐjīng guānshang le*	*zìjǐ zuò de*	*méi guānxi*	*guān mén*
关上	中文系	数学	单数	数一数	楼上
guānshang	*Zhōngwén xì*	*shùxué*	*dānshù*	*shǔ yi shǔ*	*lóushang*
大楼	生意	什么意思？	没意思	不能去	思想
dàlóu	*shēngyì*	*Shénme yìsi?*	*méi yìsi*	*bù néng qù*	*sīxiǎng*
第一次	上次	去过一次	再说一次	不能吃猪肉	
dì-yī cì	*shàng cì*	*qùguo yí cì*	*zài shuō yí cì*	*bù néng chī zhūròu*	
事情很多	什么事儿	没事儿	办事情	做事儿	没时间
shìqing hěn duō	*shénme shìr*	*méi shìr*	*bàn shìqing*	*zuò shìr*	*méi shíjiān*

20.2.2 [SC] Comment and response

1. 「红白喜事」是什么意思？/男女结婚是喜事。红是<u>血</u>的<u>颜色</u>，跟人生有关系，也是好事儿的意思。婚事是好事儿所以红也是结婚喜事的意思；女的结婚的时候<u>穿</u>红衣。白吗，白是死的意思，人死了的时候人家都穿<u>白色</u>的衣服。红白喜事是生死的意思。

2. 祖父是父亲的父亲，对吗？祖母是父亲的母亲。那母亲的父母怎么说呢？/嗯，这一方面中文和英文不一样：祖父祖母是父亲那边儿的；母亲的父亲是外祖父（或者<u>外公</u>、<u>老爷</u>），母亲的母亲是外祖母（也有人说<u>外婆</u>、<u>姥姥</u>）。因为在中国，太太是外来的，所以外祖父、外祖母的外的意思是太太那边儿的。

3. 你经常在什么地方吃中饭？/都在家里吃，自己做的；在街上吃太贵了，也不怎么好吃，所以我中午走回家去，自己做一点儿简单的饭，一边儿吃饭一边儿看报。

4. 你和他是什么关系？/他是我<u>堂弟</u>，我父亲的哥哥的儿子。我们是同祖父。英文怎么说？

5. 你这是第一次来九江吗？/不是，我来过好几次，差不多每年两三次，我在九江市经常有<u>生意</u>的事情。

6. 今天中文课有多少学生？/那我数一数：一、二、三……好像一共有十五个。/十五个不好，为什么呢，因为是单数，有一个人没有伴儿。

7. 虽然现在在中国不像以前只能生一个孩子，可以生两个孩子了，但是不能生第三个。/那<u>少数民族</u>也是这样儿吗？我听说少数民族可以生更多的。

NOTES

血	*xiě (xuè)* 'blood'
颜色/顔色	*yánsè* 'color'
穿	*chuān* 'wear'
白色	*báisè* 'white'
外公	*wàigōng* 'maternal grandfather'
老爷/老爺	*lǎoye* 'maternal grandfather'
外婆	*wàipó* 'maternal grandmother'

姥姥	lǎolao 'maternal grandmother'
堂弟	tángdì 'cousin; uncle's son'
生意	shēngyì 'business'
少数民族/少數民族	shǎoshù-mínzǔ 'minority group'

20.2.3 [SC] 少年的毛泽东

<u>毛泽东</u>是在清朝1893年十二月二十六号出生的。他的出生地是湖南<u>湘潭</u>县的
  <u>韶山</u>。你们也许都知道湖南在中国中部，是长江南边儿的一个大省。湖南
  最大的城市是<u>省府长沙</u>。韶山在湖南中部，离长沙不远，大概有几百公
  里。毛家<u>世代</u>都是农民，元朝的时候，祖先从江西搬到韶山来；他们在韶
  山养猪,种米,茶,竹子差不多有五百多年了。毛泽东的父亲虽然不能说是很
  有钱，可是他也不算<u>穷</u>。毛家的房子不小，有六间屋子，<u>泥地面</u>，<u>木扇
  窗</u>，还有一些简单的<u>家具</u>。
毛泽东本来是老三，上头有两个哥哥，但是在他还小的时候他们就死了，所
  以他成了老大。<u>后来</u>家里又生了两个弟弟，一个妹妹。兄弟姐妹的名字都
  有个泽字：毛泽东，毛泽民，毛泽潭，毛泽红。因为父亲对他不好，所以
  毛泽东小的时候住在母亲家里，那儿离韶山不太远。他一直很爱母亲，不
  喜欢父亲。小的时候，他母亲对他很好，<u>外婆</u>也对他非常好。
毛泽东八岁回到韶山上学，可是他不喜欢<u>传统</u>的<u>学校</u>，<u>于是</u>最后去了长沙一
  个比较好也比较先进的学校。在学校的时候他很<u>认真</u>，也喜欢<u>读书</u>，<u>写
  诗</u>，可是就是不喜欢数学。他十四岁就跟一个十八岁的女孩结婚了。因为
  那不是他自己要的，是父母要的，所以后来他<u>便</u>说那个女孩不能算是他太
  太，他和她没有什么关系。毛泽东离开韶山以后，又结了几次婚，最后生
  了几个孩子，从那个时候起也只回去过一两次，大多数的时间都住在北
  京，办中国<u>政府</u>的事情。

NOTES

毛泽东	Máo Zédōng
湘潭	Xiāngtán
韶山	Sháoshān
省府	shěngfǔ 'provincial capital': cf. shǒudū ~ guódū 'national capital'
长沙	Chángshā
世代	shìdài 'generation / from generation to generation'
穷	qióng 'be poor'

泥   *ní* 'mud'
地面   *dìmiàn* 'ground; floor'
木扇   *mùshàn* 'wooden fan; slats'
窗   *chuāng*: bound form of 窗户 *chuānghu* 'window'
家具   *jiājù* 'furniture'
成   *chéng* 'become; into'
后来   *hòulái* 'afterward; later'
外婆   *wàipó* 'maternal grandmother'
传统   *chuántǒng* 'traditional'
学校   *xuéxiào* 'school'
于是   *yúshì* 'as a result; hence; thereupon'
认真   *rènzhēn* 'earnest; scrupulous' ('know-real')
读书   *dúshū* 'study; read; attend school'
写诗   *xiěshī* 'write poems'
便   *biàn* 'then; in that case': cf. *suíbiàn, fāngbiàn*
政府   *zhèngfǔ* 'government'

Méijiāwù Cūn ('village'), a tea-growing village near *Hángzhōu*

20.2.4 [TC] Questions

1. 清朝是哪年到哪年，知道嗎？(不知道的話，看字典或問中國朋友。)

2. 毛澤東是哪年生的，哪年死的？

3. 他出生的地方離長江多遠？

4. 毛家的農場農業怎麼樣？

5. 他有幾個兄弟姐妹？問題爲什麼不怎麼簡單？

6. 他是個什麼樣的學生？

7. 毛澤東離開韶山以後是否常回去？

8. 他結了幾次婚？生了幾個孩子？

9. 他小的時候，上學的時候，爲什麼沒跟父親住在一起？

20.3 Third set

臥	壞	活	正	冬	冰
7+2	3+16	3+6	4+1	2+3	2+4

卧	坏				
7+2	3+4				
wò	*huài*	*huó*	*zhèng*	*dōng*	*bīng*
'lie down'	'bad'	'live; alive'	'proper; correct'	'winter'	'ice'

NOTES

a. 卧/臥 *wò* 'lie down': The simplified graph 卧 (臣 + 卜) is slightly different in form from the standard traditional graph 臥 (臣 + 人). The left-hand element is 臣 *chén* 'minister; attendant', and the graph may have originally depicted a minister prostrating himself (which provides us with a mnemonic for 'lie down'.) 卧虎藏龙/臥虎藏龍 *wòhǔ-cánglóng* ('crouching-tiger-hidden-dragon') (in other words, 'unnoticed talent') is the name of a popular Chinese martial arts film that was first shown in 2000.

b. 坏/壞 *huài* 'bad': The traditional graph 壞 consists of the radical 土 *tǔ* 'ground; soil' and an element that now appears only in other compound graphs such as 怀/懷 *huái* (where it shows a phonetic role). That element is based on 衣 (*yī* 'clothing') and originally meant 'conceal beneath the clothes'. It was formed by the insertion of material between the top and lower strokes of 衣, along the lines of 裹 *guǒ* (=衣 + 果*guǒ*) and 褒 *bāo* (=衣 + 保*bǎo*). The simplified graph substitutes 不, which is a close match to the bottom of the complex form, as well as suggestive of the meaning. (Mnemonic: For the traditional graph, 土 'soil' and the 衣 complex suggest *bad* intent; for the simplified, 不 provides the hint.)

c. 活 *huó* 'live / life' consists of the water radical and the element 舌 *shé* 'tongue'. The presence of 舌 is not original, being a simplification of a more complex element. 活 does show phonetic contact with other characters in which the 舌 element has undergone the same evolution—话 / 話 *huà*, 刮 *guā*, 括 *kuò*. (Mnemonic: Liquid 氵 on the tongue 舌: drink long and *live* long.)

d. 正 *zhèng* 'upright; proper; correct; just' is formed from 止 *zhǐ* 'foot; step; stop' and a horizontal top line (i.e., advancing to the *correct* point, and just the *right* point). It shows phonetic contact with graphs such as 政 *zhèng* and 整 *zhěng*.

e. 冬 *dōng* 'winter', with the ice radical below, is phonetic in 疼 *téng* 'ache; hurt'. Other characters with the ice radical include 凍 *dòng* 'icy; freeze' and 冰 *bīng*. The latter is constructed on semantic rather than phonetic principles. (Mnemonic: Ice for winter.)

20.3.1 [SC] Compounds and phrases

卧房	卧车	卧虎	硬卧	软卧	坏人
wòfáng	*wòchē*	*wòhǔ*	*yìngwò*	*ruǎnwò*	*huàirén*
好坏	坏蛋	坏话	坏血病	生活	活动
hǎohuài	*huàidàn* 'scoundrel'	*huàihuà*	*huàixiěbìng* 'leukemia'	*shēnghuó* 'life; livelihood'	*huódòng* 'activities'
活到老	正在吃呢	正好	正北	正面	正直
huó dào lǎo	*zhèng zài chī ne*	*zhèng hǎo*	*zhèng běi* 'due north'	*zhèngmiàn* 'obverse; right side'	*zhèngzhí* 'honest; upright'
冬天	冬瓜	冬菇	冰点	冰箱	冰淇淋
dōngtiān	*dōngguā*	*Dōnggū* 'dried winter mushrooms'	*bīngdiǎn* 'freezing point'	*bīngxiāng* 'refrigerator'	*bīngqílíng*
冰山	冰水	冰天雪地	冰冻三尺, 非一日之寒		
bīngshān	*bīngshuǐ*	*bīngtiān-xuědì* 'of a frozen landscape'	*bīngdòng sān chǐ, fēi yí rì zhī hán* 'ice frozen to three feet, not in one day of cold' [said of a deep-rooted problem]		

20.3.2 [SC] 卧冰求鲤 *Wò bīng qiú lǐ* 'Sleeping on ice to procure fresh carp'

晋朝的时候，有个叫王祥的人，他很小的时候妈妈就死了。后来他爸爸又结婚了，可是他的继母对他不太好，常常在他爸爸面前说他的坏话。坏话听多了，他爸爸也不再爱他了。有一次，王祥的继母要吃活鱼，可是那个时候正是冬天，天非常冷，河水也结了冰。在这样的天气里上哪儿去找活鱼呢？王祥听说继母要吃活鱼，他就到河边去，衣服放在河边儿，睡在冰上找鱼。他虽然冷得不得了，但是睡了一个晚上，冰就化了一点儿，他就可以用手找鲤鱼了。找到了两条鱼以后，他就回家给他妈妈做了很好吃的鱼。他这样做，非常孝敬他继母！

NOTES

晋	*Jìn* is the name of a petty state under the *Zhōu* that first gained some prominence in the 7th century BCE. It was located near present-day *Tàiyuán* in *Shānxī*; in the modern written language, 晋 is used as an abbreviated name (e.g., on license plates) for that province. The *Jìn* Dynasty was a succession of rulers that emerged in the same area much later, between 265–420 CE.
祥	*Xiáng*, as in 吉祥 *jíxiáng* 'auspicious', but here, part of a personal name
继母	*jìmǔ* 'stepmother': cf. 继父; the core meaning of 继 is 'follow; continue'
不得了	*bùdéliǎo* 'extremely'
化	*huà* 'change': as in 化学 *huàxué* 'chemistry' ('transformation-study')
鲤鱼	*lǐyú* 'carp'
孝敬	*xiàojìng* 'show respect to [one's elders]' ('be filial-respect'): cf. 孝经 *Xiàojīng* 'The Book of Filial Duty'

Rénxíng tōngdào, jìnzhǐ zuòwò 'Pedestrian underpass: no sitting or lying'

20.4 Fourth set: Weather terms

天气在安慰我们像梦够到无梦的人.

Tiānqì zài ānwèi wǒmen xiàng mèng gòu dào wú mèng de rén.

'Weather comforts us, like a dream reaching the dreamless.'

('Weather *zài* comfort us like dream reach not-have dream *de* people.')

—From the poem 灵魂游戏 *Línghún Yóuxì* 'Spirit Game', by the Chinese poet 北岛 *Běi Dǎo*

雨	雪	雲	霧	溫	度
8+0	8+3	8+4	8+11	3+10	3+6
		云	雾	温	
		2L+2	8+5	3+9	
yǔ	*xuě*	*yún*	*wù*	*wēn*	*dù*
'rain'	'snow'	'clouds'	'fog'	'warm'	'degree'

陰	陽	夜	晴	風	轉
3+8	3+9	3+5	4+8	9+0	7+11
阴	阳			风	转
2+4	2+4	2+6		4+0	4L+4
yīn	*yáng*	*yè*	*qíng*	*fēng*	*zhuǎn / zhuàn*
'female; shade'	'male; light'	'night'	'clear; fine' [of weather]	'wind'	'turn / revolve'

級	陣	區	力	向
6+3	3+7	2+9	2+0	3B+3
级	阵	区		
3L+3	2+4	2L+2		
jí	*zhèn*	*qū*	*lì*	*xiàng*
'level; rank'	'a bout of'	'region'	'strength'	'toward; to'

NOTES

a. 雨 *yǔ* 'rain', originally a representation of rain, is the radical in many graphs that represent meteorological phenomena: 雪 *xuě* 'snow', 雾/霧 *wù* 'fog', and the traditional form 雲 *yún* (but not the corresponding simplified version, 云). Others, not in our set, include the following: traditional 電 *diàn* (but not simplified 电) 'lightning; electricity', 雷 *léi* 'thunder', and 雹 *báo* 'hail' (both with one form only). In many cases, the variable element is phonetic: 云 *yún* in 雲 *yún*; 务/務 *wù* in 雾/霧 *wù*; 包 *bāo* in 雹 *báo*. 雷 broke from the pattern when phonetic 畾 *léi* was simplified to 田 (*tián*). Similar cases of reinterpretation or simplification account for most of the other exceptions. (Mnemonic: 雪 shows layers of *snow* [under the precipitation radical]; 云 is suggestive of cumulus *clouds*; 雾/霧 is a *fog* of detail!)

b. 温/溫 *wēn* forms a phonetic set with characters mostly pronounced *yùn*: 蕴/蘊, 慍/慍, 酝/醖. Even in the traditional set, 温 is sometimes written as 温, just like the standard simplified form. (Mnemonic: *Warming* water 氵 on a stove 皿.)

c. 陰, 陽 *yīn, yáng* represent female-male contrasts such as moon-sun, moist-dry, and shade-light. In the traditional, 陰 contains the so-called left ear and a right-hand element consisting of 今 *jīn* above 云 (*yún*). The traditional 陽 also shows the left ear and is phonetically linked to 場 *chǎng* and 湯 *tāng*. Traditional, informal simplifications of 陰 and 陽 as 阴 and 阳 (making use of 月 *yuè* 'moon' and 日 *rì* 'sun' in well-motivated semantic substitutions) were formalized in the new 'official' simplified set. (Mnemonic: *Shade*, represented as 云 in 陰 contrasts with 日 'sun' or *light* in 陽—a contrast that is made more explicit in the simplified graphs.)

d. 夜 *yè* 'night' contains 夕 'moon', which is obscured by a rightward slanting stroke (*nà*), as in 多, 名, and 外. Mainland dictionaries (of the simplified set) assign the first two (top) strokes as the radical rather than the traditional 夕, allowing for a more discrete division of constituents into top and bottom. (Mnemonic: A person walking in the moonlight 夕 at *night*.)

e. 晴 *qíng* 'clear; fine' [of weather], as noted earlier, is part of a large, regular phonetic set whose members include 請 *qǐng* and 清 *qīng*. (Mnemonic: 日 'sun' and 青 *qīng* allude to 清, and both suggest 'clear, fine'.)

f. 风/風 *fēng* 'wind': The traditional form has an element on its inside that is made up of the insect radical (虫) plus a top stroke (cf. 虽/雖, where the upper part is a box). This alludes to the popular association of wind to the dissemination of insects. For the simplified graph, 风, see 区/區, where the innards are also reduced to a cross. (Mnemonic: Both graphs look like kites floating in the *wind*.)

g. 转/轉 represents a pair of closely related words, *zhuǎn* 'turn; change; transmit' (the meaning relevant to weather forecasts) and *zhuàn* 'revolve; rotate; stroll'. Both graphs have the vehicle radical and the phonetic element 专/專 *zhuān*, which is also seen in 传/傳 *chuán* (as a verb), *zhuàn* (as a noun). (Mnemonic: In both graphs—though more in the traditional—both elements resemble spindles or axels that *turn* or *revolve*.)

h. 级/級 *jí* 'level; rank' contains the silk radical and a phonetic 及 *jí*, which is also seen in the simplified 极 *jí* (好极了). (Mnemonic: Silk 纟/糸 presented to pupils who advance 及 to the next *level*.)

i. 阵/陣 *zhèn* was originally 'a battle array', but now it most commonly represents a measure word for sudden events or 'bouts': 一阵雨/一陣雨, 一阵风/一陣風. Contrast with the unrelated surname 陈/陳 *Chén*. (Mnemonic: *Sudden* appearance of a vehicle 车/車 over a hill or mound, the latter represented by the so-called left ear whose full form is 阜.)

j. 区/區 *qū* 'region; area': The traditional graph contains 品 *pǐn* (itself made up three 口 *kǒu* components), and both graphs demarcate a region (which provides the mnemonic hint). 区/區 is phonetic in 驱/驅 *qū* and 躯/軀 *qū*. (Mnemonic: The outer lines demarcate a *region* that includes the various inner forms—品 or 乂.)

k. 力 *lì* 'strength; effort' is a radical in 功, 加, 助, 务, and 办 (but not in 边 or 为). Contrast with 九 and 刀. (Mnemonic: A man or woman with legs braced, pushing with all of his or her *strength*.)

l. 向 *xiàng* is said to derive from a representation of a window beneath a roof, something *to face* or *turn toward*. 向 is phonetic in a few characters, such as 响/嚮 *xiàng* and 饷/餉 *xiǎng*. 向 *xiàng* should be distinguished from 回 *huí* 'return' and 同 *tóng* 'same as / with'.

Temple incinerator (Macau). The complex character is an auspicious blend of 福, 禄, 寿/福, 祿, 壽 *fú-lù-shòu* 'fortune, salary, long life'.

20.4.1 [SC] Compounds and phrases

下大雨 *xià dàyǔ*	白云 *báiyún*	雨下得很大 *yǔ xià+de hěn dà*	在下雨 *zài xiàyǔ*	常下雨 *cháng xiàyǔ*
雨衣 *yǔyī*	云海 *yúnhǎi*	不常下雨 *bù cháng xiàyǔ*	温度 *wēndù*	风很大 *fēng hěn dà*
几年级 *jǐ niánjí*	二十三度 *èrshísān dù*	三级 *sānjí*	三年级 *sān niánjí*	毕业了 *bìyè le*
下雪 *xiàxuě*	下雾 *xiàwù*	没有风 *méiyǒu fēng*	风度 *fēngdù* 'demeanor; style'	阴天 *yīntiān*
夜里 *yèlǐ*	半夜 *bànyè* 'midnight'	晴天 *qíngtiān*	转阴 *zhuǎnyīn*	转晴 *zhuǎnqíng*
地区 *dìqū*	一阵雨 *yí zhèn yǔ*	一阵风 *yí zhèn fēng*	风力 *fēnglì*	人力 *rénlì*
力气 *lìqi* 'strength'	离心力 *líxīnlì* 'centrifugal force'	阵雨 *zhènyǔ* 'rain showers'	夜间 *yèjiān*	方向 *fāngxiàng* 'direction'
北风和太阳 *Běifēng hé Tàiyang* [a story]	市区 *shìqū* 'urban district'	百分之九十 *bǎifēn zhī jiǔshí* '90 percent'		

20.4.2 [TC] Dialogue

甲：　請問，你住在什麼地方？

乙：　我住在東風西路，離人民路不遠。

甲：　那，你怎麼來上課？

乙：　看天氣怎麼樣；太熱我就坐車來。回去因為是夜裏，我也坐車回去。

甲：　坐車要多長時間？

乙：　差不多三十分鐘。

甲：　我今天想去石林(*Shí Lín*)，跟我一塊兒去，好不好？

乙：　石林離這兒不是很遠嗎？

甲：　是很遠，但是地方很有名，我們在昆(*kūn*)明的時候不能不去！

乙：　今天有點冷，沒有太陽，明天去，行不行？

甲：　明天去也可以。

乙：　好，那我們明天去吧。

20.4.3 [SC] Weather reports

Weather reports follow a very consistent format, which makes them a good genre for beginning reading. Three examples are cited in this section; current ones can be found in most Chinese newspapers and on the Web.

<u>全国</u>部分城市<u>天气预报</u>
25日20时 到26日20时

	城市	天气	气温 (白天 ~ 夜里)
(一)	北京	雾转多云	09 ~ 17 度
(二)	上海	阴转小雨	16 ~ 21 度
(三)	天津	多云	10 ~ 19 度
(四)	广州	晴转多云	20 ~ 29 度
(五)	香港	晴	23 ~ 28 度
(六)	南宁	阴转小雨	21 ~ 27 度
(七)	海口	多云	25 ~ 29 度
(八)	桂林	多云转小雨	17 ~ 24 度
(九)	武汉	小雨转阴	16 ~ 20 度
(十)	南京	阴	14 ~ 20 度
(十一)	杭州	小雨转阴	16 ~ 22 度
(十二)	福州	多云转阴	18 ~ 25 度
(十三)	厦门	晴	19 ~ 28 度
(十四)	台北	多云转阴	20 ~ 25 度

NOTES

全国   *quán guó* 'whole country'

天气预报   *tiānqì yùbào* 'weather forecast'

Cities cited   In most cases, you can guess from the parts you know: *Xiānggǎng; Nánníng; Hǎikǒu; Guìlín; Wǔhàn; Hángzhōu; Fúzhōu; Xiàmén.*

上海<u>市区</u>今明天气预报 （七月)

天气：多云，<u>局部</u>地区阴有阵雨；温度：27°–33°；明天27°–33°；<u>风向</u>：<u>偏</u>东；风力：4–5
级，阵风6级。

NOTES

市区   *shìqū* ('city-region')
局部   *júbù* 'local'
风向   *fēngxiàng* ('wind-direction')
偏   *piān* 'inclined'

Bù suídì tǔtán, bù jiǎng cūhuà zānghuà! 'Don't spit
indiscriminately, and don't use vulgar or dirty language!'
(*Shànghǎi* 2006)

北京市区今明天气预报 （十月)

今天白天：晴转多云，<u>降水概率</u>20%，北转南风二三级，最高气温十七度。

今天<u>夜间</u>，多云转阴，降水概率60%，南转北风一二级，<u>最低气温</u>九度。

明天白天到夜间，阴转晴，降水概率20%，偏北风一二级转四五级，最高气温19度，最
<u>低气温</u>七度。

NOTES

降水(量)   *jiàngshuǐ(liàng)* 'precipitation' ('drop-water-amount')
概率   *gàilù* 'likelihood' ('approximate-ratio')
夜间   *yèjiān* 'at night' ('night-space')

最低   *zuìdī* 'lowest'
百分之二十   '20 percent': percentages are read thus; 百分之三十 '30 percent'; and so on

20.5 On the street #7

20.5.1 Support or oppose

Because Chinese characters can represent language in a very succinct form, they are particularly suited to signs, headlines, advertisements, and other contexts where space is at a premium. Pharmacies display 药/藥 *yào*, dentists 牙 *yá*, and pawnbrokers 押 *yā*—all often in a calligraphic version designed to fit the space and catch the eye. In countries such as Japan that make use of Chinese graphs to write words that originate in Chinese or are homologous with Chinese, demonstrators still use Chinese graphs to write their slogans or otherwise express their positions on issues. Korea used to make use of Chinese graphs to write words borrowed from Chinese.

Here are some basic phrases to use on your own posters.

欢迎/歡迎	*Huānyíng* [X] 'welcome [someone]'
打倒	*Dǎdǎo* [X] 'down with [someone]' ('hit-collapse')
拥护/擁護	*Yōnghù* [X] 'up with; support [someone]'
独立/獨立	[X] *dúlì* 'independence for [something]' ('alone-stand')
反对/反對	*Fǎnduì* [X] 'oppose [someone]' ('overturn-face')
要民主要自由！	*Yào mínzhǔ yào zìyóu!* 'Dcmocracy and freedom!': *mínzhǔ* ('people-host'); *zìyóu* ('self-source')
打倒帝国主义	*Dǎdǎo dìguózhǔyì!* 'Down with imperialism!' ('imperial-country-ism')
打倒资产阶级和他们的走狗！	*Dǎdǎo zīchǎn jiējí hé tāmen de zǒugǒu!* 'Down with the bourgeois class and their running dogs!'

香港 (2011): 占领中环/佔領中環 *Zhànlǐng Zhōnghuán*
'Occupy Central'

20.5.2 More signs

Signs of one kind or another are ubiquitous in China and present opportunities for some succinct reading pleasure. Here are some more to add to your repertoire.

药房/藥房	*yàofáng* 'pharmacy' ('drug-store')
美容	*měiróng* 'beautician' ('beauty-appearance')
批发/批發	*pīfā* 'wholesale' ('batch-distribute')
施工	*shīgōng* 'construction site' ('carry+out-work')

A NOTE TO THE EPIGRAPH

The first part (*Rù guó wèn jìn*), like many citations from the classics, has become a common saying and appears in dictionaries as such. The whole citation is from *Lǐ Jì*, or the "Book of Rites", also called the "Classic of Rites", a compilation of rules of social conduct and decorum. It is one of the five texts that form the core of the Confucian canon.

Unit 21 第二十一课/課 DÌ-ÈRSHÍYĪ KÈ

不知则问，不能则学。/不知則問，不能則學。

Bù zhī zé wèn, bù néng zé xué.

'If you don't know, ask; if you can't do it, learn.'

('Not know then ask, not able then learn.')

只要功夫深，铁杵磨成针。/只要功夫深，鐵杵磨成針。

Zhǐ yào gōngfu shēn, tiěchǔ mó chéng zhēn.

'With enough persistence, an iron bar can be ground into a needle.'

('Only need effort deep, iron-bar grind become needle.')

—Sayings in praise of effort and perseverance

Unit 21, the last of the character units, introduces more than sixty additional characters and completes the character foundation. This unit differs from the others in that it introduces some transitional material not already covered in the core units. This material anticipates the shift to other readings, such as the edited storybooks mentioned at the end of this unit. Additional explanation is added below as it is needed and relevant. Otherwise, the unit continues in the regular format, with five sections (rather than four) introducing about a dozen characters at a time, then progressing from words and phrases to comment and response and, in some cases, longer passages. The unit concludes, as usual, with a section on signs and slogans.

21.0 [TC] 复习/復習 *Fùxí* **'Review'**

1. 你去過北京醫院嗎？/在東城區那兒的嗎？沒去過，可是我知道去那兒怎麼走。

2. 他們現在不住在這裡了，搬走了。/搬走了？什麼時候般走的？/不知道。我們是最近才搬進來的。我們搬來的時候，他們已經搬出去了。

3. 他不錯，只學了一年就說得那麼好，真不簡單！/對啊，他說得比二年級、三年级的同學還好。不過你知道，他小的時候住過中國，所以已經會說一點兒了。

4. 聽說現在在西方離婚的比結婚的還多。/可能不是離婚的多，是結婚的少了。很多男女住在一起很久，那樣也可以算是結婚的吧。

5. "水土不服"是啥意思？"水"就是喝的，"土"就是吃的，"不服"就是不舒服，生病。意思就是客人從遠方來，吃的東西，喝的東西不一樣，<u>不適應</u>，所以很容易生病。/明白了，我<u>剛</u>來中國的時候也是這樣，上午都不舒服，過了一段時間就好了。現在已經沒有問題了。

6. 有不吃豬肉的，有不吃牛肉的，但好像不吃羊肉的比較少。/住在中東的人大多數不吃豬肉，對嗎？有的中國人不吃牛肉，可是不吃羊肉的我不太情楚。美國人吃羊肉嗎？/不多，美國人經常吃牛肉的最多，常吃羊肉的也有，但是不多。

7. 美國中部冬天非常冷，零下十度到零下二十度都有，雪下得很多，走路不行，開車很難。/中國北方也很冷，風有時候也很大，不過雪沒有美國北邊下得那麼大。

8. 我最近忙死了，功課太多了，飯也沒有好好吃，茶也沒時間喝，累得不得了了。/那，你坐一會兒吧，先喝點茶，然後咱們去吃飯，紅屋飯店離這裡很近。吃飽了以後，先把功課作完，然後好好睡個覺。

NOTES

a. 不适应/不適應 *bú shìyìng* 'get used to; suit; adapt; fit'

b. 刚/剛 *gāng* 'just now' (see the first set)

c. 啥 *shá*: In online chat rooms and other places where the language is very colloquial, the regional alternative to 什麼—啥 *shá*—is often seen.

Exercise 1

Determine the gist of the following sentences, despite the unknown characters.

1. 我正在学做饭，做着玩儿而已。	What's the speaker doing—when and why?
2. 美国的货币单位是Dollar。	What's being said about the United States?
3. 他因为婚姻关系，也有西班牙的亲戚。	Is the speaker claiming the person is Spanish?
4. 你双手手指的总数是十。	What is the meaning of 手指? Why use 十?
5. 每天来这家饭馆吃饭的人数是几千多。	What does the figure represent?
6. 语言是那一种工作必不可少的工具。	What does the job involve?
7. 她入美国籍已经两年了。	What happened two years ago?

Read the following tone groups (down, then across).

方言	搬家	看法	打开
当然	书包	进口	火车
虽然	阴天	路口	紧张
国家	鱼头	市区	认错
前边	学习	看书	看报
南方	同学	四川	电话

Hěn zhuàngguān! (*Fántǐzì*) *Xuánkōngsì* 'The Hanging Temple', 山西

21.1 First set

等	接	回	平	如	穿
6T + 6	3 + 8	3T + 3	1 + 4	3L + 3	5 + 4
děng	*jiē*	*huí*	*píng*	*rú*	*chuān*
'wait'	'meet'	'return'	'level'	'as; like'	'wear'

找　懂　　奇怪　認識　剛　甜
3 + 4　3 + 13　　3 + 5　3 + 5　7L + 7　7 + 12　2 + 8　6 + 5

懂　　　　　　认识　刚
3 + 12　　　　　　2L + 2　2 + 5　2 + 4

zhǎo　dǒng　　qí　guài　rèn　shí　gāng　tián
'find'　'understand'　'strange'　　'know [a　'just'　'sweet'
　　　　　　('strange-　person]'
　　　　　　uncanny')　('recognize-
　　　　　　　　　　　　know')

NOTES

a. 等 děng 'wait' has zhúzìtóu (竹字头/頭) as a radical; cf. 第, 算, 籍, 笑. Bamboo is used to make implements (笔/筆 and 算, the latter based on the abacus); it has regular segments that suggest periods of time or order (等, 第), and it breaks and burns with characteristic sounds (such as laughter, 笑). The original phonetic connection between the right-hand element, 寺 sì 'temple', and 等 děng is supported by other pairs, such as 待 dāi 'stay' / dài 'entertain', 诗/詩 shī 'poem', and 時 shí 'time' (simplified as 时). Note that d and s/sh are quite close in terms of position of articulation.

b. 接 jiē 'meet; answer [the phone]' combines tíshǒur ~ tíshǒupáng (提手旁) with 妾 qiè, originally 'a captured female servant' (cf. 立 lì 'stand' and 女 nǔ 'female') and by extension 'a concubine'. (Mnemonic: Female servant extending hands to meet someone.)

c. 回 huí 'return' is also a verbal measure for 'times': 怎么一回事/怎麼一回事 'what's going on'. The outer square is assigned as the radical; cf. 国/國 guó. (Mnemonic: 回 depicts a return from the perimeter to the center.)

d. 平 píng 'level' looks the part, with its level horizontal strokes. The notion of 'level' is extended to 'peace' (和平 hépíng). The top level stroke is assigned as the radical.

e. 如 rú: The graph, showing 女 'woman' (as radical) and 口 'mouth; speech', is based on the original meaning of 如 rú, which is 'follow'. Extended meanings include 'as; like; according to'. 如 is used phonetically in a few characters, such as 茹 rú and 洳 rù.

f. 穿 chuān 'wear' shows 穴 xué 'cavity' (assigned as radical) above 牙 yá 'teeth' reflecting the more general meaning of 'pierce through' or 'pass through', hence 'put on clothes; wear'. (Mnemonic: The character looks vaguely like a mannequin—neck, shoulders, two arms, a pelvic area, and two legs.)

g. 找 *zhǎo* 'find' consists of 扌 'hand' and 戈 *gē* 'spear'. The graph is obviously very similar to 我, lacking only the initial *piěr* stroke, which provides the mnemonic: *searching* for the missing stroke.

h. 懂 *dǒng* 'understand' combines the left-hand heart radical (cf. 忙) and the phonetically relevant 董 *dǒng*. The simplified form differs only in the way the inner *cǎozìtóu* is written—with three strokes (艹) rather than four.

i. 奇 *qí* 'strange; rare' has 大 as a radical over 可. (Mnemonic: *Strange* things with great 大 possibilities 可.) The graph is phonetic in 骑/騎 *qí* 'straddle; ride' (骑/騎自行車, 骑马/騎馬). 怪 *guài* 'strange; uncanny' has the left-hand heart radical (cf. 懂) and a right element (no longer an independent graph) that shows 'hand' (又) above 'ground' (土). (Mnemonic: The graph is sometimes glossed as 'hands opening up new or *strange* lands'.)

j. 认识/認識 *rènshi* 'know; recognize': Both traditional and simplified graphs are phonosemantic, with the speech radical (*yánzìpáng*) combining with sound-inspired elements. In the case of the first character, the phonetic elements are 忍 *rěn* (cf. 刃 *rèn*, 切 *rèn*) or 人 *rén*. In the case of the second character, the phonetic elements are 戠 or 只 *zhī/zhǐ* (seen in 职/職 *zhí* and 织/織 *zhī*).

k. 刚/剛 *gāng* 'strong; just; just now': The graph consists of the combining form of 刀 *dāo* 'knife'. (Mnemonic. The knife radical, as well as the solid-looking left-hand elements 冈/岡, suggest 'strong and just', with the latter meaning extended to 'precise' and 'just now'.) 冈/岡 *gāng* is the basis of a phonetic set that includes 岗/崗 *gāng* and 纲/綱 *gāng*. The traditional form, 岡, with 山 *shān* in the lower middle, should be distinguished from an entirely different graph (also traditional), 罔 *wǎng*, with 亡 *wáng* in the lower middle (cf. 忙 *máng*). 冈 *gāng* with 山 *shān*; traditional 罔 *wǎng* with 亡 *wáng*. The *gāng* set is consistently simplified with a cross; the *wǎng* set, however, is inconsistent: 惆 *wǎng* has only one form, but cf. 网/網 *wǎng* 'net'.

l. 甜 *tián* 'sweet' consists of 舌 *shé* 'tongue' (originally a representation of the tongue) and 甘 *gān* 'sweet; pleasant', said to have originally represented something held in the mouth (口), hence 'sweet to the tongue'. 甘 *gān* is phonetic in a number of rather rare characters, such as 柑 *gān* and 坩 *gān*.

21.1.1 [SC] Compounds and phrases

二等	来接我们	甜菜	一点都不甜	听不懂
èrděng	*lái jiē wǒmen*	*tián cài*	*yìdiǎn dōu bù tián*	*tīngbudǒng*
'second class'				
接客	回去	等车	觉得很奇怪	接着说
jiēkè	*huíqu*	*děng chē*	*juéde hěn qíguài*	*jiēzhe shuō*
				'continue talking'

回来 huílai	平常 píngcháng	平地 píngdì	穿上衣服 chuānshang yīfu	找钱 zhǎo qián
等一下 děngyixià	接电话 jiē diànhuà	回家 huíjiā	如果 rúguǒ	三十年如一日 sānshí nián rú yī rì
看得懂 kàndedǒng	等了一天 děngle yì tiān	甜点 tiándiǎn	奇怪的事情 qíguài de shìqing	懂了吗? Dǒng le ma?
一回事 yì huí shì	回国 huíguó	不认识她 bú rènshi tā	睡得很甜 shuì+de hěn tián	认识你真好 rènshi nǐ zhēn hǎo
不如 bùrú	如下 rú xià	刚下火车 gāng xià huǒchē	如鱼得水 rú yú dé shuǐ '[happy] as fish in water'	刚才说的 gāngcái shuō de
刚到 gāng dào	找朋友 zhǎo péngyou	奇怪的问题 qíguài de wèntí	认识几个字 rènshi jǐ ge zì	文化水平 wénhuà shuǐpíng 'cultural level'
北平 Běipíng	不平的地方 bù píng de dìfang	不认得路 bú rènde lù	男女平等 nánnǚ píngděng 'sexual equality'	甜活 tiánhuó 'cushy job'

21.1.2 [TC] Compounds and phrases

認錯人 rèncuò rén	如意 rúyì 'as one wishes'	雖然 suīrán	認不出她 rèn bu chū tā	剛要走 gāng yào zǒu
縣長 xiànzhǎng	認字 rènzì	農民 nóngmín	不認識他 bú rènshi tā	找你三塊吧 zhǎo nǐ sān kuài ba
剛好五塊 gānghǎo wǔ kuài	紅十字會 Hóngshízì Huì	找不著 zhǎobuzháo	農具 nóngjù	結兩次婚 jié liǎng cì hūn
家具 jiājù	教學 jiàoxué	直接 zhíjiē	往西直走 wǎng xī zhí zǒu	跟我沒關係 gēn wǒ méi guānxi

21.1.3 [SC] Comment and response

1. 哎(āi)，等了一个多小时，我不能再等了。/ 你先走吧，我等他们，没关系。

2. 这西瓜不错，很甜，哪里买的？/ 东门那儿，街上上午有个小车子，可以买他们的水果。

3. 你来得刚好，我正有事找你。/ 什么事？我一会儿得上课去，能不能下课以后再说？

4. 我懂一点儿日语；刚才你听不懂的是哪一部分？/ 就是他最后说的，好像是地方的名字。

5. 你听不懂就问吧，我认字是有问题，但听力还行。/ 哎，我听力真差。上课的时候，我没问题，都能听懂，但在外头，大家说得不怎么清楚，有点口音，用很多"儿"：出门儿，下本儿，什么的。听不懂。

6. 今天非常冷，风也很大，出去得多穿衣服。/ 风那么大，多穿衣服没用。听说是零下五度。还是在家里好，喝点热茶，看看书。

7. 你认识她多长时间了？/ 我们是九三年在上海认识的。我来上海学习汉语，她在酒店工作，我们是在公共汽车站等车认识的。

8. 谢谢你们来接我们。/ 别客气。你们是远方来的，应该来接你们。

9. 我今天有事儿，比平常晚一点回家，你先吃吧。/ 没关系，如果你可以八点以前回来，晚饭可以出去吃。

10. 这条路很平，车开得很舒服。/ 是很平，所以你多开一个小时，然后我们该吃饭。吃完饭以后，我开车，你睡在后头。应该夜里两三点以前到家。

11. 北京以前叫北平，对吗？/ 是啊，本来是因为城市在北边的一个平地上，所以叫北平。可是明朝，城市作首都的时候，名字叫北京。在1923年，KMT搬到南边的时候，还是用以前的名字，北平；但从1949年以后一直都用北京。

12. 今天什么时候回家？/ 今天因为有音乐会，晚一点才回家。回家以前我来找你，好不好？我们可以一起回去。

13. 奇怪，去年她汉语不如她那班的同学，可是今年说得、写得比同学好多
    了。/那不怎么奇怪。第一，她很用功。第二，她跟中国朋友在一起，
    他们说英文，她说中文。学得好，所以说得比同学都好。

NOTES

下本儿   *xiàběnr* 'invest capital' [in business]

首都   *shǒudū* 'capital city'

KMT   an abbreviation of Kuomintang, the Chinese Nationalist Party, founded by Sun
         Yat-sen in 1911; in pinyin, it would be transcribed as *Guómíndǎng*.

21.1.4 [SC] Comment and response

1. 你們是在哪兒認識的？/我們是在上海認識的，在上海火車站。

2. 我平常在街上一個小吃中心吃早點，吃粥和雞蛋。/粥啊，我也很喜歡吃
   粥，<u>加</u>點肉，青菜，很好吃。

3. 完蛋了，這車子又壞了。/對啊，那輛車已經有十五年了。你應該買輛新
   的，要不然買一輛自行車。

4. 天氣好怪啊。早上霧轉多雲，溫度零下，風力六級。/沒關係，多穿衣
   服，就好。外頭雖然有一點冷，但在河邊走走，還是很好玩兒。

NOTE

加   *jiā* 'add'

英文也可以从右到左。

21.1.5 [SC] 閱讀/阅读 *Yuèdú* 'Reading'

The reading for the first set of characters in this lesson (which is similar, but not identical, to a passage in an earlier spoken unit) includes a number of unfamiliar characters for (mostly) familiar words. Here they are listed, ahead of thc rcading, with pronunciation and, in some cases, a short commentary.

NOTES

电影	*diànyǐng*: 影; cf. 景 *jǐng* in 风景
首	*shǒu* 'head': *shǒudū* 'capital city'; also a measure for songs, poems
宿舍	*sùshè*: 舍; cf. 舒 *shū* in 舒服 and 啥 *shá*, the colloquial form of 什么
韩国	*Hánguó*
周末	*zhōumò*: cf. 末儿 'tip; end'; contrast with 木 *mù*, 本 *běn*, 未 *wèi*
棉袄	*mián'ǎo*: both with the combining form of 衣 *yī* 'clothes'
蒙古	*Měnggǔ*
年代	*niándài* 'decade'
春节	*Chūnjié*
叔叔	*shūshu* 'uncle; father's younger brother'
厨师	*chúshī*: 厨; cf. the traditional graph 樹 *shù* 'tree'
王府井	*Wángfǔjǐng*: 王府 'Prince's residence'; 井 'well', originally a representation of a traditional field system with a well in the middle
吵	*chǎo*: cf. 少 *shǎo*, 炒 *chǎo*
祝	*zhù* 'express good wishes for'

亲爱的张英, 你好:

　　我现在在北京！在去北京的飞机上不错, 看了两部电影, 听了很多首音乐。虽然很远, 　　有点不舒服, 可是很有意思。我是二月十七号到的。北京大学的孔老师来接我。我住的宿舍在北大, 离上课的地方不远。宿舍很大, 有六七个大楼。可是只有外国人能住在那里；有欧洲人, 美国人, 加拿大人, 日本人, 也有韩国人。虽然他们都懂英文, 可是因为有的同学说得不太好, 所以我们在一起, 我们平常都说中文, 很少说英文。看那么多外国人都在那里说中文, 中国人觉得很奇怪。北大的中国学生也想要跟我们说英文, 所以我们说话的时候, 他们跟我们说英文, 我们跟他们说中文。白天我们都出去上课, 吃饭, 做功课, 可是晚上回到宿舍来。周末我们去城里的小吃店吃饭, 然后去咖啡馆吃甜点。

北京冬天是从十一月到二月。非常冷，风也很大，可是不常下雪。今天是晴天，零下五度。虽然有一点冷，不过没关系，我有一件<u>棉袄</u>，那是中国人穿的衣服。我还有一顶<u>蒙古</u>帽子。中国朋友都说我像个七八十<u>年代</u>的中国人一样。

下个星期，因为是<u>春节</u>（就是外国人说的中国新年），所以中国同学都要回家过年。下星期四林老师请我去她<u>叔叔</u>的家吃饭。她叔叔是中国很有名的<u>厨师</u>，在北京大饭店工作。我们是上个星期在那儿认识他的。他六十多岁，住在<u>王府井</u>。他说在那已经生活二十五年了，虽然有点<u>吵</u>，可是他不想住别的地方。

那，我在北京已经三个星期了，觉得很好玩。还没去过长城。因为每天都忙着学习汉语，所以也许得等几个星期才能去别的地方。我这个学期上四门课，每天都有三四节课。班不大，都是小班，所以说中文的机会很多呀。功课不少，每天得听课文，学习汉字。那我只好"好好学习，天天向上"。

<u>祝</u>你新年快乐！
你的朋友，_____
2010.2.7

21.2 Second set

This set includes the character for the verbal particle *zhe,* which is discussed at length in Unit 15. The general function of V-*zhe* is to set the scene against which events take place: *shuōzhe shuōzhe* 'we were talking when'; *zhuōzi shang fàngzhe yí píng xiāngbīnjiǔ* 'a bottle of champagne had been placed on the table'; *ta xiàozhe gēn wǒ shuō* 'she smiled and said to me'; *tā zài shāfā shang zuòzhe ne* 'he was sitting on the sofa'. For details, review §15.5.

把	打	拉	拿	放
3 + 4	3 + 2	3 + 5	4 + 6	4R + 4
bǎ	*dǎ*	*lā*	*ná*	*fàng*
'take; handle'	'hit'	'pull'	'bring; take'	'put'
[focus marker]				

笑
6 + 4

跑
7 + 5

著
3 + 8

着
5 + 6

慢
3 + 11

快
3 + 4

xiào
'laugh'

pǎo
'run'

zhe/zhuó/zhāo
'wear; touch'
[verb suffix]

màn
'slow'

kuài
'fast'

畫
5 + 7

画
5 + 3

夠
3 + 8

够
3 + 8

極
4 + 8

极
4 + 3

huà
'draw; drawing'

gòu
'enough'

jí
'extreme; pole'

NOTES

a. The graphs 把 *bǎ*, 打 *dǎ*, 拉 *lā*, and 拿 *ná* all represent words that originally involved manipulation, hence the presence of 'hand', more or less intact in the case of 拿, or in the combining form in the case of the others. 把 shows clear phonetic connection with 巴 *bā* and other graphs such as 吧 *ba* and 爬 *pá* 'climb; hike'. 拉 shows phonetic contact with 垃 *lā* (as in *lājī* 'garbage') and the final particle 啦 *la* (used to represent *le + a*). 打, on the other hand, does not accord with the regular phonetic set formed with 丁 *dīng*, such as 顶/頂 *dǐng* 'top; M for hats' and 厅 *tīng* 'hall'. 拿 also does not show any affinity for the set based on 合 *hé*, such as 盒 *hé* 'box'.

b. For 放 *fàng* 'put; place', the left-hand element, 方 *fāng* is the basis of a well-populated phonetic set that includes 房 *fáng*, 访/訪 *fǎng*, 芳 *fāng*, and 旁 *páng* (the sound /p/ being quite close to /f/). The right-hand element is a common radical, as seen in the familiar 教 *jiāo/jiào* 'teaching', as well as in 政 *zhèng* (cf. *zhèngfǔ* 'government'), 敢 *gǎn* 'dare', 改 *gǎi* 'change', 收 *shōu* 'receive', and so on. (In 做 *zuò* 'do; make', the left-hand 'person' trumps.) In origin, the right-hand element is said to depict a hand holding a stick, and it is associated with forcefulness or causation (教, 政).

c. 笑 *xiào* 'laugh; smile' consists of bamboo (竹字头/頭), presumably selected for the aural association of splitting or burning bamboo with the noise of laughter (cf. English 'cracking up'), and the element 夭 *yāo*, also seen in 妖 *yāo* and 沃 *wò*. Contrast 夭, which has *piě* as its first stroke, with 天, which has *héng*. (Mnemonic: A *smile* resembles split bamboo; *laughter* is like the crackle and pop of burning bamboo.)

d. 跑 *pǎo* 'run' matches the mnemonically useful radical 足 *zú* 'leg' (originally a representation of a foot) to 包 *bāo* ('wrap / a bundle'), which is the basis for an extensive phonetic set that includes 饱/飽 *bǎo*, 胞 *bāo*, 抱 *bào*, 鲍/鮑 *bào*, and 泡 *pào*.

e. 着/著 represents a number of (ultimately related) words or word parts, including *zhe*, the common verb particle (笑着说/笑著說), *zhāo* 'make a move', *zháo* 'touch' (cf. 着急/著急 *zhāojí*, also *zháojí*), and *zhuó*, which is a formal word for 'put on clothes'. The simplified graph is actually a version of the traditional—a fluid reinterpretation of the 者 element, with no relationship whatsoever to graphs such as 看 or even 目. 者 *zhě* forms the basis of a 'broken' phonetic set that includes both 猪/豬 *zhū* 'pig' and 都 *dōu* 'all'.

f. 慢 *màn* 'slow' and 快 *kuài* 'fast' are both phonosemantic graphs with the vertical version of 'heart' as a radical and well-represented phonetic connections. For 慢, the heart radical combines with 曼 *màn*, which in turn forms a very reliable phonetic set that includes 漫, 蔓, and 鳗/鰻—all conveniently pronounced *màn* like the root element. 快 combines the heart radical with 夬 *guài*, which is rare as an independent character but forms the basis of a 'broken' phonetic set represented by graphs such as 块/塊 *kuài* on one hand and 决/決 *jué* (cf. 决定/決定 *juédìng* 'decide'), 诀/訣 *jué*, and 缺 *quē* on the other. 快 itself was also extended to represent 'speedy sticks; chopsticks', now written with the bamboo radical as 筷子 *kuàizi*, replacing another word, 箸 *zhù*, thought to have been avoided by boatmen because it sounded like 住 *zhù*, meaning 'stop' or 'get stuck'—bad news for boatmen.

g. 画/畫 *huà* 'draw; paint / drawing; painting': In both traditional and simplified graphs, 田 is assigned as a radical. The traditional graph contains 聿 *yù* (originally depicting a hand grasping a writing implement), which also appears in the traditional forms of 筆 *bǐ* 'writing implement' (but not the simplified 笔) and 書 *shū* 'book' (again, not in simplified 书). (Mnemonic: Both graphs contain what looks like an easel or a frame 田 for *drawing*.)

h. 够/夠 *gòu* 'enough': Before standardization, the traditional set wrote either 夠 or 够; the simplified set settled on the one with 多 on the right. In both cases, 夕 (one part of 多) is assigned as the radical. The non-多 element is 句, now used mainly to represent *jù* 'sentence'; formerly, it was also used for *gōu* 'hook; check mark / to hook', which accounts for its presence in the phonetic set illustrated by 狗 *gǒu* 'dog' and 苟 *gǒu*. In modern language, *gōu* 'hook' is represented by 钩/鉤 *gōu*, with 句 in the traditional and 勾 (both *gōu*). 勾 *gōu* itself has become specialized in the verbal meaning: 'cancel; cross out' (obviously related to the 'check mark' meaning). Distinguish among 句 *jù* 'sentence' (*gōu* 'hook'), 勾 *gōu* 'hook; check mark', and 勺 *sháo* 'spoon'. (Mnemonic: 多 is a lot, so 句 is added—on one side or the other—to indicate *enough* already!)

<u>Xiāngyá</u> 'inserting false teeth'

i. 极/極 *jí* 'extreme; pole': The wood radical, 木, represents a pole that supports a roof; the sense was extended to designate the geographical poles (北极/極; 南极/極) and extremes in general (好极/極了). The simplified graph substitutes a more common phonetic element, 及 (cf. 级/級 *jí*, 圾 *jī*) for a much rarer one, 亟 *jí*.

21.2.1 [SC] Compounds and phrases

把门打开	拿过来	打人	打水	不够好
bǎ mén dǎkāi	*ná guòlai*	*dǎ rén*	*dǎ shuǐ*	*bú gòu hǎo*
			'fetch water'	

跑马场	把画儿拿回去	打火机	画一张画	打个的去
pǎomǎchǎng	*bǎ huàr ná huíqu*	*dǎhuǒjī*	*huà yì zhāng huàr*	*dǎ ge dī qù*
		'a lighter'		

笑着跟我说	站着舒服	打错了	钱不够	拿走了
xiàozhe gēn wǒ shuō	*zhànzhe shūfu*	*dǎcuòle*	*qián bú gòu*	*názǒule*
		'wrong number'		

把东西放在那儿
bǎ dōngxi fàng zài nàr

多放点牛奶
duō fàng diǎnr niúnǎi

打字
dǎzì 'type'

放心
fàngxīn 'rest assured'

打个电话
dǎ ge diànhuà

拿不住东西
nábuzhù dōngxi

走得很慢
zǒu+de hěn màn

拿错了
nácuòle

开玩笑
kāi wánxiào

慢走
màn zǒu

笑起来了
xiào qǐlai le

说着说着
shuōzhe shuōzhe

画了个十字
huàle ge shí zì

快班
kuàibān

画上的美人
Huà shang de Měirén 'The Lady in the Painting'

下着雨
xiàzhe yǔ

说个笑话
shuō ge xiàohua

画得很好
huà+de hěn hǎo

非常慢
fēicháng màn

慢两分钟
màn liǎng fēn zhōng

快车
kuàichē

快乐
kuàilè

不要笑她
bú yào xiào tā

一张画儿
yì zhāng huàr

笑话
xiàohua

太阳快出来了
tàiyang kuài chūlai le

够了吗
gòu le ma

拉下水
lā xià shuǐ 'be pulled under'

北极
Běijí

拉面
lāmiàn

有三个笔画
yǒu sān ge bǐhuà

快要到了
kuài yào dào le

跑得快
pǎo+de kuài

打算
dǎsuàn

慢车
mànchē

画家
huàjiā

好极了
hǎo jíle

打酒
dǎjiǔ 'buy liquor'

不够高
bú gòu gāo

极大的
jídà de 'extremely large'

四方之极
Sìfāng zhī jí 'The Pivot of the Four Quarters'

拉丁美洲
Lādīng Měizhōu 'Latin America'

放音机
fàngyīnjī

跑了第一名
pǎole dì-yī míng

用马拉的车
yòng mǎ lā de chē

21.2.2 [TC] Compounds and phrases

畫狗畫得很好 *huà gǒu huà+de hěn hǎo*	中國畫報 *Zhōngguó Huàbào*	乙那個字只有一畫 *yǐ nèi ge zì zhǐyǒu yí huà*		畫像 *huàxiàng* 'draw a portrait'
極不好意思 *jí bù hǎo yìsi*	清楚極了 *qīngchu jíle*	極不認真 *jí bú rènzhēn*	筆畫 *bǐhuà*	走著走著 *zǒuzhe zǒuzhe*
咱們走著去吧 *zánmen zǒuzhe qù ba*	不夠清楚 *bú gòu qīngchu*	夠一個人吃 *gòu yí ge rén chī*	跑道 *pǎodào* 'runway'	不夠兩個人吃 *bú gòu liǎng ge rén chī*
找不著 *zhǎobuzháo*	找到了 *zhǎodàole*	一支筆 *yì zhī bǐ*	慢慢寫 *mànmān xiě*	寫得太快 *xiě+de tài kuài*

21.2.3 [SC] Comment and response

1. 这些菜刚够俩人吃的。/两个人吗？我刚请了两个同学，够不够四个人吃？

2. 你画的那只猪，头太大了，看起来像匹马，一点儿都不像个猪。/哪里有猪啊，我画了个象，不但头很大，每个地方都很大。

3. 我把你的行李放在屋子里，好不好？要不要先拿你想用的东西？/我来，我来。先把行李放在门后头，行吗？吃完饭以后我把东西拿上去。

4. 他走到屋子里一看，屋子里好像没人，没有家具，但是在地上，有一些已经做好的吃的东西，像拉面，饺子，水果，什么的。/那奇怪极了，是谁做的呢？屋子里只有那张画儿，画儿上只有个美丽的女人，是不是那位"画上的美人"做的呢?

5. 中文课每个星期有几节？/中文课有快班，也有慢班。有人觉得"慢班"不好听，说应该是非快班 — 开玩笑！快班一周五次，慢班一周三次。你看，快班快点儿，但不是特快。特快班有时候也有，学生很少；一周十次，很紧张。但不是每年都有。

6. 昨晚的晚会太好玩了，我差点笑死了。/笑什么？我觉得没什么意思，喝得太多，吃得太多，回到家后打不开门，等了一个小时才能进卧房睡觉，真叫人难受！

7. 三轮车，跑得快，上头坐个老太太，要五毛，给一块，你说奇怪不奇怪？/不怎么奇怪，也许她没有零钱。再说，车夫跑得快，应该多给一点钱。

8. 请把门打开，屋子里热死了。/门开着呢，你看。你坐这儿吧，这儿比较舒服，有微风。

NOTES

些   *xiē*

匹   *pǐ*: M for horses

特   *tè* 'special'

受   *shòu* 'receive; suffer'

零   *líng* 'zero'

微   *wēi* 'a small amount': cf. *Wēiruǎn* 'Microsoft'

21.3 Third set

The third set contains the 着/著 character again, but this time the focus is on its appearance in another context, where it represents a fully toned syllable *zhāo*.

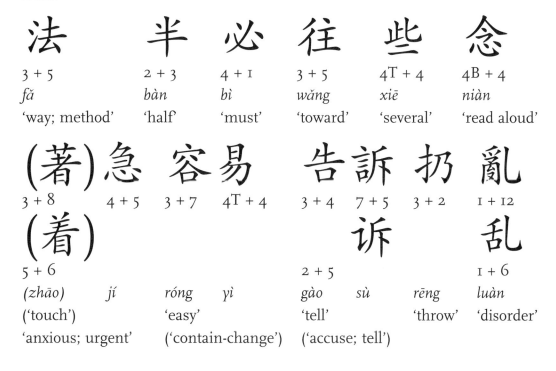

法	半	必	往	些	念
3 + 5	2 + 3	4 + 1	3 + 5	4T + 4	4B + 4
fǎ	*bàn*	*bì*	*wǎng*	*xiē*	*niàn*
'way; method'	'half'	'must'	'toward'	'several'	'read aloud'

(著) 急	容 易	告 訴	扔	亂
3 + 8	4 + 5 3 + 7	4T + 4 3 + 4	7 + 5 3 + 2	1 + 12
(着)		訴		乱
5 + 6		2 + 5		1 + 6
(zhāo) *jí*	*róng* *yì*	*gào* *sù*	*rēng*	*luàn*
('touch')	'easy'	'tell'	'throw'	'disorder'
'anxious; urgent'	('contain-change')	('accuse; tell')		

NOTES

a. 法 *fǎ* 'law; method' contains the water radical (cf. 河 *hé*, 江 *jiāng*), suggesting control, management, or channeling of water resources—meanings that fit with the core idea of method or law. The right-hand element, now represented as 去 *qù*, is a reinterpretation of what was originally 正 *zhèng* 'upright; correct', which is also a better fit with the meaning. (Mnemonic: A *method* for avoiding 去 floods 氵.)

b. 半 *bàn* 'half': The symmetry of the graph supports the meaning. The graph is categorized under radical 八 *bā* (the top two strokes), which is associated with division (as well as 'eight'). 伴 *bàn* 'partner' probably represents the same word, with the specialized meaning of 'partner' eventually differentiated by the addition of 人字旁 *rénzìpáng*.

c. 必 *bì* 'necessity' shows a line (*piě*), originally 弋 (an arrow with a string attached), through the heart, 心 *xīn*. (Mnemonic: *Necessity* leads you to go against your inclinations, 心.) 必 is phonetic in 密 *mì* 'secret'.

d. 往 *wǎng* 'toward; to' (also *wàng* in some regions). The original graph had 土 *tǔ* above 王 *wáng*, which reveals its original phonetic role. The whole was then reinterpreted, or simplified, as 主 *zhǔ*, thereby confusing 往 with another phonetic set based on 主 *zhǔ* (e.g., 注, 柱, 驻/駐, all of which are *zhù*). 王 is the basis for a phonetic set that includes 汪 *wāng*, 枉 *wǎng*, and 狂 *kuáng*. (Mnemonic: *approaching*—but not touching—the king)

e. 些 *xiē* 'several' consists of 此 *cǐ* (止 *zhǐ*, 匕 *qǐ*) above 二 *èr*, with 止 assigned as radical. 此 forms a phonetic set that includes 雌 *cí*, 疵 *cī*, and 紫 *zǐ* 'purple'. (Mnemonic: 二, *several* horizontals; 此 *several* verticals)

f. 念 *niàn* 'recall; read aloud; study' has 今 *jīn* above the radical 心. (Mnemonic: *Reading and studying*—which traditionally also involved reading aloud—is feeling 心 the past in the present 今.) 今 is the basis of a phonetic set that includes 矜, 琴, and 芩, all of which are *qín*. 念 as a whole is phonetic in a few uncommon characters, such as 捻 *nián* and 埝 *niàn*.

g. 急 *jí* 'anxious; urgent' combines 心 with a component that was originally written 及 *jí*. 着急/著急 *zhāojí* (*zháojí* for some) is literally 'touch anxiety'—'be anxious, worried'. (Mnemonic: Holding something against the heart to dispel *anxiety*.)

h. 容 *róng* 'demeanor; contain' combines the radical *bǎogàir* (宀) with 谷 *gǔ* 'valley; hollow'. 容 itself is phonetic in 溶 and 榕, both pronounced *róng*. 容 combines with 易 *yì*, originally 'change' (cf. 易经/經 *Yìjīng* 'Book of Changes') to form 容易 *róngyi* 'easy; likeable' ('containing-change'). 易 is the basis of a phonetic set that includes 踢 *tī* and 赐/賜 *cì*, though sound change has obscured any original phonetic contact.

i. 告 *gào* 'inform; announce; sue' has 口 assigned as a radical. It is phonetic in 诰/誥 *gào*, 造 *zào*, and 浩 *hào*. In the unit material, it is seen in combination with 诉/訴 *sù* 'inform; accuse', which is composed of the speech radical and 斤 (pronounced *chì*, which is not helpful). The same element appears in 拆 *chāi* 'dismantle; pull down', a character often seen around town marking buildings earmarked for demolition. (Mnemonic: Radicals for both characters, 告诉/告訴, suggest speech, hence *tell; inform*.)

j. 扔 *rēng* 'throw' combines the hand radical, 扌, with 乃, pronounced *nǎi* as an independent character, but in 扔 apparently represents the simplification of a more complex component that originally had nothing to do with 乃. 乃 *nǎi*, however, is matched with 奶 *nǎi* 'milk', and it also appears in the pictorial 孕 *yùn* (as in *huáiyùn* 'be pregnant'). (Mnemonic: 扔 has a hand for *throwing* plus a component that resembles a bow—to help you *throw*.)

k. 乱/亂 *luàn* 'disorder': The right-hand element (the radical in the *luàn* graphs, as it is in 乳 *rǔ* 'breast') has a noncombining form, 乙 (*yǐ*), that is seen in 乞 *qǐ* and 乾 *qián*. The complex left-hand element of the traditional graph, now a jumble of strokes, originally showed 'silk' and 'hands', suggesting a tangle (hence 'disorder; chaos'). The simplified graph substitutes 舌 *shé* 'tongue' for the jumble, with which it has only the initial *piě* stroke in common. (Mnemonic: The traditional graph contrasts *disorder*—the jumble on the left—with order, or the smooth line on the right; the simplified graph suggests that the tongue is the source of *chaos*.)

21.3.1 [SC] Compounds and phrases

没办法 *méi bànfǎ*	一些 *yìxiē*	急事儿 *jíshìr*	法国 *Fǎguó*	急急忙忙 *jíjí-mángmáng*	忘了告诉你 *wàngle gàosu nǐ*
半个 *bàn ge*	睡不着觉 *shuìbuzháo jiào*	往南走 *wǎng nán zǒu*	三点半 *sān diǎn bàn*	开往上海 *kāi wǎng Shànghǎi*	已经念到第 21单元 *yǐjīng niàn dao dì-21 dānyuán*
不必 *búbì*	念书 *niànshū*	不必要的 *bú bìyào de*	往前走 *wǎng qián zǒu*	可真不容易 *kě zhēn bù róngyi*	天下大乱 *tiānxià dàluàn*
一些水果 *yìxiē shuǐguǒ*	快些走 *kuài xiē zǒu*	看法 *kànfǎ*	想念他们 *xiǎngniàn tāmen*	这些东西 *zhèi xiē dōngxi*	有些什么人 *yǒu xiē shénme rén*
别着急 *bié zhāojí*	必不可少 *bìbùkěshǎo* 'indispensable'	走得很急 *zǒu + de hěn jí*	乱花钱 *luàn huā qián* 'spend recklessly'	着火了 *zháo huǒ le* 'catch on fire'	心急如火 *xīnjírúhuǒ* 'burn with impatience'

扔果皮 *rēng guǒpí*	心里乱极了 *xīnlǐ luàn jíle*	一半 *yíbàn*	扔了吧 *rēng le ba*	去告他 *qù gào tā*	现易后难 *xiānyì-hòunán*
广告	易经	美容师	笑容	把它扔出去	把信念给她听听
guǎnggào 'advertisement'	*Yì Jīng* 'Book of Changes'	*měiróngshī* 'beautician'	*xiàoróng* 'smiling face'	*bǎ tā rēng chūqu*	*bǎ xìn niàn gěi tā tīngting*

21.3.2 [TC] Compounds and phrases

三點半 *sān diǎn bàn*	半新半舊 *bànxīn-bànjiù*	舊衣服 *jiù yīfu*	舊思想 *jiù sīxiǎng*	婚姻法 *Hūnyīnfǎ* 'marriage law'	看法不對 *kànfǎ bú duì*
沒辦法 *méi bànfǎ*	往前看 *wǎng qián kàn*	往下說 *wǎng xià shuō*	開往上海 *kāiwǎng Shànghǎi* 'heading to Shanghai'	往哪兒騎 *wǎng nǎr qí*	金剛石 *jīngāngshí* 'diamond'
剛好 *gānghǎo*	認清是非 *rènqīngshìfēi*	緊急 *jǐnjí*	讓人給告了 *ràng rén gěi gào le* 'get sued by someone'	走著去 *zǒuzhe qù*	不必要的事兒 *bú bìyào de shìr*

21.3.3 [SC] Comment and response

1. 你别着急，她会开得很慢，不会有事的。/我真的很着急，你看，天气那么坏，已经下了很多雪，不下雪吧，就下雾，开车什么都看不见！

2. 来了三十多位客人，这些面怕不够吃呀。/不够的话，我们再做一些。

3. 真不容易，我想了半天，还是想不出个好听的名字。哎，真没办法。/中国狗狗的名字很简单，像丁丁、蛋蛋、点点、欢欢、四喜等等。你这只小狗是半白半黑的，那就叫它"小花"(*huā*)好了，很可爱。

4. 急事先办，不急的可以放一放。什么意思？/意思就是先做最着急的事儿。急事儿是什么？急事儿是紧急的事情。把紧急的事情先做完了以后，再做不急的事情。懂我的意思吗？

5. 车到山前必有路是什么意思？/意思是如果已经来到了山前，必定会有山上的路。意思是：事情到了一定的时候，必然有办法。比方说：这事儿，你别着急，车到山前必有路，一定会有办法的。

6. 请你告诉我到火车站怎么走？/火车站？火车站很近。你往南走五分钟，在十字路口儿那儿往左走，在前头一百米那就是火车站了。

7. 这怎么念："不要—什么地—乱扔果皮"。/那是"不要随(suí)地乱扔果皮"。果皮你知道，那是吃水果等等，不能吃的那些部分。乱就是没有条理，是非不分；比方说：乱说，乱来，乱吃，等等。不要随地乱扔果皮。随地就是 — 嗯，怎么说 — 就是每个地方，<u>任何</u>地方。"不要随地乱扔果皮"就是东西用完了以后，你不要仍在地上。

8. 快要上课的时候老师跟你们说什么呢？他说："上课"。你们就站起来跟他说："老师好"。然后呢？你们得站着，对吧？坐着不行。为什么呢？因为要是你们有点累的话，坐着很容易睡觉。站着说外语更好些。<u>当你们说对话的时候</u>，老师经常说："站着可以，坐着也可以"。这时候你们才可以坐下。

9. 你别把我的东西放乱了。/哦，对不起，地方不够大，我想把你的东西都放在旁边儿，<u>这样腾出空地够两个人念书</u>。

NOTES

做一些	*zuòyixiē*: Many speakers would prefer to use 煮一些, using the more specific word 煮 *zhǔ* 'boil; cook'.
任何	*rènhé*: 'any, whatever'
当……的时候	*dāng . . . de shíhou*: a more formal version of the 'when' construction
对话	*duìhuà* 'dialogues' ('facing-speech')
这样腾出空地够两个人念书	*téngchū kōngdì* 'clear away a space for'

Zhàntái bú shì yóulèchǎng. 'The platform isn't a playground.'

21.4 Fourth set

鳥	談	賣	帶	讓	舊
11 + 0	7 + 8	7 + 8	3 + 8	7 + 17	6 + 11
鸟	谈	卖	带	让	旧
5 + 0	2 + 8	2 + 6	3 + 6	2 + 3	1 + 4
niǎo	*tán*	*mài*	*dài*	*ràng*	*jiù*
'bird'	'converse'	'sell'	'belt / take; bring'	'yield; make; let'	'old; used'

船	越	替	久
6 + 5	7 + 5	4 + 8	1 + 2
chuán	*yuè*	*tì*	*jiǔ*
'boat'	'exceed; the more'	'for; in place of'	'long time'

NOTES

a. 乌/鳥 *niǎo* 'bird' is one of a number of animal characters, such as 马/馬 *mǎ* 'horse', 象 *xiàng* 'elephant', 鼠 *shǔ* 'mouse', 龙/龍 *lóng* 'dragon', and 鱼/魚 *yú* 'fish', whose pictorial origins are still vaguely discernible and which have radical status (cf. §13.7 in the elementary volume.) The simplified graph, which reflects traditional calligraphic forms, reduces the number of strokes by half while keeping a family resemblance to the original—an ideal simplification. 乌/鳥 is assigned the radical in many graphs for bird names: cf. 鸭/鴨 *yā* 'duck', 鸦/雅 *yā* 'crow', 鸽/鴿 *gē* 'dove'.

b. 谈/談 *tán* 'converse; chat' combines the speech radical (讠/言) with 炎 *yán* 'inflamed; -itis' (made up of two 火 components, appropriately). 炎 is the basis for the phonetic set that includes 淡 *dàn* 'shallow', 痰 *tán* 'phlegm' (cf. 吐痰 *tǔtán* 'expectorate'), and 氮 *dàn* 'nitrogen'. (Mnemonic: 言 + 炎 suggests hot topics for *discussion*.)

c. 卖/賣 *mài* 'sell' is instantly recognizable as a relative of 买/買 *mǎi* 'buy'. The traditional graph has the transaction radical, 贝/貝, said to have originally depicted a cowrie shell, which was once used as currency along China's southern coast. 贝/貝 shows up in characters such as 财/財 *cái* 'wealth', 贸/貿 *mào* 'trade', and 资/資 *zī* 'charges; capital'. The simplified graph substitutes 头 for the complicated innards, but it keeps the top to retain a family resemblance to the original. (Mnemonic: The hat, 卖/賣, marks a specialist, the one *selling*; the buyer, 买/買, wears no hat.)

d. 带/帶 *dài* 'belt / carry with; bring; take': The top parts resemble a belt or sash, reinforced by the radical, 巾 'cloth'. From 'sash' or 'belt' come meanings such as 'bring' and 'lead'.

e. 让/讓 *ràng* 'yield; allow; let; make': The traditional graph has speech plus a complex component, 襄 *xiāng*, that is the basis of a phonetic set including 娘/孃 *niáng*, 酿/釀 *niàng*, 嚷 *rāng*, 瓤 *ráng*, and 壤 *rǎng*. Fortunately, the simplified form substitutes a simpler, though less apt, phonetic element—上.

f. 旧/舊 *jiù* 'old; used': The traditional graph combines 臼 *jiù* with 萑 *huán* (cf. 歡 *huān*), and 臼 is assigned as radical despite the phonetic association; cf. 舅 *jiù*, in which it is also the radical, and 舂 *chōng* and 插 *chà*, where it is not. (Mnemonic: 臼 in the traditional form shows a box coming apart at the seams, hence *old*; the simplified 旧 shows the side falling off.)

g. 船 *chuán* 'boat' has 舟 *zhōu*, which originally depicted a kind of boat and is now common as a radical in boat words: 航 *háng* 'navigate' (cf. 航空公司 *hángkōng gōngsī* 'airline company'), 舱/艙 *cāng* 'cabin', and 舰/艦 *jiàn* 'warship'. The right-hand component is seen in 沿 *yán* and 铅/鉛 *qiān* 'lead', and it should be distinguished from the right-hand component of 般 *bān* (*yìbān* 'in general') and 搬 *bān* 'move'. (Mnemonic: 舟 looks vaguely like a *boat*; the right-hand element in 船 is sealed at the bottom, so it floats—versus 般.)

h. 越 *yuè* 'exceed; the more' combines 走 *zǒu* as a radical with a right-hand element that is also pronounced *yuè* (cf. 钺/鉞 *yuè*) and originally depicted the weapon known as a halberd—a kind of axe (an extension to 戈 *gē* 'spear'); cf. 成 *chéng* 'become' in the fifth set of this unit, which has a different extension to 戈. (Mnemonic: 走 walking with a weapon and getting *more and more* exhausted.)

i. 替 *tì* 'in place of' consists of two 夫 *fū* 'person; man' components and the horizontal 曰 (rather than the vertical 日 *rì*), which is the designated radical. Originally, the graph showed two 立 components above a 自; the whole graph was later simplified to its current form. (Mnemonic: One person夫 *replacing* another夫.)

j. 久 *jiǔ* 'long time': This character is said to have originally been a person (人 *rén*) with a hindrance, hence he or she is slowed down and requires a longer duration. Even if not precisely so, this provides us with a mnemonic. The graph is phonetic in 玖 *jiǔ*, 疚 *jiù*, and 灸 *jiǔ*. Contrast with 夕 *xī*, 外 *wài*, and 入 *rù*.

21.4.1 [SC] Compounds and phrases

带东西	旧衣服	两只船	越来越快	热带	谈话
dài dōngxi	*jiù yīfu*	*liǎng zhī chuán*	*yuè lái yuè kuài*	*rèdài*	*tánhuà*
那只鸟	不久	飞着的鸟儿	书包带	没人能替他	多久
nà zhī niǎo	*bù jiǔ*	*fēizhe de niǎor*	*shūbāodài*	*méi rén néng tì tā*	*duō jiǔ*
她是船长	两本旧书	早起的鸟儿	谈一个问题	好久不见	旧事
tā shi chuánzhǎng	*liǎng běn jiùshū*	*zǎo qǐ de niǎor*	*tán yí ge wèntí*	*hǎo jiǔ bú jiàn*	*jiùshì*
水越来越高	让位	谁的船快？	鸟儿就飞走	谈话	他把她让进屋里
shuǐ yuè lái yuè gāo	*ràng wèi*	*shéi de chuán kuài*	*niǎor jiù fēizǒu*	*tánhuà*	*tā bǎ tā ràng jìn wū lǐ*
他是个船工	船不慢	替死鬼	很久以前	带鱼	把船拿到河里
tā shi ge chuángōng 'he's a boatman'	*chuán bú màn*	*tìsǐguǐ* 'scapegoat'	*hěn jiǔ yǐqián*	*dàiyú* 'ribbonfish'	*bǎ chuán ná dao hé lǐ*

替她们着急　　我替你去　　鸟儿的毛　　　代替别人上班　　　　　　五号替他
上场

tì tāmen　　　　wǒ tì nǐ qù　　niǎor de máo　　dàitì biérén　　　　　wǔ hào tì tā
zhāojí　　　　　　　　　　　　　　　　　　　shàngbān　　　　　　shàng chǎng
'number
five takes
the field for
him'

脸上也带着笑的样子　　　　长城一带　　正在谈天　　飞着的鸟儿　越想越觉
得没意思
Liǎn shang yě dàizhe xiào de　Cháng Chéng　zhèngzài　　fēizhe de niǎor　yuè xiǎng
yàngzi　　　　　　　　　　yí dài　　　tántiān　　　　　　　　yuè juéde
méi yìsi

21.4.2 [TC] Compounds and phrases

談談心談談愛　　談天說地　　面談　　　　會談　　　　　做買賣
tántán xīn tántán　tántiān-shuōdì　miàntán　　huìtán　　　　zuò
ài　　　　　　　　　　　　'interview'　　'hold discussions'　mǎimài

賣國　　　　賣唱　　　　舊車　　　　舊思想　　　　舊家具
màiguó　　　màichàng　　jiùchē　　　jiùsīxiǎng　　jiù jiājù
'betray one's　'sing for a
country'　　living'

帶路　　　　長江一帶　　我告訴你　　帶25公斤行李
dàilù　　　　Cháng Jiāng　wǒ gàosu nǐ　dài 25 gōngjīn xíngli
'show the way'　yídài

她讓人給告了.　心裡亂極了　出了個亂子　　接到了發來的告急電
Tā ràng rén gěi　xīnlǐ luàn jíle　chūle ge luànzi　jiēdàole fālái de gàojídiàn
gào le.　　　　　　　　　'got into some　'received the urgent tele-
'She was sued by　　　　difficulties'　gram that was sent'
someone.'

常亂說話	報紙	手工紙	紙黃金紙白銀
cháng luàn	*bàozhǐ*	*shǒugōngzhǐ*	*zhǐhuángjīn*
shuōhuà		'handcrafted paper'	*zhǐbáiyín*

臉蛋	三花臉兒	臉上畫的黑點
liǎndàn	*sānhuāliǎnr*	*liǎn shang huà de*
'cheeks'	'opera clown;	*hēidiǎn*
	ugly face'	'black dots painted
		on the face'

21.4.3 [SC] Comment and response

1. 在木船上工作的人是什么人？/在木船上工作的人，那是不是个船夫？或是个船户？船户、船夫，差不多。但船夫是在水上以船为家的人，跟船员有点不同。船员是在船上工作的人员。船只，船只是什么？船只[zhī]就是船的意思。船夫也有人叫船老大。

2. 这件毛衣才买了一年，已经穿得很旧了。/一分钱，一分货。货就是东西的意思。/你的意思是东西越贵越好。/那是我的意思？我想不一定越贵越好，可是有关系。很便宜的毛衣也许不会穿很久。

3. 那位老太太每天去买报纸不是因为要看报，是因为要跟人们谈天。/那好，老人不应该从早到晚都在家里，应该出门，找朋友，做事，买些东西，跟人们谈谈。

4. <u>走鹃</u>不会飞但跑得很快。/是啊，是南加州，墨[mò]西哥的一种鸟。听说自行车跑不过它。

5. 你最好替我们去问问有没有人民币。如果有的话，那我们想买五千元。/你卖美金吗？/是啊。美金；大概一千六到七百块。

6. 他自己不着急，你何必替他着急？/他第一次跑马拉松(sōng)，跑二十七英里那么远，爸爸不能不替他着急！

7. 阿林，你可不可以带新同学去见他们的老师？/现在吗？他们是不是都有同个老师？/都是中文系的孔老师。他在办公室里等你们。/好，咱们走吧。带你们到中文系。

8. "早起的鸟儿有虫吃"，你同意不同意？/你的意思是早睡觉早起来比晚睡觉晚起来好？对鸟来说，也许这样说有道理，因为虫子是早起所以鸟也得早起。但我自己觉得晚睡晚起也好，只要你睡的时间不越过七八个小时。

9. 你看，报上说在中国，越贵的车卖得越好，像宾利、<u>劳斯莱斯</u>、还有刚进入(rù)中国不久的<u>阿斯顿马丁</u>。/只买贵的不买对的！中国的车市是这样；什么贵买什么，越贵越火!

NOTES

走鹃	zǒujuān 'roadrunner': cf. 杜鹃 dùjuān 'cuckoo'
虫(子)	chóng(zi) 'insect'
宾利	Bīnlì
劳斯莱斯	Láosīláisī
阿斯顿马丁	Āsīdùn Mǎdīng

21.4.4 [TC] Comment and response

1. 新的放在上頭，舊的放在底下。/何必把舊的放在底下呢？舊的可以扔出去，沒用了。/等一下，等一下，讓我想一想。雖然是舊的，可是我還能用，不要把舊東西扔了，放在底下就行了。

2. 你知道"晚安 不能亂說嗎？/為什麼不能亂說？/我告訴你：晚安的拼音是ＷＡＮＡＮ：每個字母都說成一個字：W＝我，A＝愛，等等。晚安就是我愛你愛你。/亂說！哪裡有人會這樣想的？

3. 第二天他帶著兩個人到王大山家去了。見著王大山，他告訴他：國王叫他們每天送兩只鳥兒去，一定要在吃晚飯以前送到。/國王晚飯平常吃鳥兒嗎。很奇怪！

4. 我要跟你談一談。/談什麼？/我看你有兩輛自行車，你可不可以賣給我一輛？/那讓我想一想。本來有一輛是給我姐姐騎的，但她很少來這兒，用得比較少。那我送給你，好了，不要錢，反正是輛舊的。

5. 你是否願意這個男子成為你的丈夫？/我願意。/好。那，你是否願意這個女子成為你的妻子？/我願意。/好，恭喜你們結為夫妻。

21.5 Fifth set

成	怕	臉	紙	發	願
4 + 2	3 + 5	4 + 13	6 + 4	5 + 7	9 + 10
		脸	纸	发	愿
		4 + 7	3 + 4	2 + 3	4 + 10
chéng	*pà*	*liǎn*	*zhǐ*	*fā*	*yuàn*
'become; into'	'afraid'	'face'	'paper'	'issue; start'	'willing; wish'

唱	歌	送	底	吹	黑
3 + 8	4 + 10	3 + 6	3 + 5	3 + 4	12 + 0
chàng	*gē*	*sòng*	*dǐ*	*chuī*	*hēi*
'sing'	'song'	'give a gift; escort'	'base; under'	'blow'	'black'

NOTES

a. 成 *chéng* 'become; change into' consists of the radical 戈 *gē* 'spear' (cf. 我 *wǒ*, 或 *huò*) and a kneeling extension to the left. The graph forms a phonetic set that includes 城 *chéng* 'city', as well as 盛 *chéng* (*shèng*) and 诚/誠 *chéng*. 成 shows just one of a number of very similar left-leaning extensions that can be added to 戈. Others include 戊 *wù* (the fifth of the ten celestial stems, 甲乙丙丁戊), 戌 *xū*, 戍 *shù*, 戎 *róng*, and the right-hand side of 越 *yuè* that no longer occurs as an independent graph. [Mnemonic: Modification of the spear *into* other weapons.]

b. 怕 *pà* 'fear; be afraid' combines the heart radical with 白 *bái* 'white', the basis of an extensive phonetic set: 伯 *bó* (伯父 *bófù*), 怕 *pà*, 拍 *pāi*, 迫 *pǎi* and *pò*. (Mnemonic: Heart *fearful*; face white with *fear*.)

c. 脸/臉 *liǎn* 'face' combines the flesh radical 肉 *ròu* (in its left-side form) with 金/僉 *qiān*, the basis for the phonetic set that includes 签/簽 *qiān*, 剑/劍 *jiàn*, and 险/險 *xiǎn*. (Mnemonic: 金/僉 resembles a face, as confirmed by the flesh radical.)

d. 纸/紙 *zhǐ* 'paper' combines the silk radical (paper was high quality in ancient times) with 氏 *shì* 'clan', which shows phonetic contact with a few other graphs, such as 舐 *shì*. 氏 should be distinguished from 氐 *dī*, with the extra stroke on the bottom, which forms a more substantial phonetic set that includes 底 *dǐ*, 抵 *dǐ*, and 低 *dī*. (Mnemonic: association of silk and *paper*; 氏 resembles a writing desk)

e. 发/發 *fā* 'issue; start': The traditional form has the relatively rare radical formed by the top five strokes and glossed as 'climb' (cf. 癸 *guǐ*, the last of the Ten Heavenly Stems, and 登 *dēng*). The simplified form completely reworks the graph, ignoring its historical provenance and adding strokes to 友 *yǒu* 'friend' to create a graph that is barely relatable to the original. 发 is also the simplified version of 髮 *fà* 'hair'; therefore, traditional 發 *fā* and 髮 *fà* merge to 发 *fā* and *fà*. The traditional graph contains 弓 *gōng* 'bow', an allusion to the core meaning of 'issue; start'. The right-hand inner element is seen in 搬 *bān*.

f. 愿/願 *yuàn* 'willing': Both graphs contain 原 *yuán* (cf. 源 *yuán* 'source; origin'), but the simplified form shifts from 页/頁 *yè* 'page / leaf of a door' to the heart radical, which seems more attuned to the meaning of 'willing'.

g. 唱 *chàng* 'sing' consists of the mouth radical (口) and 昌 *chāng*; cf. 倡 *chàng*, 娼 *chāng*, 猖 *chāng*. (Mnemonic: Song, emanating 口 from a stout-bodied opera *singer* 昌.) 歌 *gē* 'song' has 欠 *qiàn* 'owe' as the radical (cf. 吹 *chuī*, 次 *cì*, 歡/欢 *huān*, and 砍 *kǎn*), along with 哥 *gē* 'older brother'. (Mnemonic: Older brother, with arms spread, singing a love *song*.)

h. 送 *sòng* 'present a gift; escort; give a ride to': The graph is composed of the travel radical 辶 (cf. 边/邊 *biān*, 过/過 *guò*, 远/遠 *yuǎn*, 还/還 *hái* and *huán* 'return', and 进/進 *jìn*) and 关 *guān*, which also happens to be the simplified version of 關 *guān* 'close'. (Mnemonic: 辶 for movement, and 关 resembles a delivery man; hence *escort* and *present*.)

i. 底 *dǐ* 'under; below; end' combines the three-stroke radical, often glossed as 'shelter' (seen also in 度 *dù*, 店 *diàn*, and traditional—but not simplified—廁/厠 *cè*) and 氐 *dī* (not 氏 *shì*), the core of the phonetic set cited in note d. (Mnemonic: *Under* a roof, with the dot marking *below*.)

j. 吹 *chuī* 'blow' combines radical 口 with 欠, pronounced *qiàn* on its own meaning 'owe'. 欠 forms a series that shows vestigial phonetic connections; for example, 炊 *chuī* 'cook' and 次 *cì*. It is more common as a radical (cf. 歌 and others listed in note g.) (Mnemonic: *Blowing* through the mouth 口; 欠 resembles a person beneath a wind vane.)

k. 黑 *hēi* 'black': The original form of the graph is said to show specks of soot on a window (which is a sufficiently good mnemonic for the meaning). The character is a unitary form (hence the designation 12 + 0) that appears as a radical in characters such as 點 *diǎn* (but not simplified 点), 墨 *mò* 'ink', and 默 *mò* 'silent'.

21.5.1 [SC] Compounds and phrases

心里有点怕	黑马	纸作的鸟儿	不愿意卖	吹了一口气
xīnlǐ yǒu diǎn pà	*hēimǎ*	*zhǐ zuò de niǎor*	*bú yuànyi mài*	*chuīle yì kǒu qì* 'exhale a sigh of relief'
唱得很好	发现	不怕慢	唱歌	送去以后
chàng+de hěn hǎo	*fāxiàn* 'discover'	*bú pà màn*	*chànggē*	*sòngqu yǐhòu*

头发 *tóufa*	发明 *fāmíng*	吹牛 *chuīniú* 'brag'	出发 *chūfā* 'start [a journey]'	不用怕 *bú yòng pà*
白纸 *báizhǐ*	没脸 *méi liǎn* 'lack face'	成人 *chéngrén* 'adult'	民歌 *míngē*	底下 *dǐxià*
天不怕，地不怕 *tiān bú pà, dì bú pà*	红脸 *hóngliǎn*	愿意不愿意 *yuànyi bú yuànyi*	纸老虎 *zhǐ laohù* 'paper tiger'	成功 *chénggōng*
天黑了 *tiān hēi le*	年底 *niándǐ*	吹火 *chuī huǒ*	脸蛋 *liǎndàn* 'cheek'	他成了一个船员 *tā chéngle yí ge chuányuán*
恭喜发财 *gōngxǐ fācái* [New Year's greeting]	成语 *chéngyǔ* 'four-character idiom'	唱片 *chàngpiàn* 'a record'	黑市 *hēishì* 'black market'	黑白分明 *hēibáifēnmíng*
风吹雨打 *fēng chuī yǔ dǎ*	黑夜 *hēi yè*	成果 *chéngguǒ* 'results; fruit'	自觉自愿 *zìjuézìyuàn* 'voluntarily'	四分之一叫一成 *sì fēn zhī yī jiào yì chéng*
这件事吹了. *Zhè jiàn shì chuī le.* 'It fell through.'	歌手 *gēshǒu* 'singer'	笑脸 *xiàoliǎn*	唱本 *chàngběn*	发电子邮件 *fā diànzǐ yóujiàn*

21.5.2 [SC] Comment and response

1. 他的家住在城外，离工作的地方不远。他每天早上上班的路上，可以看
   看山，看看水，有时候还唱唱歌。/唱歌？唱的也许是民歌吧。/没错，
   唱的有的是民歌，有的也不是。我听他唱过的有"东方红"、"东山<u>飘</u>雨西
   山晴"、"<u>阳光</u>总在风雨后"、"小城故事"等。/那么多呀！他像是个歌手
   吧！

2. 让我为你唱一首歌！/什么歌？/"我不愿让你一个人"，听过吗？/当然听过，五月天的。五月天，台湾的，五个成员，主唱是阿信，还有两个吉他手，一个贝斯，一个鼓手。唱的是"心中无别人"（无念 wú，是没有的意思），还有其他的。他们以前是SoBand –很奇怪的名字。你为什么要唱"我不愿让你一个人"那首？/因为我最近跟女朋友吹了。很难过。

3. 阿妹，小毕在找你，看起来很着急。她急成那个样子，必定是有要紧的事儿要告诉你！/那难怪，我两三个星期都没有见到她了。他有什么事儿现在要找我呢？

4. 我要把这些东西都扔了，没用了。/别扔，别扔，还是有用的，你给我，我可以把东西拿走，我有用，有的我自己要，那些家具我可以送给同学，他们房子里没什么家具。

5. 请问，这个字是不是念"东"？　水"东"成冰？水就是开水的水，喝水的水；冰就是放在杯里的冰块。我看第二个字，右边是个东字，东南西北的东，所以应该念东，对吗？/差不多，可是那个字不是平声，是去声，念 dòng，"水冻成冰"。你懂这个意思吗？/懂，水经过非常冷的一段时间就会冻成冰，经过很热的一段时间就会热成汽。

6. 天不怕，地不怕，只怕外国人说中国话。我很喜欢那个说法。/你太客气了，你和同学们说得已经很不错啦，哪里还怕外国人说中国话？/开玩笑。就是我们的口音好，用法还是有问题。所以还得接着说一句话：活到老，学到老，还有三分学不到。

7. 洗脸，是每个人每天必须做的事情，但不要以为洗脸是件很简单的事情。/你开玩笑吧，洗脸哪里是不简单的事？脸上有什么黑黑的，用手把水放在脸上，这样。很快就把黑黑的洗出来。/好极了。我的意思是你应该洗洗脸。现在洗好了，没问题。走吧。

8. 你那个手机发电子邮件要钱吗？/我这个有免费发邮件的软件，发多少都是免费的。/那你能不能替我发一个邮件？/行，发给谁？/发给陈老师，告诉他飞机六点才到，我先带客人到酒店，然后送他们到他那儿，大概八点到。谢谢！

9. 那两个人在门外头，看见她用纸做了两只纸鸟儿。鸟儿做好了以后，她对着纸鸟儿吹了一口气，两只鸟儿就飞起来了。/你说的故事我听过。

做纸乌儿，吹一口气的是个<u>美丽</u>的女人，就是"画儿上的美人"，对吗？在看她的那两个男人是国王的下手，他们本来得找两只乌儿给国王，但因为乌儿都飞走了，他们找不着什么乌儿，怕国王会生气，美人就用纸给他们做了两只。最后他们把乌儿送到国王那儿，就没有问题了。

10. 头发为什么白？有什么办法让白头发<u>变</u>黑呢？/你这个问题很奇怪！你怕有白头发吗？白头发很好看，长白发也很美。<u>何必</u>把白变黑？<u>年轻人</u>是黑头发，老年人是白头发，应该这样子。男女40岁以后，白发越来越多，没办法。

11. 本人在广东，十月底要去北京。看天气预报白天最高温度15-18度，夜里，4-6。应该带些什么样的衣服呢？要带大衣吗？/十月底天气还不会太冷，大衣是还用不着穿，但是毛衣要穿的。你是南方人，还是带一两件毛衣吧，那些衣服也<u>足够</u>了。

NOTES

飘	*piāo*	'flutter; drift about'
阳光	*yángguāng*	'sunlight'
主唱	*zhǔchàng*	'lead singer'
吉他	*jítā*	
贝斯	*bèisī*	
鼓手	*gǔshǒu*	'drummer'
平声	*píngshēng*	'level tone'
一段	*yí duàn*	'section; segment'
邮件	*yóujiàn*	'e-mail'
免费	*miǎnfèi*	'free of charge' ('avoid payment')
软件	*ruǎnjiàn*	'software'
故事	*gùshi*	'story'
美丽	*měilì*	'beautiful'
变	*biàn*	'change'
何必	*hébì*	'why is it necessary'
年轻人	*niánqīngrén*	'youth; young people'
足够	*zúgòu*	'sufficient'

21.6 [TC/SC] On the street #8

21.6.1 Restaurant signs for regional cuisine

川鲁粤家常菜	*Chuān-Lǔ-Yuè Jiāchángcài* [TC]
川滇粤	*Chuān-Diān-Yuè* [TC]

NOTES

川 = 四川

鲁/鲁 *Lǔ* = 山东/東 (北方)

粤/粤 *Yuè* = 广/廣东

滇 *Diān* = 云/雲南

清真涮羊肉   *Qīngzhēn Shuànyángròu* [SC = TC]

NOTES

清真   *qīngzhēn* 'purity; Islam; Muslim; kosher'

涮   *shuàn* 'rinse; cook thin slices of meat rapidly': a Muslim specialty

21.6.2 Restaurant names

For generic reference to restaurants in Chinese, the most common words are probably *cāntīng*, *fàndiàn*, and *fànguǎnr*. Restaurant names, however, can include a host of other words depending on size, region, and many other factors. These include *jiǔdiàn*, *jiǔjiā*, *jiǔlóu*, *lóu*, *fàndiàn*, *diàn*, *cāntīng*, *cānguǎn*, and *fànzhuāng*. Here are some examples from all over the world.

大日子酒家	'Great Day Restaurant' [TC = SC]
康乐酒家	康乐 *kānglè* 'wholesome; peaceful and happy' [SC]
海鲜酒家	海鲜 *hǎixiān* 'seafood' ('sea-fresh') [SC]
新星酒家:火锅	新星 *xīnxīng* 'new star'; 火锅 *huǒguō* 'hot pot' [SC]
红宝石大酒店	红宝石 *hóngbǎoshí* 'ruby' [TC]
幸运楼	幸运 *xìngyùn* 'good fortune' [SC]
饺子楼	[SC]
美味樓	美味 *měiwèi* 'delicious food' [TC]
花园饭店	花园 *huāyuán* 'garden' ('flower-garden') [SC]
烧鸭店	烧鸭 *shāoyā* 'roast duck' [SC]

Kǎiyuè Jiǔjiā 'The Hyatt?' (*Hūhéhàotè*)

21.6.3 Miscellaneous signs

外卖	*wàimài* '[food] to go' ('out-sell') [SC]
粥面粉饭	*zhōu-miàn-fěn-fàn* 'gruel noodles; wheat vermicelli' ('bean, rice, sweet potato starch-rice') [SC]
卡拉ＯＫ夜總會	*Kǎlā-OK Yèzǒnghuì* 'karaoke nightclub' [TC]
金山銀行	*yínháng* 'bank' ('silver-business') [TC]
中国人民邮政	*yóuzhèng* 'post office' ('post-government') [SC]
烟酒	*yānjiǔ* 'tobacco and wine' [SC]
旅馆	*lǚguǎn* 'hotel' [SC]
淋浴	*línyù* 'showers' [SC]
发/髮	*fà* 'hair(cuts)' [SC/TC]
眼镜公司	*yǎnjìng* 'glasses' ('eye-mirror') [SC]
打字,复印,照相,扫描	*dǎzì, fùyìn, zhàoxiàng, sǎomiáo* 'typing, copying, photos, scanning' [SC]

21.6.4 A public notice [SC = TC]

文明方便，清新自然

wénmíng fāngbiàn, qīngxīn zìrán

A civic notice, urging people to behave well

('in a civil and civilized fashion, with a fresh and pleasing manner')

NOTES

wénmíng	'civilization; culture / cultured; proper behavior'
fāngbiàn	'convenient'
qīngxīn	'fresh and new'
zìrán	'natural'

结束语/結束語 *Jiéshùyǔ* 'The end' ('conclude-language')

This concludes the character lessons. By now, you have come to understand the principles of the writing system, you have gotten used to a system that uses characters as a medium to convey information, and you have a basic repertoire of some 550 characters. At this point, it is recommended that you proceed with material that has a strong narrative structure, such as traditional stories—which also convey interesting cultural content. Yale University Press has published a number of such works for students, including *The Lady in the Painting* (画上的美人/畫上的美人 *Huàshang de Měirén*), an adaptation of a traditional folk tale, and *Strange Stories from a Chinese Studio* (聊斋故事/聊齋故事 *Liáozhāi Gùshi*), which contains simplified versions of twenty tales adapted from the Chinese classic *Liáozhāi Zhìyì* '*Strange Tales from a Chinese Studio*'. Teachers will know of other options that are at an appropriate level. Regardless of the choice of material, it will make sense for most of you to read primarily in the simplified character set, observing the relationship between the simplified and traditional versions of new characters and occasionally reading or rereading continuous text in the traditional set.

吉祥如意

jíxiáng-rúyì

'May you have good fortune and realize your desires.'

Zhōngyú jiéshù le! 'Finished at last!'

Appendix 1 MENUS AND DINING

Contents

A: The menu

B: Usage

A: The menu

1. A sample menu

This sample menu is a compilation of many menus, both from within China and abroad. The dishes are organized in the usual way—by type (appetizers, seafood, stir-fried, pork dishes, and so on)—and each is named, first in Chinese (pinyin), then in English, and finally in characters (simplified then traditional). The English generally includes a word-for-word gloss (in parentheses) and, where possible, a typical name for the dish; for example, *fānqié-chǎojīdàn* 'tomato omelet' ('tomato fried-eggs'). If additional information is included, then it is placed after a colon: *bàngbàngjī* 'shredded boiled chicken': with spicy sauce, served cold.

As you would imagine, the names of dishes and the dishes themselves vary widely over the vast world of Chinese cuisine. The menu that follows serves to give you a feel for the range and nomenclature of Chinese dishes—but one should be prepared for a lot of variation.

With all the linguistic help, this menu is obviously a far cry from an authentic document. Nevertheless, it should help you transition to the real thing. There are far too many dishes to remember, but even reciting the names aloud is a useful way of getting used to them and the range of possibilities. You will want to remember favorites from each group to add to the ones already encountered in both volumes of *Learning Chinese*. The menu can also be used in classroom activities, with classmates taking the role of servers and guests trying to decide on an order. Part B of this appendix, with notes on usage and sample dialogues, will guide you toward such activities.

菜单/菜單

1. *Lěnghūnlèi* (= *lěngcàilèi* 冷菜类/冷菜類)   冷荤类/冷荤類
   '(cold) appetizers'

   pīnpánr 'appetizers; hors d'oeuvres'   拼盘儿/拼盤兒
     ('put+together-dish')

   làbáicài 'hot pickled cabbage' ('spicy-cabbage')   辣白菜

   málà-yāzhǎng ('numb-spicy duck-feet')   麻辣鸭掌/麻辣鴨掌

   málà-ěrsī ('numb-spicy ear-shreds')   麻辣耳丝/麻辣耳絲

   sōnghuā = *pídàn* 'preserved eggs'   松花; 皮蛋
     ('pine-flower / skin-egg')

   Shāndōng-shāojī ('Shandong cooked-chicken')   山东烧鸡/山東燒雞

   xūnyú ('smoked-fish')   熏 ~ 燻鱼/熏鱼

   bànyāzhǎng ('mixed-duck-feet')   拌鸭掌/拌鴨掌

   bànsānxiān ('mixed-three-fresh')   拌三鲜/拌三鮮

   bànhǎizhé ('mixed-jellyfish')   拌海蛰/拌海蟄

   wǔxiāng-niúròu ('five-spice-beef')   五香牛肉

   làhuángguā 'cucumber with chilies'   辣黄瓜/辣黃瓜
     ('spicy-yellow-gourd')

   bàngbàngjī 'shredded boiled chicken': with   棒棒鸡/棒棒雞
     spicy sauce, served cold

   báiqiējī 'chicken poached in soup stock'   白切鸡/白切雞
     ('white-cut-chicken')

   Sìchuān-pàocài ('Sichuan+pickles')   四川泡菜

   dōngjī ('jellied-chicken')   冻鸡/凍雞

2. *Hǎixiānlèi* 'fresh seafood'   海鲜类/海鮮類
   qīngdùn-níqiū 'clear-stew loach': loach or   清炖泥鳅/清燉泥鰍
     smelt, a fish, stewed in clear broth

tángcùyú 'sweet and sour fish'
    ('sugar-vinegar-fish')   糖醋鱼/糖醋魚

Xīhú-cùyú 'West Lake fish'
    ('West-Lake vinegar-fish')   西湖醋鱼/西湖醋魚

wǔliǔyú 'sweet-and-sour fish pieces'
    ('five-willow-fish')   五柳鱼/五柳魚

sōngshǔyú ('squirrel-fish'): a fried whole fish,   松鼠鱼/松鼠魚
    usually carp, that looks like a squirrel

huóyú-sānchī ('live-fish three-eat'): a fish   活鱼三吃/活魚三吃
    cooked three ways as soup, with sweet
    sauce, and with brown sauce

gānshāo-jìyú 'steamed carp' ('dry-cooked-carp')   干烧鲫鱼/乾燒鯽魚

chǎoyúpiàn ('stir-fried-fish-slices')   炒鱼片/炒鱼片

tángcù-yúpiàn 'sweet-and-sour fish'   糖醋鱼片/糖醋鱼片
    ('sugar-vinegar fish-slices'): Cantonese

tángcù-quányú 'sweet-and-sour whole fish'   糖醋全鱼/糖醋全鱼
    ('sugar-vinegar whole-fish'): Cantonese

gānzhá-míngxiā 'dry-fried prawns'   干炸明虾/乾炸明蝦
    ('dry-fried clear-prawn')

guōbā-xiārénr (~ *xiārénr-guōbā*) 'shrimp   锅巴虾仁/鍋巴蝦仁
    over scorched rice'
    ('pan-crust shrimp-meat'):
    'Bombs over Moscow'

Dòngtíng-xiāpiàn   洞庭虾片/洞庭蝦片
    ('Dongting [Lake] shrimp-slices')

xuědòu-xiārénr ('snow-peas shrimp-meat')   雪豆虾仁/雪豆蝦仁

cuìpí-xiāqiú 'crispy shrimp balls'   脆皮虾球/脆皮蝦球
    ('crisp-skin shrimp-ball')

qīngzhēng-hémán ('steamed river-eel')   清蒸河鳗/清蒸河鰻

bàochǎo-yóuyújuǎn 'quick-fried squid rolls'   爆炒鱿鱼卷/爆炒鱿鱼捲
    ('quick-stir-fried squid-rolls')

hóngshāo-jiǎyú 'braised soft-shelled turtle'   红烧甲鱼/紅燒甲魚
    ('braised carapace-fish'): Nanjing region

sānsī-yúchì 'shark's fin with shredded   三丝鱼翅/三絲魚翅
   chicken' ('three-shreds fish-fins')

sānxiān-hǎishēn 'sea cucumber with shredded   三鲜海参/三鮮海參
   pork, bamboo shoots, and chicken'
   ('three-fresh sea slug')

3. *Bàochǎolèi* 'quick stir-fried'   爆炒类/爆炒類
   chǎoyāohuā 'fried pig kidney'   炒腰花
      ('stir-fried-kidney-flowers')
   chǎozhūgān ('stir-fried-pig-liver')   炒猪肝/炒豬肝
   bàosānzhēn 'fried chicken giblets and pork   爆三珍
      stomach' ('quick-fried-three-treasures')
   chǎojīdīng 'fried diced chicken'   炒鸡丁/炒雞丁
      ('stir-fried-chicken-cubes')
   bàojīqiú ('quick-fried-chicken-balls')   爆鸡球/ 爆雞球
   jiàngbào-tiánjī 'frog legs sautéed in duck   酱爆田鸡/醬爆田雞
      sauce' ('sauce-fast-fried field-chicken')
   bàosānyàng 'fried pork kidney, liver, and   爆三样/爆三樣
      other fried meat' ('quick-fry-three-kinds')

4. *Ròulèi* 'meat' [pork]   肉类/肉類
    jīngjiàng-ròusī ('Beijing-sauce meat-shreds')   京酱肉丝/京醬肉絲
    dōngsǔn-chǎoròusī ('winter-bamboo shoots   冬笋炒肉丝/冬筍炒肉絲
        stir-fried-meat-shred')
    cōngbào-niúròu 'beef with green onions'   葱爆牛肉/蔥爆牛肉
        ('onions-quick-fried beef')
    hóngshāo-dǔkuài 'braised pork stomach'   红烧肚块/紅燒肚塊
        ('red-braised-stomach-pieces')
    huíguōròu 'double-cooked pork'   回锅肉/回鍋肉
        ('return-wok-meat')
    jiàngbàoròu 'pork sautéed in duck sauce'   酱爆肉/醬爆肉
        ('sauce-fast-fried-meat')
    nánjiān-wánzi 'southern-style fried   南煎丸子
        meatballs' ('south-light-fry balls')
    quánjiāfú ('complete-home-fortune'):   全家福
        like chop suey
    gānbèi-sìsī 'scallops and four meats or   干贝四丝/乾貝四絲
        vegetables' ('scallop four-shreds')
    gúlǎoròu 'sweet-and-sour pork': Cantonese   咕老肉
    mùxūròu 'shredded pork with vegetables   木须肉/木須肉
        and egg' ('wood-whiskers-meat'):
        'moo shu'
    tángcù-páigǔ ('sugar-vinegar spareribs')   糖醋排骨
    méicài-kòuròu ('mustard-green stewed   梅菜扣肉
        pork'): Hakka dish

5. *Yóuzhálèi* 'oil-fried'   油炸类/油炸類
    zházǐjī ('deep-fried-young-chicken')   炸子鸡/炸子雞
    zhábákuài ('deep-fried-eight-pieces')   炸八块/炸八塊
    qīngzhá-féicháng ('clear-deep-fried   清炸肥肠/清炸肥腸
        fat-intestines')
    zházhēngān 'deep-fried chicken giblets'   炸珍肝
        ('deep-fried-treasure-liver')
    zhápáigǔ ('deep-fried-spareribs')   炸排骨

6. *Jīyālèi* 'chicken, duck, and frog'　　　　　　鸡鸭类/雞鴨類
   hóngshāojī ('red-cooked-chicken')　　　　　　红烧鸡/紅燒雞
   tiánsuān-jīkuài ('sweet-sour chicken-pieces')　　甜酸鸡块/甜酸雞塊
   gōngbǎo-jīdīng 'kung-pao chicken'　　　　　　宫保鸡丁/宮保雞丁
   　　('gongbao chicken-cubes'): chicken cubes,
   　　chili, and peanuts, stir-fried
   jiàngbào-jīdīng ('sauce-quick-fry chicken-cubes')　酱爆鸡丁/醬爆雞丁
   yóulín-zǐjī ('oil-baste young-chicken')　　　　油淋子鸡/油淋子雞
   máogū-jīpiàn 'moo goo gai pan' ('mushroom　　毛菇鸡片/毛菇雞片
   　　chicken-slice')
   yāoguǒ-jīdīng ('cashew chicken-cubes')　　　腰果鸡丁/腰果雞丁
   shícài-jīqiú ('seasonal-vegetables chicken-balls')　时菜鸡球/時菜雞球
   zhábākuài ('deep-fried-eight-pieces'):　　　　炸八块/炸八塊
   　　Beijing style
   Zuǒgōngjī 'General Tso's chicken'　　　　　　佐公鸡/佐公雞
   　　('Zuo-duke-chicken'): also *Zuǒzōng-tángjī*;　　(佐宗棠鸡)/(佐宗棠雞)
   　　chicken pieces with chili, ginger, garlic
   fúróng-jīpiàn ('lotus-chicken-slices')　　　　芙蓉鸡片/芙蓉雞片
   xiāngsūyā ('aromatic-crisp-duck')　　　　　香酥鸭/香酥鴨
   Běijīng-kǎoyā 'Peking duck'　　　　　　　北京烤鸭/北京烤鴨
   　　('Beijing-roast-duck')
   chǎoyāzhǎng ('stir-fried-duck-feet')　　　　炒鸭掌/炒鴨掌
   làzi-tiánjī 'frog legs in hot sauce'　　　　　辣子田鸡/辣子田雞
   　　('chili-young field-chicken')

7. *Sùcàilèi* (*Shūcàilèi* 蔬菜类/蔬菜類)　　　　素菜类/素菜類
   　　'vegetables; vegetarian'
   háoyóu-jièlán ('oyster-sauce Chinese-broccoli')　蚝油芥兰/蠔油芥蘭
   yúxiāng-qiézi ('fish-aroma eggplant')　　　　鱼香茄子/魚香茄子
   chǎo'èrdōng (~ *shāo'èrdōng*) 'bamboo shoots　炒二冬（烧二冬/
   　　and dried mushrooms'　　　　　　　　　　烧二冬）
   　　('stir-fried-two-winter')

chǎosāndōng (~ shāosāndōng) 'bamboo shoots with mushrooms and preserved cabbage' ('stir-fried-three-winter')   炒三冬（烧三冬/烧三冬）

páshuāngcài 'cabbage and mustard greens' ('boiled-pair-vegetables')   扒双菜/扒雙菜

jīyóu-báicài ('chicken-fat cabbage')   鸡油白菜/雞油白菜

sùshíjǐn ('vegetable-assortment')   素什锦/素什錦

fānqié-chǎojīdàn 'tomato omelet' ('tomato-fried-eggs')   番茄炒鸡蛋/番茄炒雞蛋

jiācháng-dòufu 'homestyle tofu' ('home-frequent-tofu')   家常豆腐

hóngshāo-dòufu 'braised tofu' ('red-braised-tofu')   红烧豆腐/紅燒豆腐

mápó-dòufu 'Mother Po's tofu' ('numb-old+woman tofu'): beancurd cubes, minced pork, spicy sauce, and Sichuan 'numbing' pepper   麻婆豆腐

dōnggū-dòufu ('mushroom tofu')   冬菇豆腐

8. Shāguō 'earthenware pot'   沙锅/沙鍋

shāguō-yútóu ('fish-head')   沙锅鱼头/沙鍋魚頭

shāguō-shīzitóu ('lion-head'): large meatballs stewed with cabbage leaves   沙锅狮子头/沙鍋獅子頭

shāguō-shíjǐn ('vegetable assortment')   沙锅什锦/沙鍋什錦

shāguō-dòufu ('tofu')   沙锅豆腐/沙鍋豆腐

shāguō-sānxiān ('three fresh')   沙锅三鲜/沙鍋三鮮

9. *Huǒguō* 'hot pot; fondue' ('fire-pot') 火锅/火鍋
   shíjǐn-huǒguō ('assortment hot-pot') 什锦火锅/什錦火鍋
   sānxiān-huǒguō ('three-fresh hot-pot') 三鲜火锅/三鮮火鍋

10. *Tānglèi* 'soup' 汤类/湯類
   bàoyútāng ('abalone') 鲍鱼汤/鮑魚湯
   cuānyāzhǎng 'duck feet soup' ('drop in boiling water-duck-feet') 氽鸭掌/氽鴨掌
   sānxiāntāng ('three-fresh-soup'): with shrimp, pork, and chicken 三鲜汤/三鮮湯
   suānlàtāng 'hot-and-sour soup' ('sour-hot-soup') 酸辣汤/酸辣湯
   dànhuātāng 'egg-drop soup' ('egg-flower-soup'): more often known as *jīdàntāng* in China 蛋花汤/蛋花湯 (鸡蛋汤/雞蛋湯)
   cuānwánzi ('drop in boiling water-meatballs') 氽丸子/氽丸子
   zhūgāntāng ('pig-liver-soup') 猪肝汤/豬肝湯
   húntuntāng 'wonton soup' 馄吞汤/餛吞湯
   jiācháng-dòufutāng ('home-regular tofu-soup') 家常豆腐汤/家常豆腐湯
   zhàcài-ròusītāng ('pickled-cabbage pork-shreds-soup') 榨菜肉丝汤/榨菜肉絲湯

báicài-dòufutāng ('white-cabbage tofu-soup')   白菜豆腐汤/白菜豆腐湯

huǒtuǐ-dōnggūtāng ('ham mushroom-soup')   火腿冬菇汤/火腿冬菇湯

11. *Miànlèi* 'noodles' [often divided into *tāngmiàn*   面类/麵類
    'noodle soup' and *lāomiàn* 'dry noodles']

    ròusī-chǎomiàn ('meat-shreds   肉丝炒面/肉絲炒麵
    stir-fried-noodles')

    zhájiàngmiàn 'noodles with bean paste and   炸酱面/炸醬麵
    pork' ('fried-sauce-noodles')

    shíjǐn-chǎomiàn ('assorted stir-fried-noodles')   什锦炒面/什錦炒麵

    dàlǔmiàn ('big-stewed-noodles')   大卤面/大鹵麵

    páigǔmiàn ('ribs-noodles')   排骨面/排骨麵

    sānxiānmiàn (three-fresh-noodles')   三鲜面/三鮮麵

    dàndànmiàn 'noodles with spicy sesame   担担面/擔擔麵
    sauce': Sichuan

    ròusī-liángmiàn ('meat-shred cold-noodle')   肉丝凉面/肉絲涼麵

    ròusī-tāngmiàn ('meat-shred soup-noodle')   肉丝汤面/肉絲湯麵

    chāshāo-tāngmiàn ('red+braised soup-noodle')   叉烧汤面/叉燒湯麵

    yúpiàn-tāngmiàn ('fish-slice soup-noodle')   鱼片汤面/魚片湯麵

    xiāqiú-tāngmiàn ('shrimp-ball soup-noodle')   虾球汤面/蝦球湯麵

    gèshì-lāomiàn 'lo mein' ('any-style lo mein'):   各式捞面/各式撈麵
    with pork, beef, chicken, shrimp,
    or vegetables

    běnlóu-lāomiàn 'house lo mein'   本楼捞面/本樓撈麵
    ('local-restaurant lo mein')

    gānchǎo-niúhé 'dry noodles' ('dry-stir-fried   干炒牛河/乾炒牛河
    beef-flat rice noodles)

    chǐjiāo-niúhé 'noodles with beef and black   豉椒牛河/豉椒牛河
    bean sauce' ('black bean-pepper beef-flat
    rice noodles')

12. *Zhǔshílèi* 'staples, rice dishes'   主食类/主食類
    ('main-food-type)

    chāshāo-chǎofàn ('roast-pork fried-rice')   义烧炒饭/义燒炒飯

yúpiàn-chǎofàn ('fish-slices fried-rice')   鱼片炒饭/魚片炒飯

Yángzhōu-chǎofàn ('Yangzhou fried-rice')   扬州炒饭/揚州炒飯

xiārénr-chǎofàn ('shrimp-meat fried-rice')   虾仁儿炒饭/蝦仁兒炒飯

sānxiān-chǎofàn ('three-fresh fried-rice')   三鲜炒饭/三鮮炒飯

13. *Diǎnxīnlèi* 'light fare' [i.e., Cantonese dim   点心类/點心類
     sum and light fare from other regions]

    jiǎozi 'dumplings'   饺子/餃子

    shuǐjiǎo 'boiled dumplings ('water-dumplings')   水饺/水餃

    zhēngjiǎo 'steamed dumplings'   蒸饺/蒸餃
       ('steamed-dumplings')

    bāozi 'steamed buns'   包子

    xiǎolóngbāo 'small steamed buns'   小笼包/小籠包
       ('little-steamer-bun')

    guōtiēr 'pot stickers' ('pot-stick')   锅贴儿/鍋貼兒

    shāomài 'steamed, open ravioli or   烧卖/燒賣
       dumplings' ('cook-sell')

    chūnjuǎnr ('spring-rolls')   春卷儿/春卷兒

    jiānbǐng 'Chinese pancakes' ('fried-pancake')   煎饼/煎餅

xiànrbǐng 'meat-filled chapati'   馅儿饼/餡兒餅
  ('stuffing-chapati')

báobǐng = jiāchángbǐng 'thin chapati'   薄饼/薄餅

shāobǐng ('cooked+chapati')   烧饼/燒餅

mántou 'steamed white buns; steamed bread'   馒头/饅頭

huājuǎnr ('flower-twists'): a type of bread   花卷儿/花卷兒
  or bun

yóutiáo ('oil-lengths'): sometimes called   油条/油條
  Chinese doughnuts and eaten with zhōu,
  shāobǐng, and so on

zòngzi: glutinous rice and savories in a   粽子
  banana leaf packet

zhōu 'porridge; gruel': jīzhōu   粥; 鸡粥/雞粥
  'chicken porridge'

14. Tiándiǎnlèi 'desserts; sweets'   甜点类/甜點類

  bābǎofàn ('eight-jewel-rice')   八宝饭/八寶飯

  hǔpò-liánzǐ 'lotus seeds steamed in sweet   琥珀莲子/琥珀蓮子
    sauce' ('amber lotus-seeds')

  básī-xiāngjiāo 'candied bananas'   拔丝香蕉/拔絲香蕉
    ('pull-silk-bananas')

  xìngrénr-dòufu 'almond tofu'   杏仁儿豆腐/杏仁兒豆腐

NOTES

a. 面类/麵類 *Miànlèi*: *Miàn* generally means 'noodles' or pasta made from wheat flour, but it may also include 米粉/米粉 *mǐfěn* 'rice-flour noodles' (also called 河粉 *héfěn*) and, in Southeast Asia, 粿条/粿條 *guōtiáo* ['kwey teow' in Hokkien]. 汤面/湯麵 *tāngmiàn* 'noodle soup' can be contrasted with 捞面/撈麵 *lāomiàn* ('ladled+out-noodles'), such as 'lo mein', served without the soup and in dishes such as 牛肉面/牛肉麵 *niúròumiàn*.

b. 主食类/主食類 *zhǔshílèi* 'staples' ('main-food-type'), sometimes called 饭类/飯類 *fànlèi*, are dishes served on or with rice. They are not usually eaten alone.

c. 甜点类/甜點類 *tiándiǎnlèi*: Traditionally, desserts would not be part of an ordinary meal, and even with banquets, what counts as a dessert is usually an attractive platter of fresh fruit. However, with increasing affluence, sweet dishes eaten as a snack between meals or in the evening or as dessert in restaurants are becoming more and more popular. In addition to traditional sweet snacks such as 豆花 *dòuhuā* with cane sugar, shops that sell cakes, doughnuts, and Southeast Asian desserts made with sticky sweet rice are proliferating.

2. Names of dishes

Descriptive names, in which the parts give some clue to the dish:

炒鸡丁/炒雞丁 *chǎojīdīng*	('stir-fried-chicken-cubes')
榨菜肉丝汤/榨菜肉絲湯 *zhàcài-ròusītāng*	('pickled-cabbage meat-shreds-soup')
海参-北菇-扒大鸭/ 海參-北菇-扒大鴨 *hǎishēn-běigū-pádàyā*	('sea-cucumber northern-mushrooms braised-big-duck')

Dishes incorporating proper names:

扬州炒饭/揚州炒飯 *Yángzhōu-chǎofàn*	'Yangzhou fried rice': named for *Yángzhōu* on the *Yángzǐjiāng*, or *Cháng Jiāng*, east of *Nánjīng*
东坡肉 *Dōngpōròu*	'Dongpo's pork': a fatty pork dish associated with—and possibly created by—the Song Dynasty poet *Sū Shì*, generally known as *Sū Dōngpō* 'Su of the East Bank' [of the Yangtze, the site of his house]
西湖醋鱼/西湖醋魚 *Xīhú-cùyú*	('West Lake vinegar fish'): named for West Lake in *Hángzhōu*

Dishes with numbers: 二冬 *èrdōng*, 三鲜/三鮮 *sānxiān*, 八宝/八寶 *bābǎo*, 三珍 *sānzhēn*:

烧二冬/燒二冬 *shāo'èrdōng*	('cooked-two-winters'): the two are usually *dōnggū* 'winter mushrooms' and *dōngsǔn* 'winter bamboo shoots'
三鲜海参/三鮮海參 *sānxiān-hǎishēn,*	'sea cucumber' ('three-fresh sea-slug'): this is actually an animal served with shredded pork, bamboo shoots, and chicken
干贝四丝/乾貝四絲 *gānbèi-sìsī*	('scallops four-shreds'): scallops with four meats/vegetables

Poetically or allusively named dishes:

蚂蚁上树/螞蟻上樹 *máyǐ-shàngshù*	('ants climb-tree'): spicy ground beef sauce poured over deep-fried bean threads (*fěnsī*); The dish is named for the black specks that appear on the noodles.
狮子头/獅子頭 *shīzitóu*	('lion-head'): large meatballs stewed with cabbage leaves, resembling a lion's head
佐公鸡/佐公雞 *Zuǒgōngjī*	('Zuo-duke-chicken'): often called 'General Tso's chicken'; a dish said to have been created in the United States by a cook from the Cantonese region of China
罗汉扒大鸭/羅漢扒大鴨 *Luóhàn-pádàyā*	('saint braised-big-duck'): *Luóhàn* (Arahant in Sanskrit) was a Buddhist worthy
佛跳墙/佛跳牆 *Fótiàoqiáng*	('Buddha-jumps-wall'): a stew of meats and dried ingredients served in a big jar. A Fujianese dish, so-called because even the Buddha—a vegetarian—would jump over a wall to eat some.

Chinese dishes associated with a region or a regional cuisine and often promoted as 地方风味菜/地方風味菜 *dìfāng fēngwèi cài* 'dishes with regional tastes':

过桥米线/過橋米線 *guòqiáo-mǐxiàn*	('cross-bridge-rice-strands'): associated with Kunming, Yunnan
毛家菜 *Máojiācài*	('Mao-home-dishes'): Hunan countryside dishes, supposedly the sort of things that Mao Zedong enjoyed growing up: *hóngshāoròu* 'braised beef'
狗不理包子 *gǒubùlǐ bāozi*	('dog-not-obey dumplings'): from Tianjin
耳朵鸭炸糕/耳朵鴨炸糕 *ěrduo-yāzhágāo*	('ear duck-fried cakes'): sweet and deep-fried cake; another specialty of Tianjin

羊肉泡馍/羊肉泡饃 *yángròu-pàomó*	('lamb meat-broth'): a specialty of Xi'an
腌肉/醃肉 *yānròu*	'salted pressed pork': associated with Zhenjiang, Jiangsu

3. Some general menu terms

什锦/錦 *shíjǐn*	'assortment of; mix of': sometimes represented on menus as 'subgum', a spelling based on the Cantonese pronunciation
红/紅 *hóng*	'red': usually meaning 'cooked in soy sauce'; cf. *hóngshāo* 红烧/紅燒 'red cooked', which means simmered in soy sauce
鱼/魚香 *yúxiāng*	'fish-scented': = tasty; garlic sauce
豉汁 *chǐzhī*	'black bean sauce'
豉椒 *chǐjiāo*	'black bean peppers'
咖喱 *gālí*	'curry'
蚝/蠔油 *háoyóu*	'oyster sauce'
宫保 *gōngbǎo*	'keeper of the palace' ('palace-keeper'): cooked with chilies and peanuts; also written as 宫宝/寶 'treasure of the palace'
酱/醬爆 *jiàngbào*	('sauce-quick-fried'): usually means cooked with a bean-paste sauce
三丝/絲 *sānsī*	'three-shredded [items]'
二冬 *èrdōng*	'two-winter [vegetables]': also *shuāngdōng* 双冬/雙冬 'pair of winter'
时菜/時菜 *shícài*	'seasonal vegetables' ('time-vegetables')
麻辣 *málà*	'numb-spicy hot': cooked with *huājiāo* 花椒 'Sichuan pepper', chili, and sesame oil
珍 *zhēn*	'treasure': usually means 'giblets'
家常 *jiācháng*	'homestyle' ('home-frequent')

4. Methods of cooking (*pēngtiáo fāngfǎ*)

bàn	'mix': especially of various cold appetizers; *bànhǎizhé* 'mixed jellyfish'
bào	'quick fry': *bàoyāohuār* ('quick-fry-kidney-flower')
chǎo	'stir fry [in a little oil]': *chǎofàn*; *chǎomiàn*
cuān	'boil in soup for a short time': *cuānwánzi* 'boiled meatballs'
dùn	'boil in water, low heat; stew': *dùnniúròu* 'stewed beef'
hóngshāo	'boil in soy sauce; braise' ('red-cook'): *hóngshāo-qiézi* 'braised eggplant'
huì	'boil in water and (thicken with) soy sauce': *huìxiārénr* 'braised shrimp'
jiān	'shallow-fry [in a little oil]': *jiānyú* 'fried fish'
jiàng	'boil in a little soy sauce': *jiàngbào-jīdīng* 'fried chicken cubes'
kǎo	'bake; roast; toast': *kǎomiànbāo* 'toast'; *kǎoyā* 'roast duck'
kòu	'steam in a mold': *kòuròu* 'potted meat'
pá	'boil or steam, then thicken with starch': *páhǎishēn* 'braised sea slug'
pēng	'sautée [in very hot oil]': *pēngdàxiā* 'sautéed prawns'
shāo	'fry in light vegetable oil, stirring': *shāosānsī* ('cook-three-shredded')
tángcù	deep fry, with sweet and sour sauce added ('sugar-vinegar'): *tángcùyú*
xūn	'smoke [food] after boiling': *xūnyú* 'smoked fish'
zhá	'deep fry [in deep, hot oil]': *zhájī* 'fried chicken'
zhēng	(or *qīngzhēng*) 'steam over water': *qīngzhēngyú* 'steamed fish'
zhǔ	'boil; cook': [general term]; *shuǐzhǔ-niúròu* 'boiled beef'; Sichuan

5. Ways of cutting (*qiēfǎ*)

dīng	'cubes':	*jiàngbào-jīdīng* 'fried chicken cubes'
piàn	'slices':	*yúpiàn* 'sliced fish'
qiú	'ball; curl':	*chǎoxiāqiú* 'fried shrimp balls ('curls of shrimp')'
sī	'shredded':	*ròusī-chǎomiàn* 'fried noodles with shredded pork'

B: Usage

1. In restaurants

MENUS   Chinese menus, *càidān* ('dish-list'), often look like a playbook for a cooking competition; there might be a dozen dishes listed for each of a dozen categories of food. Chinese may examine the menu in detail when arranging dishes for a banquet, but for ordinary meals, if you observe, you will find that Chinese patrons often don't spend much time looking at the menu. Instead, they negotiate with the server about dishes, asking what is in season, what the specialties of the house are, how fat the crabs are or how big the fish, and at the same time check on costs. Ideally, they then make a selection based on years of experience, choosing food that is fresh and flavorful, while also balancing textures, colors, and cooking methods. The foreigner, by contrast, is extremely handicapped. Not only are menus hard to read, but the foreigner often eats alone, which limits the variety of dishes with which he or she is familiar. The foreigner will also obviously not be familiar with the regional specialties and seasonal foods.

UTENSILS   Utensils—not those in the kitchen but the ones on the table—include the following (measure words are in brackets): *kuàizi* [*shuāng*] 'chopsticks' [pair]; *sháor* or *sháozi* [*bǎ*] 'small spoon'; *cānjīn* [*tiáo*] 'table napkin' ('food-cloth'); *bēizi* [*gè*] 'glass'; *wǎn* [*gè*] 'bowl'; *pánzi* [*gè*] 'plate; dish'; *diézi* [*gè*] 'small plate; dish'. If you are eating at a non-Chinese restaurant in China, then you may get Western utensils: *dāozi* [*bǎ*] 'knife', *chāzi* [*bǎ*] 'fork', *dāochā* 'knife and fork'.

> *Qǐng zài lái yì shuāng kuàizi.*   'Please bring another pair of chopsticks.'

Xiǎo.jiě, zài lái yí ge xiǎowǎn, yí ge xiǎosháor.	'Miss, another bowl and spoon.'
Máfan nǐ zài huàn ge bēizi, zhèi ge pò le.	'May I bother you for another glass; this one's cracked.'

SERVERS: WAITERS AND WAITRESSES   *Fúwùyuán* is a fairly neutral term for a male or female server in China (but not in Taiwan or overseas communities). Alternatively, *xiānsheng* or *xiǎo.jiě* are used for male and female servers, respectively. Local patrons might use kin terms, such as *xiǎomèi* 'little sister' for young servers.

Fúwùyuán, wǒmen diǎn cài.	'We'd like to order please.' [This is equivalent to asking for a menu.]
Nǐmen yǒu shénme shícài?	'What seasonal vegetables do you have?'
Nǐmen zhèr yǒu shénme náshǒu cài?	'What specialties do you have here?'
Xiè<zi> féi bu féi?	'How are the crabs? ('crabs fat-not-fat')
Xiànzài, shénme yú zuì féi?	'What kind of fish is best ('plump') these days?'
Yǒu méiyǒu qīngcài, wǒ bù chī ròu.	'Do you have any vegetable dishes; I don't eat meat.'
Qǐng bú yào tài là.	'Not too hot please.'
Gòu bu gòu sì ge rén chī?	'Is that enough for four?'
Bú gòu wǒmen zài diǎn, hǎo ma?	'If it's not enough, we'll order more, okay?'
Zài lái yì wǎn mǐfàn.	'Bring another bowl of rice.'
Zhēn guòyǐn.	'That really hits the spot.' ('really pass-craving')
Xiǎo.jiě, jiézhàng ~ mǎidān.	'Miss, check please.'
Báizhǎnjī hǎoxiàng méi shàng, huàdiào.	'I don't think the chicken poached in soup stock came; take it off the bill.'

shícài	'seasonal food' ('timely-food')
náshǒu cài	'special; expert; signature [dishes]' ('take-hand')
diǎn <cài>	'order <food>': also *jiào cài*
zài lái . . .	'bring another . . .'
féi	'fatty; rich; sleek'
mǎidān	'the bill / pay the bill' ('buy-list'): originally from Cantonese but now common in Mandarin
báizhǎnjī	('white-chopped-chicken'): chicken poached in soup stock and served cold; also called *báiqiējī* (as on the previous menu)
huàdiào	'cross it off [the bill]' ('delete-fall')

2. At homes
a. Before sitting down

Lái, suíbiàn zuòle jǐ ge xiǎocài, bù zhīdao hé bu hé nǐ de kǒuwèir.	'Here, I've put together a few dishes; I'm not sure you'll like them.'
Gěi nǐ tiān máfan le.	'I've put you to a lot of trouble.'

b. Inviting a guest to eat at the beginning of the meal

Qǐng yòng cài.	'Help yourself.'
Wa, hǎo fēngshèng de.	'Wow, what a feast.'

c. Seating is important, and if you are offered a seat of honor next to the host, then you can decline ritually before accepting the inevitable

Lái, zuò zhèr, zuò zhèr.	'Come, sit here.'
Bù gǎndāng.	'No, I couldn't.'
Bù, zuò zhèr.	'No, sit here.'
Hǎo, hǎo, xièxie.	'Okay, thanks.'

d. Being aware of the vast differences in cuisine and eating habits, Chinese may wonder if you can cope with Chinese food.

Zhōngguó cài nǐ chīdeguàn ma?	'Can you eat Chinese food?'
Dāngrán chīdeguàn, hěn xǐhuan.	'Of course, I love it. In Holland, we
Wǒmen zài Hélán jīngcháng	often eat in Chinese restaurants,
zài Zhōngguó fànguǎnr chīfàn,	though the food there isn't so
dàn nàr de cài bù zěnme	authentic, and it's not as good as
dìdào, bú xiàng zài zhèr chī	eating here.'
de nàme hǎo.	
Zhè shi pīnpánr.	'Here are some cold dishes.'
Wa, nàme duō ya.	'Wow, so many.'
Zhè shi bànyāzhǎng, bànhǎizhé,	'There's [list of dishes].'
làhuángguā, báiqiējī.	
A, quán shi dìdào de Zhōngguó	'Ah, this is truly authentic Chinese
cài.	food.'

e. Your host will want to make sure you are not holding back out of politeness; ultimately, you may want to accept a little more to show how good the food is. Fortunately, with Chinese food, it's not the amount but the flavors and textures, so you can always take a little more. On special occasions—rather than just a daily meal—one eats less rice. In fact, it's good to leave some rice in the bowl at the end of the meal to show you've had enough.

Chī a, chī a, bié xiánzhe.	'Eat up; don't hold back.'
Xièxie, xièxie, chībǎo le.	'I'm full, thanks.'
Bié jiànwài, duō chī yìdiǎnr ~	'Don't be a stranger; have some
Bié kèqi, zài lái yìdiǎnr.	more.'
Hǎo, hǎo, jiù yìdiǎnr.	'Okay, just a bit then.'

f. Out of politeness or modesty, the host may find fault with the food. Obviously, this is to be vigorously denied.

Cài zěnmeyàng, xián bu xián?	'How's the food? Is it a bit salty?'
Bù, xiándàn zhènghǎo, hěn hǎochī.	'No, it's just right, very tasty.'

g. At a formal meal, and especially at a banquet, there will be toasts, with glasses held up with two hands. Toasts are usually reciprocal, so you might counter with 'to your health'.

Lái, wǒ lái jìng ge jiǔ. Wèi nǐmen xuéyè yǒu chéng, gānbēi!	'I'd like to propose a toast: here's to the success of your studies. Bottoms up!'
Xièxie nín, yě zhù nín jiànkāng.	'Thank you; your health.'
Xièxie nǐmen de rèqíng kuǎndài. Lái, wǒmen gān yì bēi.	'Thank you for your kind hospitality. Here, a toast!'
Nǐ tài kèqi le.	'You shouldn't.'

3. A sample conversation

Wáng [W] = 'the host'
Shǐmìsī [Sm] = 'Smith'
xiǎo.jiě [X] = 'the waitress'

Smith and his classmates, who are studying in Kunming, have traveled to Beijing on their break. They're meeting up with an old friend of Smith's named Wang, an ebullient fellow who loves to entertain foreign guests. He has invited Smith and his two classmates to dinner at a popular local restaurant. Smith does the talking for the guests and tries to keep Wang's natural generosity in check.

W:	*Nǐmen jīntiān xiǎng chī yìdiǎnr shénme?*	'What would you like to have today?'
Sm:	*Suíbiàn, suíbiàn.*	'Oh, whatever, anything.'
W:	*Āi, bié suíbiàn a, jīntiān gěi nǐmen jiēfēng! Wǒ qǐngkè, nǐ jiu bié kèqi le. Fàngxīn de diǎn cài, xǐhuan chī shénme jiu diǎn shénme.*	'Hey, no 'whatevering'; today we're welcoming you! I'm inviting, so relax. Don't worry about ordering; order whatever you like.'
Sm:	*Bié, bié, bié tài pòfèi le, suíbiàn chī yìdiǎnr déle!*	'Don't spend too much, let's just have a little something and that'll do!'

W: *Nà zěnme xíng a? Nǐmen*   'What do you mean? You're a
     shi yuǎnfāng lái de kèrén,   guest from a long way off; we
     bù néng dàimàn le!   can't neglect our duty.'

Sm: *Wǒmen bú huì diǎn cài, háishi*   'We can't order; better you do it.
     nǐ lái ba. Kèsuízhǔbiàn.   We'll just go along with you.'

W: *Hǎo ba, nǐmen xǐhuan chī*   'Okay, do you like seafood? Or
     hǎixiān ne? Háishi xǐhuan   meat?'
     chī ròulèi de cài?

Sm: *Píngshí chī de tǐng suíbiàn,*   'Generally, we're not at all fussy;
     zhǔyào shi shūcài.   we're basically into vegetables.'

W: *Nà, zánmen xiān lái jǐ ge*   'Okay, let's have some
     sùcài. Xiǎo.jiě!   vegetarian food first. Miss!'

X: *Xiānsheng, diǎncài ma?*   'You're ordering, sir?'

W: *Nǐmen zhèr de sùcài, něi ge*   'What's your best vegetarian
     zuì náshǒu?   dish here?'

X: *Gānbiān-sìjìdòu, háoyóu-jièlán,*   'Stir-fried string beans, broccoli
     ng . . . jiācháng-dòufu,   in oyster sauce, uh, home-
     sùshíjǐn.   cooked tofu, vegetable platter.'

W: *Nà, jiu lái ge jiācháng-dòufu,*   'So, bring a home-cooked tofu
     yí ge sùshíjǐn. Āi, xiǎo.jiě,   and a vegetable platter. Say,
     nǐmen zhèr yǒu miànjin ma?   do you have gluten here?'

X: *Yǒu, yǒu dōngguā-miànjin,*   'Yes, we have winter-melon
     dúmiànjin, ng . . .   gluten, plain gluten, uh . . .'

W: *Lái ge dúmiànjin ba.*   'Bring a plain gluten, okay?'

X: *Xiānsheng hái yǒu yìdiǎnr*   'What else will you have, sir?'
     shénme?

W: *Lǎo Shǐ, nǐmen zài Měiguó*   'Smith, in America you always
     zǒng chī niúròu, duì me?   eat beef, right? So bring an
     Nà, lái ge lóngxū-niúròu;   asparagus beef. Uh . . . what's
     ng . . . xiànzài, shénme   a good fish?'
     yú zuì féi?

X:	*Ng, hóngshāo-mùyú, qīngzhēng-guìyú, gānshāo-jìyú.*	'Uh, red-braised cod, steamed salmon, steamed carp.'
W:	*Hǎo, hǎo, lái ge qīngzhēng-guìyú.*	'Okay, bring the steamed carp.'
Sm:	*Xíng le, xíng le, tài duō le, wǒmen chībuliǎo!*	'That'll do, that's too much, we won't be able to eat it all.'
W:	*Méi wèntí, chīdeliǎo.*	'No problem, we'll manage.'
X:	*Shuǐjiǔ yào bu yào?*	'Do you want water or wine?'
Sm:	*Lái diǎnr liángshuǐ jiu xíng le.*	'Just bring some water and that'll be fine.'
W:	*Chīfàn nǎr yǒu bù hē jiǔ de? Zài Zhōngguó, chīfàn méiyǒu guāng hē liángshuǐ de! Jīntiān ràng wǒmen chángchang Zhōngguó báijiǔ. Xiǎo.jiě, nǐmen zhèr yǒu shénme míngjiǔ?*	'How can you have a meal without wine? In China, we don't just drink cold water. Today, let's try some Chinese white liquor. Miss, what sort of quality wines do you have here?'
X:	*Wǒmen shénme míngjiǔ dōu yǒu, yǒu Máotái, yǒu Wǔliángyè, Měnggǔwáng.*	'We have all the well-known wines: Maotai, Five Grain, Mongol King.'
W:	*Yǒu xiǎopíngr de ma?*	'Do you have small bottles?'
X:	*Yǒu èr liǎng zhuāng de hé bàn jīn zhuāng de.*	'We have two-ounce bottles and half-jin bottles.'
W:	*Bàn jīn zhuāng de Máotái hé Wǔliángyè, yí yàng lái yì píngr.*	'A half-jin bottle of Maotai and Five Grain, onc of cach.'
X:	*Hái yào yìdiǎnr shénme ne?*	'And what else?'
W:	*Hǎo, hǎo, bú gòu de huà wǒmen zài lái.*	'Okay, if it's not enough, then we'll order more later.'
Sm:	*Hǎo le, zámen jiè zhèi ge jīhuì hǎohǎo liáoliao.*	'Okay, let's take this opportunity to have a good chat!'

SHĒNGCÍBIǍO

jiēfēng	'welcome someone after a journey' ('meet-wind')
pòfèi	'incur expense; spend too much money' ('break-expenses')
déle!	'that's plenty; that's enough' ('get-LE')
yuǎnfāng	'distant place; afar'
dàimàn	'neglect a guest': *dàimàn le* 'I've been a poor host'
kèsuí-zhǔbiàn	'go along with' ('guest-follow host-convenience'): the expression is based on *suíbiàn* and the opposition of *zhǔ* 'host' and *kè* 'guest'
Píngshí chī de tǐng suíbiàn.	'I'm usually pretty easygoing [about food].'
zhǔyào	'main; chief; major' ('host-need'): *zhǔyào shi shūcài* 'mainly vegetarian dishes'
sùcài	'vegetable dish' ('plain-dish'): *chīsù* 'be a vegetarian'; *shūcài* is literally 'vegetables'; *sùcài* is literally a 'plain dish', but by implication, it is also a vegetable dish.
guāng	'be smooth; be bare / solely; only': *méiyǒu guāng hē liángshuǐ de* 'there aren't people who only drink cold water [with their meals]'; 'people don't just drink cold water [with meals]'
èr liǎng zhuāng	'two-ounce capacity': *zhuāng* 'hold; load'

NOTES

a. *Miànjin* 'gluten': Barbara Tropp, in her book *The Modern Art of Chinese Cooking: Techniques and Recipes* (1982), called *miànjin* a 'mock meat', a category that covers "a variety of products made variously from wheat gluten and soybeans that are flavored and fashioned to resemble meat" (p. 553).

b. *Yuǎnfāng*: part of the opening section of the *Analects* of Confucius: *Yǒu péng zì yuǎnfāng lái, bú yì lè hū?* This has been translated by Arthur Waley as "That friends should come to one from afar, is this not after all, delightful?"

c. *Liángshuǐ*: Traditionally, Chinese would not drink water with food, especially not cold water, which would be regarded as bad for the health. However, customs are changing, and cold drinks are more common, even with food.

d. Dishes mentioned:

干煸四季豆/乾煸四季豆
　gānbiān-sìjìdòu

蚝油芥兰/蠔油芥蘭
　háoyóu jièlán

家常豆腐 jiācháng-dòufu

素什锦/素什錦 sùshíjǐn

冬瓜面筋 dōngguā-miànjin

独面筋/獨面筋 dúmiànjin

龙须牛肉/龍鬚牛肉
　lóngxū-niúròu

红烧目鱼/紅燒目魚
　hóngshāo-mùyú

清蒸鲑鱼/清蒸鮭魚
　qīngzhēng-guìyú

干烧鲫鱼/干燒鯽魚
　gānshāo-jìyú

'dry-cooked string beans': with
　seasonings and stir fried until the
　liquid evaporates; a Sichuan dish

'Chinese broccoli in oyster sauce'

'home-cooked tofu'

'vegetarian platter'

'winter melon gluten'

'plain gluten'

'asparagus beef' ('dragon-whiskers
　beef')

'red-braised cod'

'steamed salmon'

'steamed carp'

Appendix 2 MEASURE WORDS

Appendix 2 contains a list of the more common measure words, including all of those encountered in the two volumes of *Learning Chinese*. Units of currency, weight, volume, or other quantities—which are predictable—are not included. Ultimately, finding the measure for a particular noun requires reference to one of the dictionaries (or other more specialized reference works) that includes measure words in noun entries.

bǎ	for items with handles	
	Nèi bǎ hóng de shi wǒ de.	'The red one's mine.' [umbrella]
	Sān bǎ yǐzi bú gòu.	'Three chairs aren't enough.'
	Nǐ nèi bǎ dāo hǎo lìhai.	'That's a formidable knife you have.'
bān	for regularly scheduled transport	
	Měi tiān zhǐyǒu liǎng bān.	'Only two trips/flights a day.'
bāo	pack of	
	Yì bāo yān bā kuài wǔ.	'A pack of cigarettes is ¥8.50.'
běn	for bound items	
	Wǒ zhǐyǒu liǎng běn.	'I only have two.' [dictionaries]
	Mǎi <yì> běn Zhōngguó dìtú ba.	'Why not buy a Chinese atlas?'
céng	floor; story	
	Shi yí dòng liù céng lóu de fángzi.	'It's a six-story building.'
	Tāmen zài dì-liù céng.	'They're on the sixth floor.'
chǎng	for shows, movies, plays	
	Jīntiān qī diǎn yǒu yì chǎng.	'There's a show tonight at 7:00.'

chuàn	bunch; string of	
	Nèi chuàn yàoshi shi shéi de?	'Whose keys are those?'
	Yí chuàn duōshao qián?	'How much for a bunch [of bananas]?'
dài	bag of	
	Yí dài sān máo.	'Thirty cents a bag.'
dào	course (of food)	
	Dì-yī dào bú cùo, kěshì dì-èr wǒ juéde wèidào bú tài hǎo	'The first course wasn't bad, but the second didn't taste so good, I thought.'
dǐng	for things with points, tops	
	Tā xiǎng mǎi yì dǐng hóng màozi.	'She wants to buy a red hat.'
	Chuáng shang yǒu yì dǐng wénzhàng.	'There was a mosquito net over the bed.'
dòng	for buildings	
	Shi yí dòng liù céng lóu de fángzi.	'It's a six-story building.'
duàn	for parts, sections	
	Dì-yī duàn, nǐ niàn gěi wǒmen tīngting, hǎo bu hǎo?	'Read the first paragraph for us, okay?'
dùn	for meals	
	Tā měitiān zhǐ chī liǎng dùn fàn.	'He only eats two meals a day.'
duǒ	for flowers	
	Mǎi yì duǒ huā gěi tā ba.	'Why don't you buy her a flower?'
fèn	for newspapers; copies	
	Qǐng mǎi èrshí fèn; shí fèn bú gòu.	'Please buy twenty copies; ten are not enough.'
fēng	for letters	
	Jīntiān xiěle sān fēng Zhōngwén xìn le.	'Today, I've written three letters in Chinese.'

fù	for things that come in pairs; emotions	
	yí fù yǎnjìng; yí fù pūkèpái	'a pair of eyes'; 'a deck of cards'
	yí fù xiàoliǎn	'a smiling face'
gè	for people; things; the general (and default) M	
	liǎng ge Zhōngguó péngyou	'two Chinese friends'
	sì ge cài yí ge tāng	'four dishes and a soup'
	yí ge wèntí	'a question; problem'
	sì ge dōngxi	'four things'
	něi ge chéngshì	'which city'
jiā	for companies, businesses	
	Zài nèi jiā gōngsī gōngzuò hěn xīnkǔ.	'It's tough working for that company.'
	Nèi jiā fànguǎnr zěnmeyàng?	'How's that restaurant?'
jià	for airplanes, contraptions, constructions	
	Nǐ kàn nèi jià fēijī, nàme dī!	'Look at that plane; it's so low!'
	Nèi liǎng jià zhàoxiàngjī, yí jià chūle wèntí.	'One of those two cameras has a problem.'
jiàn	for items of business, clothing, luggage	
	Wǒ hái děi bàn yí jiàn shìqing.	'I still have to do one more thing.'
	Zhǐyǒu yí jiàn xíngli.	'There's only one piece of luggage.'
	Nèi jiàn tàofú hěn piàoliang.	'That's a pretty suit.'
jié	segment; for classes	
	Yì jié kè yào jǐ fēn zhōng.	'How long does a class take?'

jù	for sentences	
	Nǐ shuō yí jù huà, jiù xíng. (cf. *Shuō yí ge jùzi.*)	'One sentence will be enough.' (cf. 'Say a sentence.')
	Tā xiěle jǐ jù zhìxiè de huà.	'She wrote a few words of thanks.'
kē	for tufts, trees	
	yì kē shù	'a tree'
kǒu	for people in surveys	
	Jiā lǐ yǒu liù kǒu rén.	'There are six in my family.'
liàng	for vehicles	
	Zài Měiguó yǒu liǎng liàng chē de bù shǎo!	'In the United States, there are quite a lot of people with two cars.'
mén	for courses of study	
	Yǒurén dú liù-qī mén kè.	'Some people take six or seven courses.'
pǐ	for horses	
	yì pǐ mǎ	'a horse'
piān	for articles, stories	
	yì piān wénzhāng	'an article'
	yì piān gùshi	'a story'
piàn	slice of, expanse of	
	yí piàn miànbāo	'a slice of bread'
shù	bouquet, bunch, bundle	
	Tāmen qǐng nǐ chīfàn, nà, nǐ kě.yǐ mǎi yí shù huā gěi tāmen.	'If they invite you to dinner, you can buy them a bouquet of flowers.'
suǒ	for buildings; cf. *dòng*	
	Nàr yǒu liǎng suǒ xuéxiào.	'There are a couple schools there.'
	Nǐ kàn, nèi suǒ shi tāmen de.	'Look, that one's theirs.' [house]

tái	for appliances, machines; also plays, performances ('platform')	
	Fángjiān li yǒu liǎng tái diànshì, yě yǒu yì tái diànnǎo.	'There are two TVs and a computer in the room.'
táng	period [in school]; class	
	Wǒ xiàwǔ hái yǒu liǎng táng kè.	'I still have two more classes in the afternoon.'
tàng	journey	
	Wǒmen qùle liǎng tàng.	'We went there twice.'
tiáo	for long, sinuous things (roads, rivers, fish, some animals, news items [i.e., that used to appear on ticker tape])	
	Zhōngguó yǒu liǎng tiáo dà hé.	'China has two main rivers.'
	Zhèi tiáo xīnwén hěn yǒu yìsi.	'Here's an interesting item of news.'
	Liǎng zhī jī, yì tiáo yú.	'Two chickens and a fish.'
tóu	head of [cattle]	
	yì tóu niú	'a cow'
wèi	polite M for people	
	Nín <shi> něi wèi?	'Who is it, please?'
	Zhèi wèi shi wǒ de lǎoshī.	'This is my teacher.'
zhāng	for flat things	
	Wǒ mǎile liǎng zhāng [piào].	'I bought two [tickets].'
	Kànkan zhèi zhāng dìtú ba.	'Why don't you take a look at this map?'
zhèn	bout of, burst of	
	Zhèi zhèn fēng hěn lìhai.	'That was quite a gust!'
	yí zhèn yǔ (cf. *zhènyǔ*)	'a shower of rain' (cf. 'rain showers')

zhī	for certain animals	
	yì zhī māo / gǒu / niǎo / jī	'a cat' / 'dog / 'bird' / 'chicken'
zhī	for stubby things, such as pens and candles	
	liǎng zhī xiāngyān	'two cigarettes'
	yì zhī bǐ, liǎng zhī qiānbǐ	'a pen; two pencils'
zuò	for structures, mountains	
	Chéngshì de nánbianr yǒu yí zuò qiáo.	'There's a bridge at the southern end of town.'
	Xībianr yǒu yí zuò shān.	'There's a mountain in the west.'

Appendix 3 CHARACTER LISTS

Appendix 3 provides a list of all the characters formally presented in the character units of both volumes of *Learning Chinese* (but not the extra characters that are underlined and only appear irregularly in the texts and examples). There are three sections.

Section A lists characters from the simplified set with pinyin pronunciation. The list is organized by total number of strokes. To find a particular character, count the strokes, find the section, and then scan along the row(s) for the character. Only those pronunciations that are relevant for *Learning Chinese* are given. (差, for example can, in different compounds, be pronounced *chà*, *chā*, *chāi*, or *cī*, but only the first two are relevant: *chà* in 差不多 and *chā* in 时/時差.) Tones that are grammatically conditioned (*bù*, *bú*) or variant pronunciations of a single word (*nǎ* ~ *něi*) are not included.

Section B matches traditional graphs to their simplified counterparts in those cases where the two are significantly different. Differences that involve only the form of the radical (such as 谈/談) are not included in the list. Again, the characters are organized by total number of strokes.

Section C presents some general features of the simplification process that have given rise to the simplified set.

A. Simplified character list

1 / 2 strokes

一	二	十	儿	人	几	七	八	九	了	力
yī	*èr*	*shí*	*ér*	*rén*	*jǐ*	*qī*	*bā*	*jiǔ*	*liǎo*	*lì*
									le	

3 strokes

三	么	个	子	川	大	山	门	习	已	也
sān	*me*	*gè*	*zǐ*	*chuān*	*dà*	*shān*	*mén*	*xí*	*yǐ*	*yě*

上	下	女	小	马	飞	工	千	万	己	久
shàng	*xià*	*nǚ*	*xiǎo*	*mǎ*	*fēi*	*gōng*	*qiān*	*wàn*	*jǐ*	*jiǔ*

4 strokes

五	六	月	日	今	天	王	毛	不	太	中
wǔ	liù	yuè	rì	jīn	tiān	wáng	máo	bù	tài	zhōng

文	以	什	手	书	车	气	方	从	见	斤
wén	yǐ	shén shí	shǒu	shū	chē	qì	fāng	cóng	jiàn	jīn

少	比	孔	水	长	火	友	片	公	午	为
shǎo	bǐ	kǒng	shuǐ	cháng zhǎng	huǒ	yǒu	piàn	gōng	wǔ	wèi wéi

父	办	牛	开	厅	云	风	区	认
fù	bàn	niú	kāi	tīng	yún	fēng	qū	rèn

5 strokes

四	号	白	他	们	生	对	可	东	包	叫
sì	hào	bái	tā	men	shēng	duì	kě	dōng	bāo	jiào

去	外	北	边	本	电	瓜	目	汉	用	功
qù	wài	běi	biān	běn	diàn	guā	mù	hàn	yòng	gōng

母	节	头	市	兄	业	只	出	民	奶	写
mǔ	jié	tóu	shì	xiōng	yè	zhǐ zhī	chū	mín	nǎi	xiě

乐	左	右	正	冬	平	打	半	必	扔	鸟
lè yuè	zuǒ	yòu	zhèng	dōng	píng	dǎ	bàn	bì	rēng	niǎo

让	旧	发
ràng	jiù	fā fà

6 strokes

年	她	吗	好	忙	吃	有	师	在	那	西
nián	tā	ma	hǎo hào	máng	chī	yǒu	shī	zài	nà	xī

机 jī	伞 sǎn	字 zì	行 xíng háng	名 míng	地 dì de	过 guò	安 ān	州 zhōu	百 bǎi	再 zài
多 duō	衣 yī	先 xiān	早 zǎo	买 mǎi	同 tóng	问 wèn	场 chǎng	自 zì	会 huì	共 gòng
因 yīn	欢 huān	岁 suì	妈 mā	后 hòu	江 jiāng	羊 yáng	肉 ròu	考 kǎo	米 mǐ	毕 bì
许 xǔ	件 jiàn	级 jí	汤 tāng	吸 xī	竹 zhú	农 nóng	死 sǐ	红 hóng	关 guān	次 cì
冰 bīng	阴 yīn	阳 yáng	老 lǎo	向 xiàng	回 huí	如 rú	刚 gāng	成 chéng		

7 strokes

李 lǐ	我 wǒ	你 nǐ	冷 lěng	还 hái	没 méi	男 nán	陈 chén	张 zhāng	这 zhè	报 bào
但 dàn	走 zǒu	来 lái	吧 ba	两 liǎng	近 jìn	远 yuǎn	别 bié	忘 wàng	里 lǐ	块 kuài
听 tīng	坐 zuò	汽 qì	住 zhù	作 zuò	每 měi	位 wèi	应 yīng	系 xì	更 gèng	进 jìn
弟 dì	言 yán	条 tiáo	鸡 jī	时 shí	间 jiān	否 fǒu	医 yī	县 xiàn	坏 huài	找 zhǎo
识 shí	把 bǎ	快 kuài	极 jí	往 wǎng	告 gào	诉 sù	乱 luàn	纸 zhǐ	吹 chuī	

8 strokes

明 míng	周 zhōu	杯 bēi	姓 xìng	呢 ne	饭 fàn	经 jīng	的 de dī	学, xué	现, xiàn	典 diǎn
国 guó	英 yīng	京 jīng	到 dào	非 fēi	话 huà	码 mǎ	杯 bēi	服 fú	姐 jiě	朋 péng

所	爸	定	该	厕	河	试	房	炒	鱼	或
suǒ	bà	dìng	gāi	cè	hé	shì	fáng	chǎo	yú	huò

者	和	玩	店	妹	知	具	单	直	雨	夜
zhě	hé	wán	diàn	mèi	zhī	jù	dān	zhí	yǔ	yè

转	事	奇	怪	拉	放	画	法	些	念	易
zhuǎn zhuàn	shì	qí	guài	lā	fàng	huà	fǎ	xiē	niàn	yì

卖	怕	底	卧
mài	pà	dǐ	wò

9 strokes

昨	很	是	点	怎	前	看	哪	贵	美	南
zuó	hěn	shì	diǎn	zěn	qián	kàn	nǎ	guì	měi	nán

省	说	茶	洗	觉	客	要	钟	星	总	城
shěng	shuō	chá	xǐ	jué jiào	kè	yào	zhōng	xīng	zǒng	chéng

孩	语	面	虾	饺	给	差	院	音	祖	养
hái	yǔ	miàn	xiā	jiǎo	gěi	chà chā	yuàn	yīn	zǔ	yǎng

虽	屋	结	亲	思	活	度	穿	急	带	送
suī	wū	jié	qīn	sī	huó	dù	chuān	jí	dài	sòng

种
zhǒng zhòng

10 strokes

饿	热	班	课	都	谁	高	样	难	紧	笔
è	rè	bān	kè	dōu dū	shéi	gāo	yàng	nán	jǐn	bǐ

起	海	部	离	家	酒	请	铁	较	站	哥
qǐ	*hǎi*	*bù*	*lí*	*jiā*	*jiǔ*	*qǐng*	*tiě*	*jiào*	*zhàn*	*gē*

真	爱	候	旁	烟	病	能	拿	笑	容	谈
zhēn	*ài*	*hòu*	*páng*	*yān*	*bìng*	*néng*	*ná*	*xiào*	*róng*	*tán*

11 strokes

累	第	您	常	得	晚	清	做	菜	理	蛋
lèi	*dì*	*nín*	*cháng*	*děi*	*wǎn*	*qīng*	*zuò*	*cài*	*lǐ*	*dàn*
				dé de						

教	馆	猪	婚	情	雪	接	甜	着	够	船
jiāo	*guǎn*	*zhū*	*hūn*	*qíng*	*xuě*	*jiē*	*tián*	*zhāo*	*gòu*	*chuán*
jiào								*zhe*		

脸	唱
liǎn	*chàng*

12 strokes

喝	舒	最	帽	就	街	期	湖	谢	粥	朝
hē	*shū*	*zuì*	*mào*	*jiù*	*jiē*	*qī*	*hú*	*xiè*	*zhōu*	*cháo*

道	然	晴	渴	等	越	替	黑	温
dào	*rán*	*qíng*	*kě*	*děng*	*yuè*	*tì*	*hēi*	*wēn*

13 strokes

想	错	睡	楚	路	概	像	跟	搬	简	意
xiǎng	*cuò*	*shuì*	*chǔ*	*lù*	*gài*	*xiàng*	*gēn*	*bān*	*jiǎn*	*yì*

数	雾	楼	跑
shù	*wù*	*lóu*	*pǎo*
shǔ			

14 or more strokes

算	题	澡	籍	慢	愿	歌	懂
suàn	*tí*	*zǎo*	*jí*	*màn*	*yuàn*	*gē*	*dǒng*

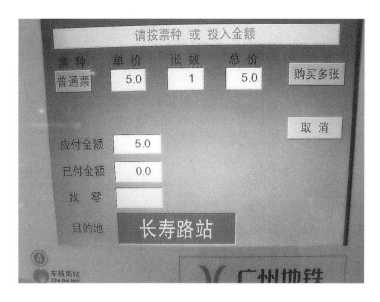

Guǎngzhōu Dìtiězhàn: Dào Chángshòulùzhàn, yì zhāng wǔ kuài.

B. Traditional to simplified list [TC over SC]

7 strokes

車	見	沒
车	见	没

8 strokes

兒	門	長	東	兩	臥
儿	门	长	东	两	卧

9 strokes

甚	為	風	後	係	飛
什	为	风	后	系	飞

10 strokes

個	馬	書	師	這	時	剛	畢	氣
个	马	书	师	这	时	刚	毕	气

11 strokes

習	從	區	陰	陳	張	進	條	過	著
习	从	区	阴	陈	张	进	条	过	着
國	魚	鳥	帶	夠					
国	鱼	鸟	带	够					

12 strokes

幾	開	傘	買	湯	陽	報	裡	廁	單	貴
几	开	伞	买	汤	阳	报	里	厕	单	贵
筆	畫	雲	場							
笔	画	云	场							

13 strokes

號	電	節	業	會	歲	農	遠	經
号	电	节	业	会	岁	农	远	经
愛	煙	溫	極	亂	萬	塊		
爱	烟	温	极	乱	万	块		

14 strokes

麼	對	漢	種	認	緊
么	对	汉	种	认	紧

15 strokes

寫	樂	蝦	養	樣	數	樓	豬	賣
写	乐	虾	养	样	数	楼	猪	卖

16 strokes

辦	頭	機	還	學	親	錢	縣
办	头	机	还	学	亲	钱	县

17 strokes

應	點	總	雖	臉	舊
应	点	总	虽	脸	旧

18 strokes

邊	雞	醫	轉	發	離
边	鸡	医	转	发	离

19 strokes

壞	難	霧	識	願
坏	难	雾	识	愿

20 or more strokes

關	廳	歡	聽	覺	麵	鐵	讓	鐘
关	厅	欢	听	觉	面	铁	让	钟

C. Principles of simplification

This section displays the general relationships between traditional and simplified characters in terms of processes such as omission and replacement.

1. Regular simplification of radicals (most common)

Notice that the simplification of radicals applies only to elements that appear in certain positions in compound graphs—not to those same elements as independent graphs.

言/讠	請/请	誰/谁	But: 言/言
食/饣	飯/饭	餓/饿	But: 食/食
糸/纟	紙/纸	紅/红	But: 累/累
門/门	們/们	問/问	
見/见	現/现	視/视	
馬/马	嗎/吗	媽/妈	
車/车	輕/轻	輛/辆	
金/钅	錢/钱	錯/错	But: 鑒/鉴

2. Omitting parts

氣/气	電/电	點/点	兒/儿
條/条	時/时	雖/虽	親/亲
開/开	飛/飞	習/习	產/产
廣/广	歷/么	從/从	隨/随

3. Substitution of a simpler element for a more complex one
The simpler element is not a character (though it may be part of one).

熱/热	學/学	風/风	傘/伞
應/应	單/单	農/农	錢/钱

The simpler element is a character, but it was not chosen for its sound.

這/这 *zhèr*	(文 *wén*)	會/会 *huì*	(云 *yún*)
歲/岁 *suì*	(山 *shān*; 夕 *xī*)	邊/边 *biān*	(力 *lì*)
還/还 *hái*	(不 *bù*)	國/国 *guó*	(玉 *yù*)
孫/孙 *sūn*	(小 *xiǎo*)	過/过 *guò*	(寸 *cùn*)
亂/乱 *luàn*	(舌 *shé*)		

The element 又 *yòu* 'again' is a particularly common substitute for complex parts.

歡/欢	對/对	漢/汉
樹/树	雞/鸡	難/难

Partial phonetic substitution—in which sound is the main factor in the simplification.

種/种 *zhǒng*	(中 *zhōng*)	蘋/苹 *píng*	(平 *píng*)
華/华 *huá*	(化 *huà*)	樣/样 *yàng*	(羊 *yáng*)
認/认 *rèn*	(人 *rén*)	極/极 *jí*	(及 *jí*)
幾/几 *jǐ*	(几 *jī* or *jǐ*)	識/识 *shí*	(只 *zhī* or *zhǐ*)
進/进 *jìn*	(井 *jǐng*)	聽/听 *tīng*	(斤 *jīn*)

Complete phonetic substitution (rare)—a simpler character of the same or similar sound replaces a more complicated one.

幾/几 *jǐ*	(几 *jī* or *jǐ*)	後/后 *hòu*	(后 *hòu*)

Semantic replacement (relatively rare)—the simpler element is a character chosen for its meaning rather than sound.

壞/坏 *huài* 'bad'	(不 *bù*)
體/体 *tǐ* 'body; trunk'	(本 *běn* 'root; trunk')
愛/爱 *ài* 'love'	(友 *yǒu* 'friend')

4. Simplifications that preserve general shape—'gestalts'

馬/马	長/长	總/总
單/单	興/兴	帶/带
寫/写	農/农	湯/汤
買/买	為/为	樂/乐

5. Cases involving mergers or near mergers in which a single character has come to represent words originally represented with several

Complete mergers:

隻	枝	只	all written 只
zhī	*zhī*	*zhǐ*	read *zhī* or *zhǐ* according to context

幹	乾	干	all written 干
gàn	*gān*	*gān*	read *gàn* or *gān* according to context

Near mergers (with example compound words):

廣/广 *guǎng* (*Guǎngzhōu*)	廠/厂 *chǎng* (*gōngchǎng*)
為/为 *wèi* (*yīnwèi*)	辦/办 *bàn* (*bànfǎ*)
蘇/苏 *sū* (*Sūzhōu*)	邊/边 *biān* (*běibianr*)
頭/头 *tóu* (*tóu téng*)	買/头 *mǎi* (*mǎi dōngxi*)
賣/卖 *mài* (*mài bu mài?*)	實/实 *shí* (*shíjì shang* 'in fact')

Appendix 4

The small numbers indicate the order of the stroke; their position on the line shows the onset (and hence, the direction). TC and SC indicate traditional and simplified characters; only relevant pronunciations are given.

Unit 20 Characters

cháo

zhī

dào

zǔ

bān

zhú

suàn

(TC) xiàn

(SC) xiàn

(TC) nóng

(SC) nóng

(TC) yǎng

(SC) yǎng

(TC) zhū

(SC) zhū

(TC) zhǒng, zhòng

(SC) zhǒng, zhòng

(TC) suī

(SC) suī   rán   (TC) jiǎn

(SC) jiǎn   (TC) dān   (SC) dān

wū   jù   sǐ

(TC) hóng   (SC) hóng   (TC) zhí

(SC) *zhí*

(TC) *jié*

(SC) *jié*

hūn

(TC) *qīn*

(SC) *qīn*

jǐ

(TC) *guān*

(SC) *guān*

(TC) *xì*

(SC) *xì*

(TC) *shù, shǔ*

(SC) shù, shǔ

yì

sī

néng

cì

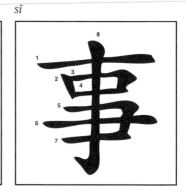
shì

qíng

(TC) wò

(SC) wò

(TC) huài

(SC) huài

huó

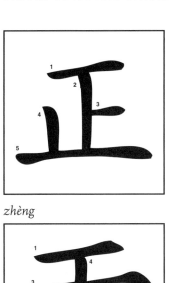

zhèng

dōng

bīng

yǔ

xuě

(TC) yún

(SC) yún

(TC) wù

(SC) wù

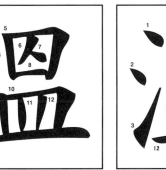

(TC) wēn

(SC) wēn

dù

(TC) yīn   *(SC) yīn*   *(TC) yáng*

(SC) yáng   *yè*   *qíng*

(TC) fēng   *(SC) fēng*   *(TC) zhuǎn, zhuàn*

(SC) zhuǎn, zhuàn   *(TC) jí*   *(SC) jí*

(TC) zhèn

(SC) zhèn

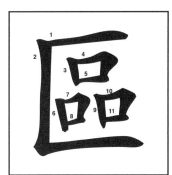

(TC) qū

(SC) qū

lì

xiàng

Unit 21 characters

děng

jiē

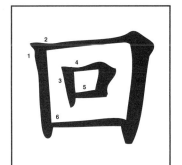

huí

píng

rú

chuān

zhǎo

(TC) dǒng

(SC) dǒng

qí

guài

(TC) rèn

(SC) rèn

(TC) shí

(SC) shí

(TC) gāng

(SC) gāng

tián

bǎ

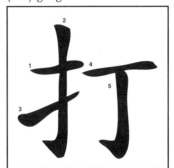

dǎ

lā

fàng

ná

xiào

pǎo

(TC) zhāo~zháo, zhe

(SC) zhāo~zháo, zhe

màn

kuài

(TC) huà

(SC) huà

(TC) gòu

(SC) gòu

(TC) jí

(SC) jí

fǎ

bàn

bì

wǎng

xiē

niàn

jí

róng

yì

gào

(TC) sù

(SC) sù

rēng

(TC) luàn

(SC) luàn

(TC)niǎo

(SC) niǎo

(TC) tán

(SC) tán

(TC) mài

(SC) mài

(TC) dài

(SC) dài

(TC) ràng

(SC) ràng

(TC) jiù

(SC) jiù

chuán

yuè

tì

jiǔ

chéng

pà

(TC) *liǎn*

(SC) *liǎn*

(TC) *zhǐ*

(SC) *zhǐ*

(TC) *fā*

(SC) *fā*

(TC) *yuàn*

(SC) *yuàn*

chàng

gē

sòng

dǐ

chuī

hēi

REFERENCES

Bei Dao. 2000. *Unlock: Poems by Bei Dao.* Trans. by Eliot Weinberger and Iona Man-Cheong. New York: New Directions.

Chao, Yuen Ren. 1968. *Readings in sayable Chinese.* 3 vols. San Francisco: Asian Language Publications.

Confucius. 1938. *The analects of Confucius.* Trans. by Arthur Waley. New York: Macmillan.

DeFrancis, John, ed. 2003. *ABC Chinese-English comprehensive dictionary.* Honolulu: University of Hawai'i Press.

Sài Miào'ěr, Wéi Kèduō, and Samuel Victor Constant. 2004. *Calls, sounds and merchandise of the Peking street peddlers.* Beijing: Beijing Library Press.

Tropp, Barbara. 1982. *The modern art of Chinese cooking: Techniques and recipes.* New York: William Morrow Cookbooks.

Wang, Yinglin. 1963. *San tzu ching: Elementary Chinese,* 2nd ed. Trans. by Herbert A. Giles. New York: Ungar.

CUMULATIVE INDEX